HISTORIC PHOTOS OF
ALASKA

Text and Captions by Dermot Cole

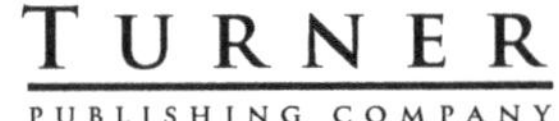
TURNER
PUBLISHING COMPANY

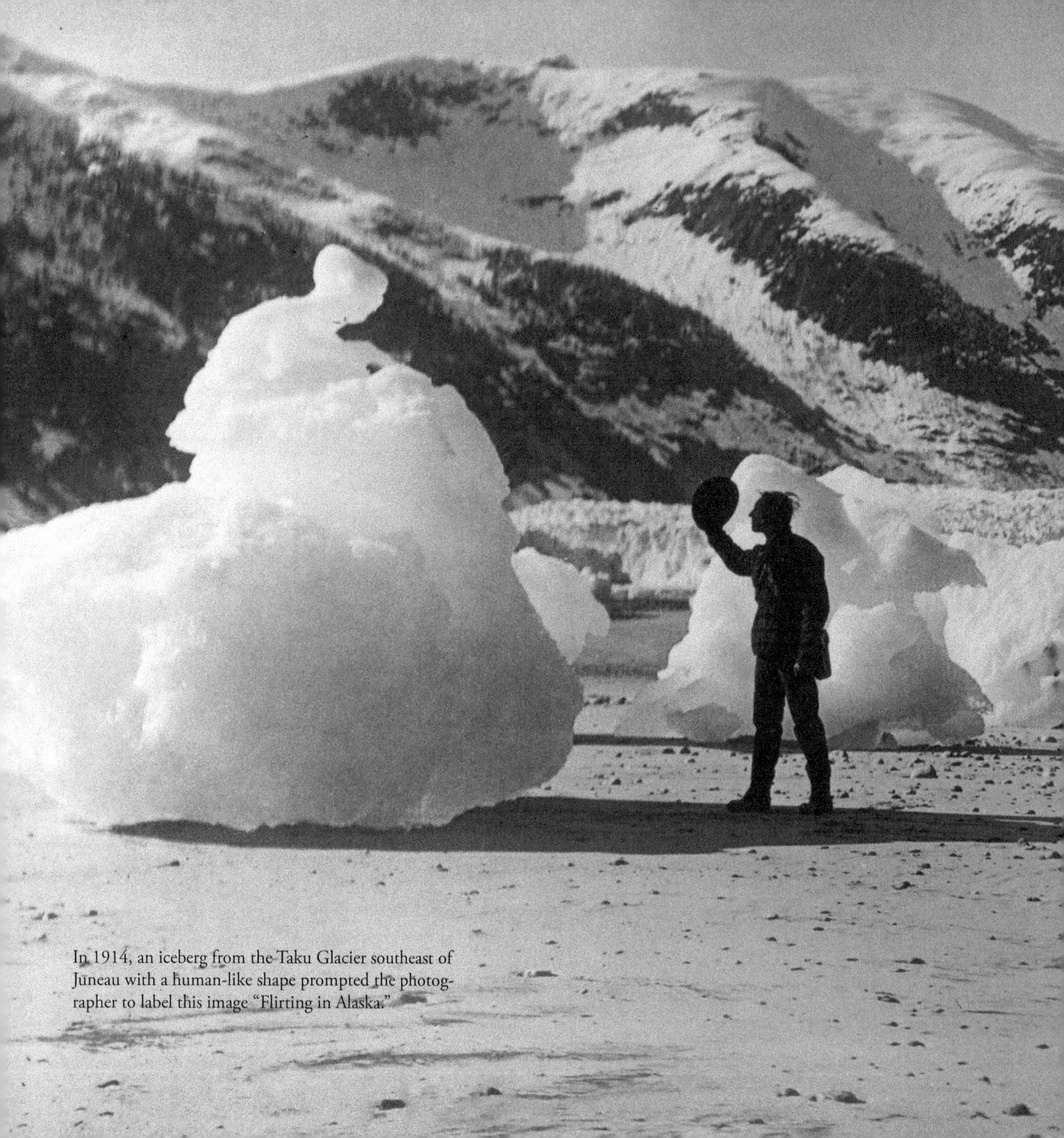

In 1914, an iceberg from the Taku Glacier southeast of Juneau with a human-like shape prompted the photographer to label this image "Flirting in Alaska."

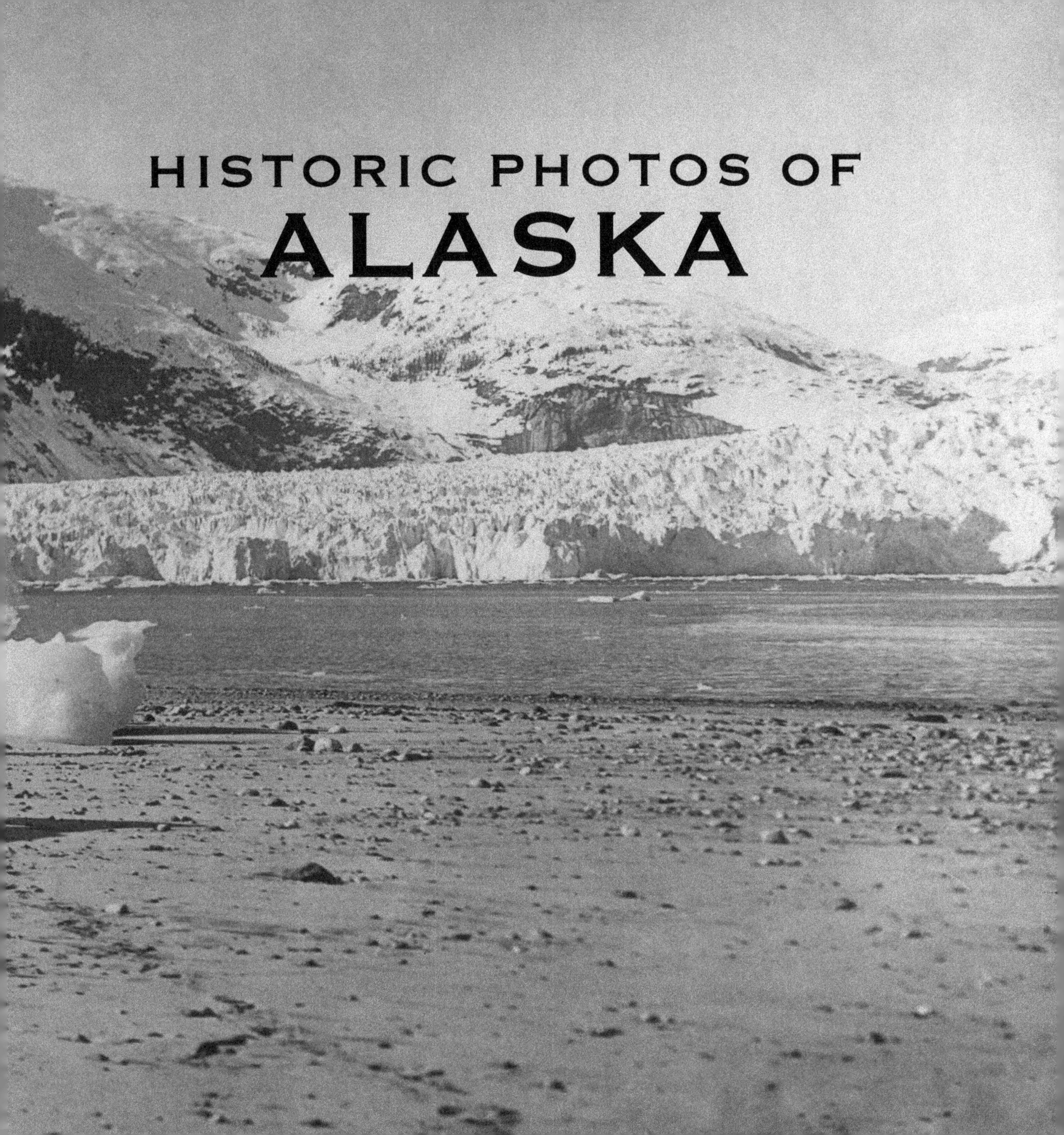

HISTORIC PHOTOS OF
ALASKA

Turner Publishing Company
www.turnerpublishing.com

Historic Photos of Alaska

Library of Congress Control Number: 2007938665

ISBN-13: 978-1-59652-424-8

Printed in the United States of America

ISBN 978-1-68442-000-1 (hc)

Contents

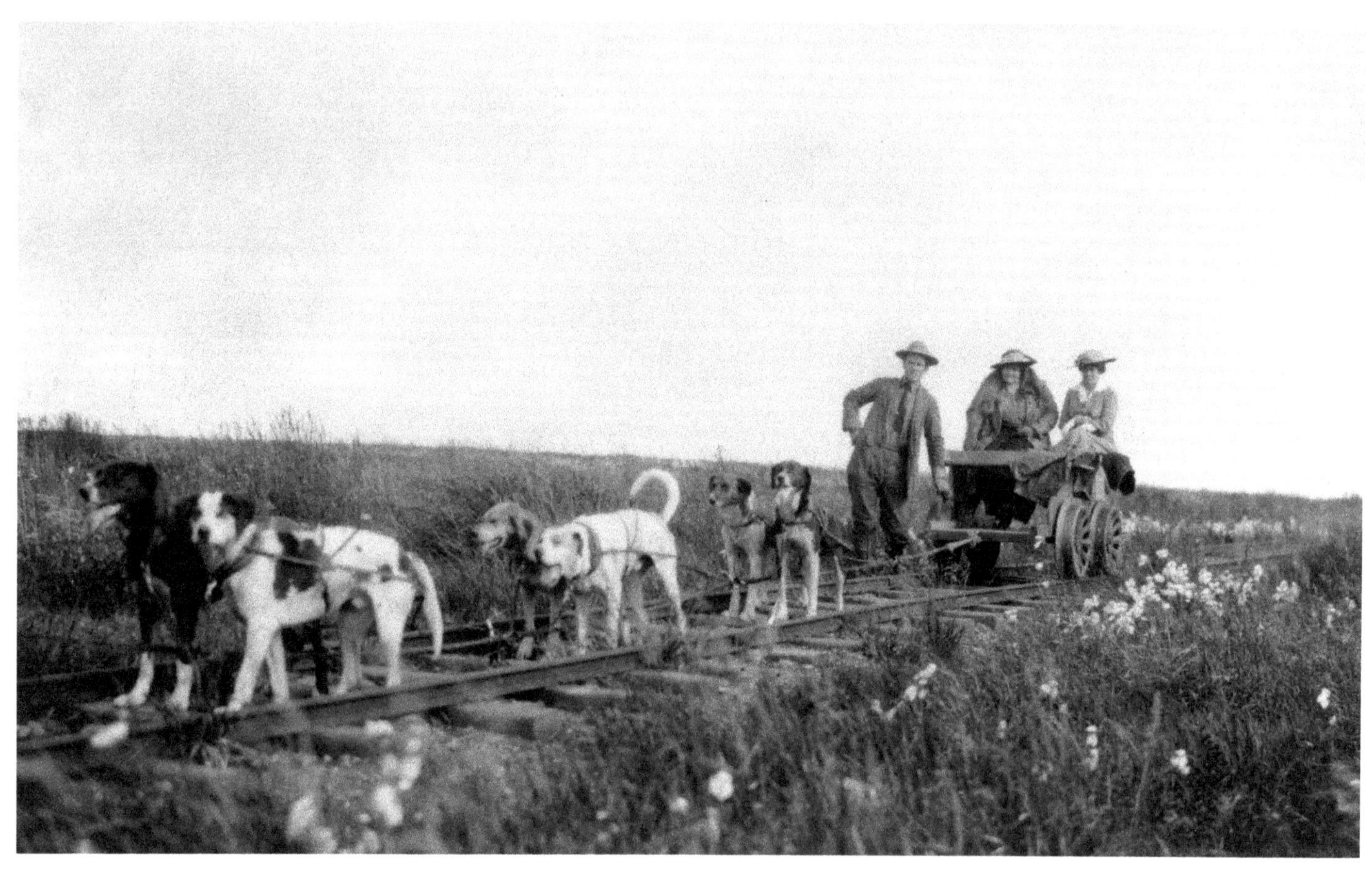

It was more common in the years before World War I to see dogs pulling carts on the train tracks of the Seward Peninsula than it was to see locomotives, which were in short supply.

Acknowledgments

This volume, *Historic Photos of Alaska,* is the result of the cooperation and efforts of many individuals, organizations, and corporations. It is with great thanks that we acknowledge the valuable contribution of the following for their generous support:

Alaska State Library

Anchorage Museum at Rasmuson Center

Library of Congress

Rasmuson Library
University of Alaska, Fairbanks

University of Alaska Anchorage Consortium Library

Preface

As Alaska prepares to celebrate the fiftieth anniversary of its admission to the Union as the forty-ninth state, there is more than a passing interest in considering where we've come from.

That is the purpose of this volume of historic photos of Alaska, which presents an overview of life in Alaska under the American flag. From the time of "Seward's Folly" to the development of a modern state providing a substantial share of the nation's oil production, Alaska has undergone a dramatic transformation.

But the wild lands, mountains, rivers, and vast expanses where moose and bears outnumber humans remain part of a timeless and spectacular landscape, where a photo from 1870 might not be all that different from 1970 except for the signs of age on the negative and the camera equipment available to the photographer.

On these pages, there are photos of Native Alaskans practicing centuries-old traditions and gold miners seeking fortunes from the earth, of military campaigns and community celebrations through the decades.

President Dwight D. Eisenhower signed the proclamation admitting Alaska on January 3, 1959. One of the editorial writers who took note of the new state's admission into the Union in 1959 commented that "Alaska is not so much in the present as in the future." It is also deeply rooted in the past.

Much has changed during the five decades of statehood. The state motto remains "North to the Future," but a real understanding of what comes next must be accompanied by knowledge of what has passed.

Life in Alaska is a unique experience and these photographs, gathered from a variety of archival collections, provide a hint of contrasts and contradictions.

Alaska is more than twice the size of the next largest state, yet its population would fit snugly into the suburbs of many American cities.

The book is arranged chronologically. The first section features photos from the late 1800s until 1905. The next section takes in the years between 1906 and 1919, when the drive for self-government began. Part three deals with the era between the world wars and the final section features the military and construction booms that created the foundation of modern Alaska.

In each section we attempt to show not only how people made a living, but what they did for recreation and how they interacted with the land and wildlife. This volume contains images of some of the most scenic areas in the world, as well as striking photos of people who mastered the art of living with a harsh climate and adapting to conditions that others would have found intolerable.

Even today, with satellite television, shopping malls, and the latest in technology available to the residents of Anchorage or Fairbanks—influences that are making parts of the state more and more like the rest of the country—the wilderness is right next door. For many people in the forty-ninth state, that's what makes all the difference.

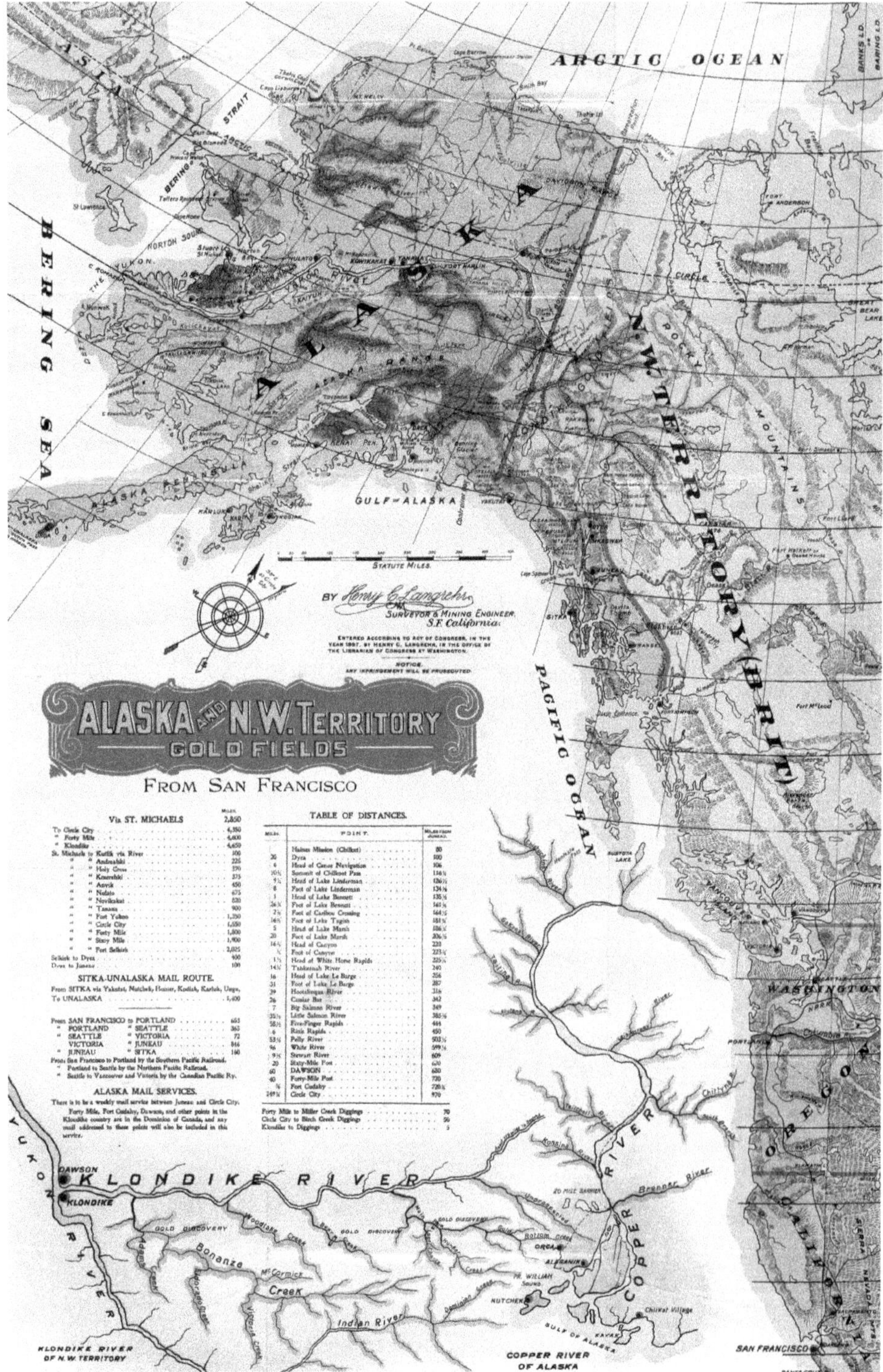

The immensity of Alaska is difficult to grasp. This 1897 map shows its size in relation to the states of Washington, Oregon, and California.

The Alaska Purchase

(1867–1905)

In 1867, Secretary of State William H. Seward and Russian representative Baron Eduard de Stoeckel worked out one of the great real estate deals of all time—great for the United States. The treaty to purchase the Russian lands on the North American continent for $7.2 million in gold won approval from the U.S. Senate in short order.

The United States took formal possession of what was to be known as Alaska on October 18, 1867, a land with about 30,000 Eskimo, Indian, and Aleut residents spread across a vast area twice the size of Texas.

The sale meant little to the aboriginal residents of Alaska, who had not been asked or informed about the transfer from Russia to the U.S. In the Interior of Alaska there was no official government presence for many years and the Alaska Natives mostly ruled themselves with customs and traditions that had evolved over centuries.

The American flag was raised at Sitka in 1867, but development was slow to arrive in the northland. It took seventeen years for the military government to be replaced with a bare-bones civilian government. In 1884, Congress called for a court system in Alaska and a governor, who would operate as much as possible under the laws of Oregon.

In 1896, rapid change began to arrive because gold was discovered in Canada's Yukon Territory. Tens of thousands of people started out for the Klondike in the latter years of the nineteenth century, many of them arriving on ships that unloaded at Skagway, for the journey over the Chilkoot Trail. Mining meant money and suddenly the United States began to pay attention to its farthest-north possession.

Most of the sojourners never made it to the Klondike or Alaska, but the Dawson gold strike was followed in rapid order by gold finds at Nome in 1899 and in Fairbanks in 1902. Traditional miners' meetings, which had served as the law of the land in the Western states, were held in the new Alaska mining towns, followed by more formal government structures.

The population of Alaska doubled between 1890 and 1900, pushing toward 65,000 and higher. The gold rush era was on and Alaska would never be the same.

In the first complete history of early Alaska, historian Hubert Howe Bancroft summed up the controversy about the purchase. Writing in 1886, he said, "experience has proved that the territory was well worth the sum paid for it, though at first it was believed to be almost valueless."

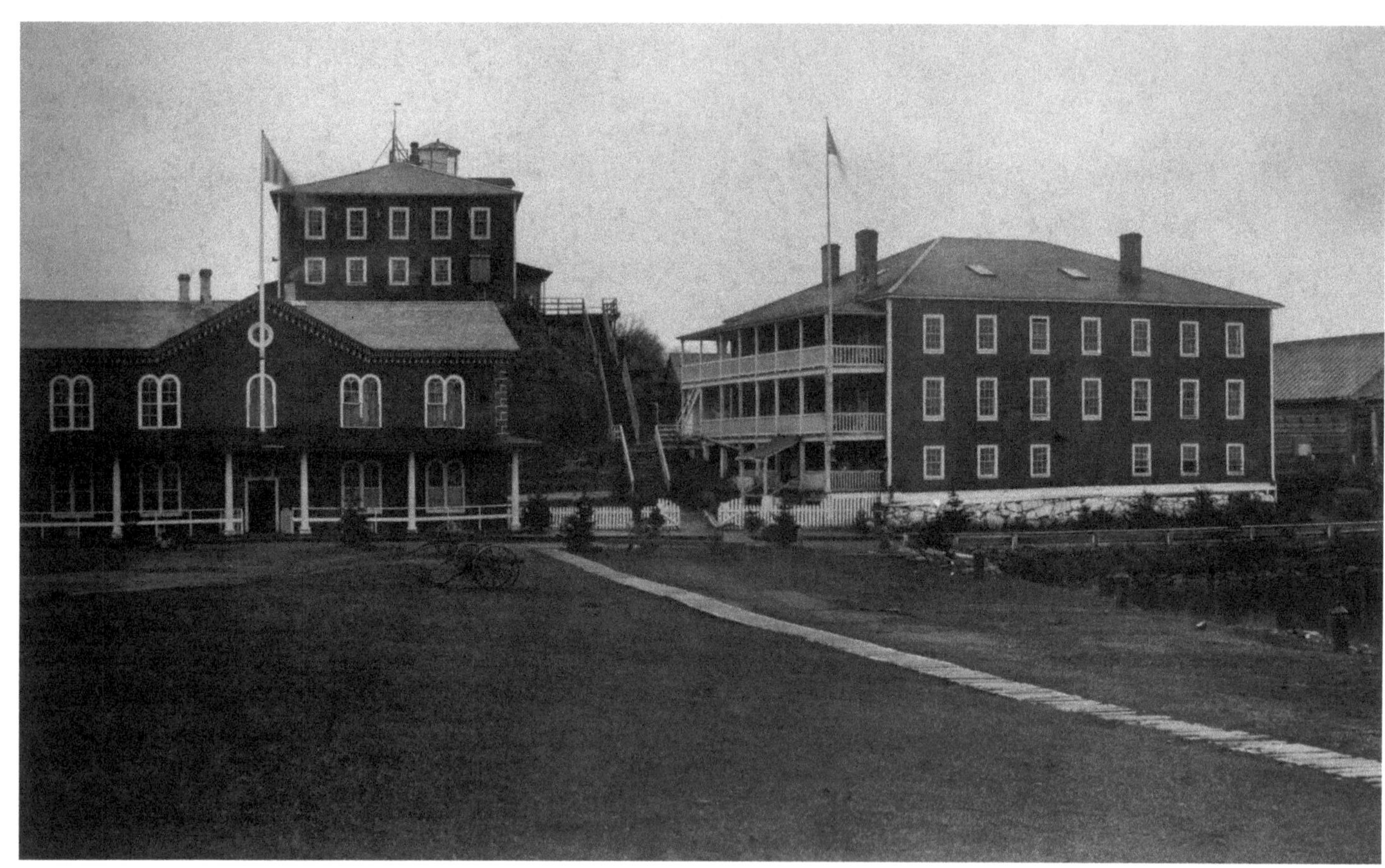

After the purchase of Alaska, the fledgling American presence took shape around this complex of Russian-built structures in Sitka, with the customs house at left, a barracks at right and "Baranov's Castle" on the hilltop, former home of the governor of Russian America, which was destroyed by fire in 1894, about a decade after this photograph was taken.

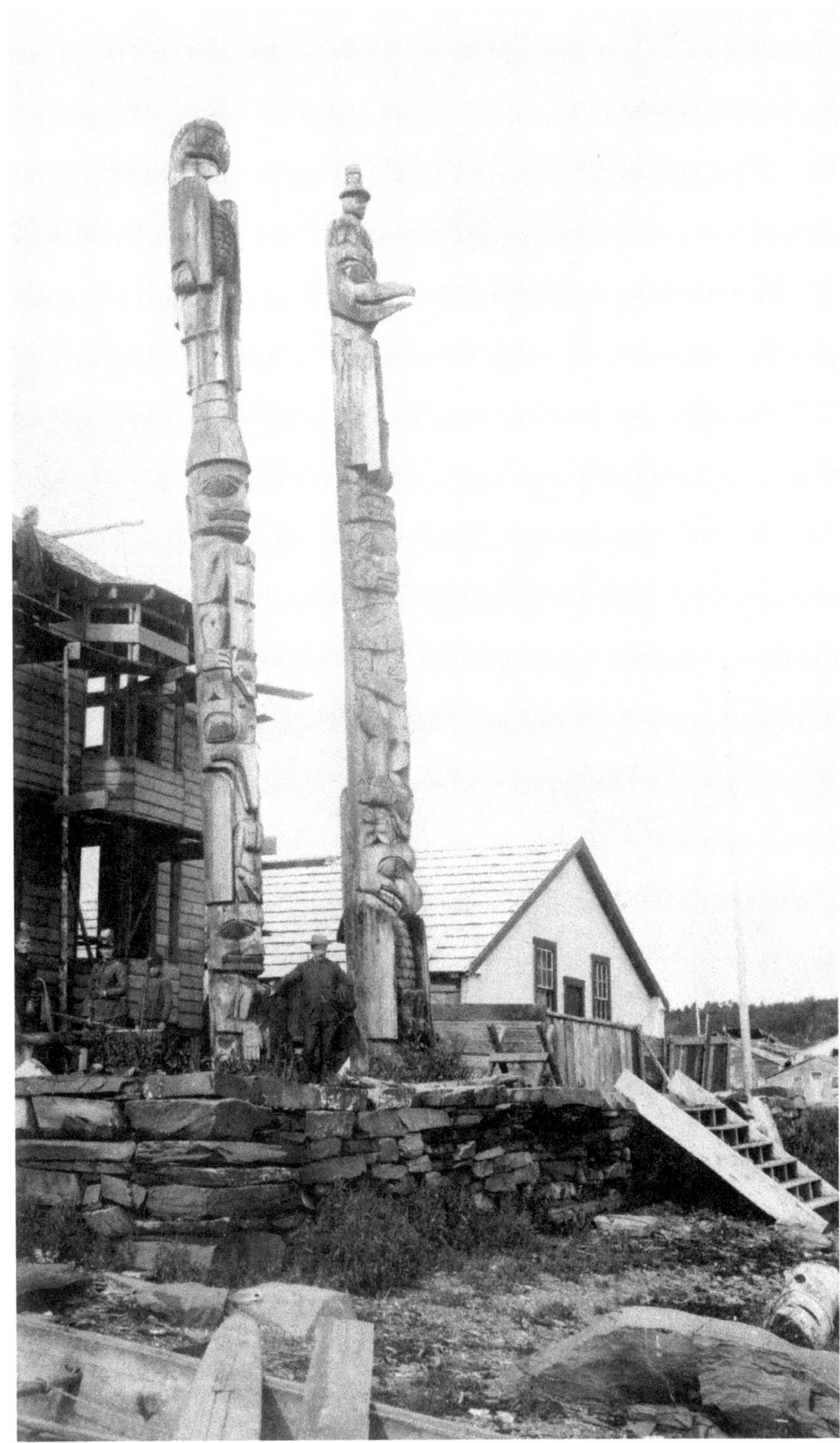

The Tlingit and Haida peoples of southeast Alaska carved totem poles from spruce or cedar, often to tell the tale of an important event or to honor an individual. This art form was much in evidence in 1887 when this image was photographed.

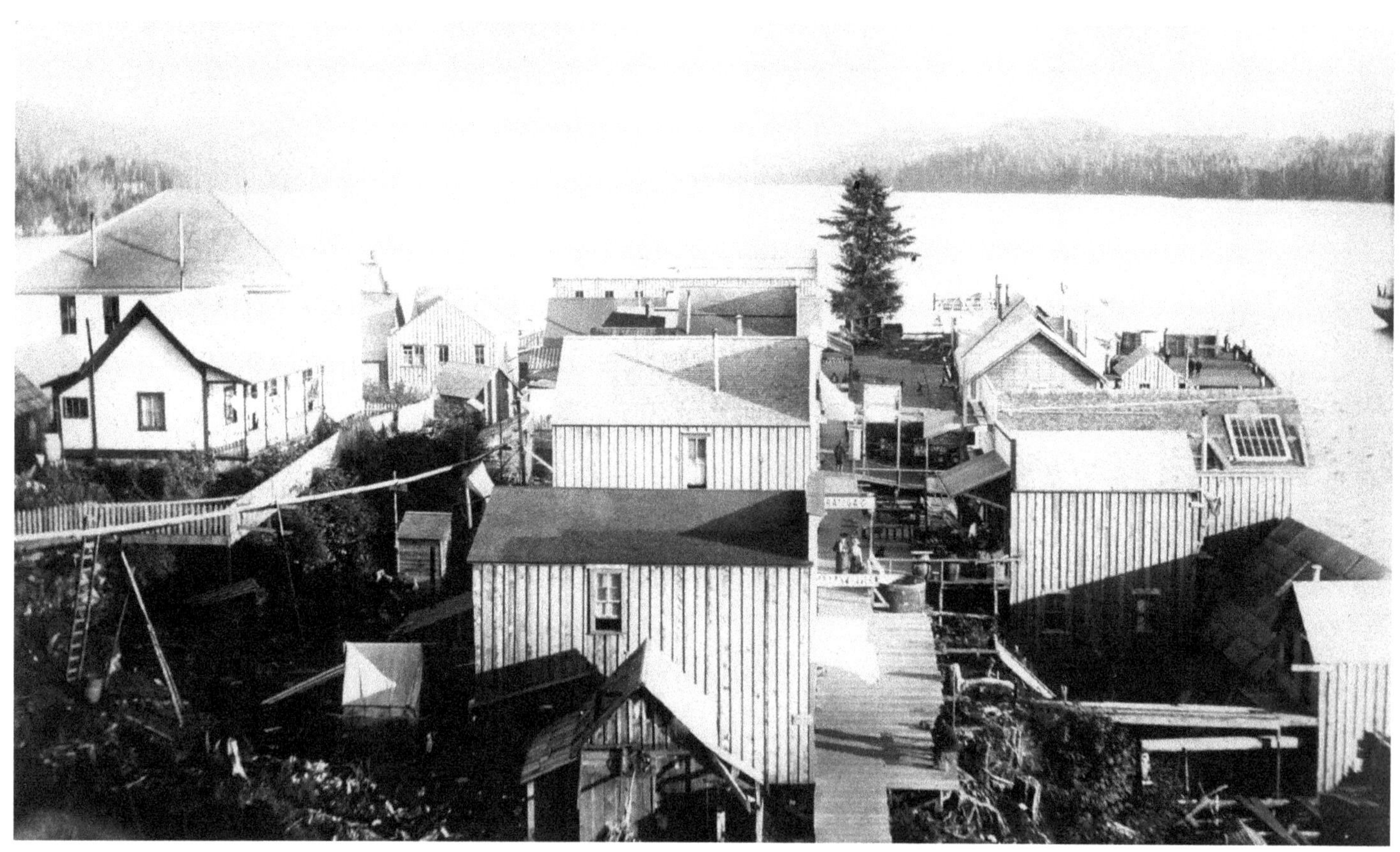

Gold and salmon attracted settlers to Ketchikan, where the lack of level ground led to crowded conditions along the waterfront. Boardwalks connected houses and businesses around the turn of the century.

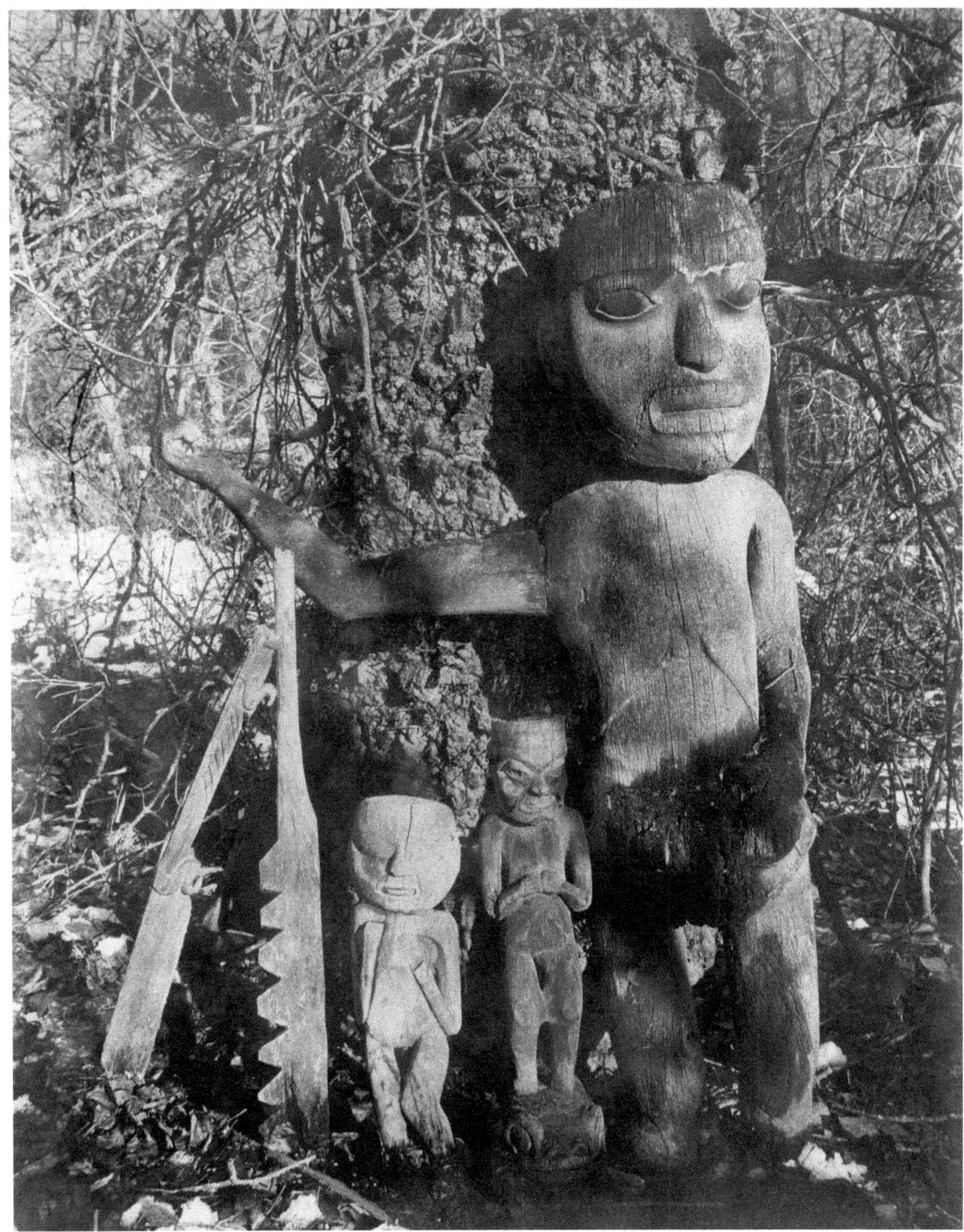

Wooden guardians at the grave of a shaman in Chilkat, placed there by Tlingit Indians who believed the images protected the remains of the shaman and his possessions from evil spirits.

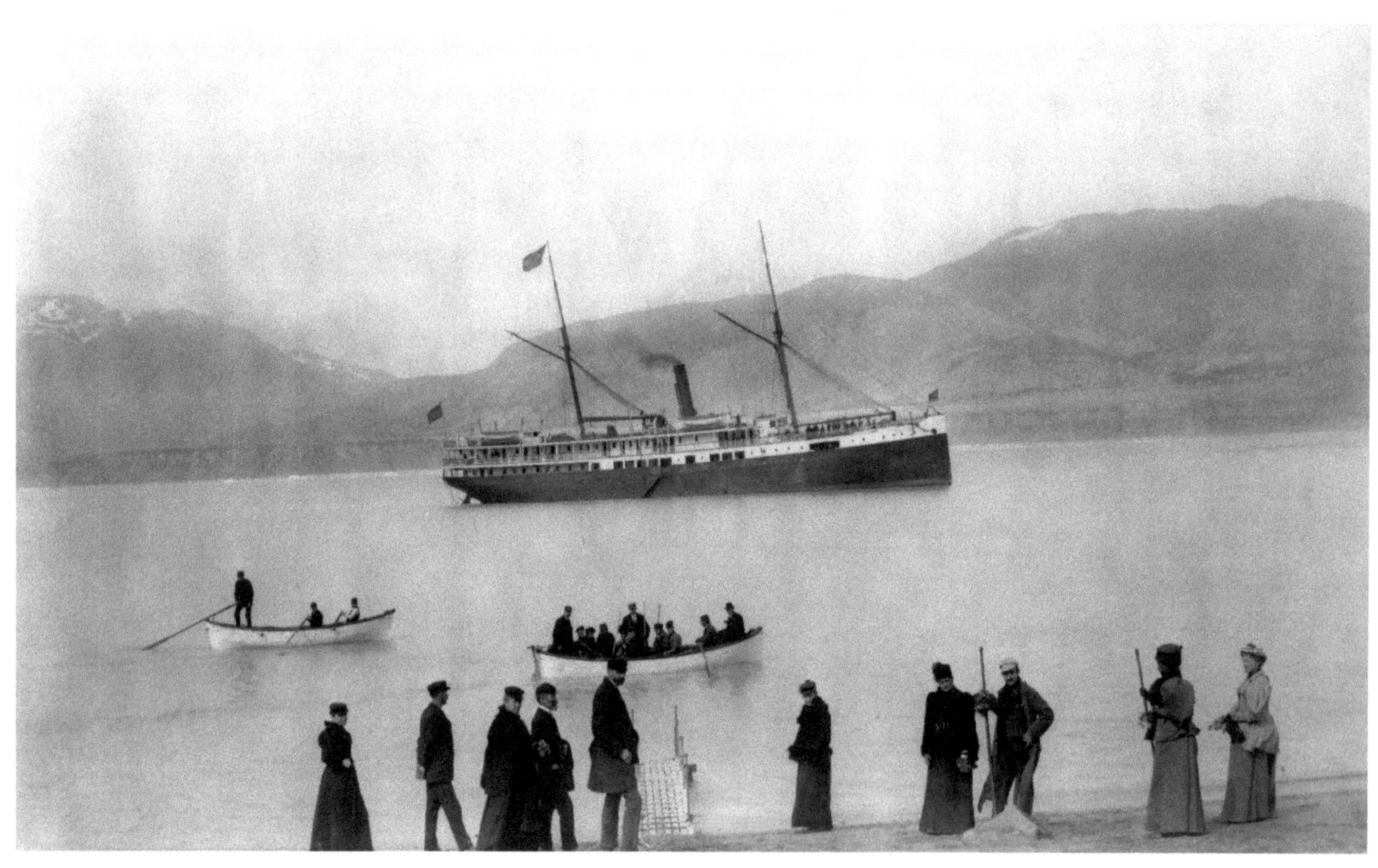

Passengers from the S.S. *Topeka,* traveling the protected waters of the Inside Passage in 1895, go ashore near the Muir Glacier for a sightseeing excursion in what is today part of Glacier Bay National Monument. The naturalist John Muir had explored the area less than twenty years earlier, writing of a "solitude of ice and snow and newborn rocks, dim, dreary, mysterious."

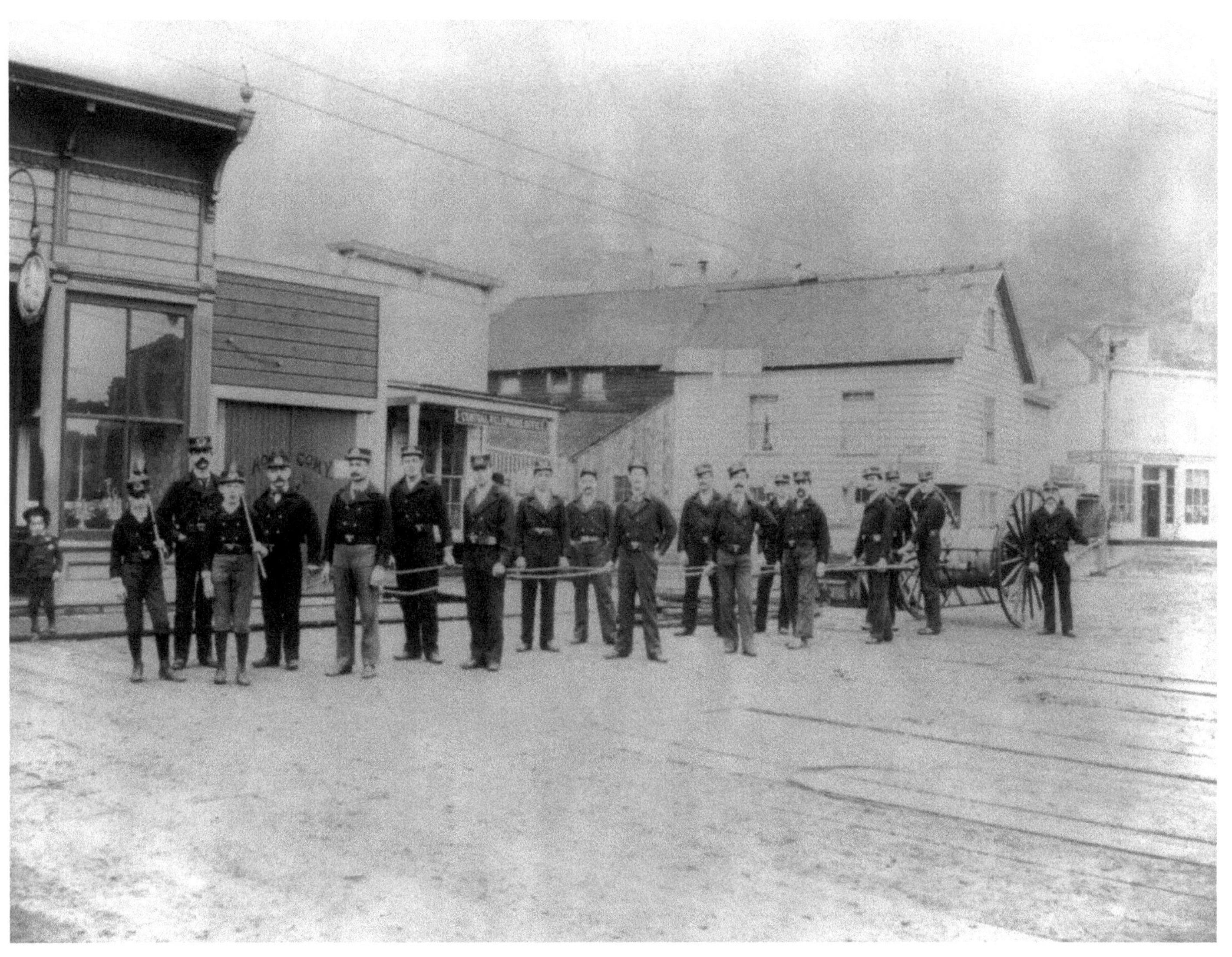

Fire was a constant threat in every part of Alaska, especially when stoves crackled to fend off winter's chill. Hose Company No. 1 of the Juneau fire brigade stands ready to roll in the 1890s, before anyone had heard of a fire truck.

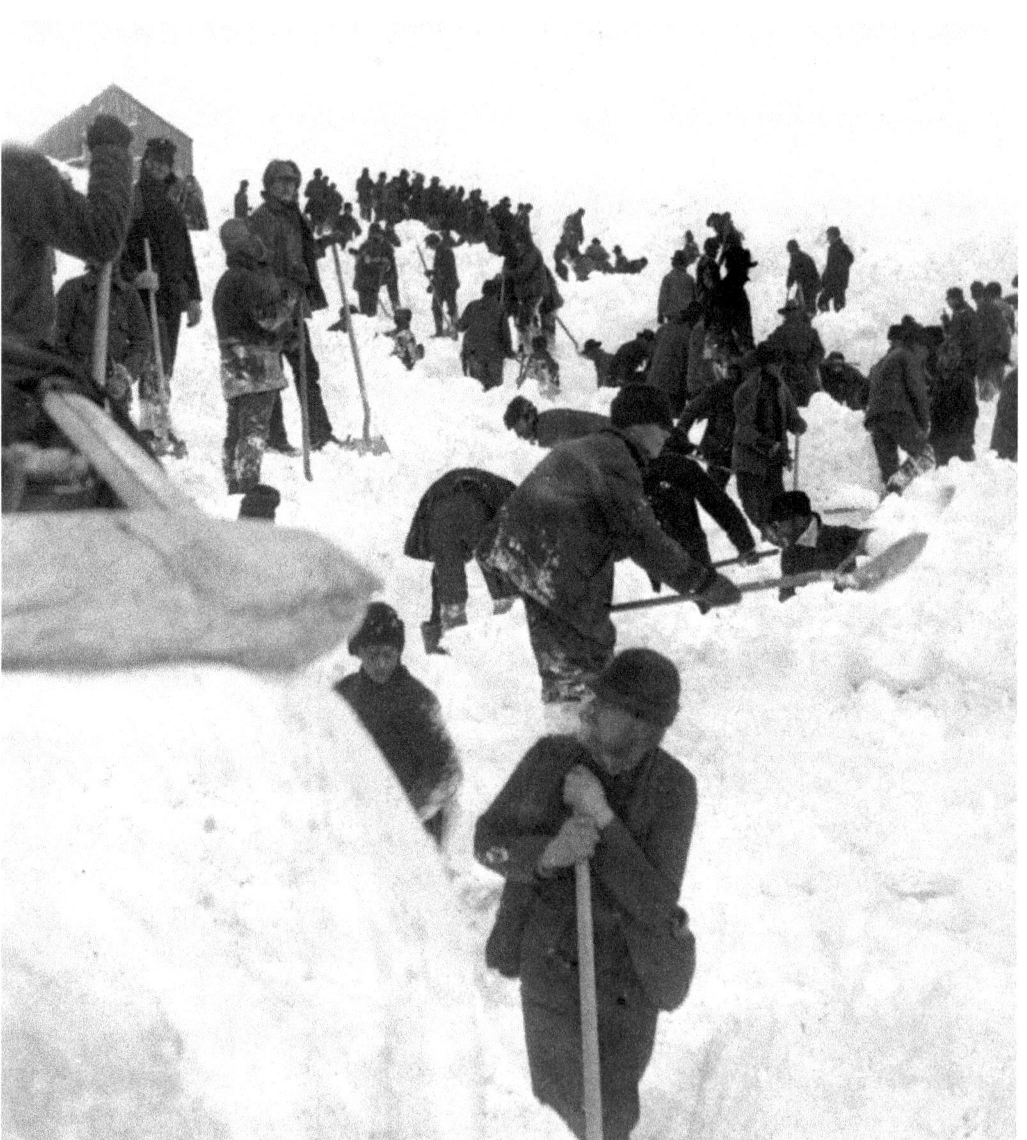

Stampeders—gold-seekers "stampeding" to the newly discovered gold fields—search for the dead after an avalanche on Palm Sunday in 1898 that claimed the lives of men struggling to reach the Klondike Gold Rush over Chilkoot Pass. Over the course of two days, as many as seventy people died in a series of avalanches.

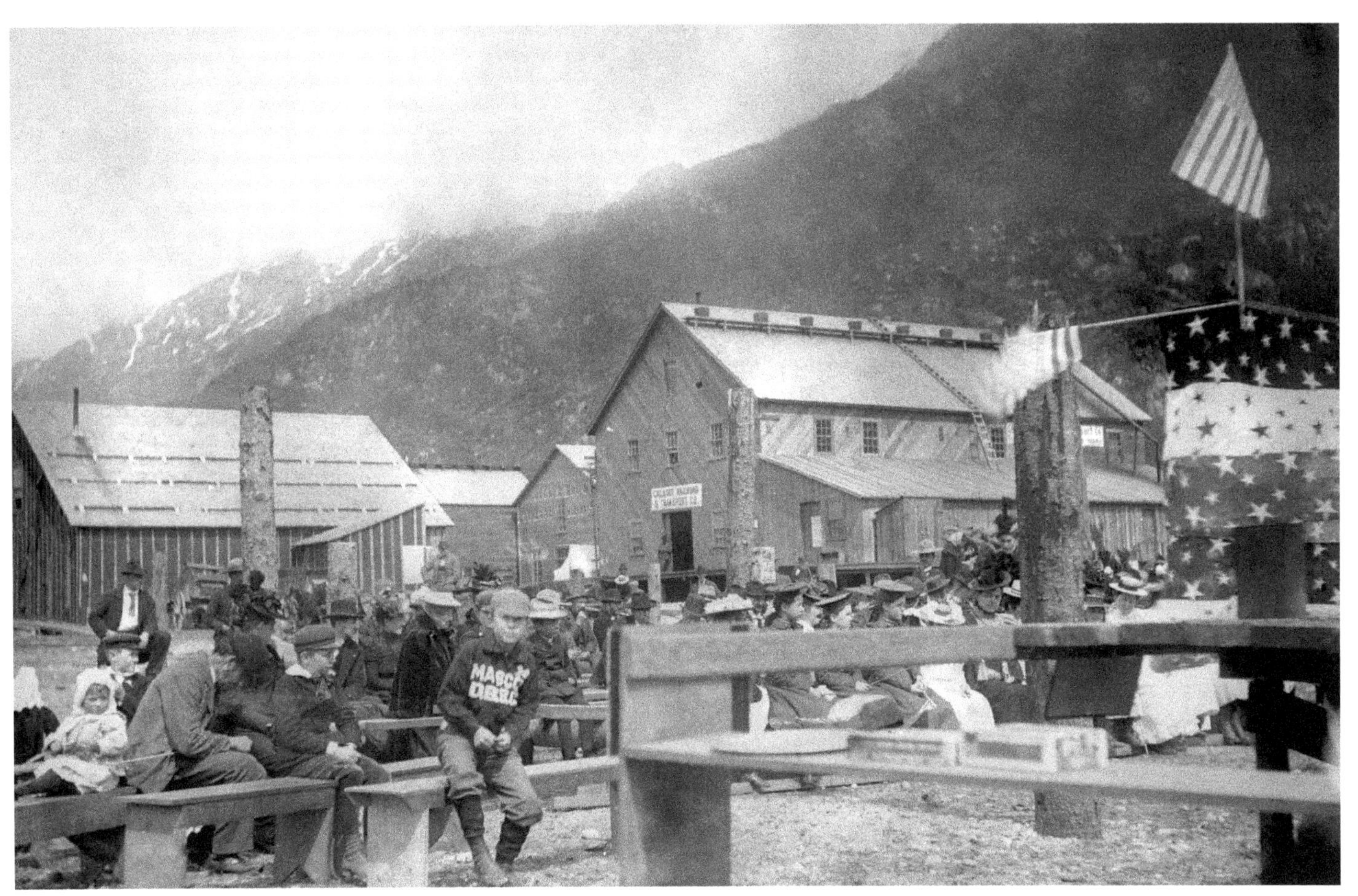

Dyea, at the foot of Chilkoot Trail, was a short-lived boomtown. Thousands passed through on their way to the Klondike, but even the most gold-hungry paused on July 4, 1898, to celebrate.

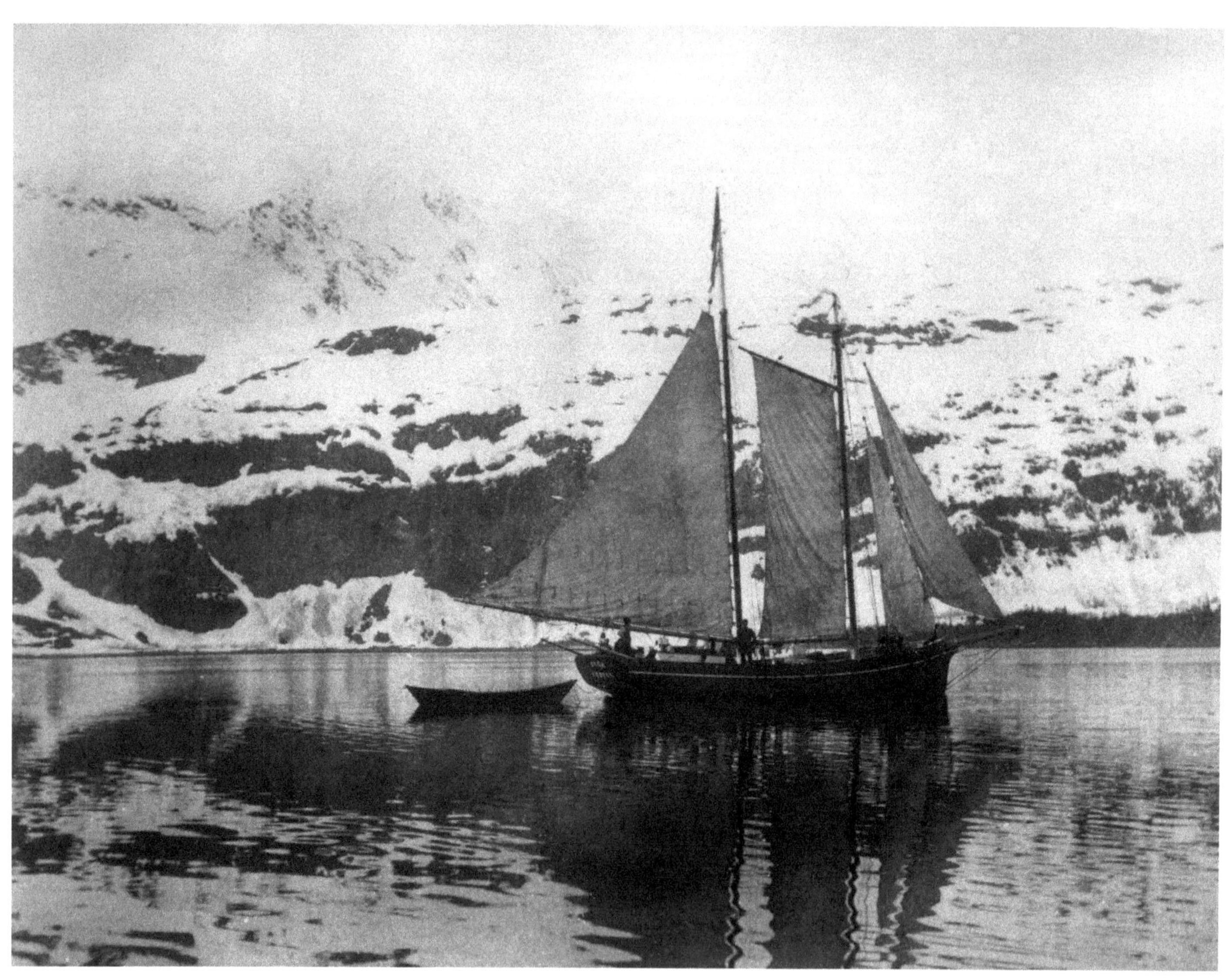

The schooner *Olga,* which sailed far and wide along Alaska's coast, tows a small dinghy during the 1898 Edwin F. Glenn Army Expedition to Cook Inlet. The Glenn Highway is named for him.

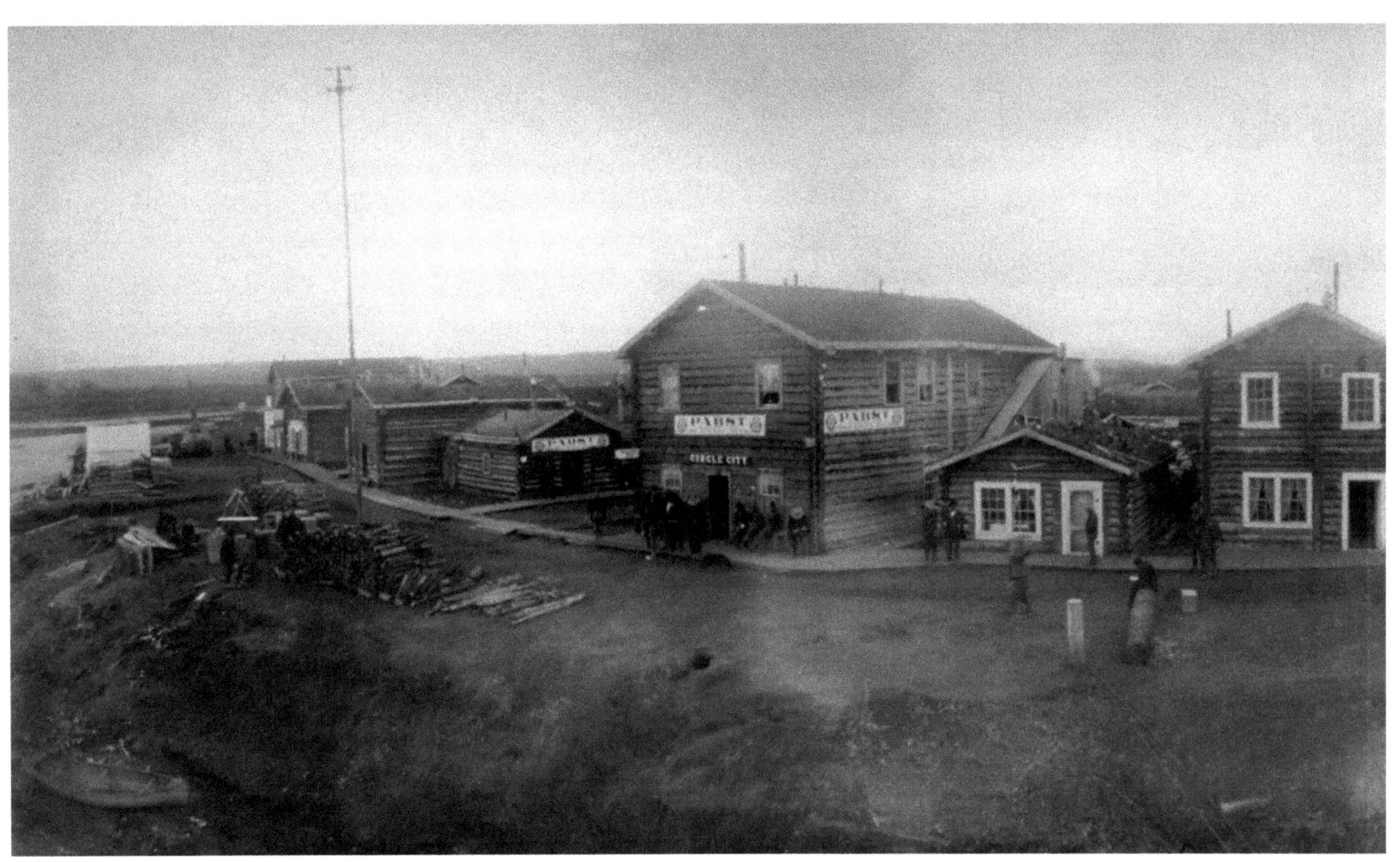

Circle City, on the Yukon River, was said to be the largest log-cabin town in the world during the peak of its gold boom in 1896, but most of its seven hundred residents left upon hearing the electrifying news that gold was discovered across the border in the Klondike, touching off a stampede that grabbed headlines around the world.

Railroad tycoon Edward Harriman led an expedition to Alaska in 1899 that stopped in Cape Fox, a village near Ketchikan on the southeast coast that had been abandoned five years earlier. Harriman's group took totem poles and other artifacts to museums in the "Lower 48" states. The items were returned a century later when the expedition's route was retraced, an event that became the subject of a public television special.

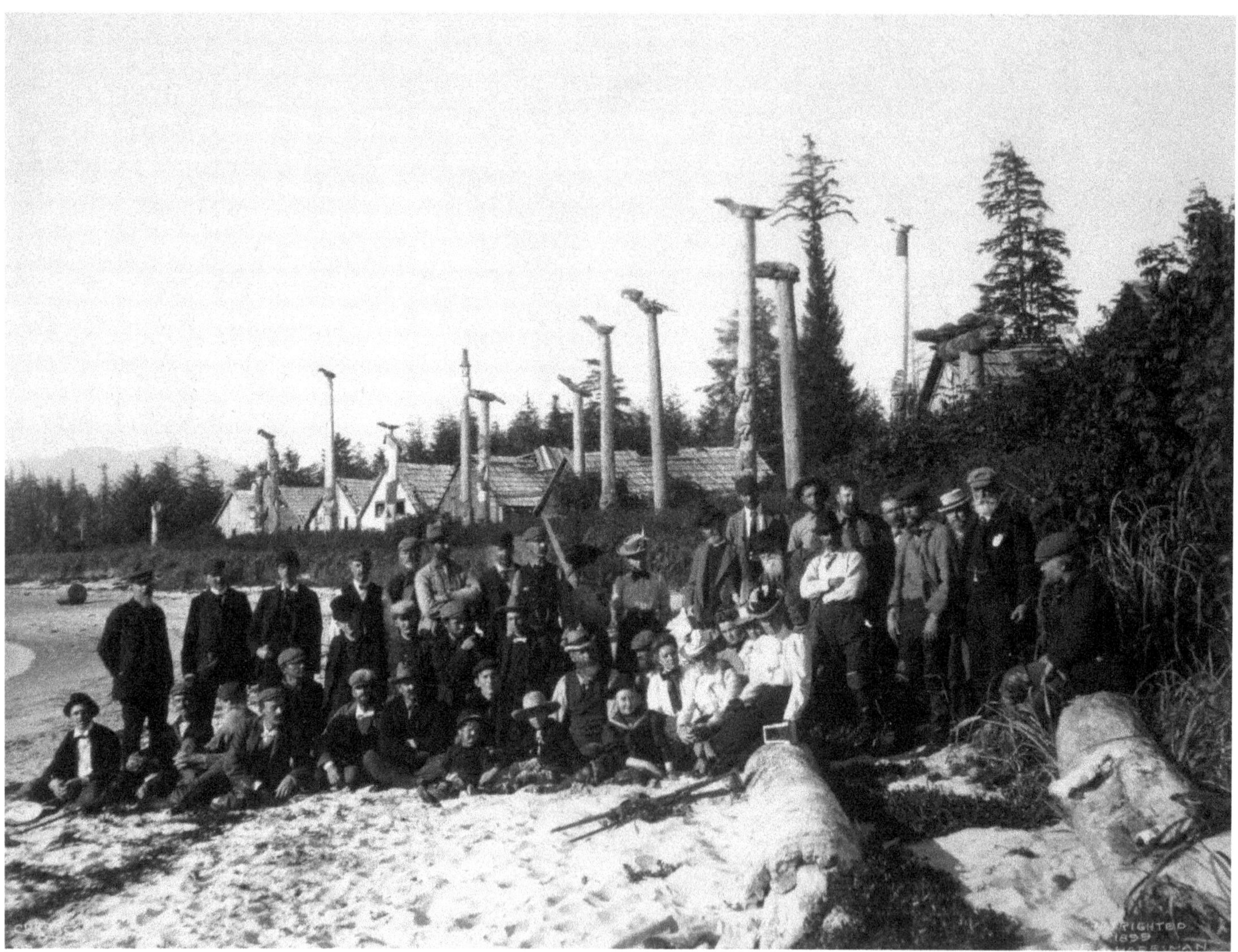

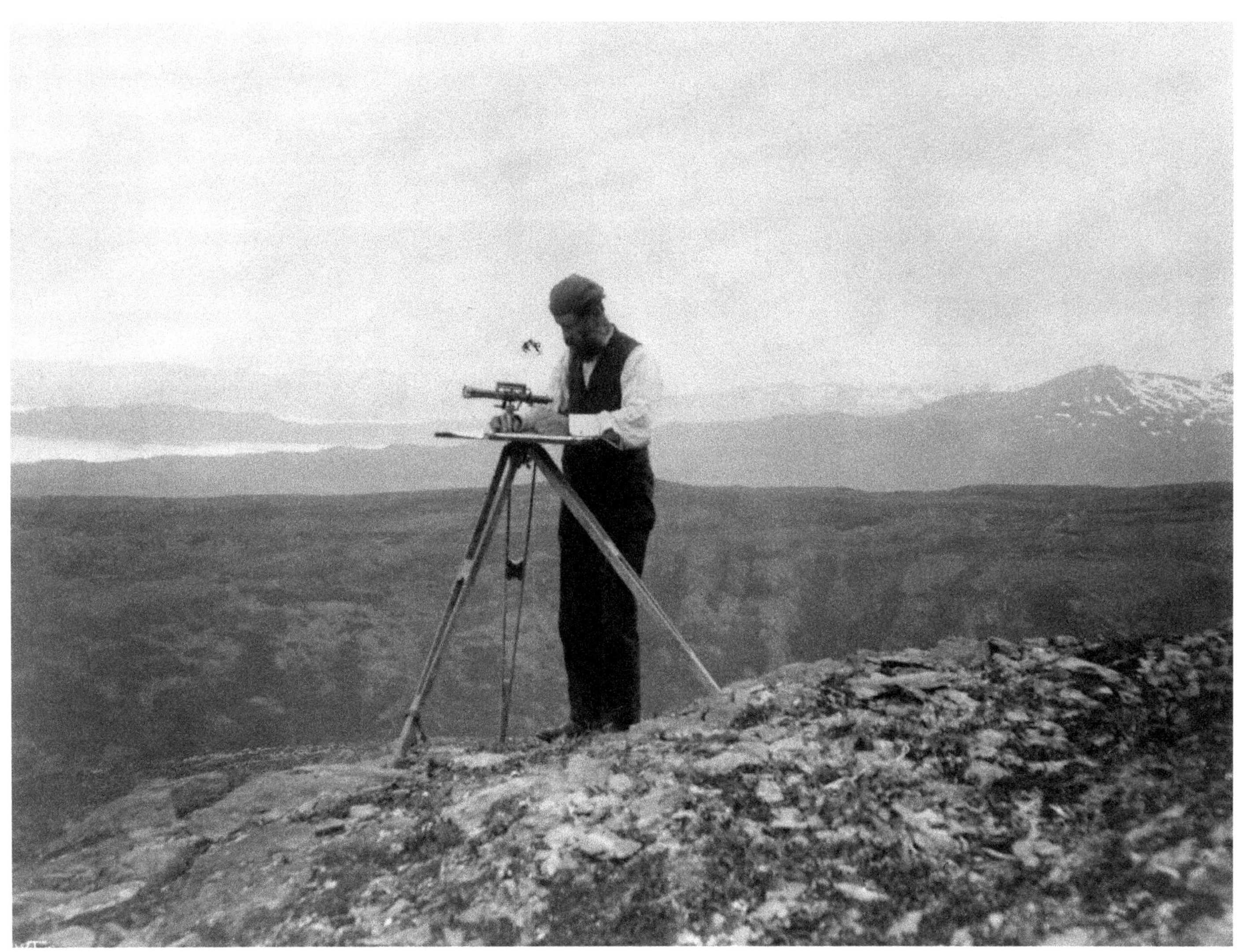

A surveyor takes his bearings along the mountainous coast of Alaska during the Harriman Expedition.

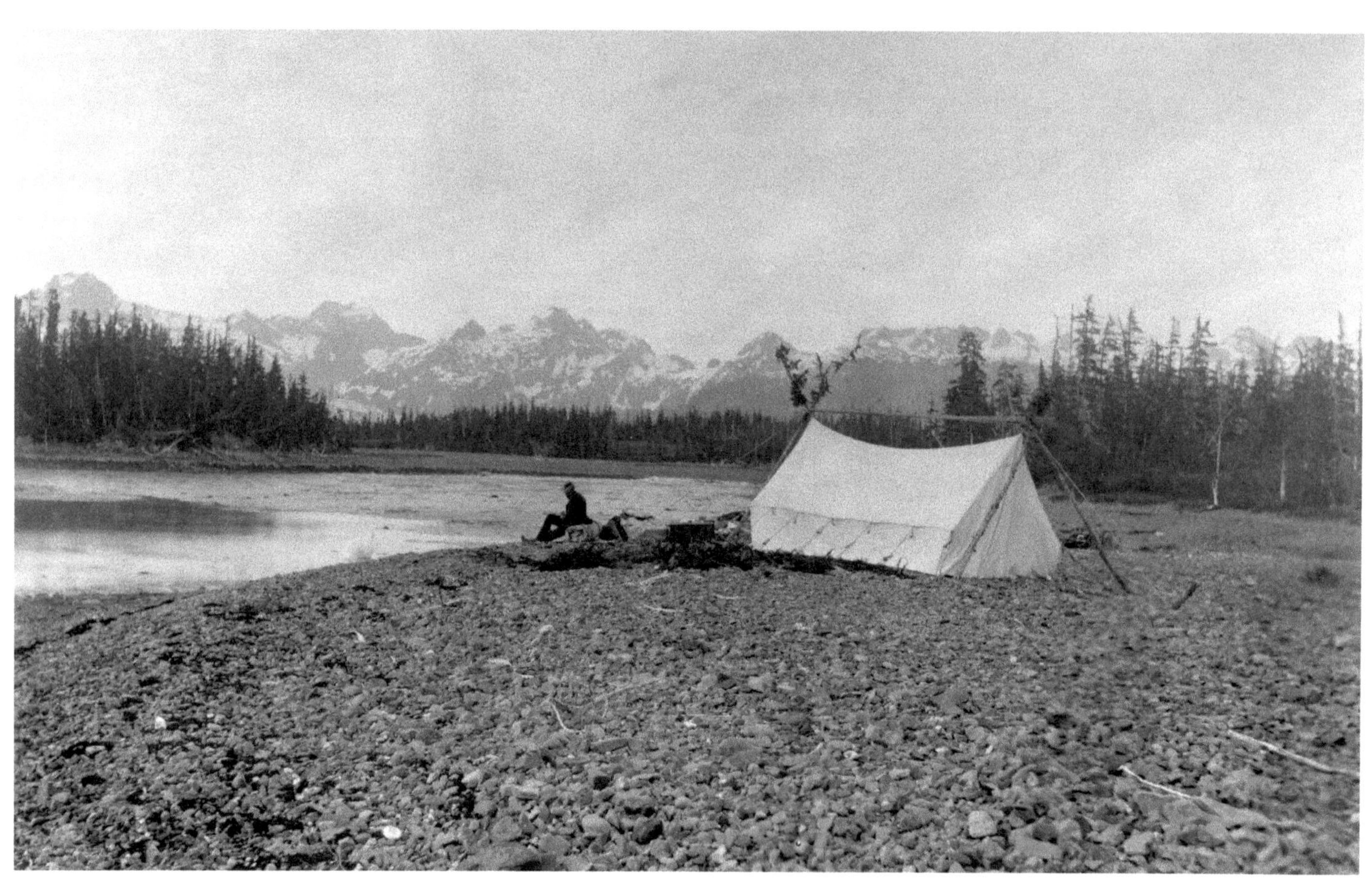

A gravel bar, open to breezes that helped keep the mosquitoes at bay, provided an excellent campsite during the Harriman Expedition. The camper is believed to be Bernhard Fernow, the first appointed chief of the U.S. Forest Service.

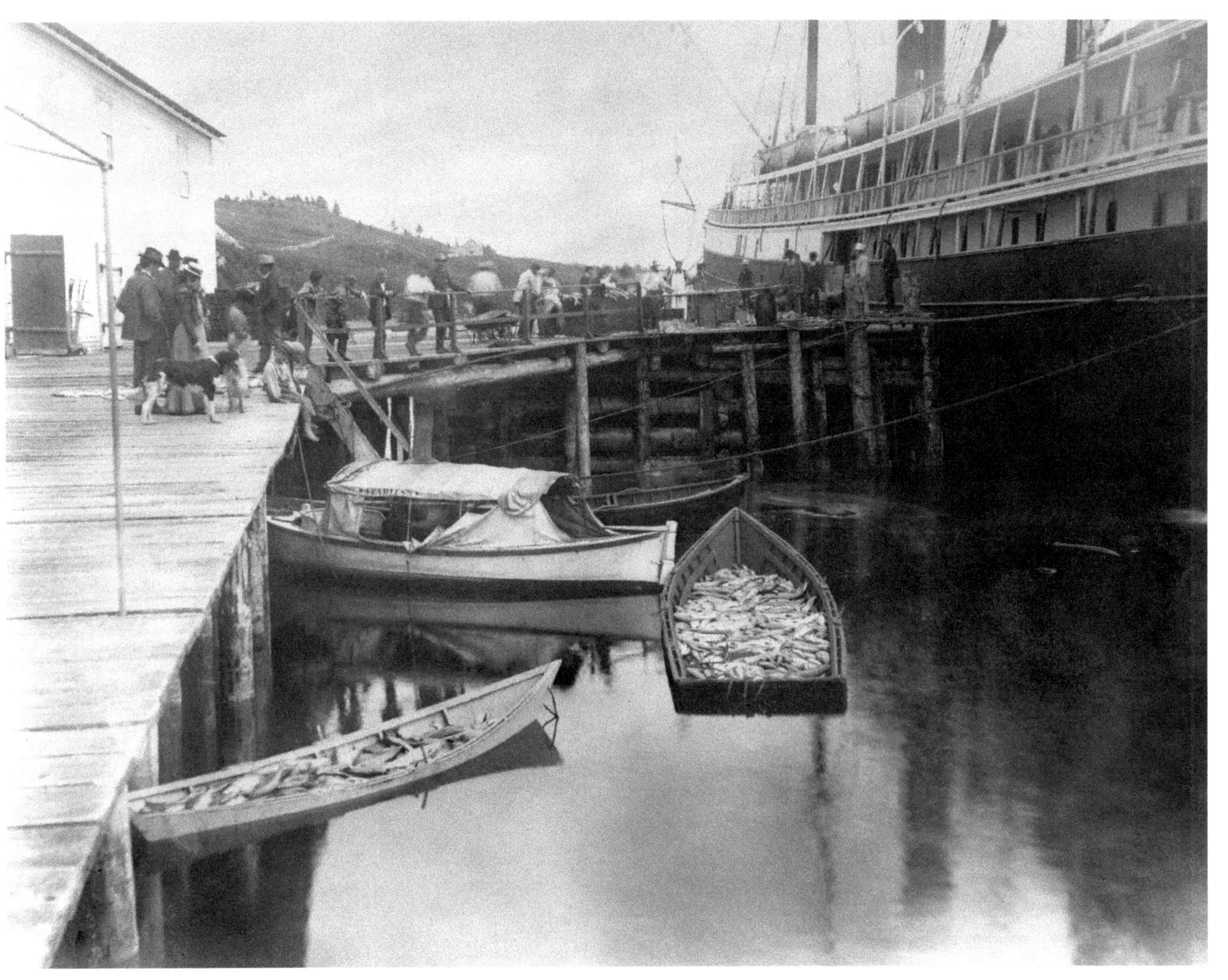

The scientists, artists, and hunters traveling with Harriman's Expedition disembark in a village, possibly Sitka, where small boats teeming with fish testify to the bounty of Alaska's waters.

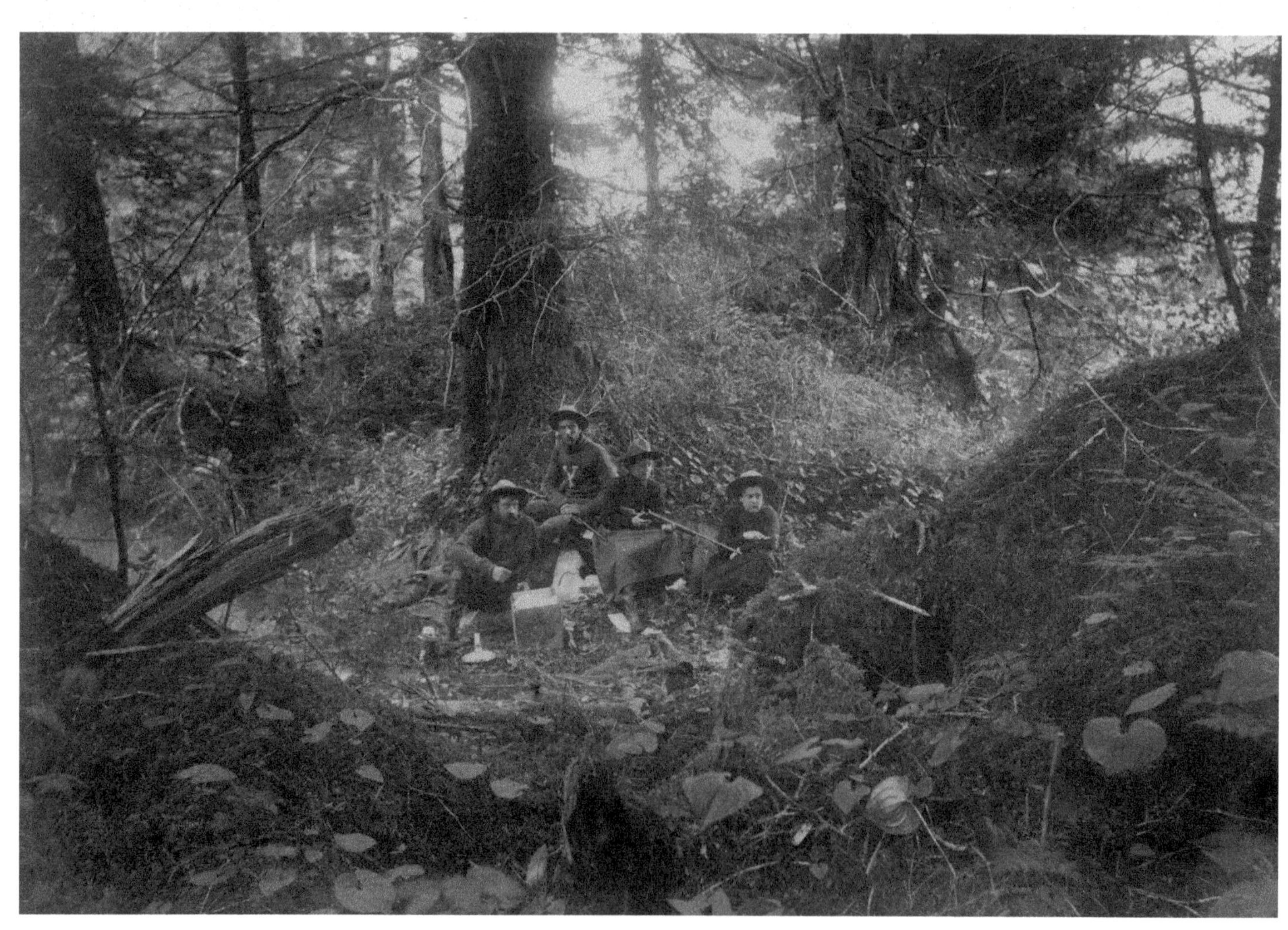

The rain forest of southeast Alaska is marked by dense vegetation and a rich, green landscape, in which some saw vast, undeveloped timber resources and others saw a region worthy of preservation.

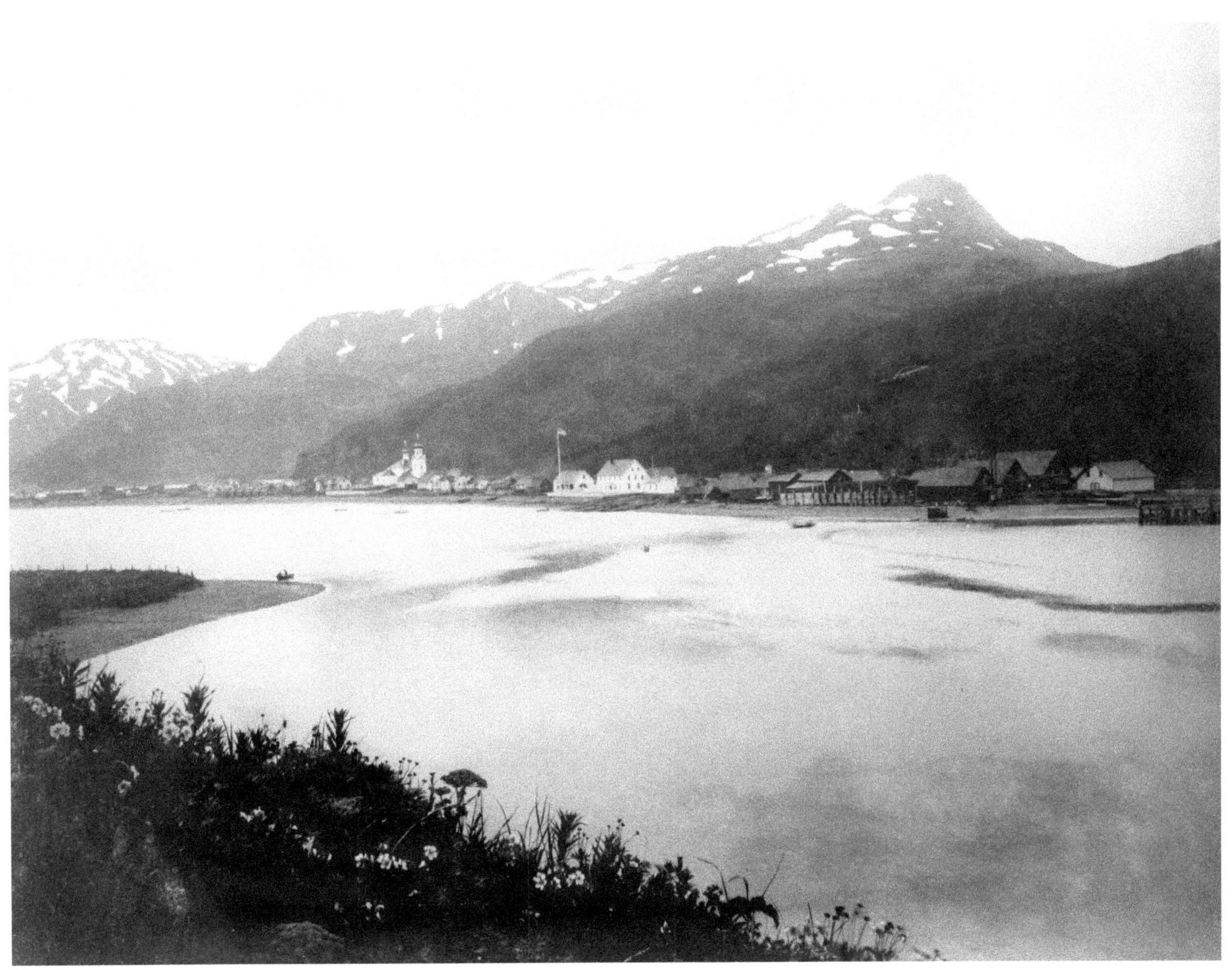

Unalaska, the commercial center of the Aleutians in the nineteenth century, gained its name from an Aleut word meaning "dwelling together harmoniously."

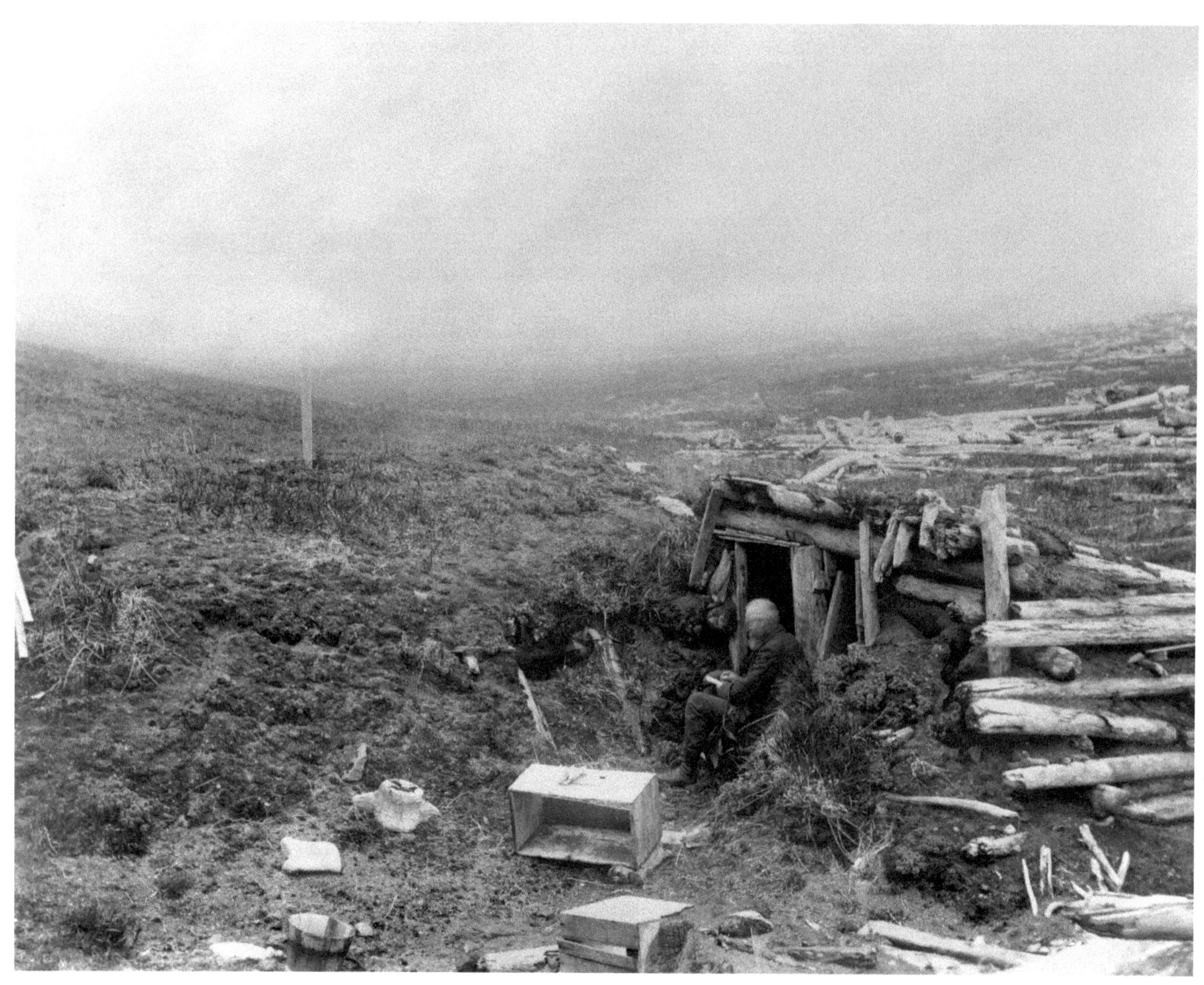

Driftwood and a cave dug into the tundra provide a rudimentary shelter for an old man in 1899.

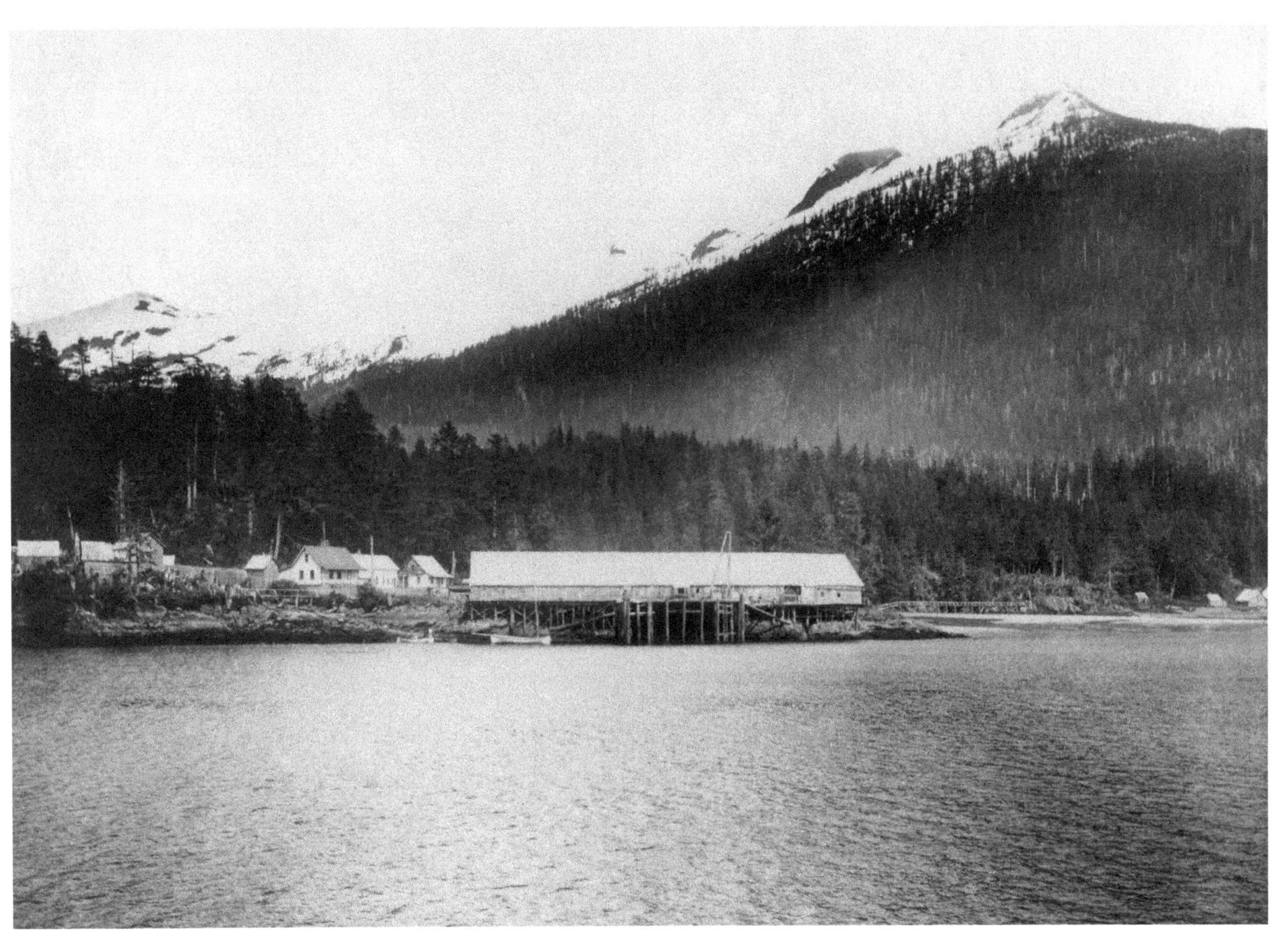

The Ketchikan waterfront in 1899, thirteen years after the town's first salmon cannery was established.

The sun gleams through the clouds above Resurrection Bay on the Kenai Peninsula.

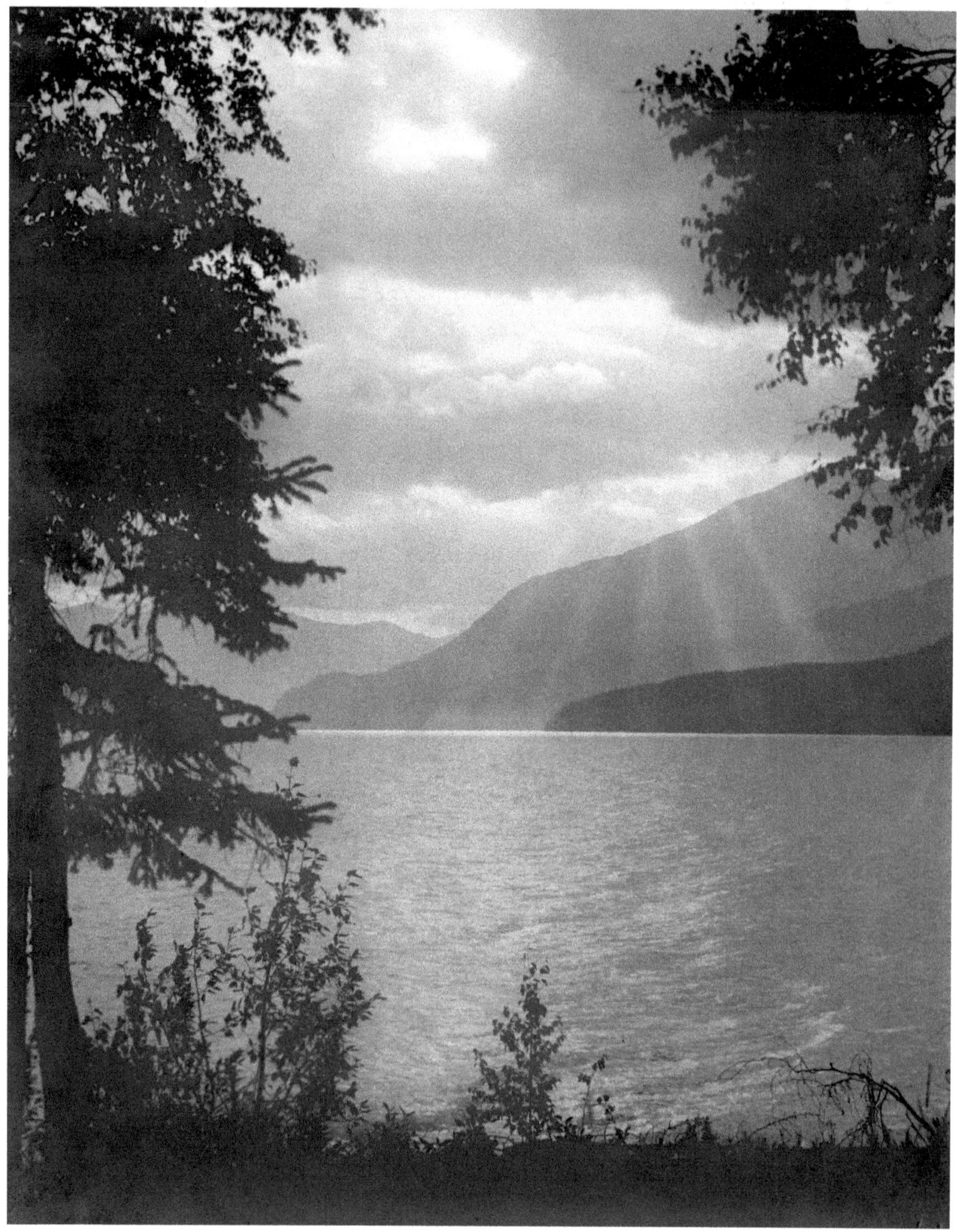

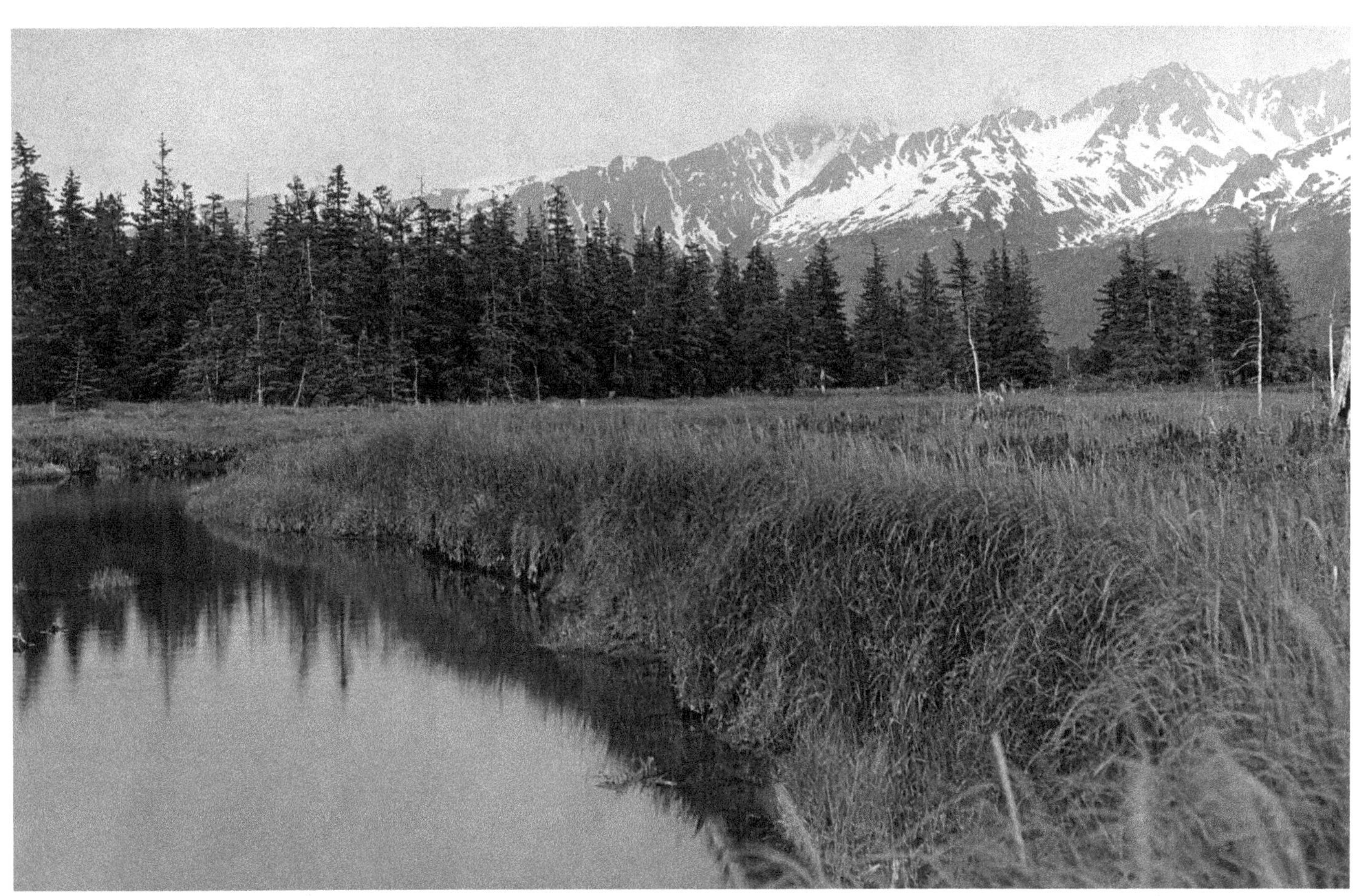

Magnificent scenery looms at the head of Resurrection Bay, which was named by Russian explorer Alexander Baranov in 1792 because it provided him shelter during a fierce storm on Russia's Sunday of the Resurrection.

A cable system in Nome provided a way to transfer passengers and freight from the shore to ships that couldn't get closer to the coast because of shallow water.

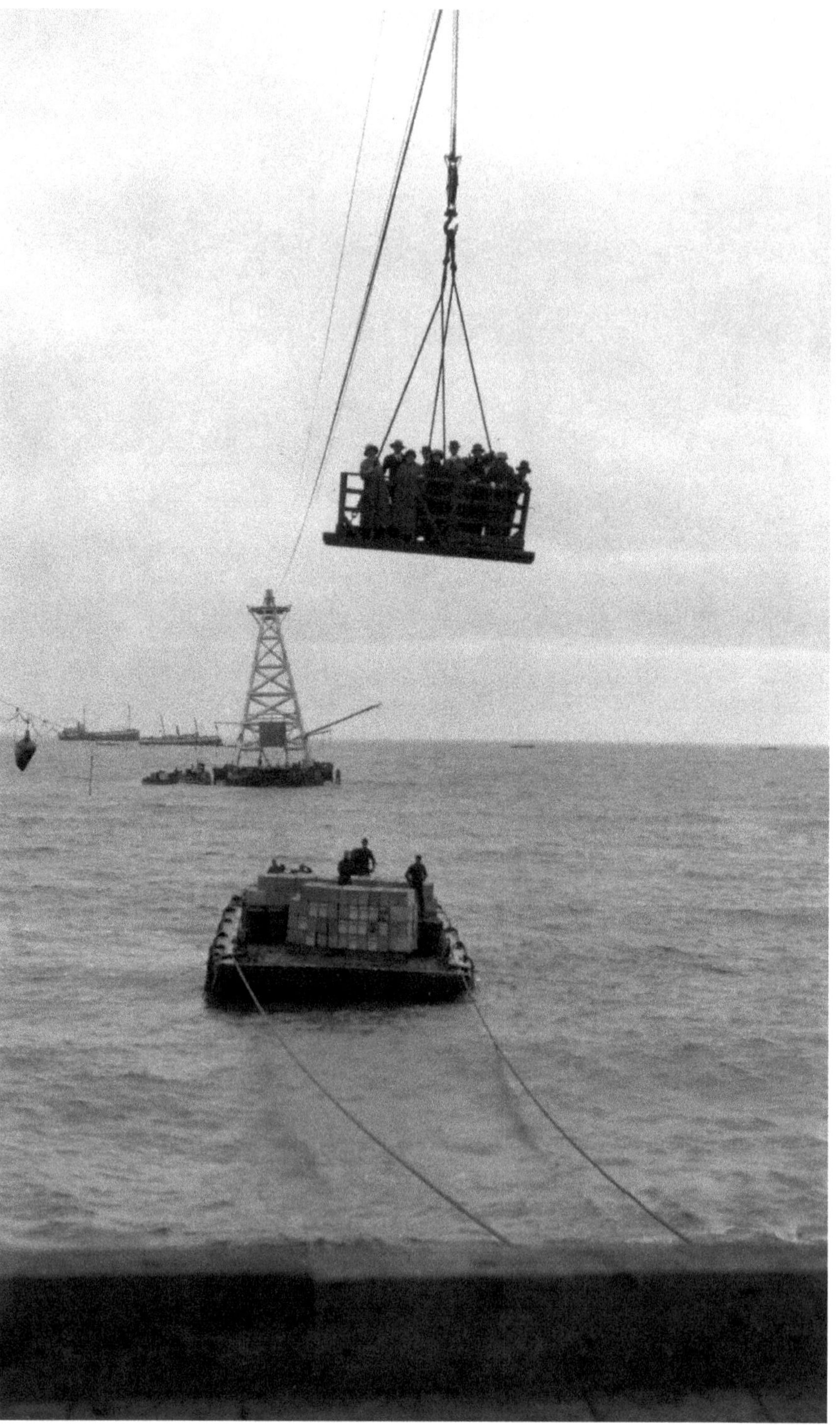

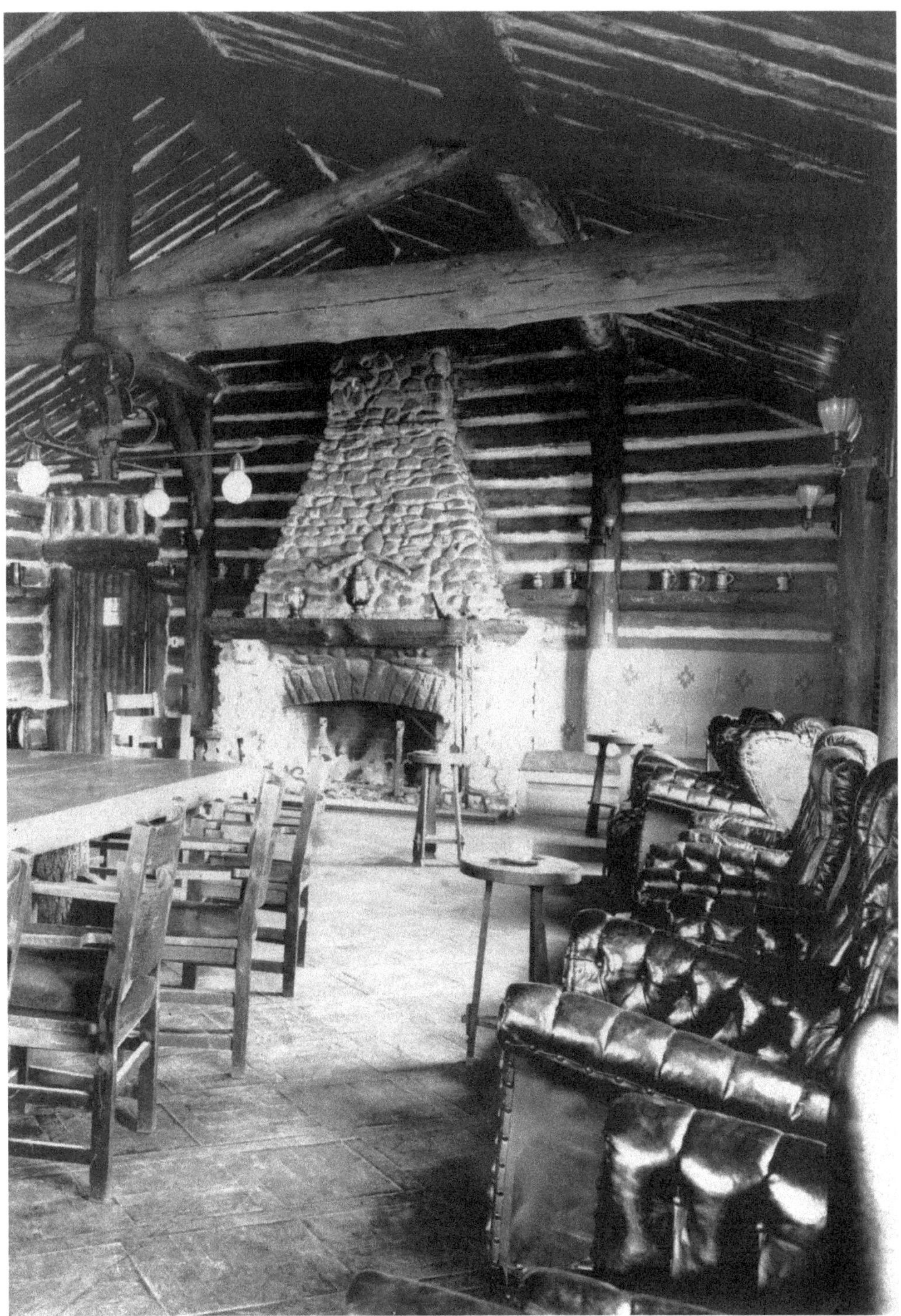

The Log Cabin Club of Nome about 1900, said to be the most northerly clubhouse in America.

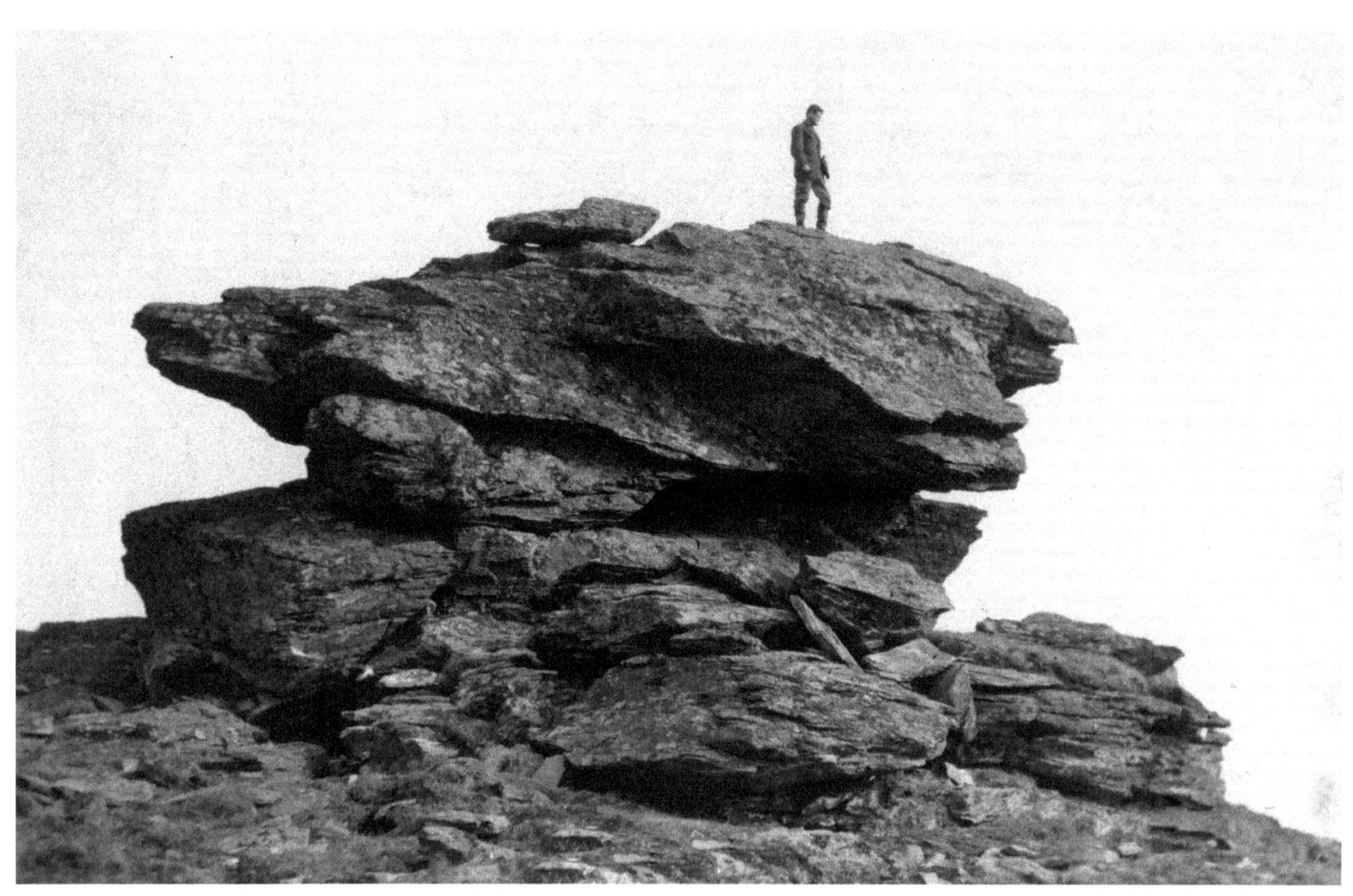

A climber takes in the view of the treeless Seward Peninsula landscape from Anvil Rock in the early 1900s.

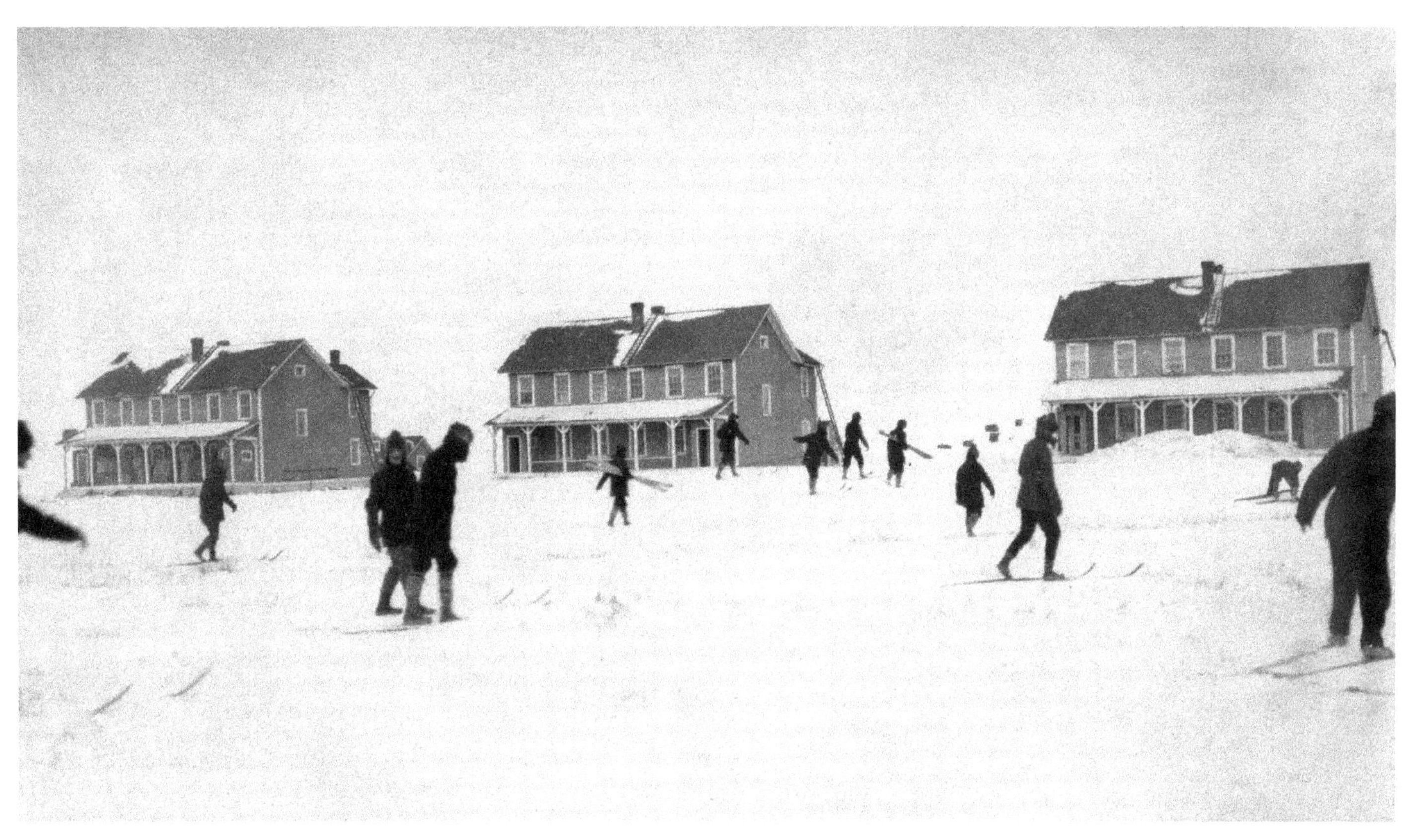

Soldiers at the U.S. Army post at St. Michael in the early 1900s strap on skis and make their way over the snow without benefit of poles.

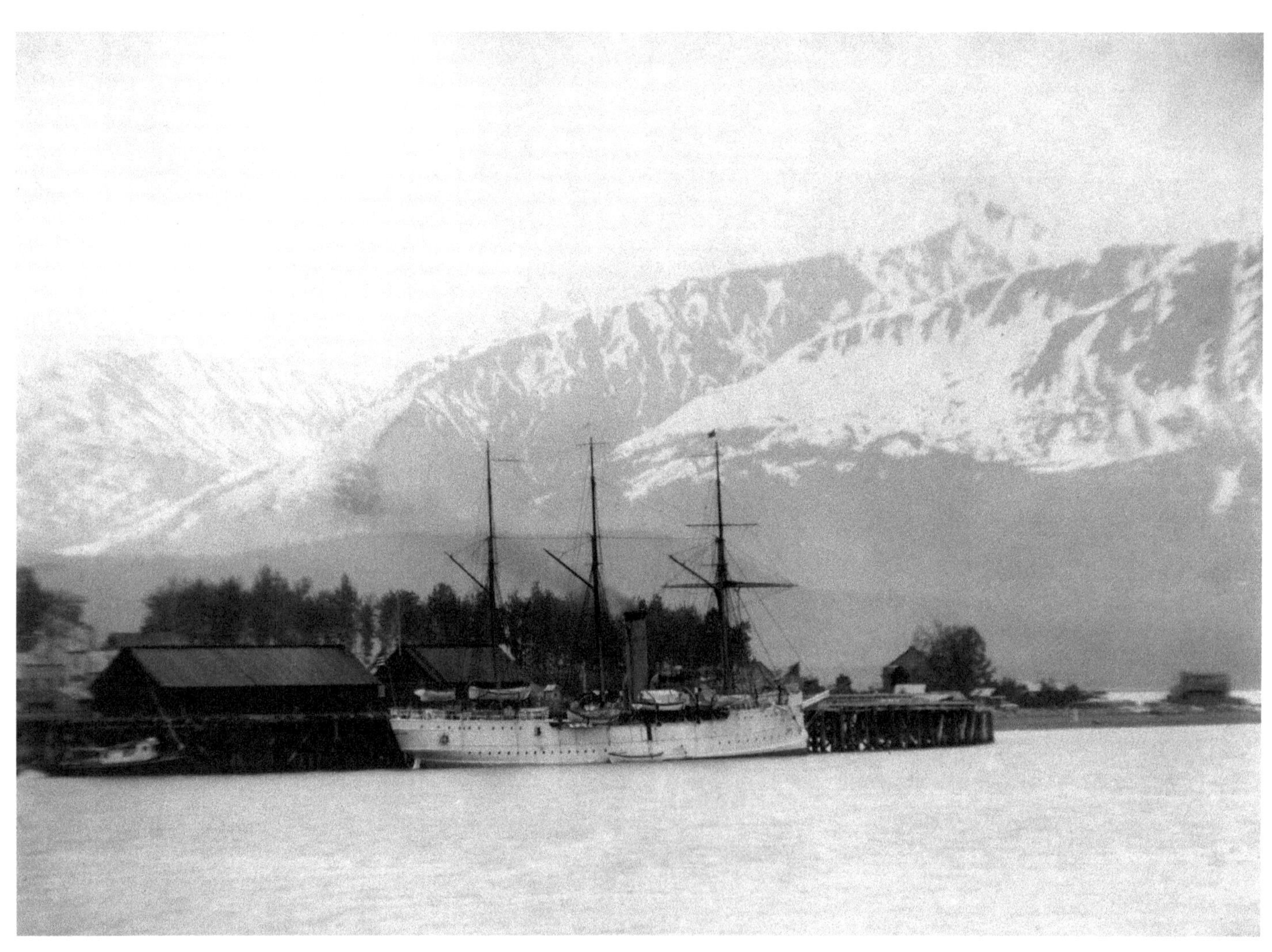

The revenue cutter *McCulloch* docks at Seward after being sent to Alaska in 1906 to enforce regulations on fur sealing (seal hunting).

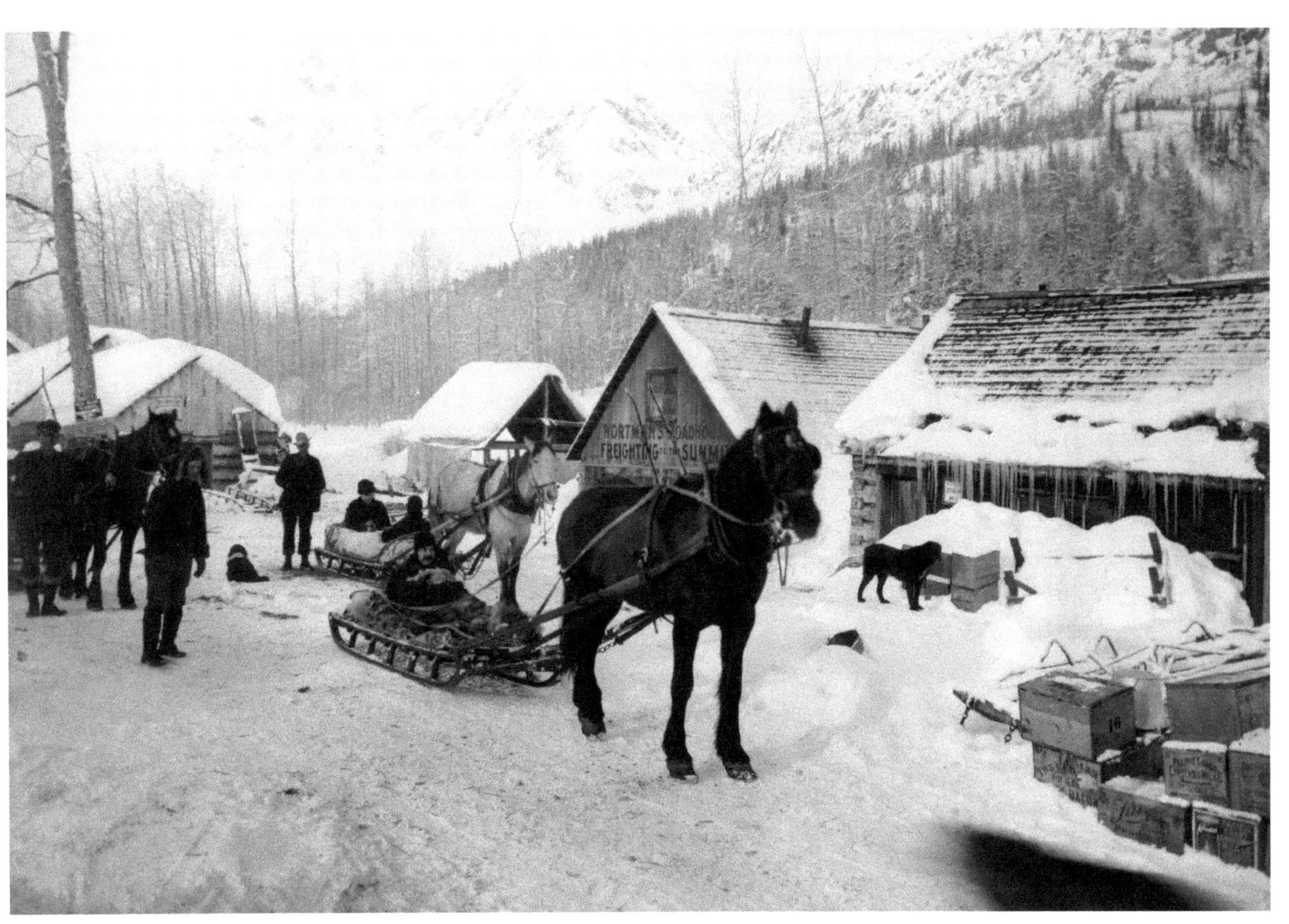

Horse-drawn sleds provide winter access from Wortman's Roadhouse, outside of Valdez, through the Chugach Mountains.

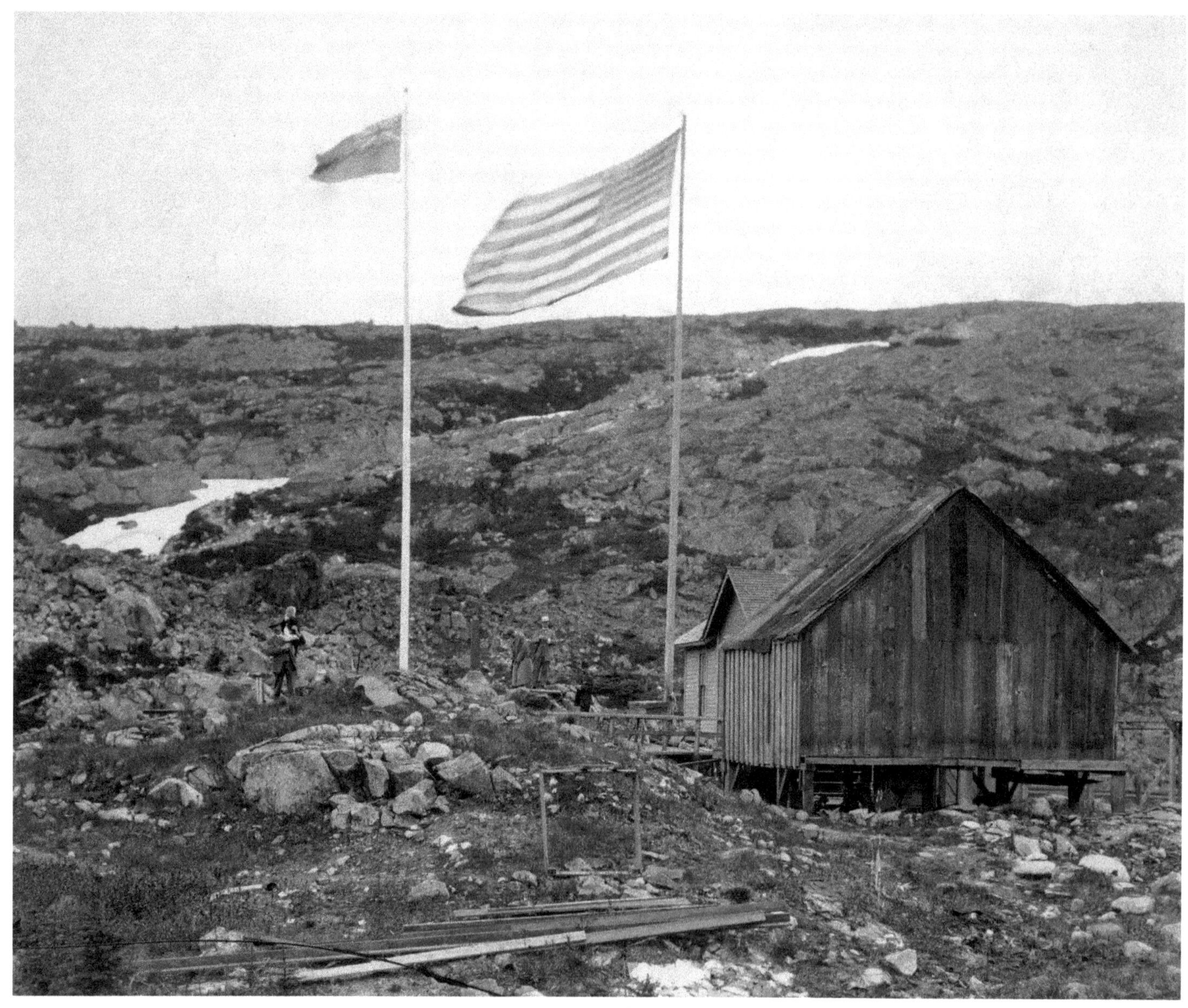

The obelisk between the flags marks a mountain-pass border between Alaska and the Yukon Territory.

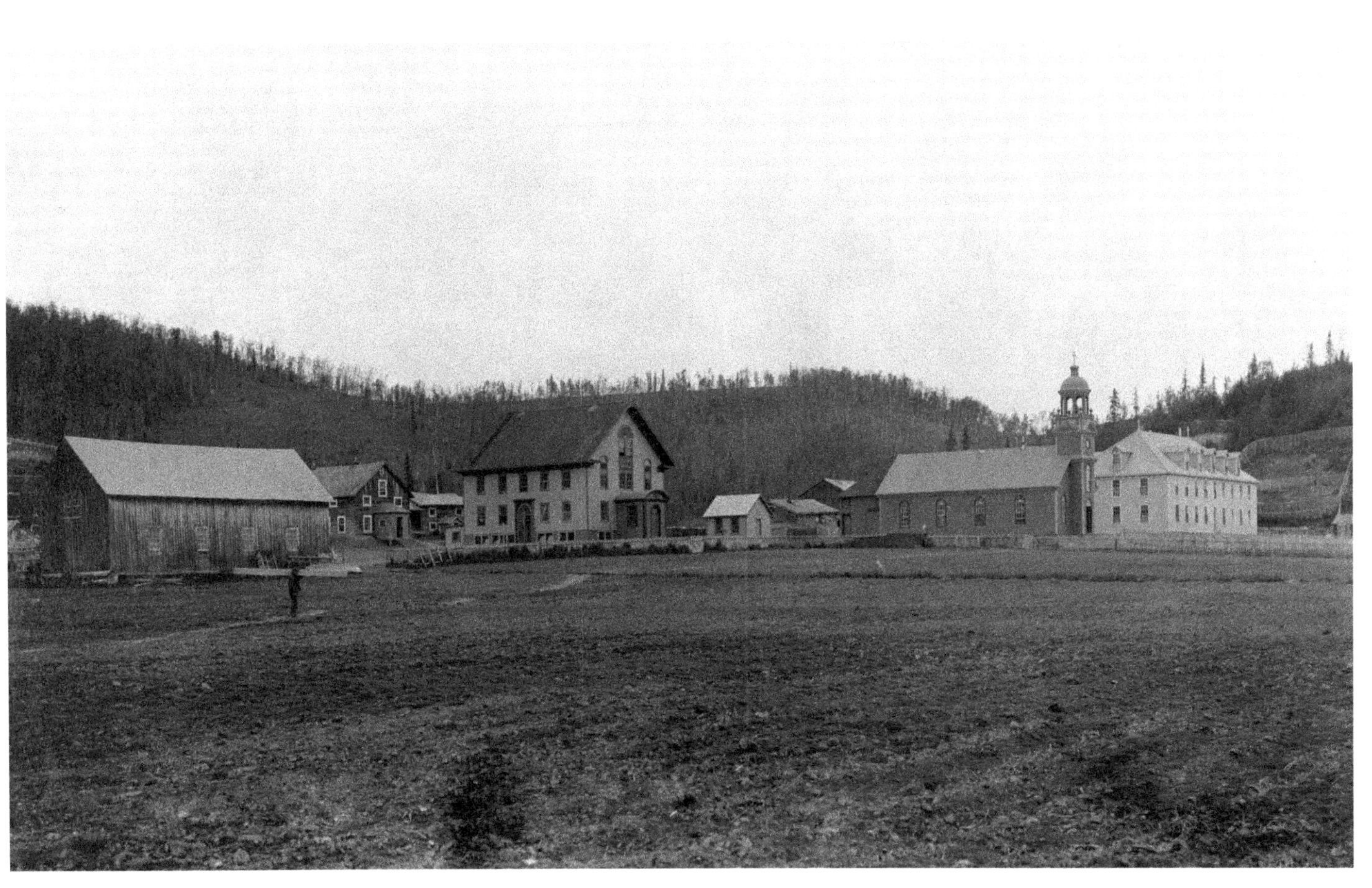

Holy Cross Mission on the Yukon River was established by the Catholic Church in 1888 as a regional center for church operations and a boarding school.

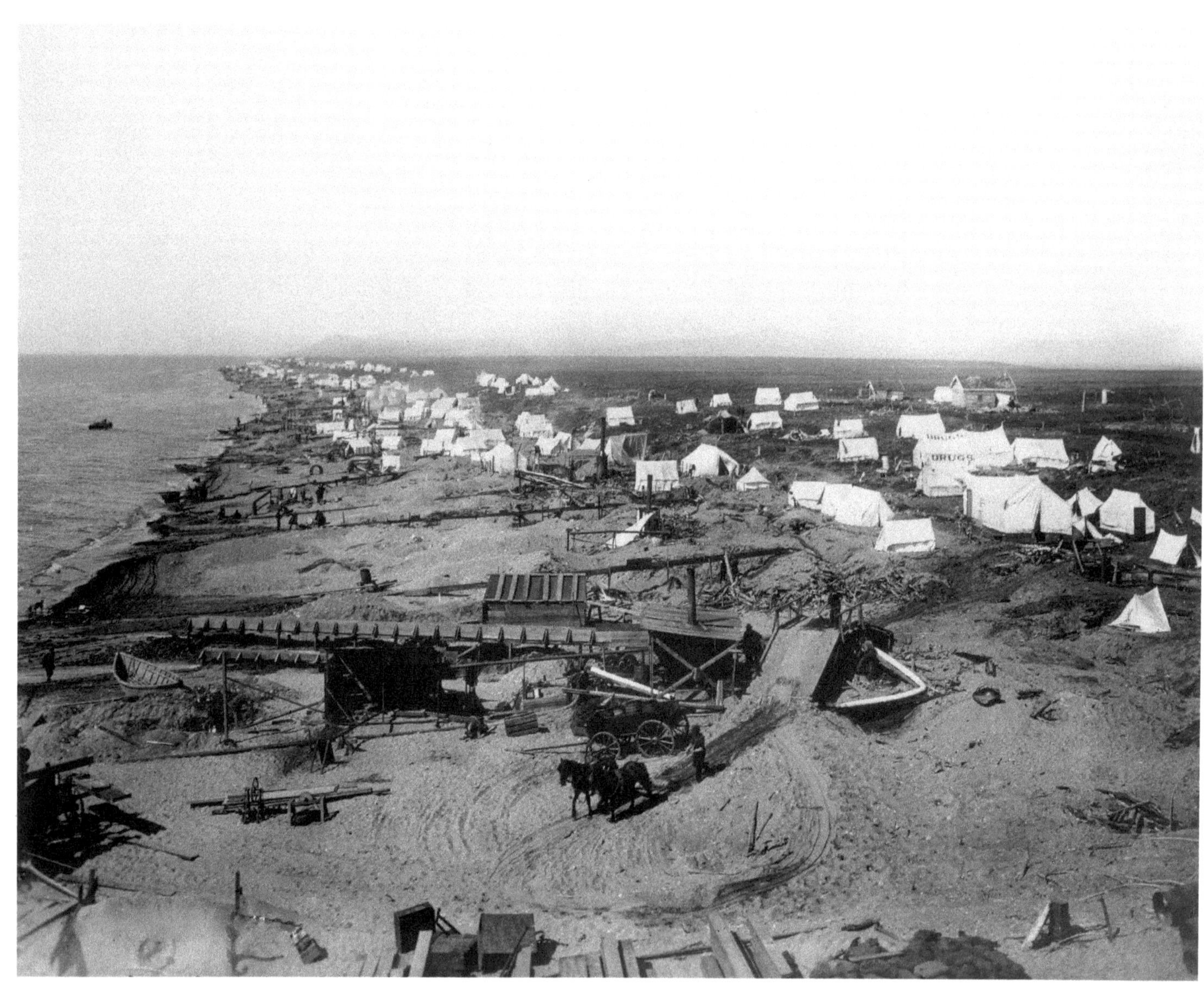

The golden beach at Nome attracted thousands of stampeders who panned for the precious metal along every foot of the shore in the summer of 1900.

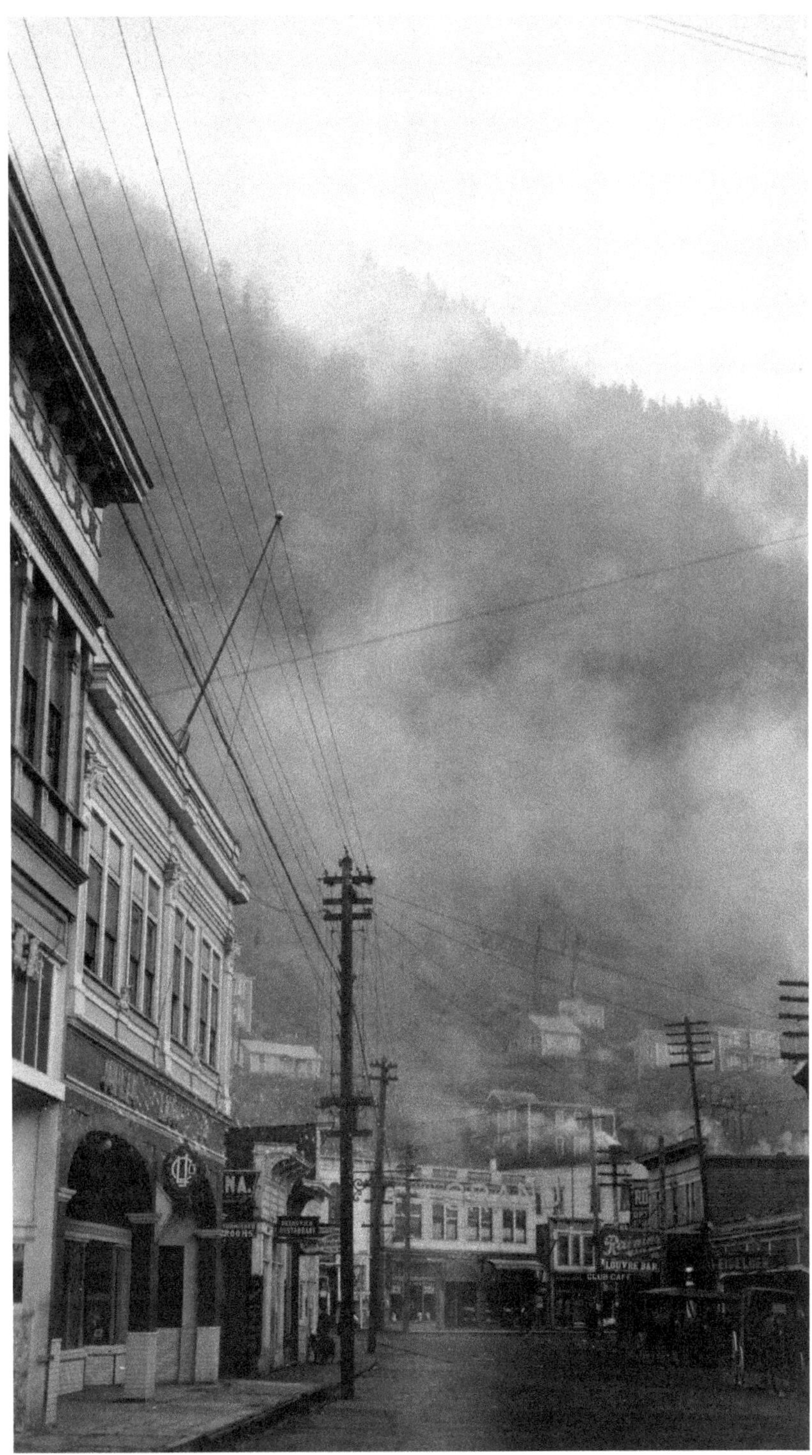

Clouds cling to the hillsides bordering Juneau's main commercial district, where the Delmonico Restaurant could be found across the street from the Louvre Bar.

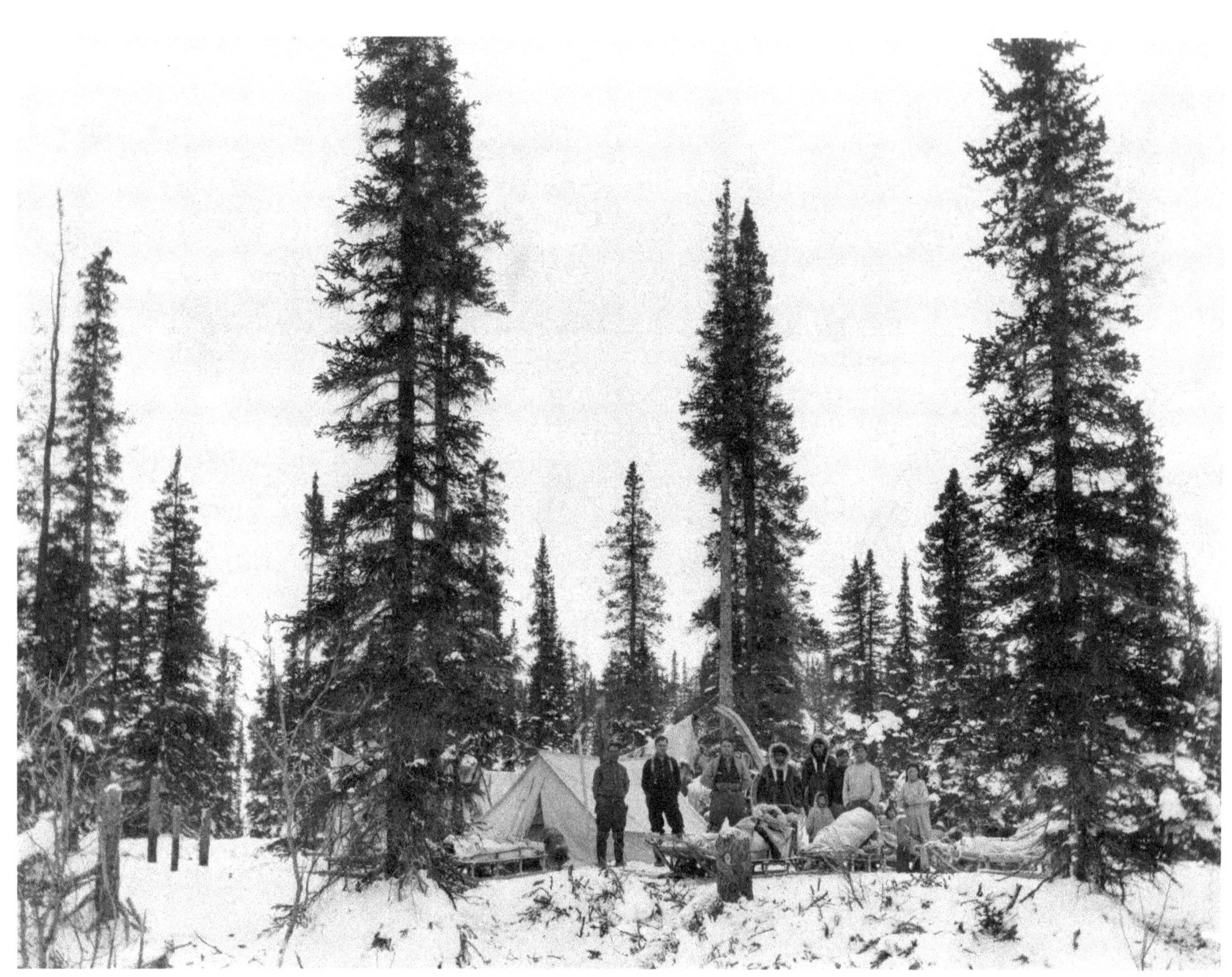

A winter camp north of the Arctic Circle, where travel by dog team required men, women, and children to be ready for severe temperatures.

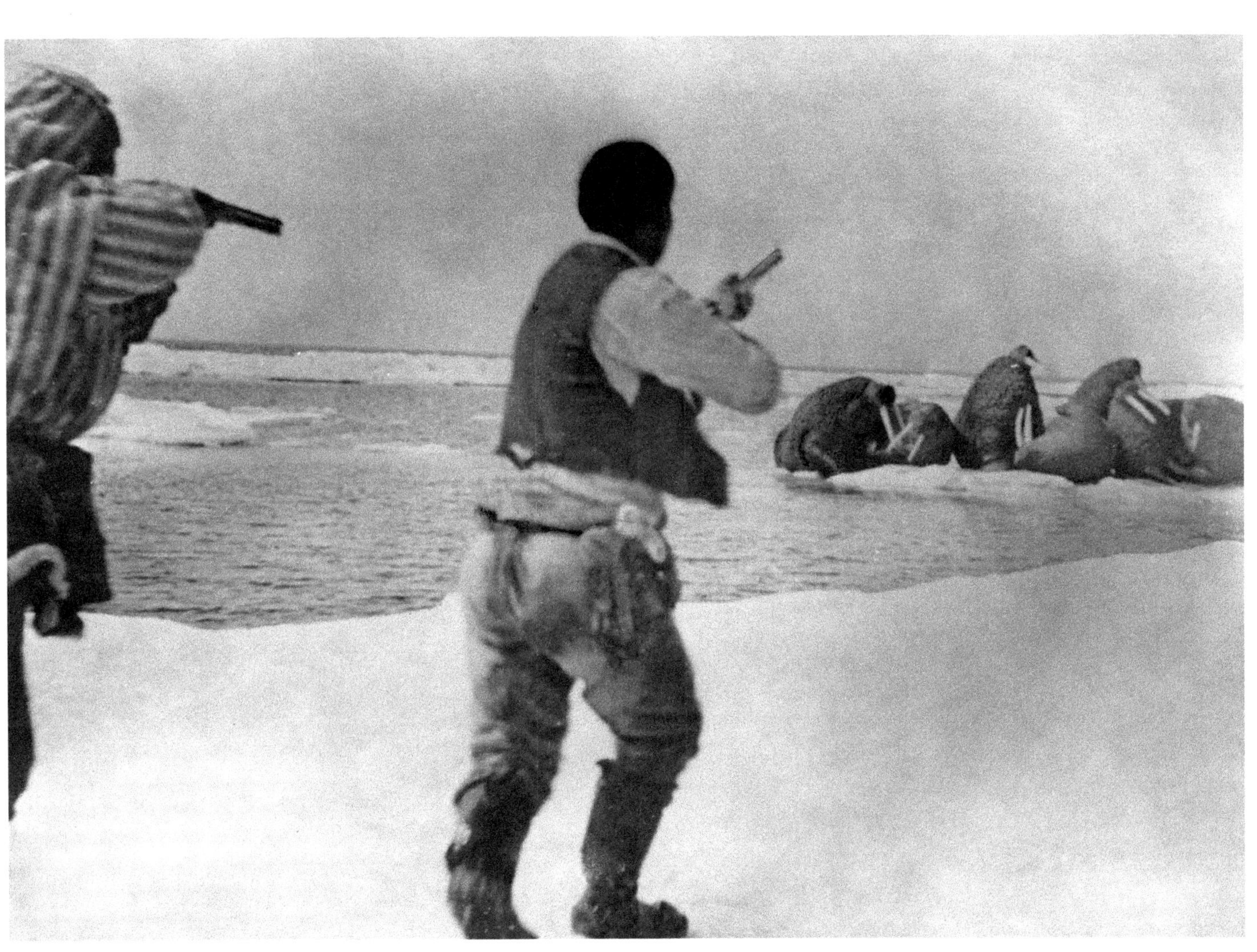

Eskimo hunters take aim at walruses on an ice floe. The adult bulls may weigh nearly two tons. They were usually hunted near the end of summer.

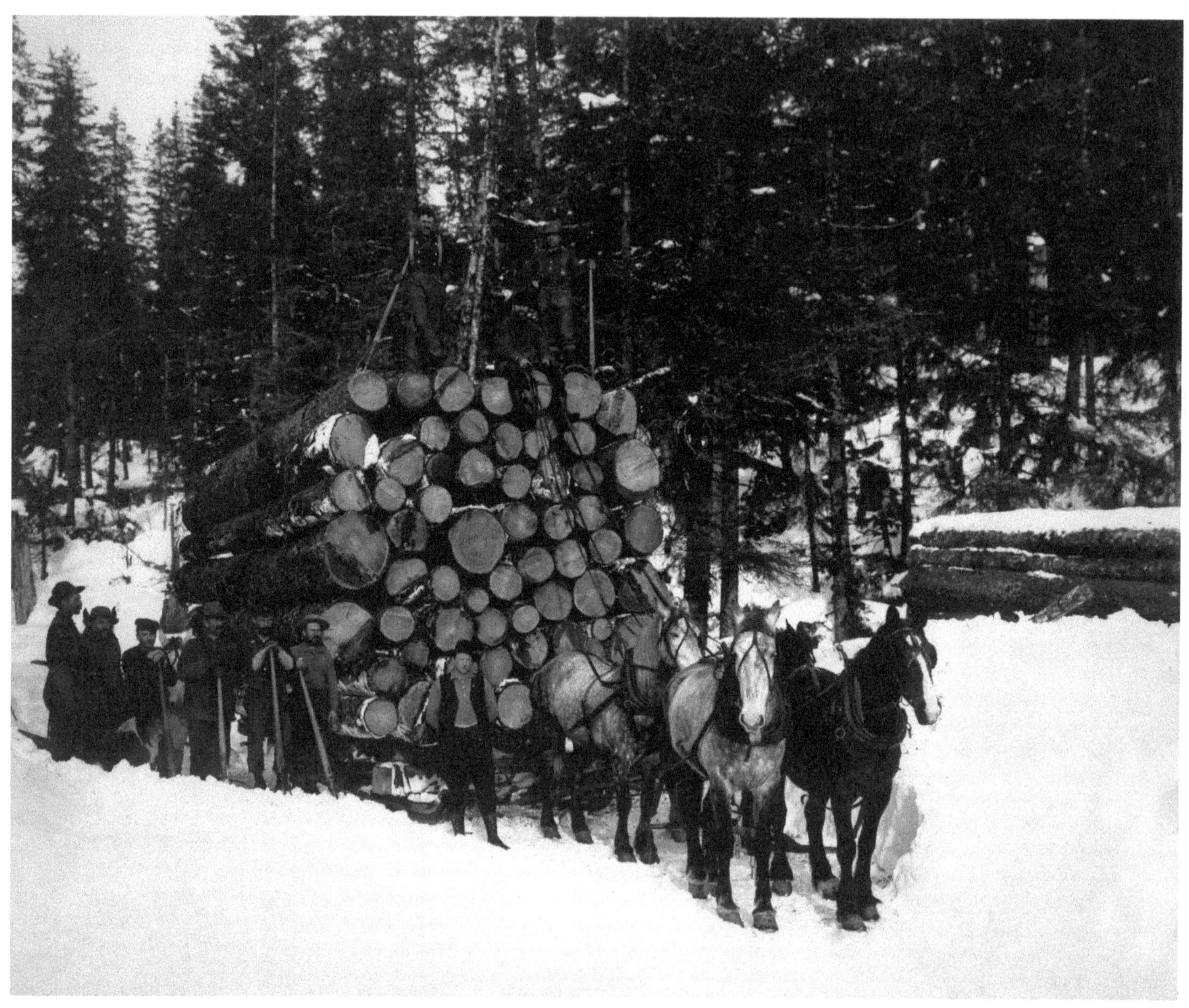

Nine woodcutters and four horses take a break while hauling tons of timber along the railroad right-of-way thirty-five miles from Seward.

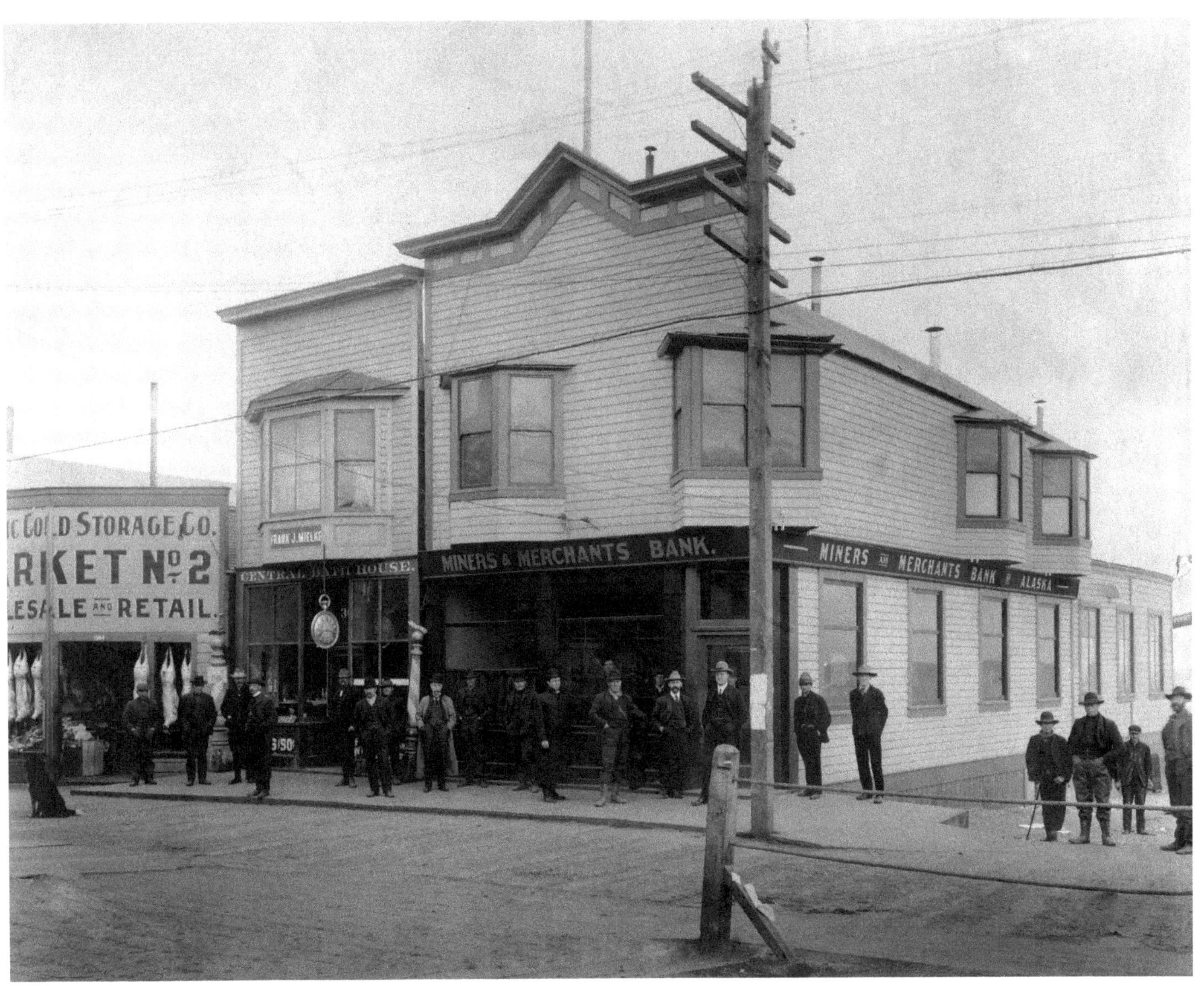

The Miners and Merchants Bank of Alaska, photographed in Nome on September 23, 1905. The bank handled millions of dollars of gold dust every year during the heyday of the Nome gold rush.

Valdez, the main gateway to Interior Alaska in the early 1900s, as seen from the bay. The mountains prompted comparisons with Switzerland.

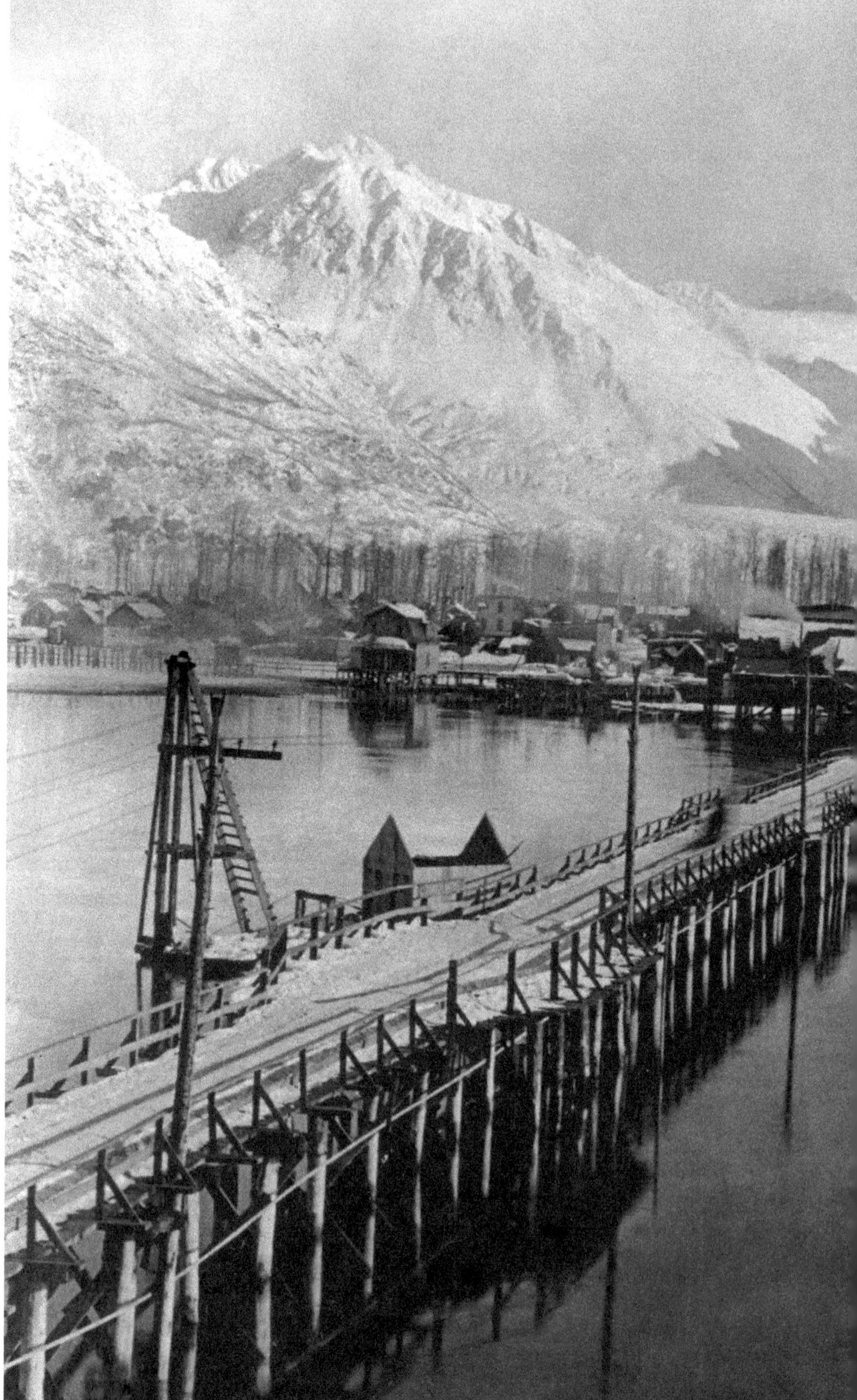

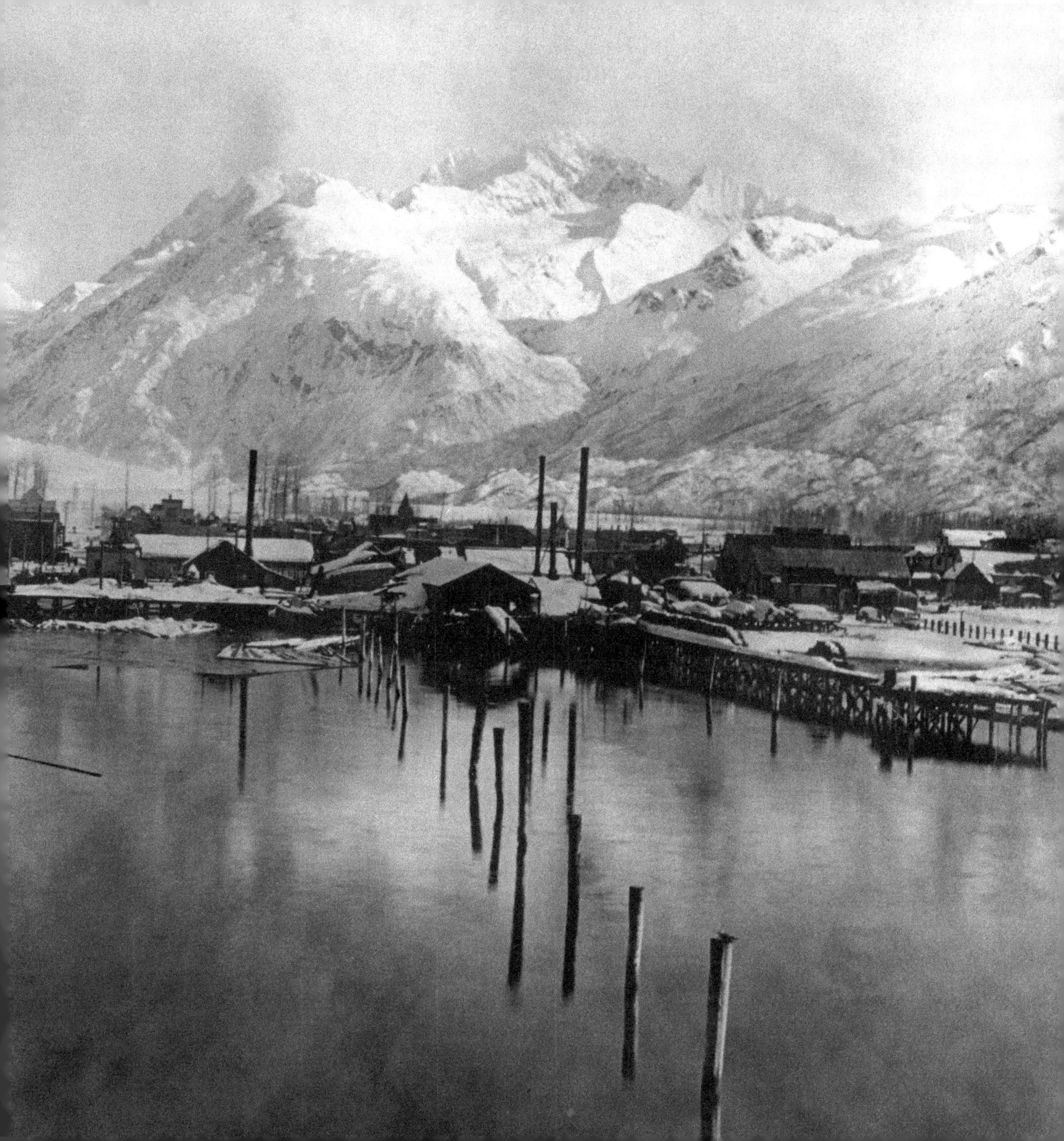

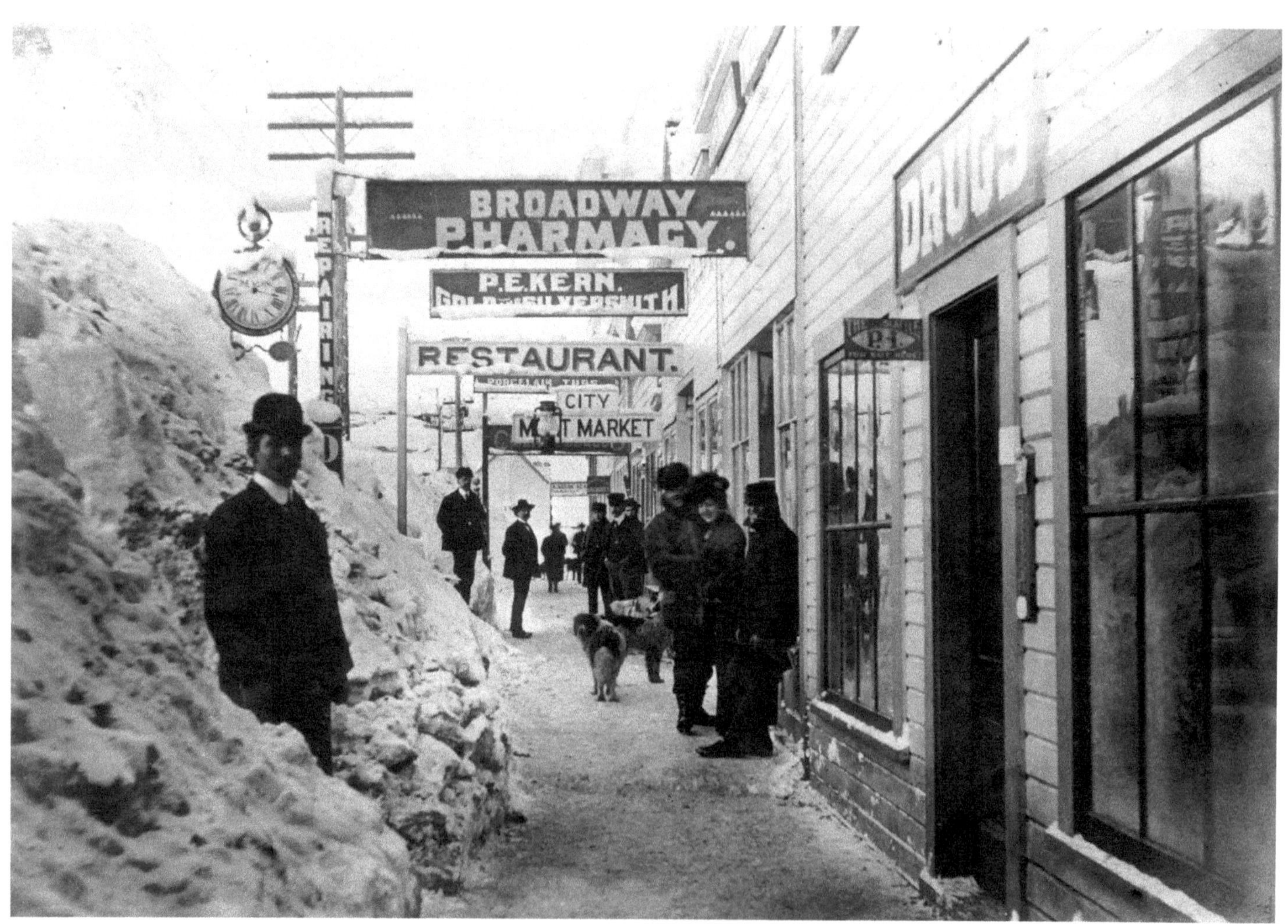

Valdez received 325 inches of snow in an average winter, and keeping the sidewalks clear was sometimes a real fight before the advent of motorized snow-clearing equipment.

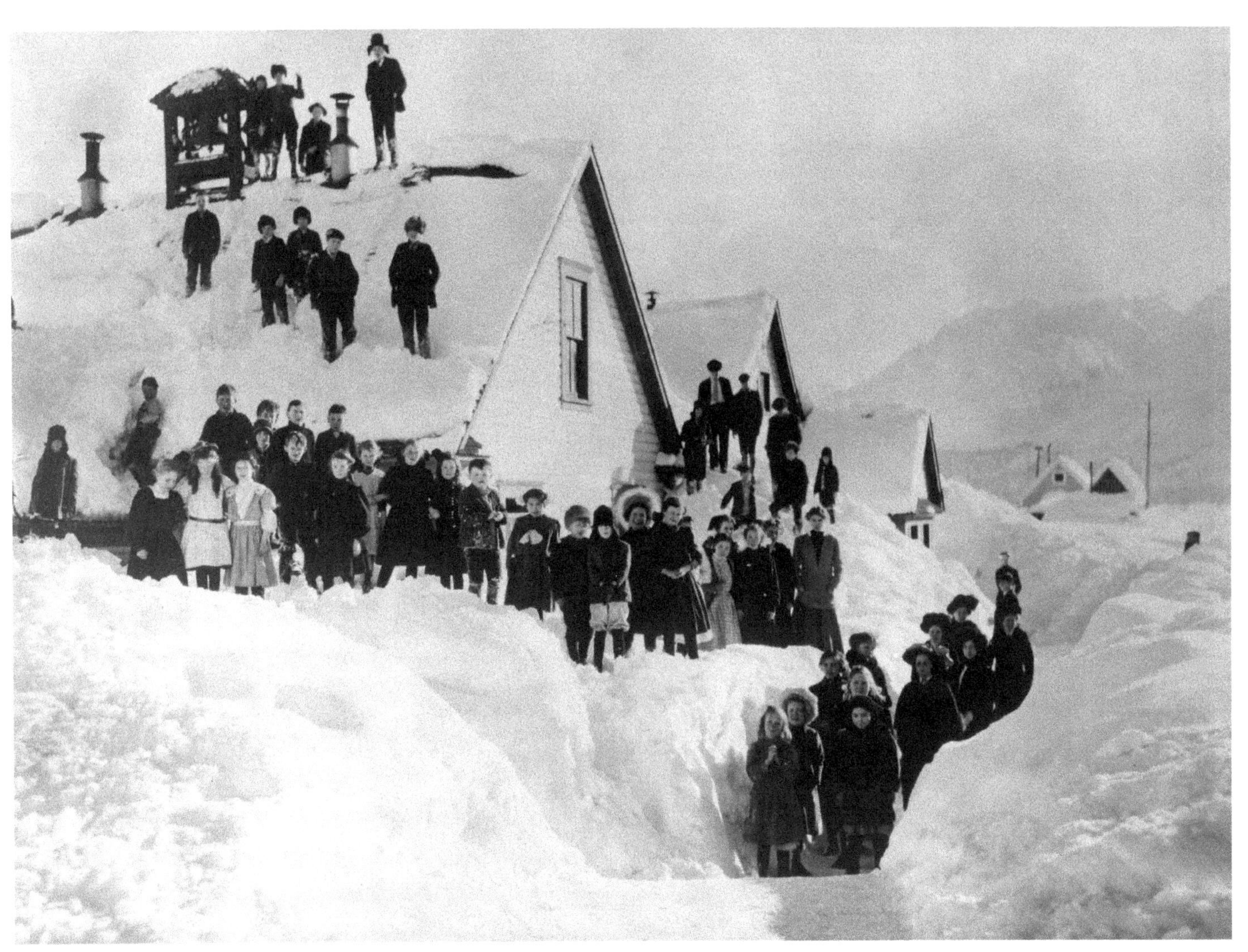

Heavy snow in Valdez in 1903 made it an easy matter to climb up on the roof of the schoolhouse.

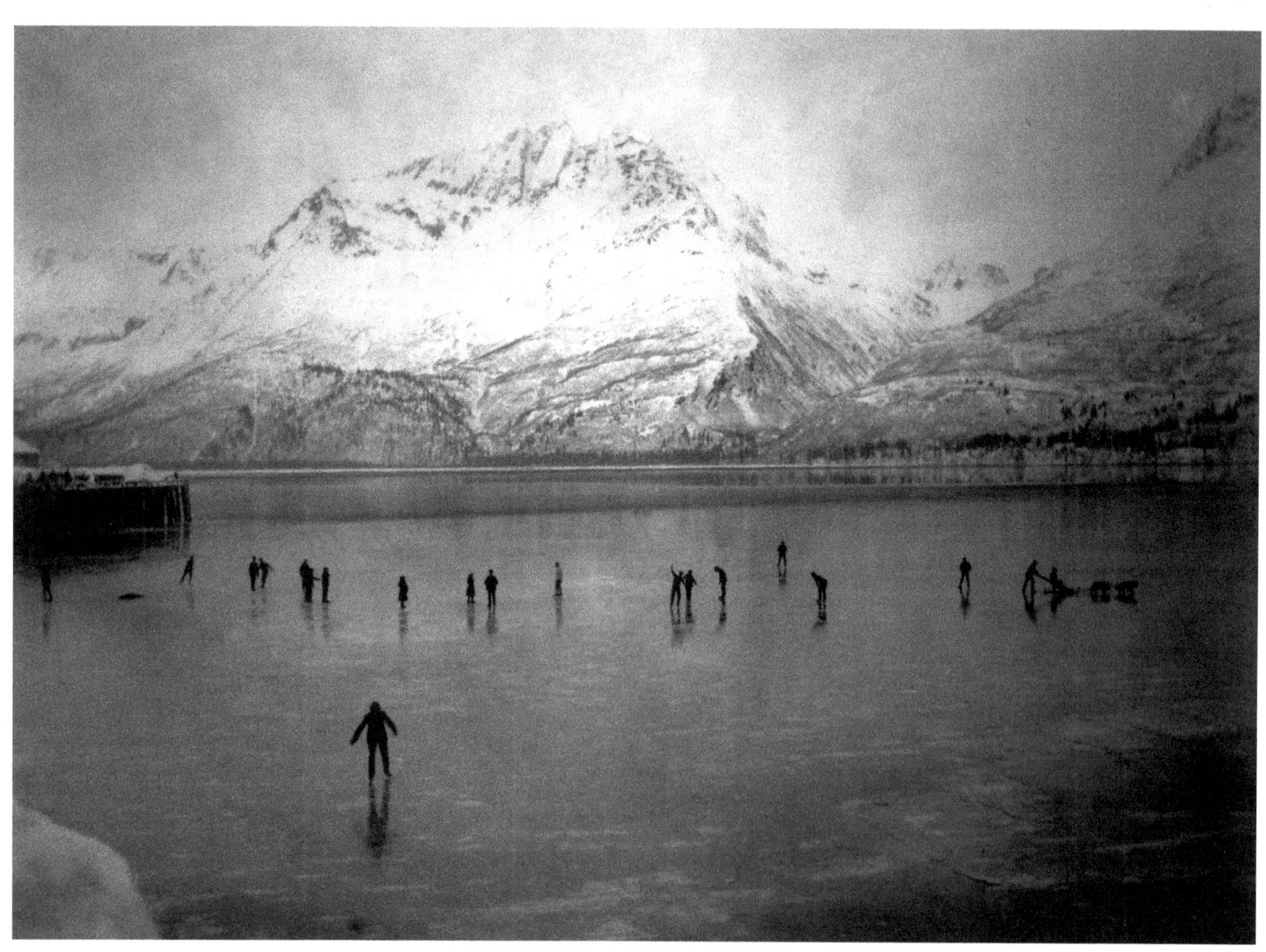

Photographer P. S. Hunt, who created the best visual record of life in early Valdez, classified this scene as a "freak of Alaska weather." It was cold enough that the harbor, normally ice-free, had built up sufficient ice along the shore to permit skating on January 15, 1905.

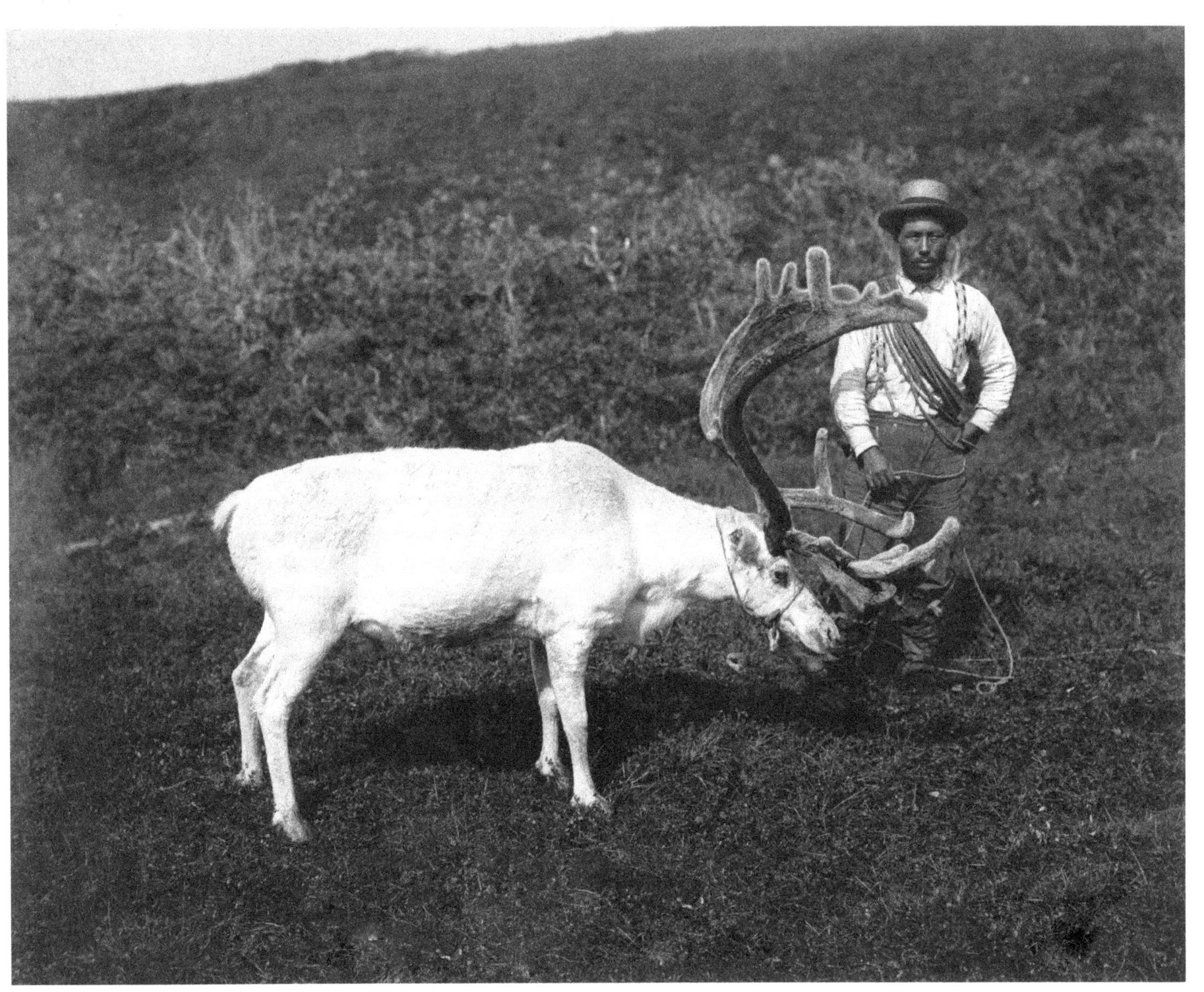

An Eskimo reindeer herder with his "rebellious captive" in western Alaska. The reindeer population would peak at more than 640,000 in the 1930s.

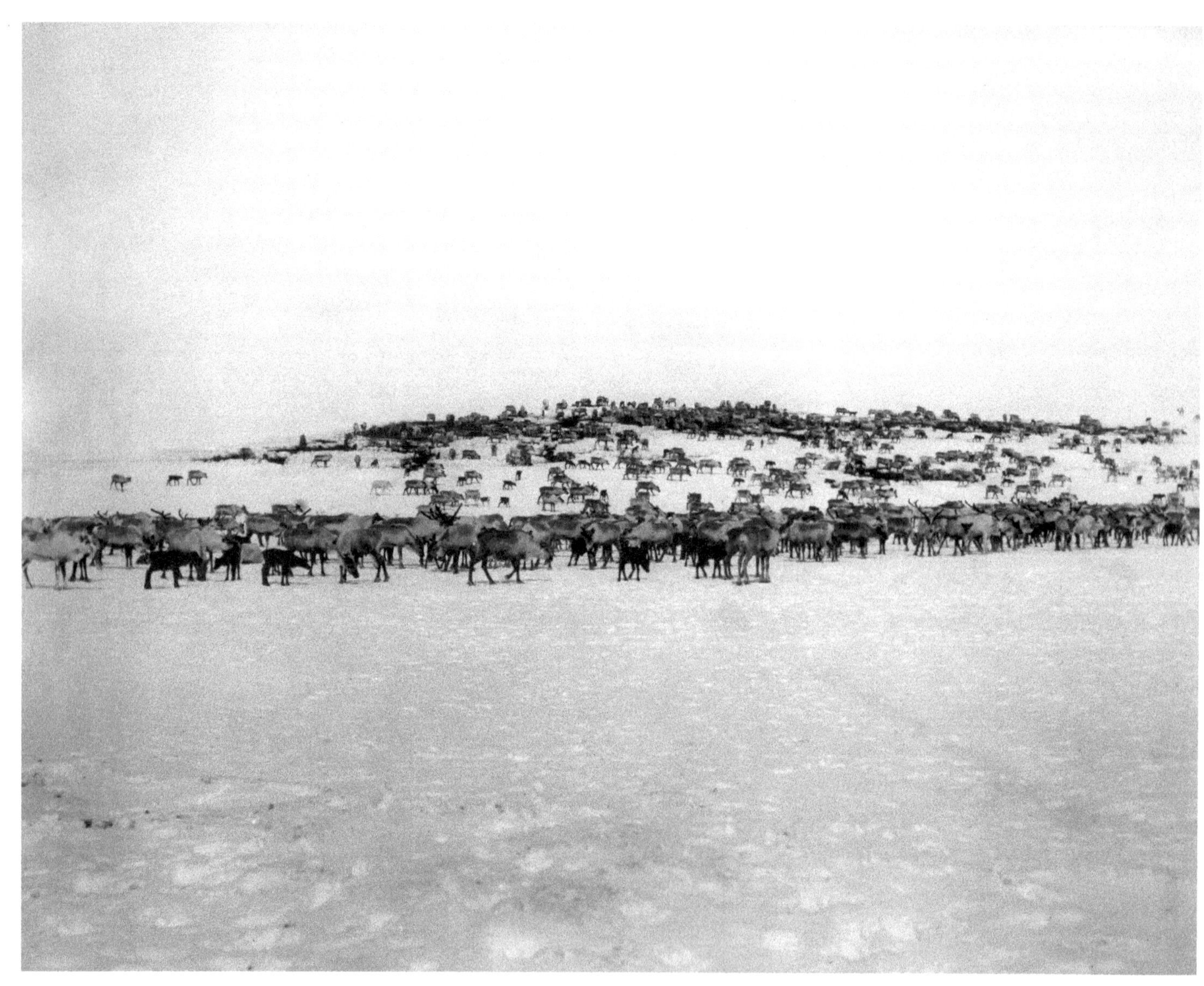

Reindeer became part of the Seward Peninsula's ecosystem in 1892 when Alaska's general agent for education, Sheldon Jackson, began importing 1,300 of them from Siberia. The vast herds provided a source of meat and income for hundreds of Eskimos employed by the Lomen Brothers of Nome from 1913 to the 1930s.

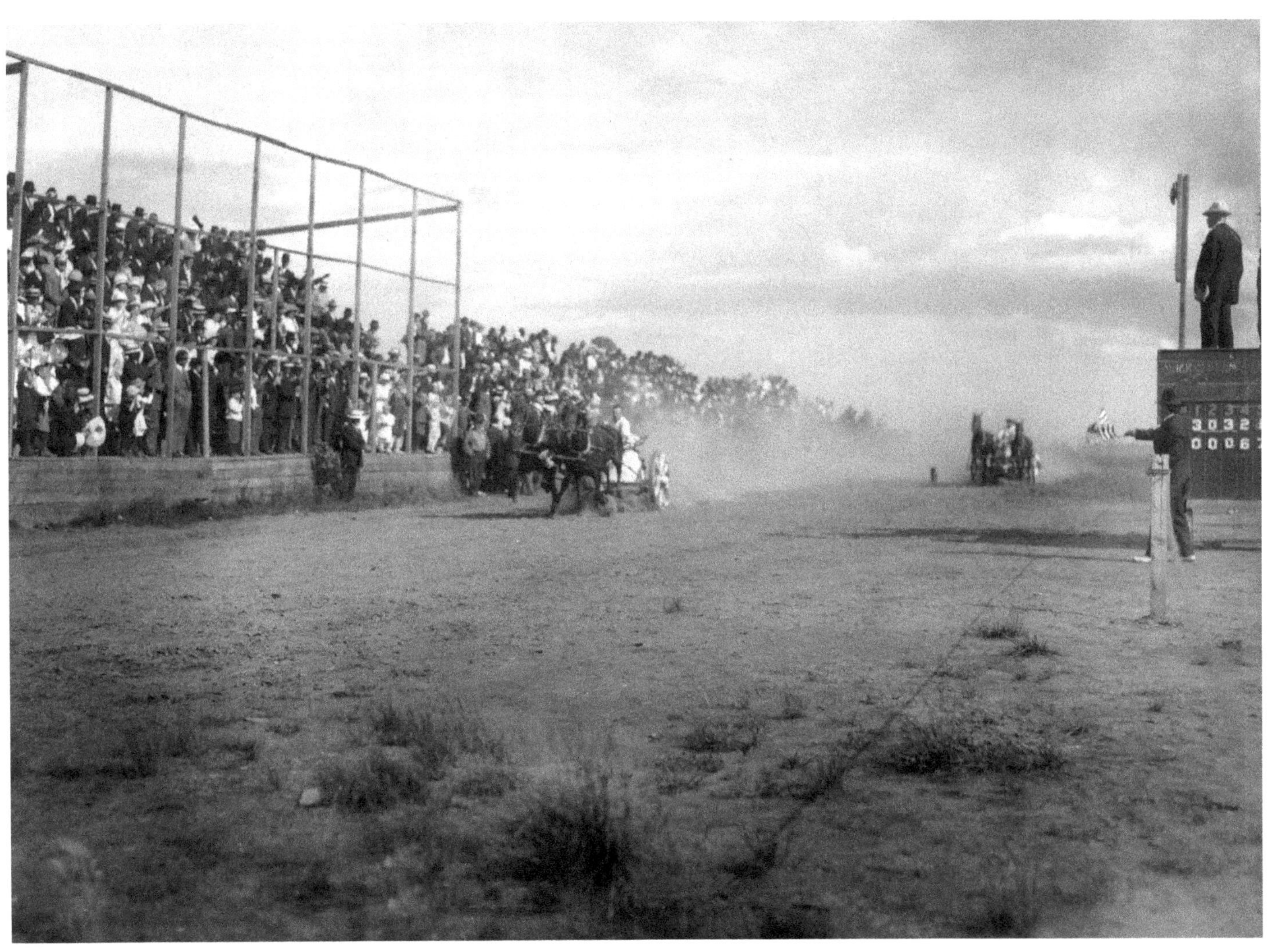

The Fourth of July Festivities in Fairbanks in the early 1900s included chariot races on the baseball field.

A Native trapper and two canine companions in a hand-built canoe full of hides.

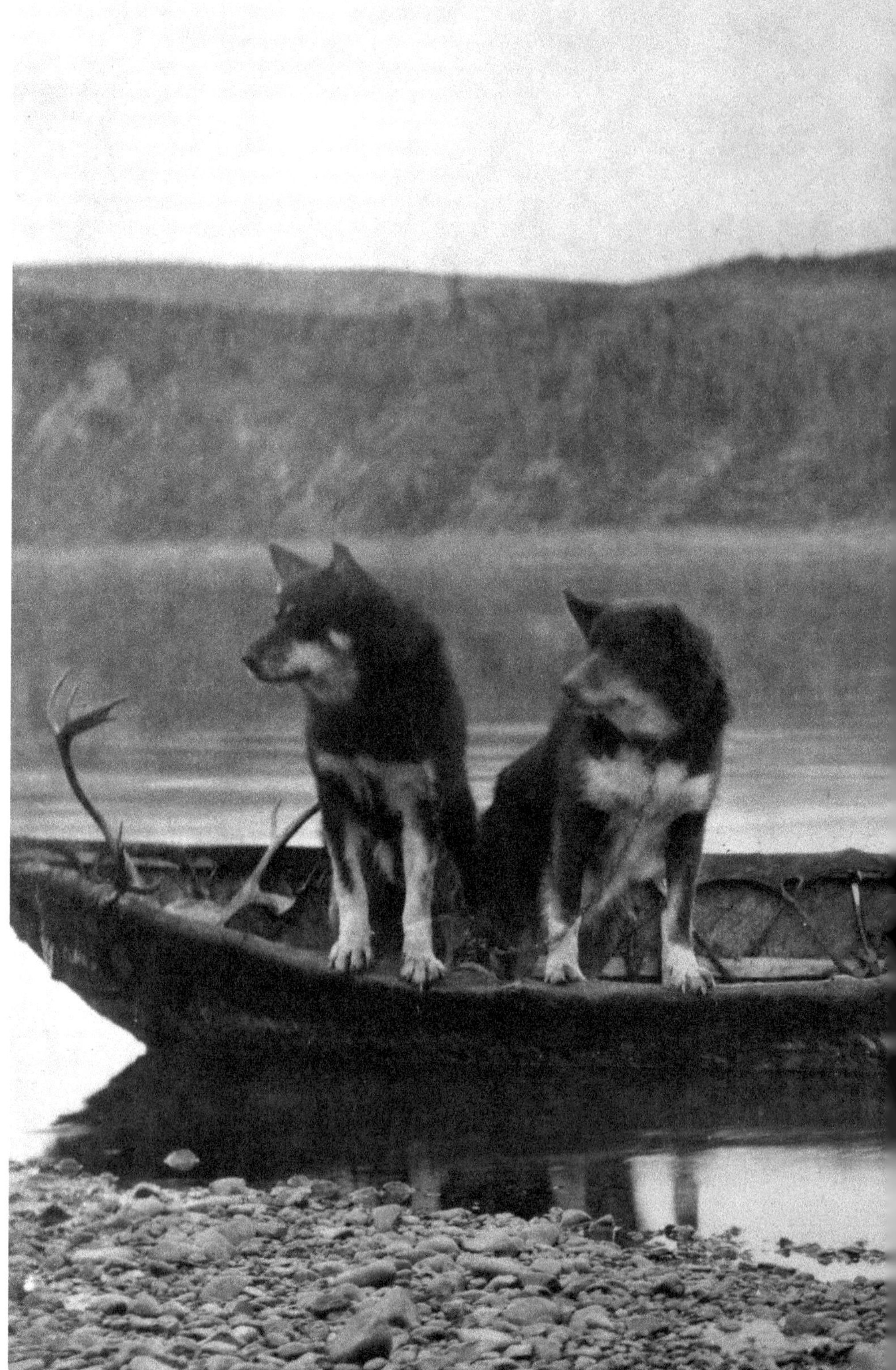

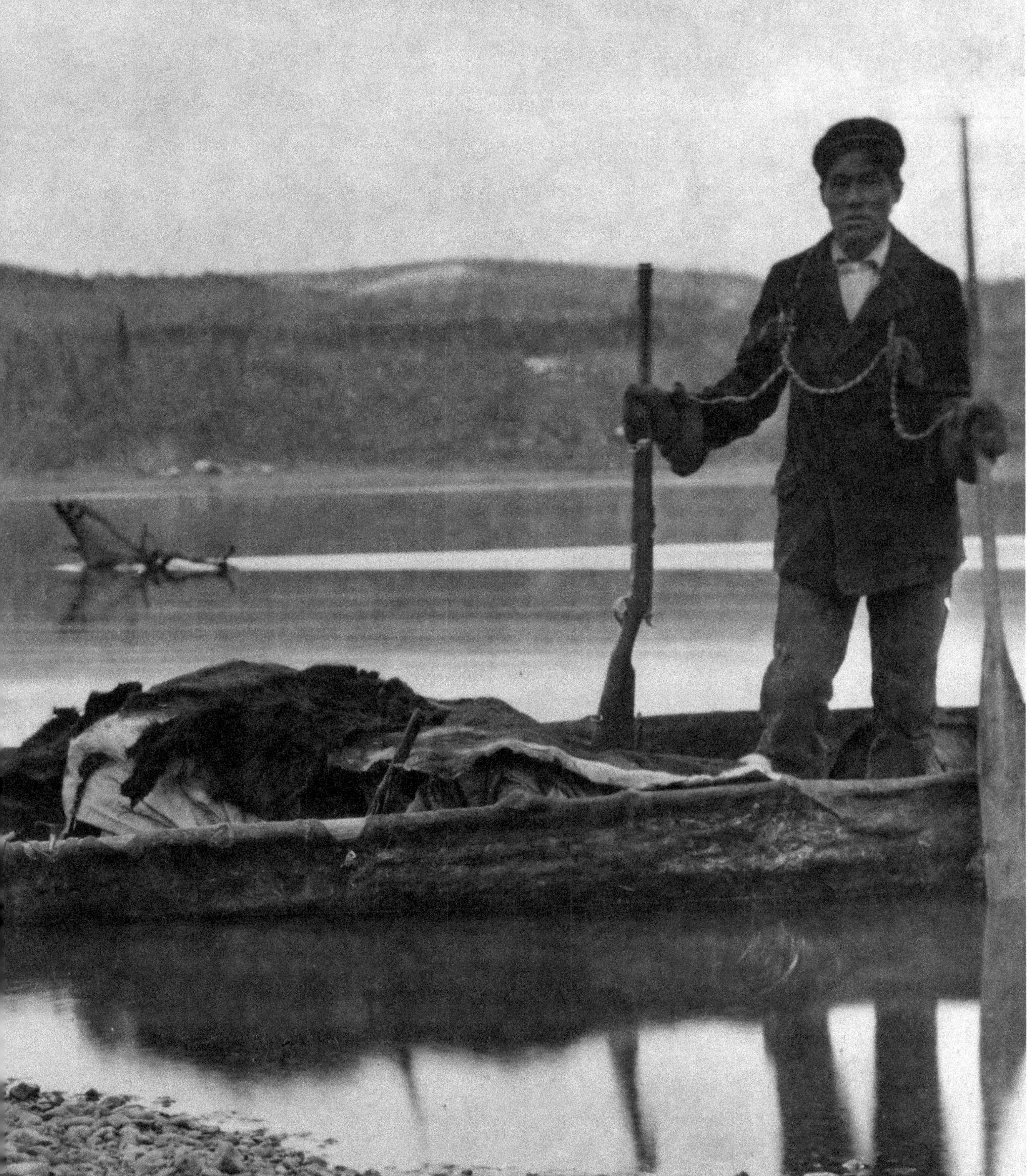

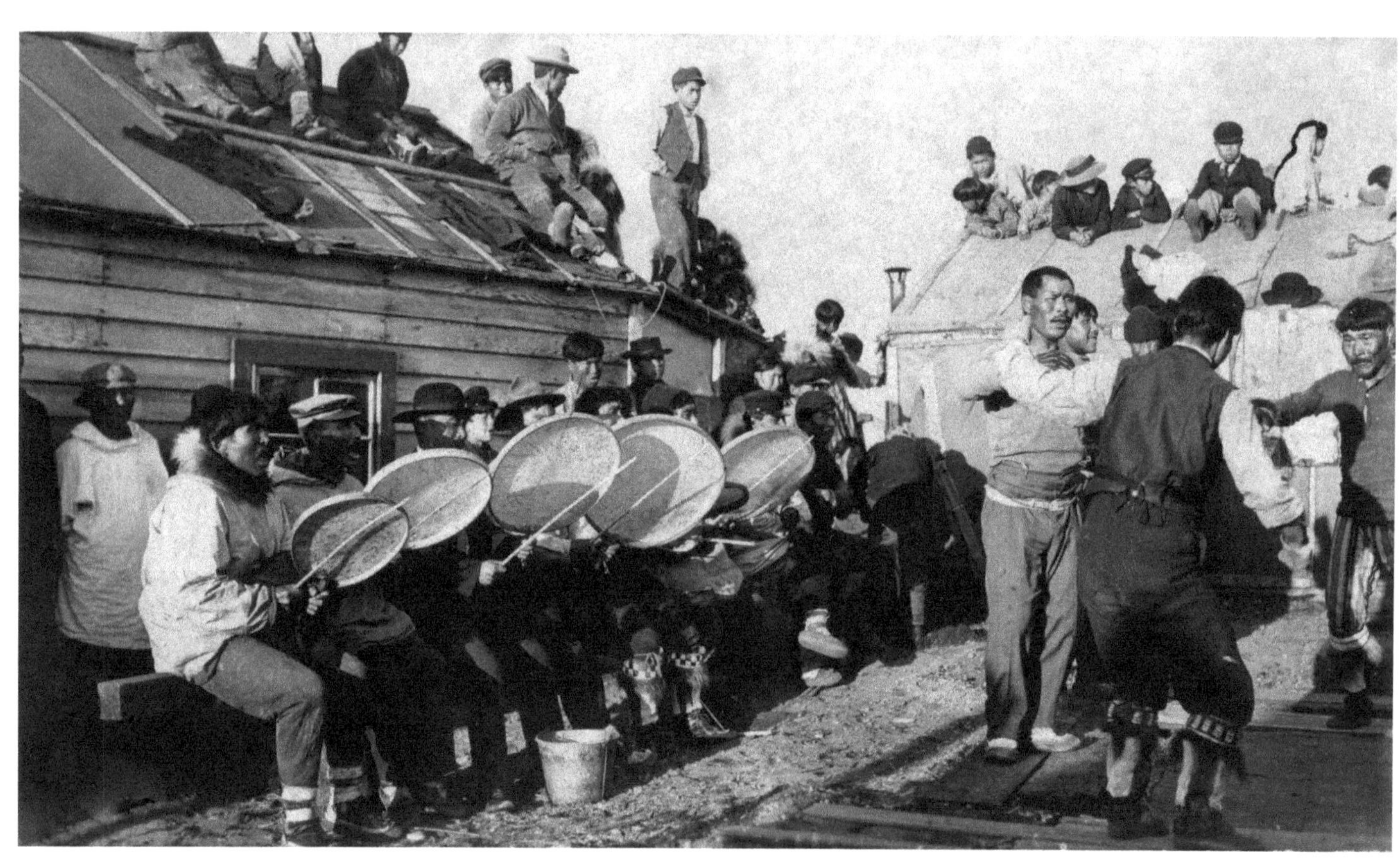

Attracting an audience on the rooftops, Eskimo drummers and dancers perform one of their most enduring and important cultural traditions.

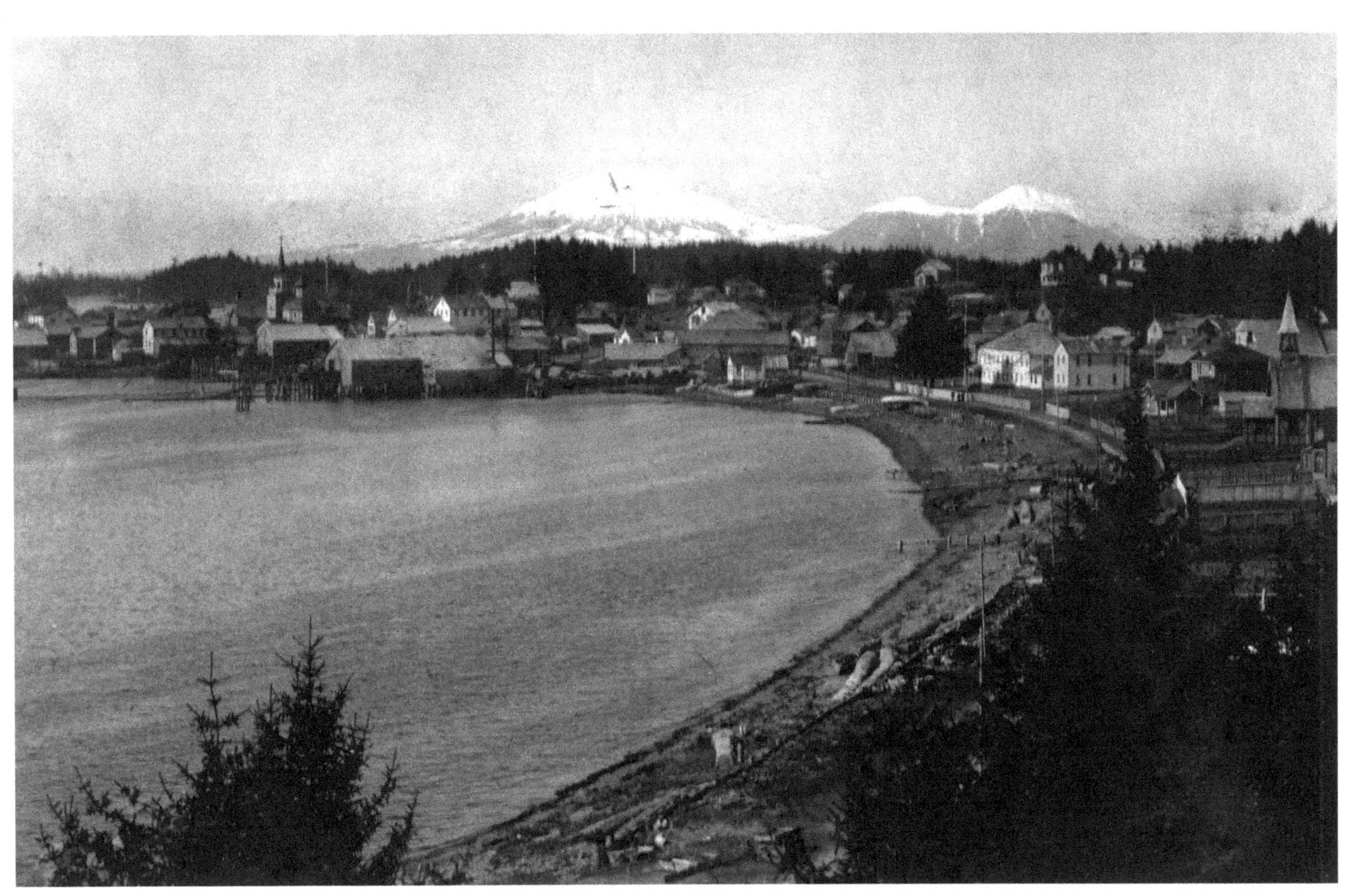

The Sitka waterfront in the early twentieth century, with Mount Edgecumbe in the background.

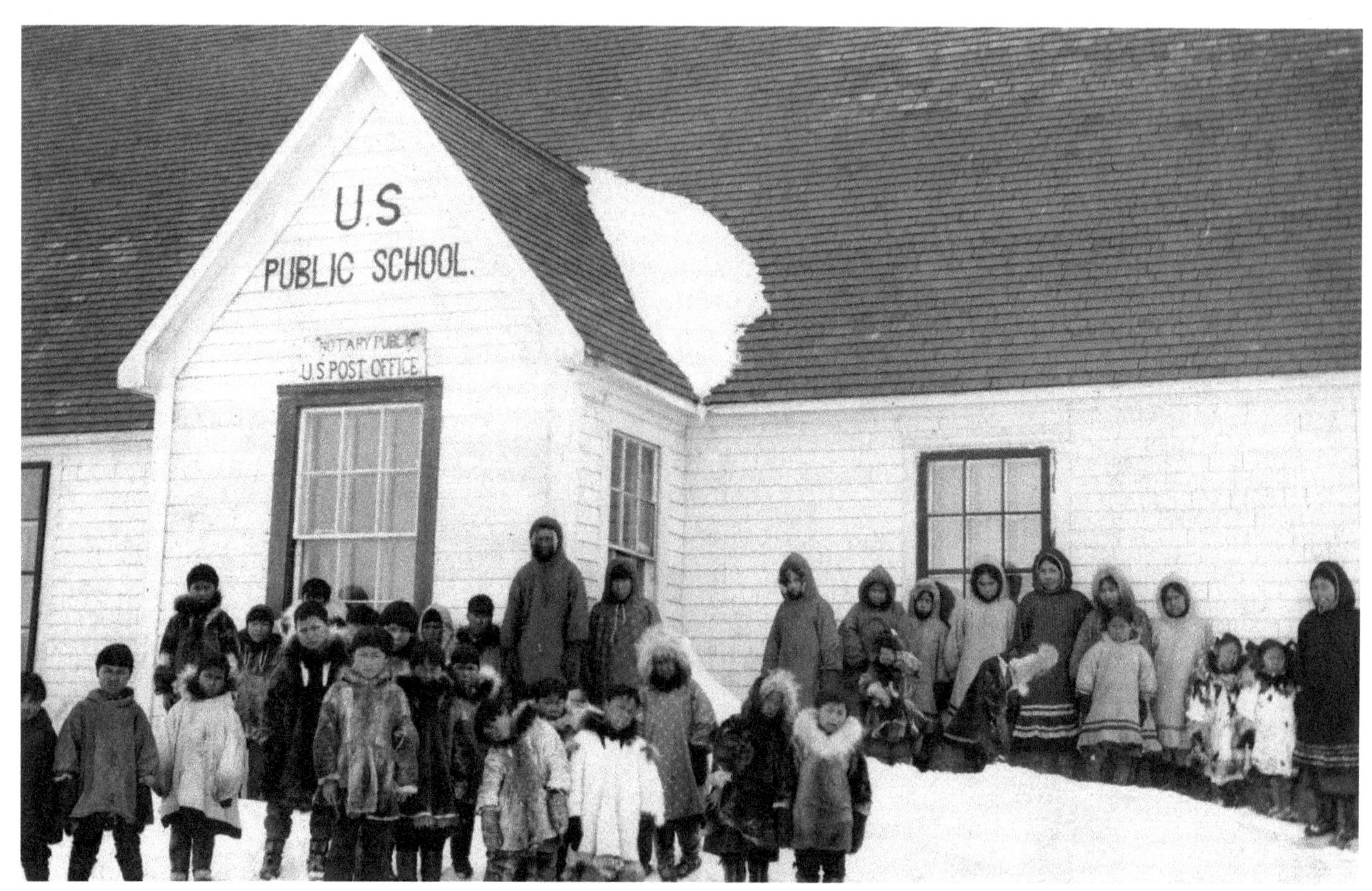

Eskimo students and their teachers stand outside their school on Cape Prince of Wales at the western edge of the Seward Peninsula.

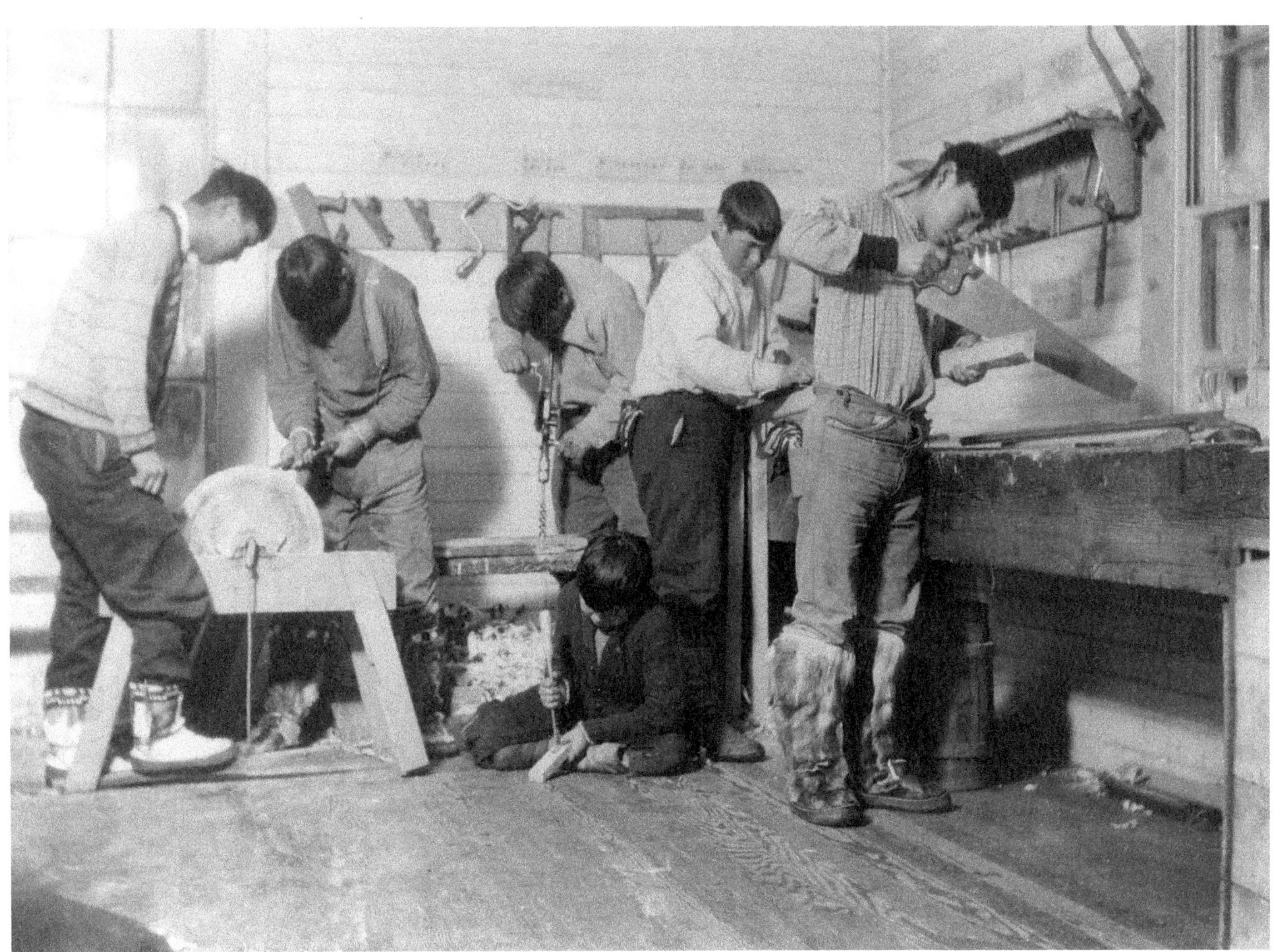

Eskimo students practice their carpentry skills in wood shop at a school in the early 1900s.

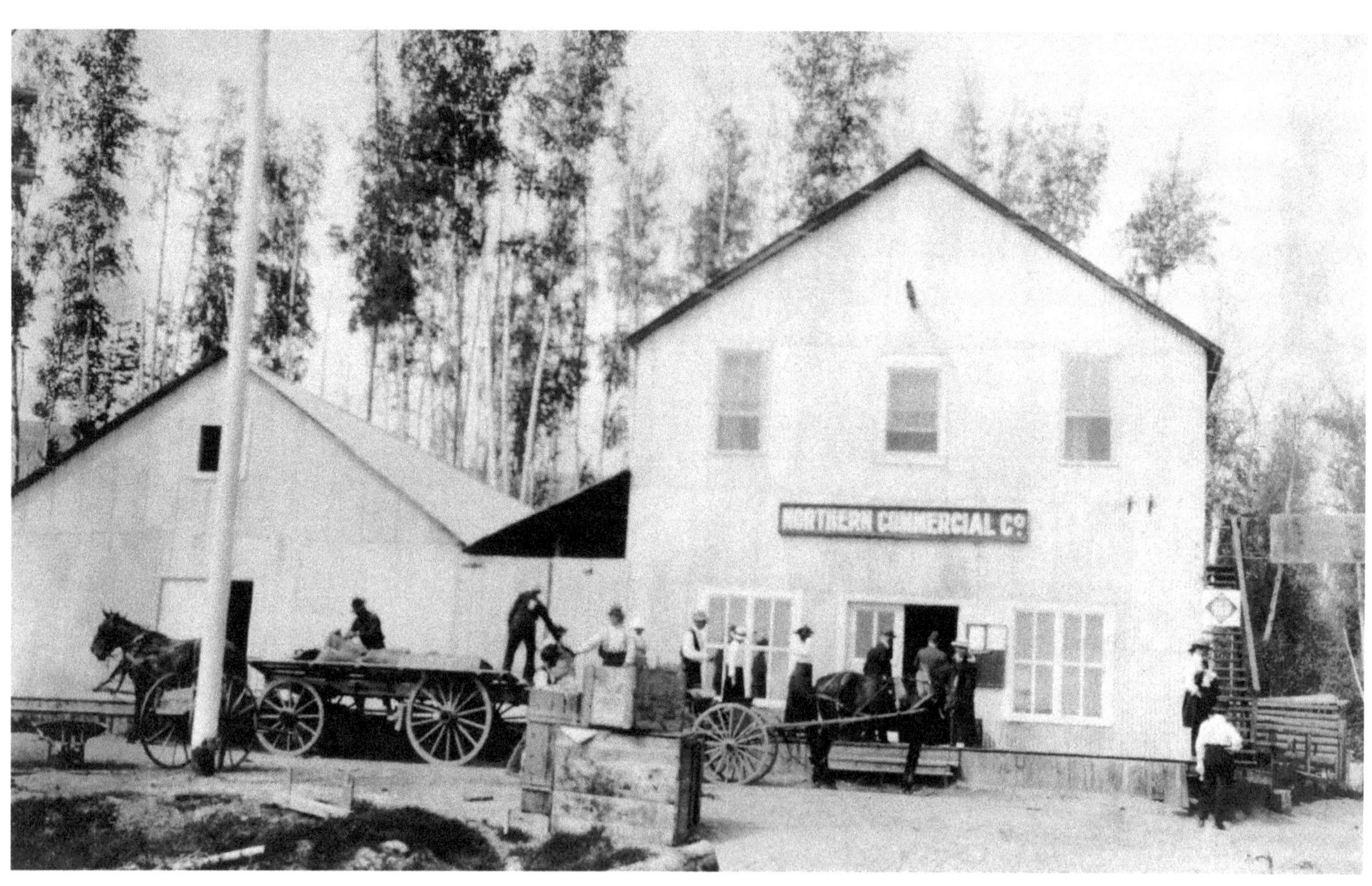

The Northern Commercial Co. had stores in villages and towns across Alaska, providing everything from hardware and furnishings to food.

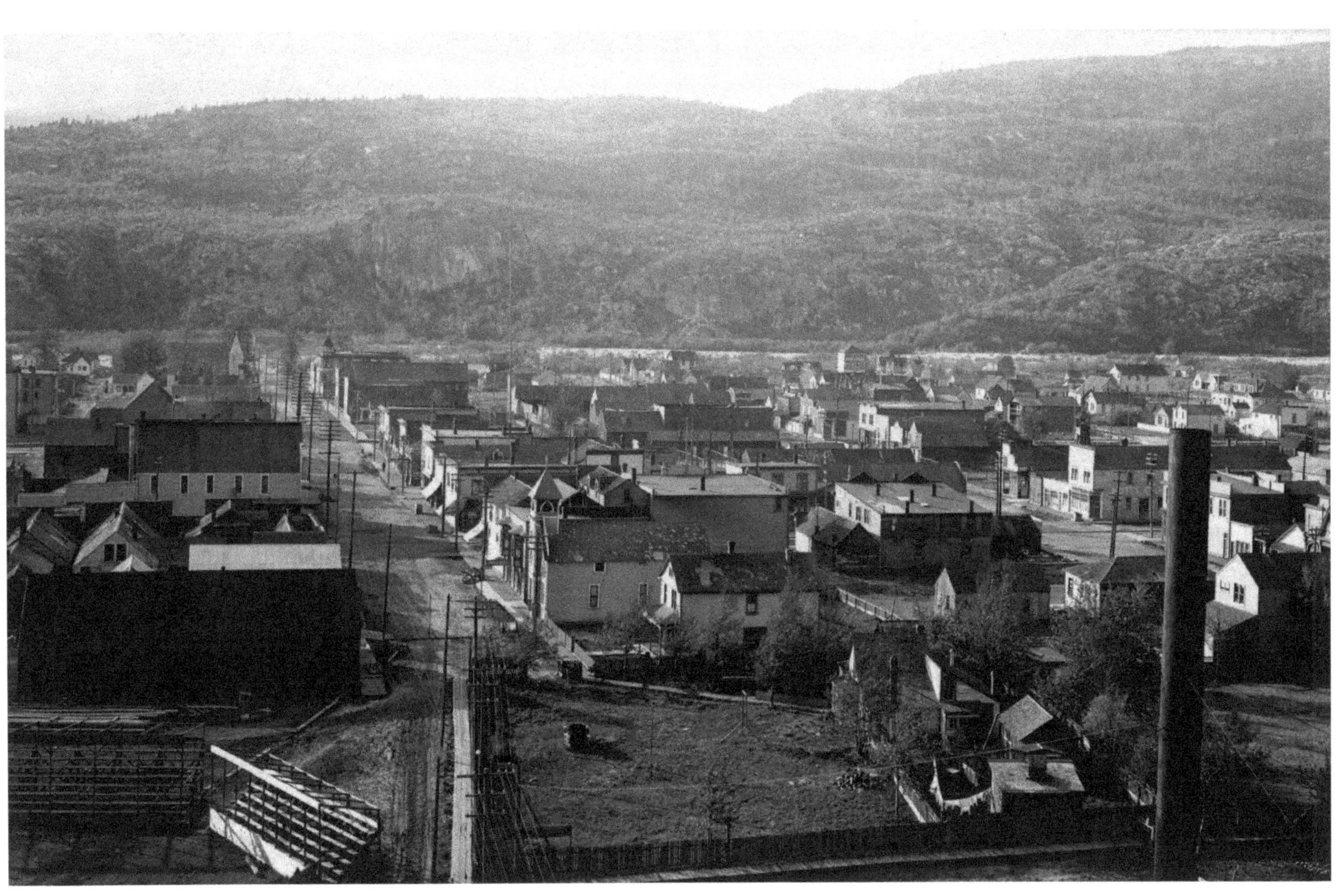

Skagway, founded at the head of Taiya Inlet after the discovery of gold in the Klondike in 1896, was the first incorporated city in Alaska, achieving that status just after Congress gave communities in Alaska the authority to incorporate. It remained an important gateway community in the decades that followed.

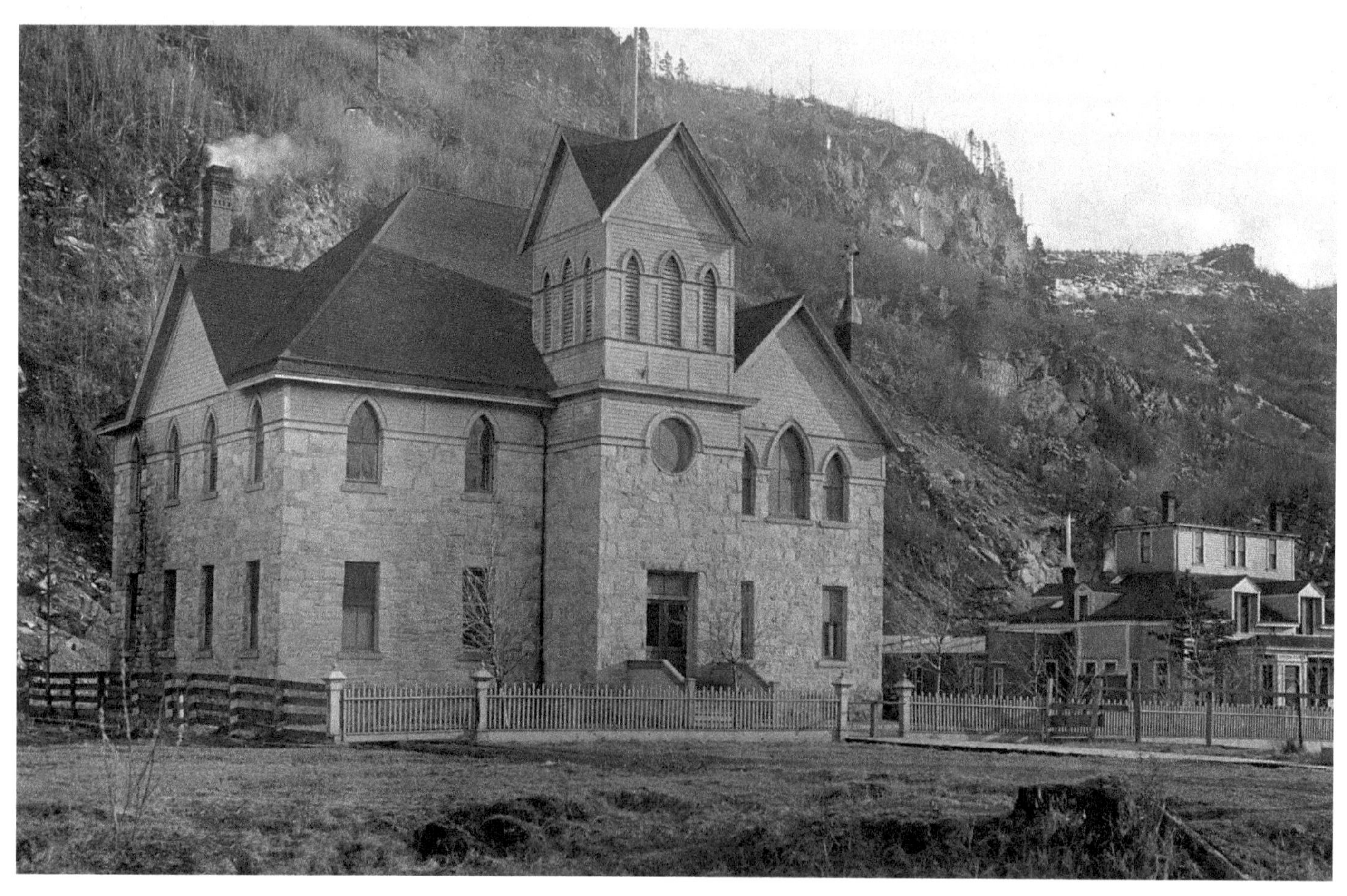

The McCabe Building in Skagway, built to house a Methodist college, was sold to the government and served as the courthouse for more than a half-century. Today the building is home to a museum and city hall.

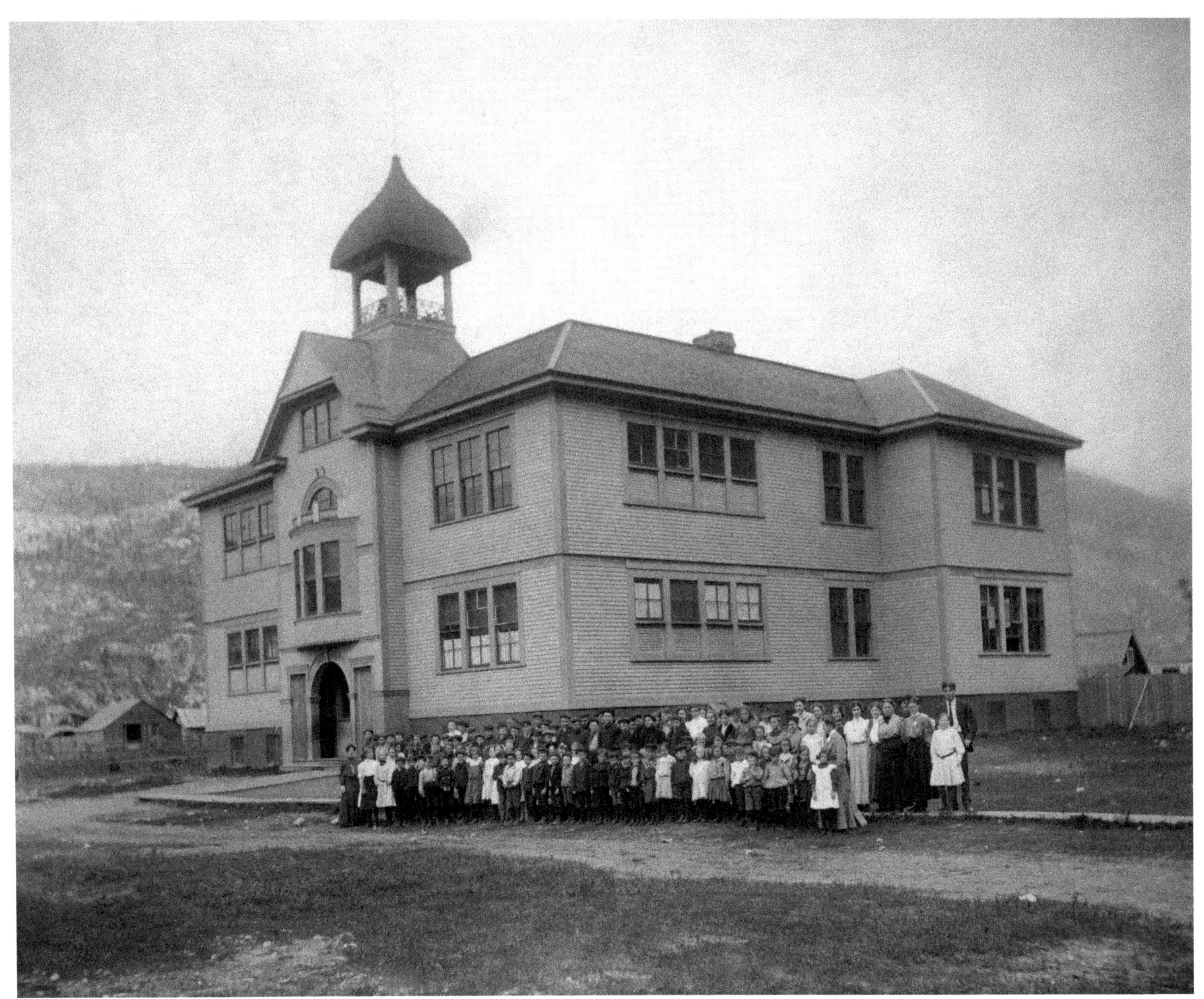

The students and teachers of the Skagway Public School gather for a group photo, August 29, 1906, at the beginning of a new school year.

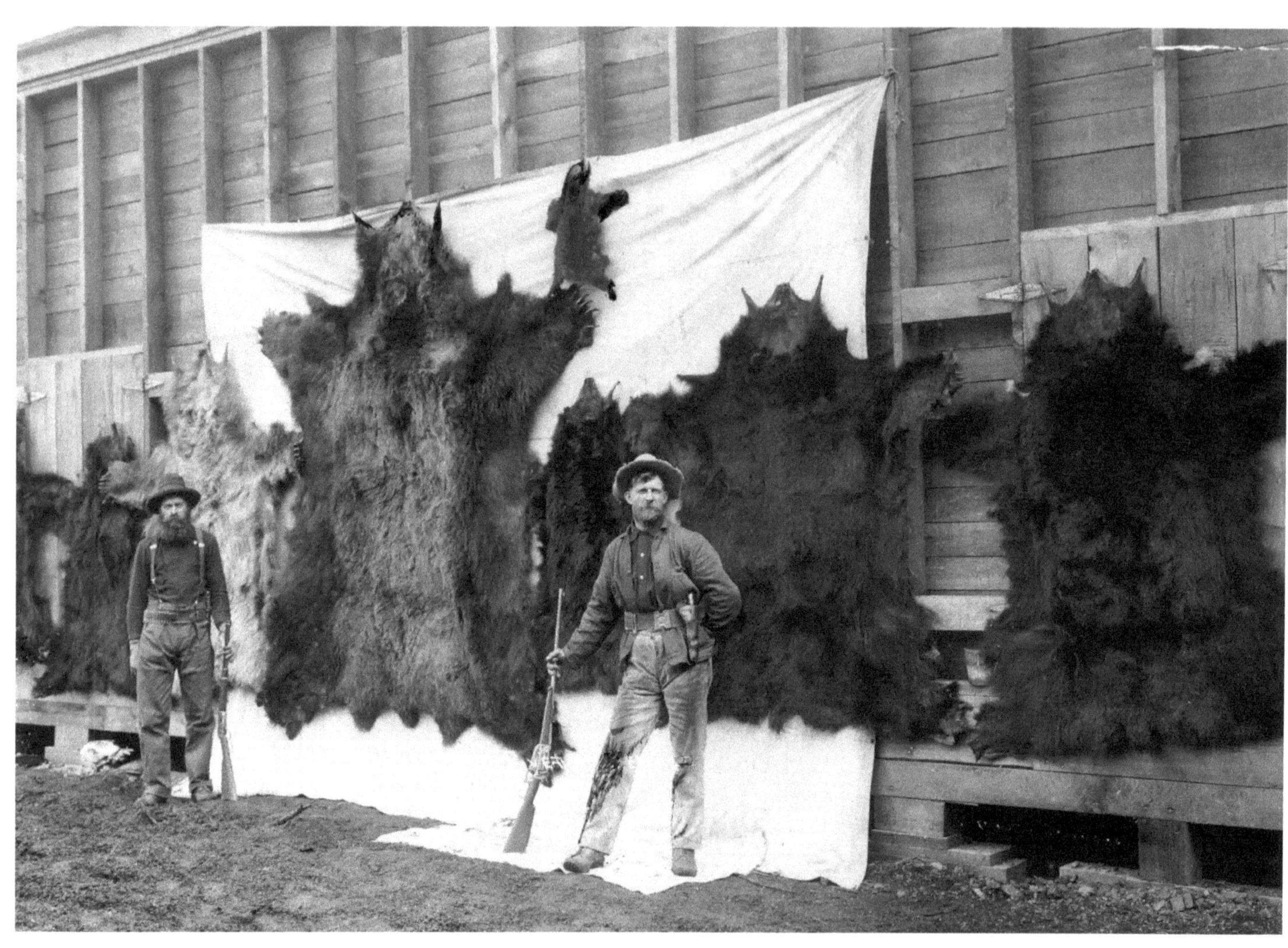

Hunters pose with the skins of bears and other animals they killed, after a 1906 hunting trip along the Snow River outside of Seward.

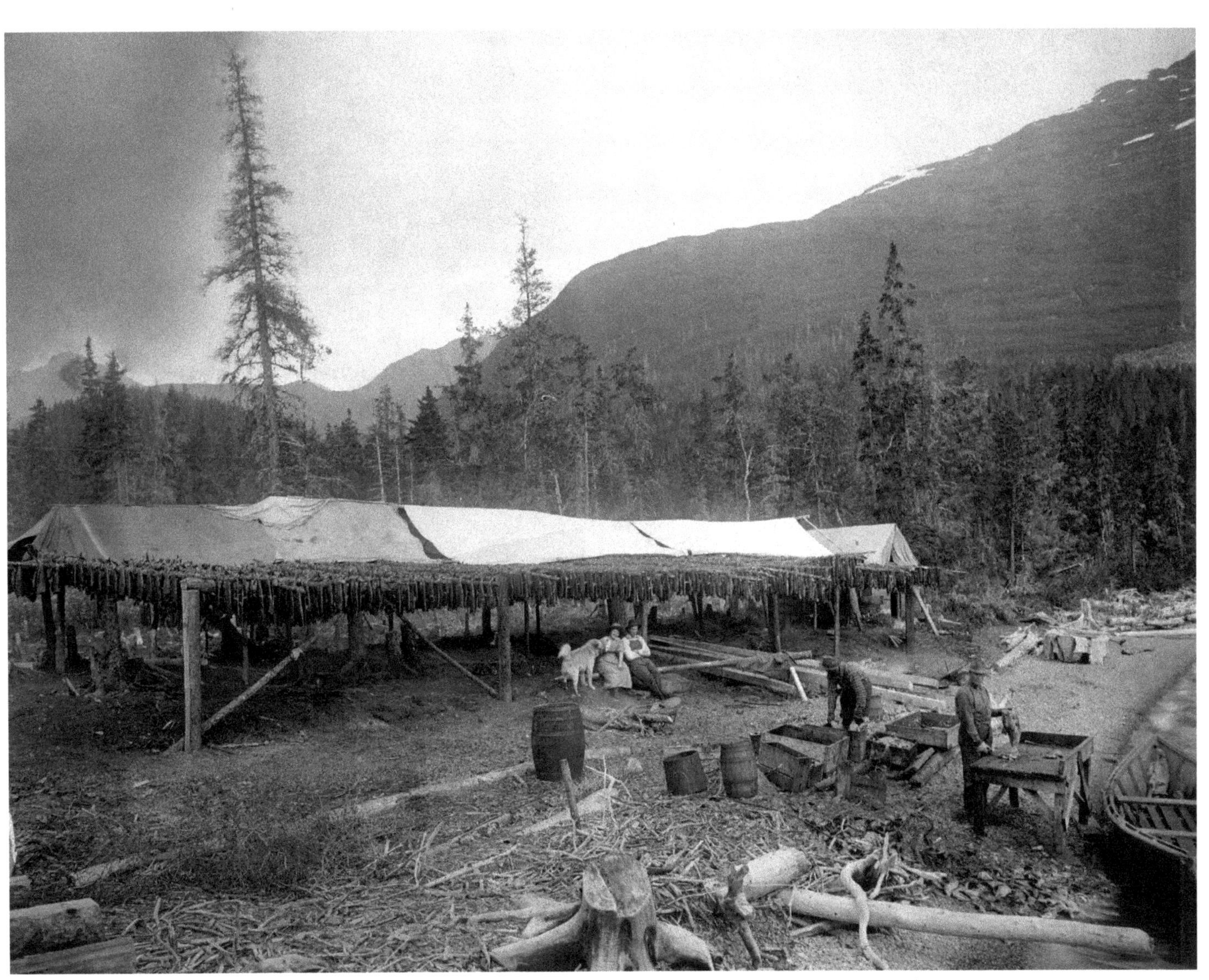

The ideal way to preserve fish in Alaska was to cut them and air-dry them in the summer at a riverside fish camp.

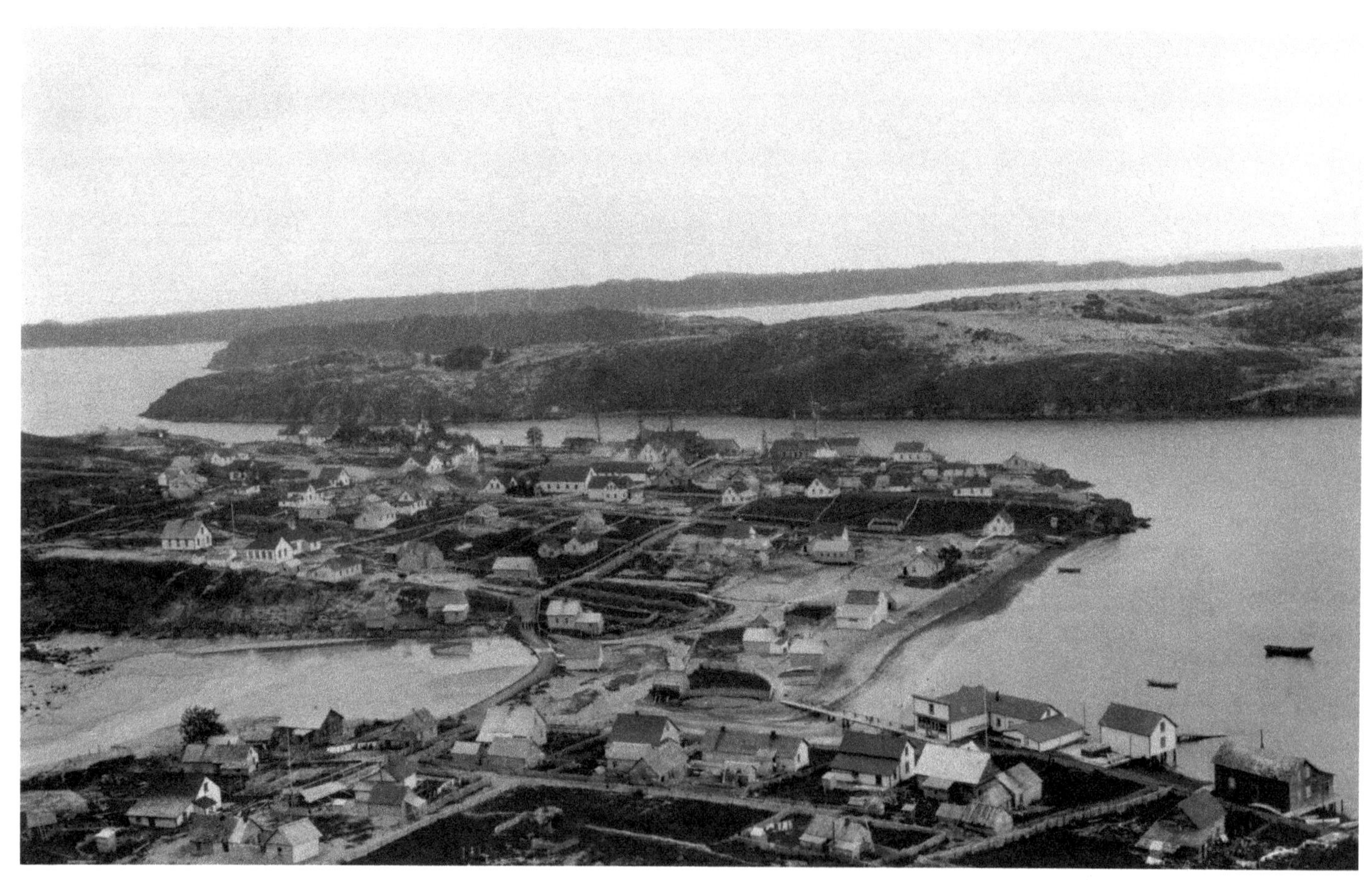

A bird's-eye view of Kodiak, an important fishing port on the largest island in Alaska.

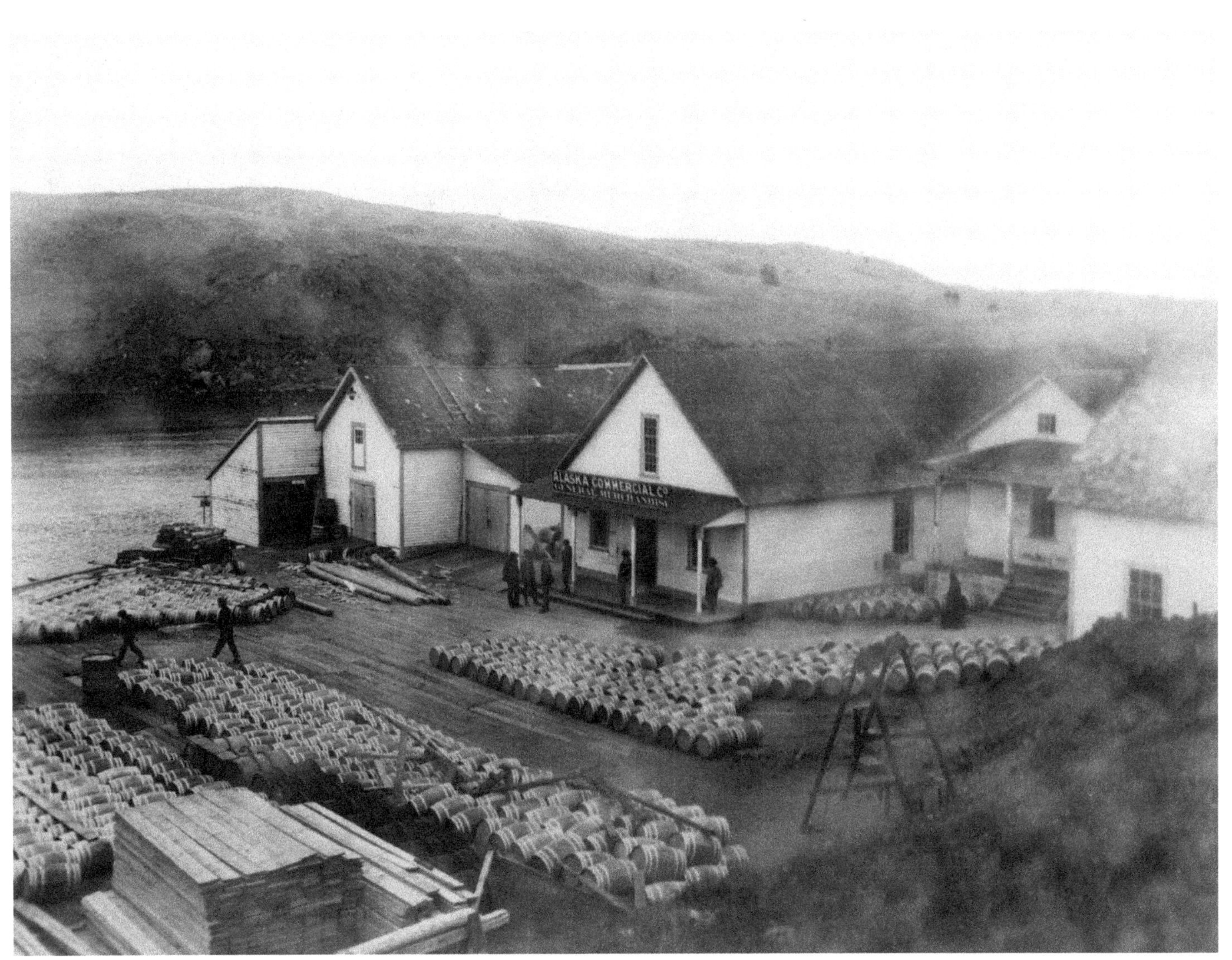

An Alaska Commercial Co. store on Kodiak Island.

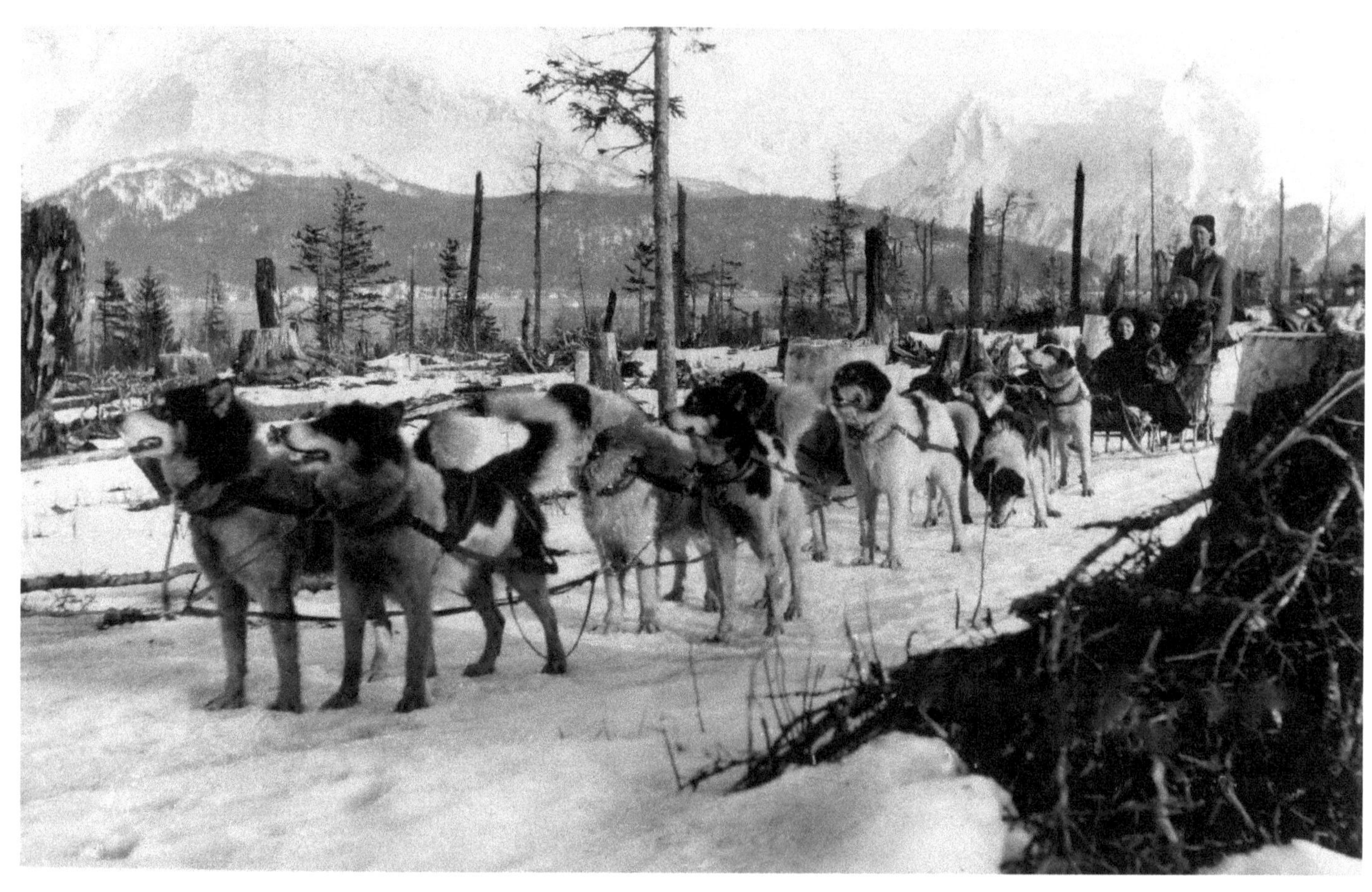

The first dog team to make the arduous journey from Nome to Seward, in 1909, traveling over part of what would become known as the Iditarod National Historic Trail.

THE TERRITORY OF ALASKA

(1906–1919)

After the Nome gold rush on the Bering Sea coast in 1900 and the gold strike that led to the founding of Fairbanks in 1902, many of the new arrivals began to think of establishing permanent communities.

There were still thousands who wanted to get rich and get out, but the desire to build businesses, schools, and churches prompted others to adopt Alaska as their home.

By 1910 Fairbanks was the largest town in Alaska, boasting electric lights, running water in the summer months, newspapers, hotels, bars, a telephone system, and a young population eager for a challenge. Pressure for more local control over what happened in Alaska finally led to an act of Congress in 1912 that created the Territory of Alaska.

The first legislature met in Juneau a year later. Some of the new lawmakers required nearly two months to travel to the new capital, proceeding by foot, dog team, and ship. Expressing the egalitarian impulse of the frontier, the first act of the legislature was to grant women the right to vote.

One of the most pressing needs was for reliable transportation. In summer the major rivers became Alaska's most effective highways, with passengers or freight traveling on one of dozens of large stern-wheelers that plied the major waterways. It was typically a slow and expensive proposition. Things were more difficult in the long winters, when dog teams or horse-drawn sleighs were the main options and the weather could be brutal, with temperatures down to sixty below zero in the Interior.

When the federal government built the Alaska Railroad from Seward to Fairbanks, a project that began in 1914 and continued until 1923, conditions began to change. The project took years longer than expected because of the slowdown caused by World War I, but upon its completion a future was assured for Fairbanks, and Christmas mail would no longer be delivered the following June.

Anchorage was born as a tent city, an Alaska Railroad construction camp, but within a quarter-century it would emerge as the commercial and population center of Alaska.

The Fairbanks Public School, the subject of great pride among citizens of the gold rush town, featured steam heat, electricity, and a cupola that provided a view of the Tanana Valley.

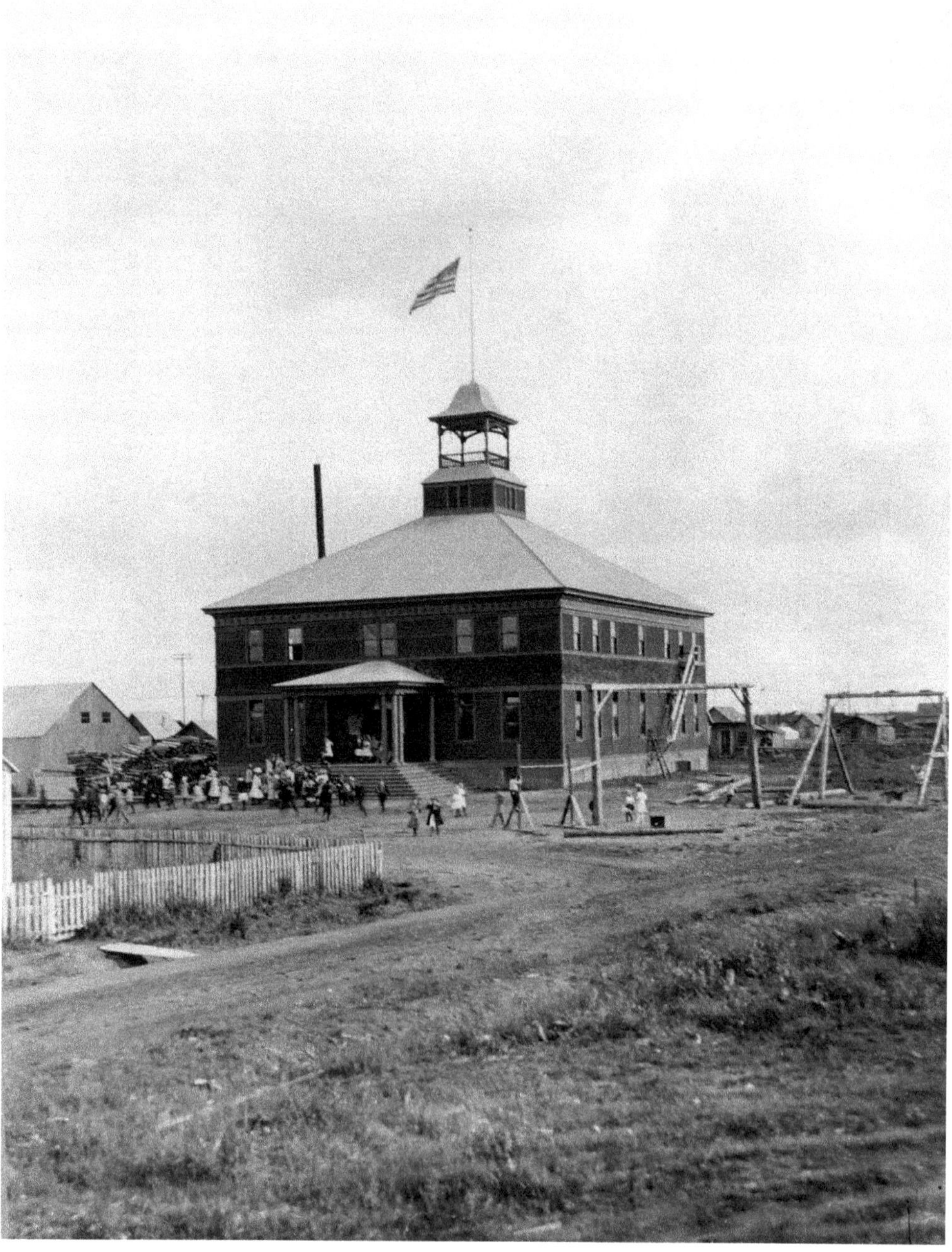

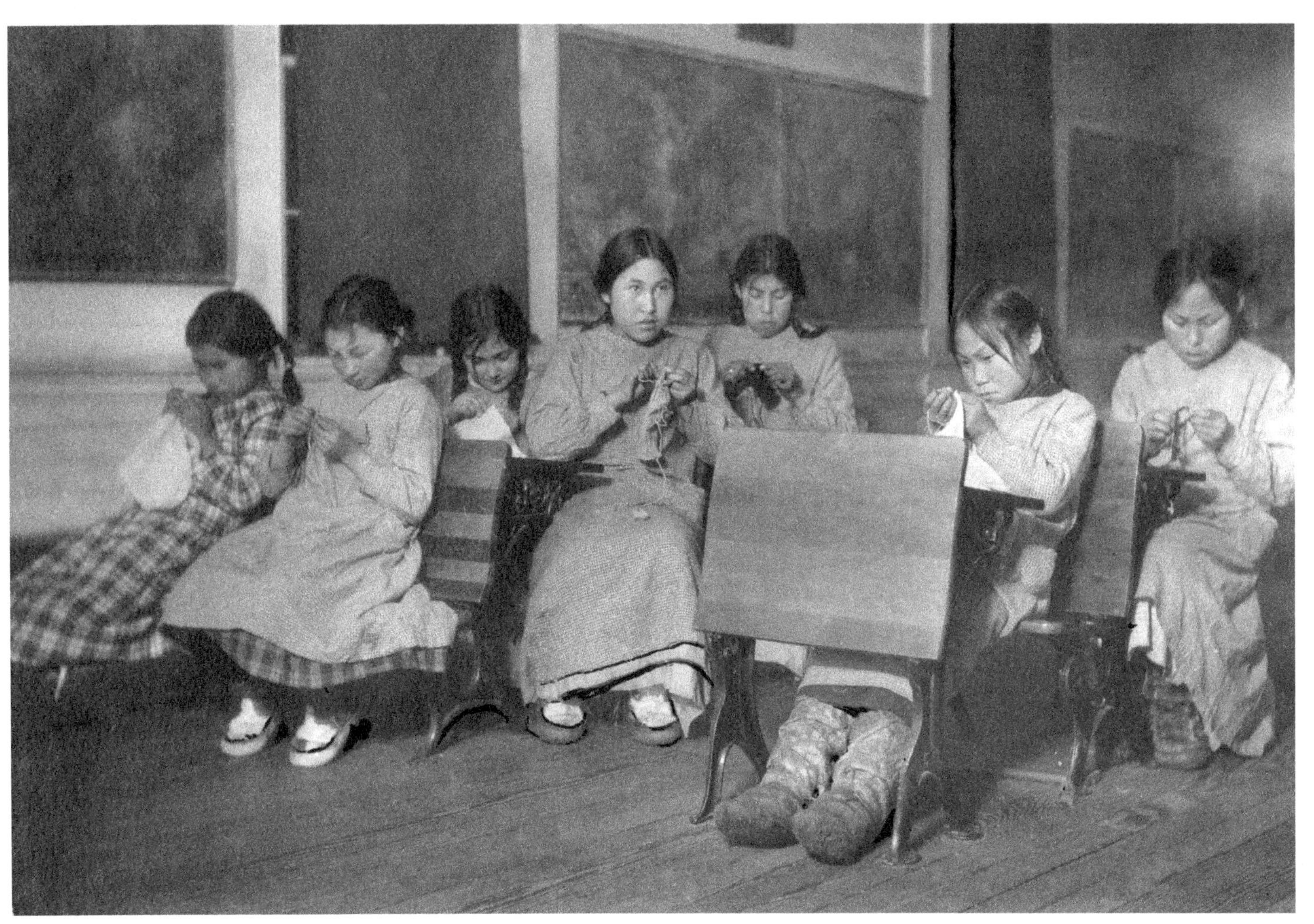

Eskimo girls in the Barrow Public School practice their sewing skills in class.

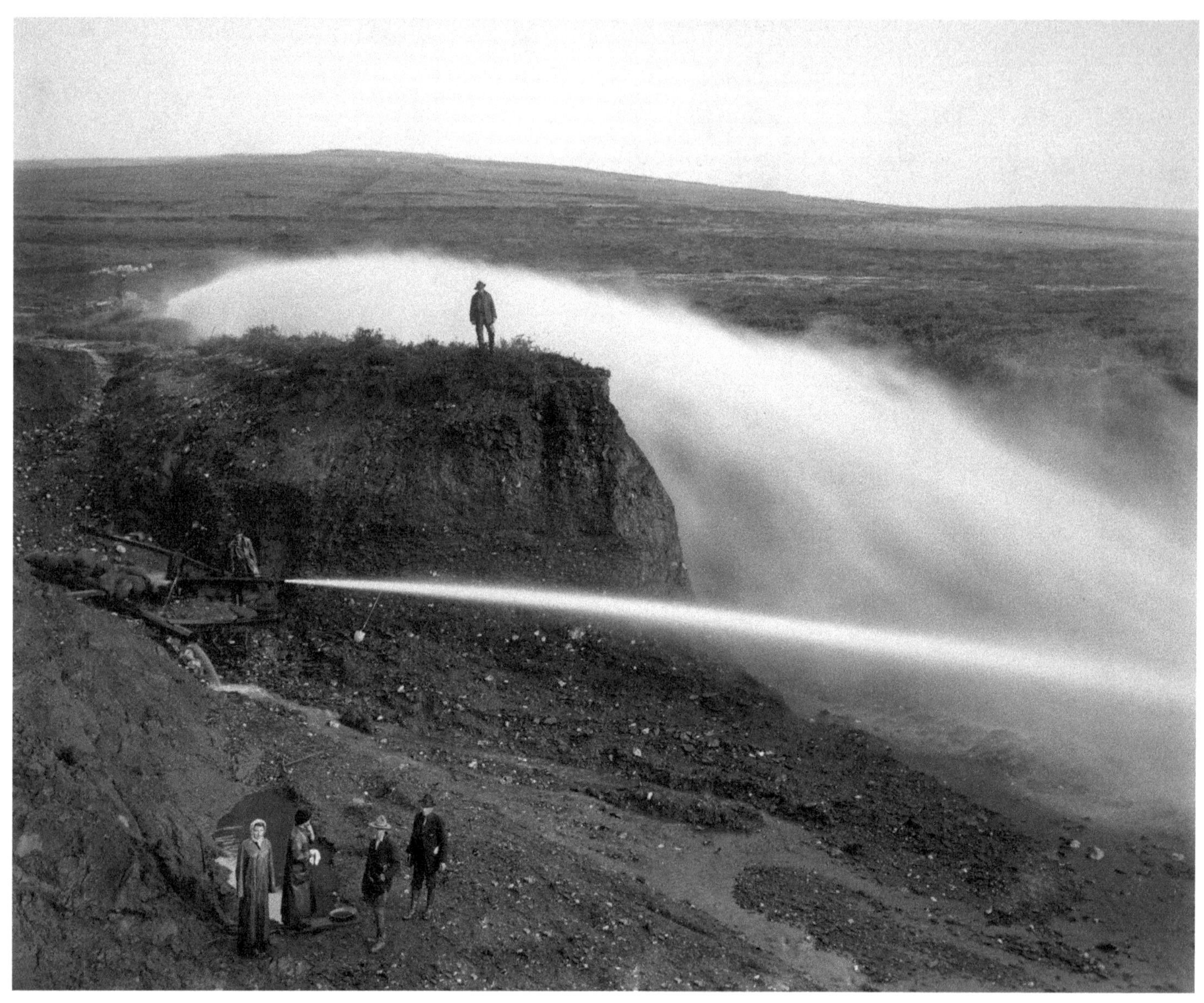

The high-pressure water nozzles known as "giants" eat into the layers of soil and rock above gold-bearing gravels in a mining operation on Glacier Creek in 1910.

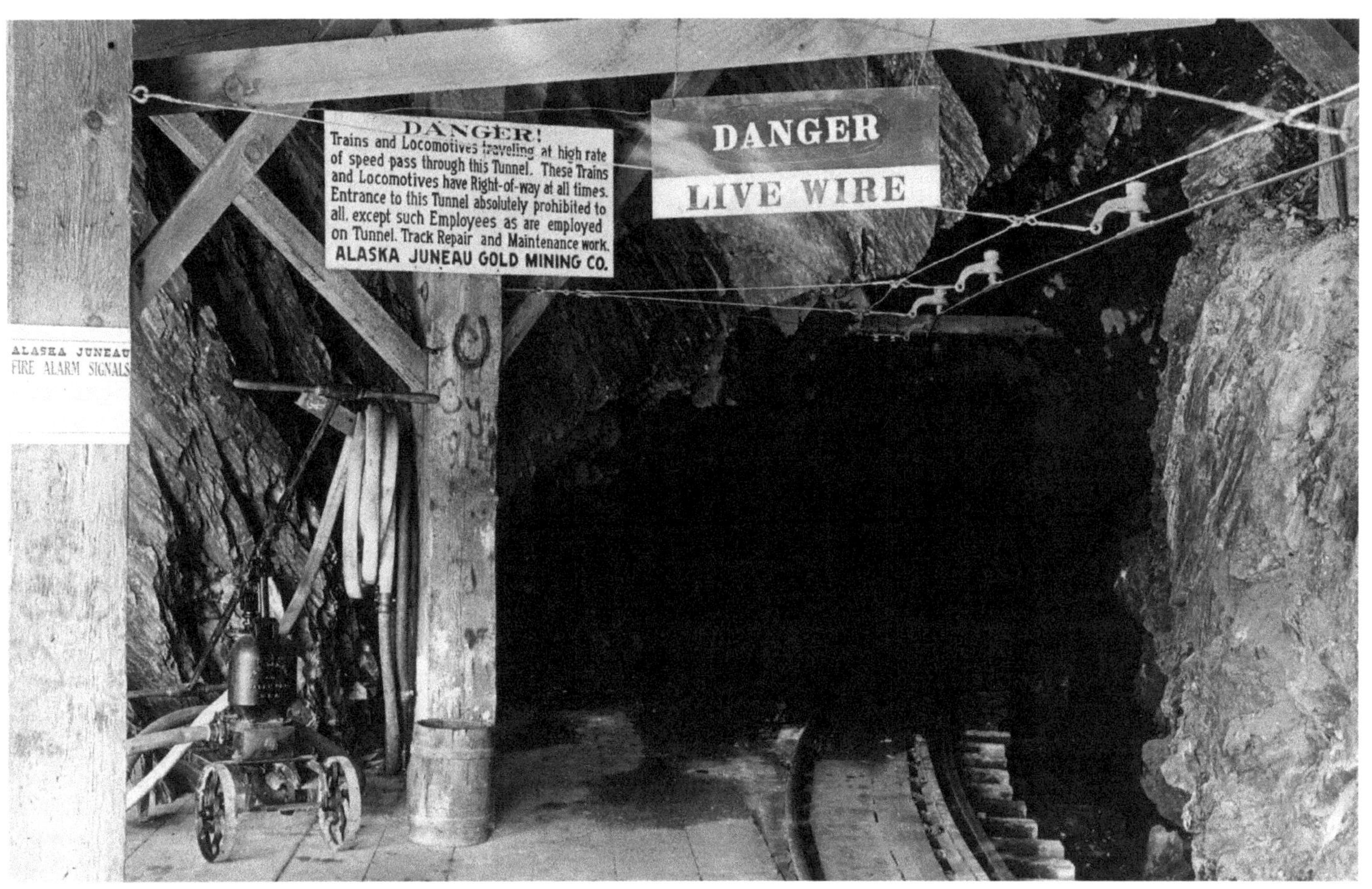

Miners working underground in the Alaska-Juneau Gold Mine had to be alert at all times for trains hauling ore to the mine entrance. The mine produced more than $80 million in gold before it closed in 1944.

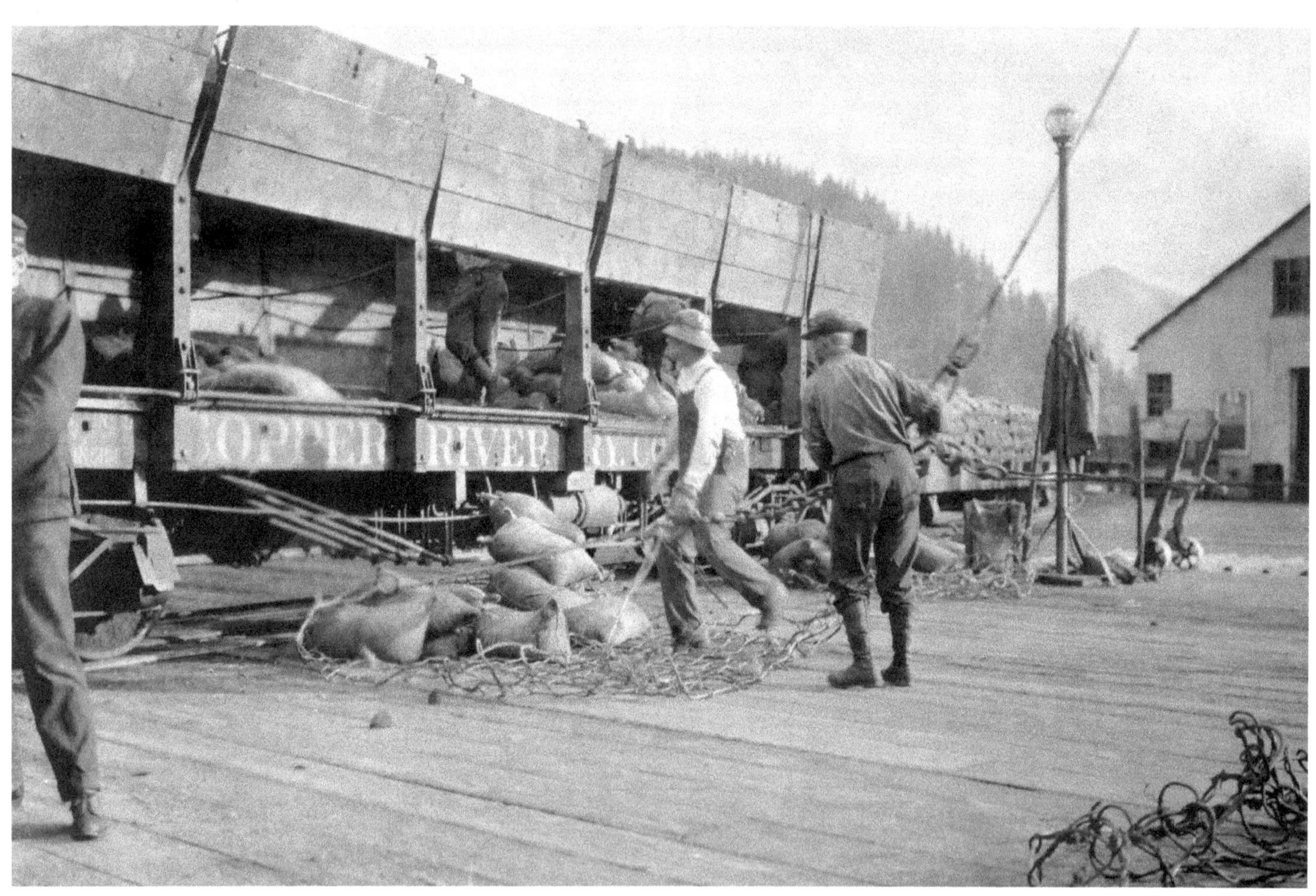

Bags of copper ore are loaded on a freight car of the Copper River Railway, built to connect copper mines with the port at Cordova.

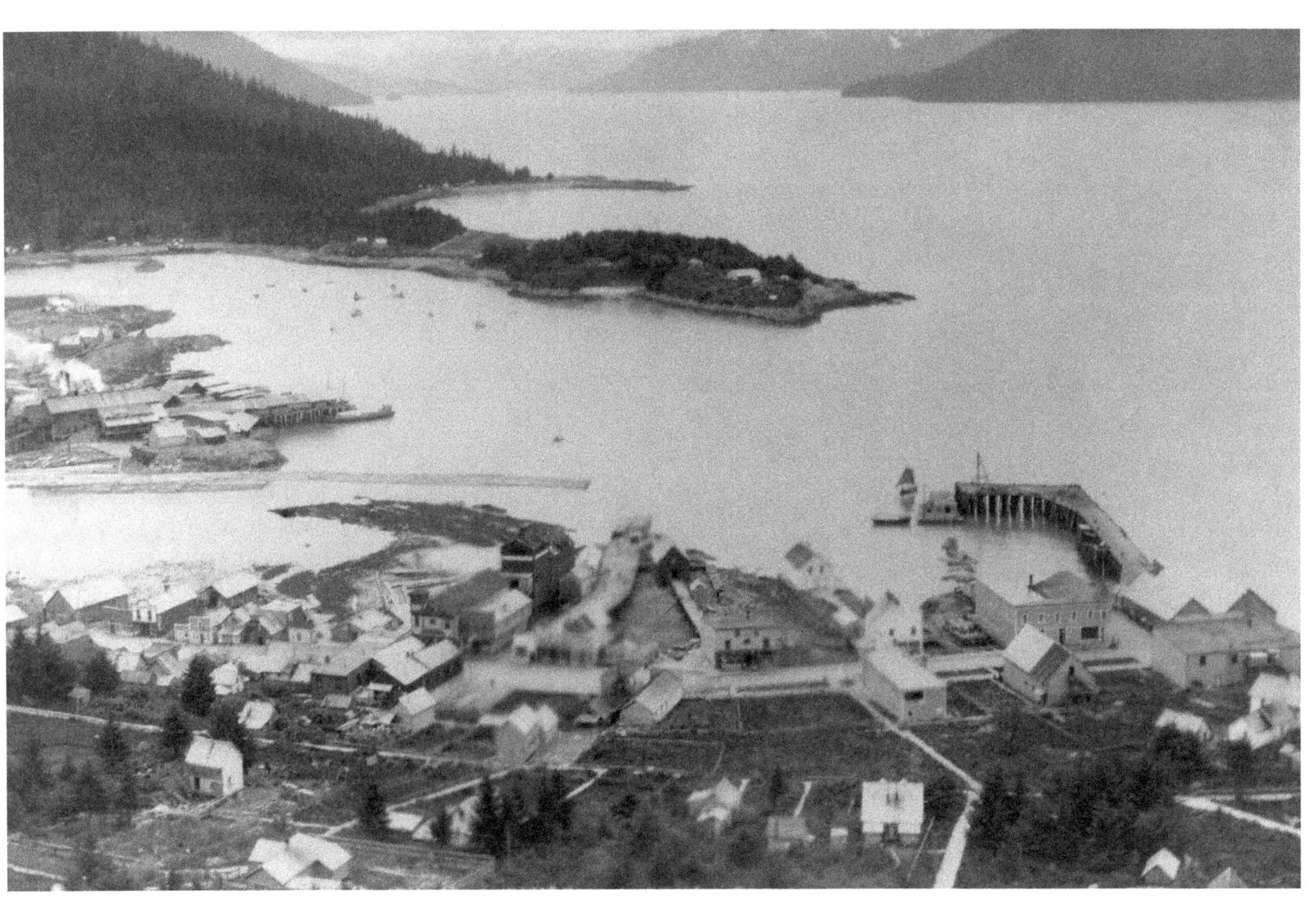

Looking down upon Wrangell, an important fishing and timber center and one of the oldest non-Native communities in Alaska.

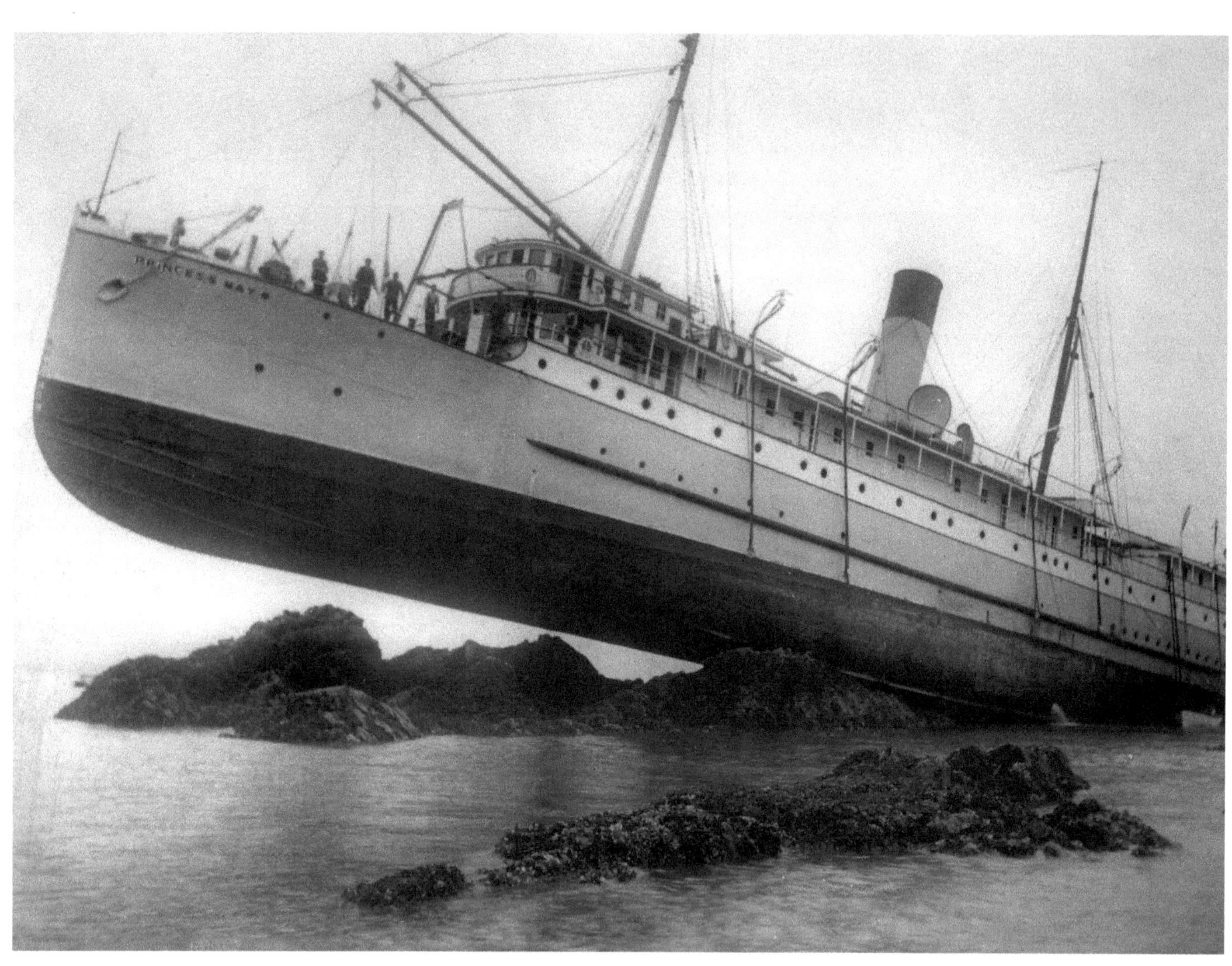

The captain of the *Princess May* encountered heavy fog on August 5, 1910, and ran onto the rocks of Sentinel Island, north of Juneau. No one died and after extensive repairs, the *Princess May* returned to service.

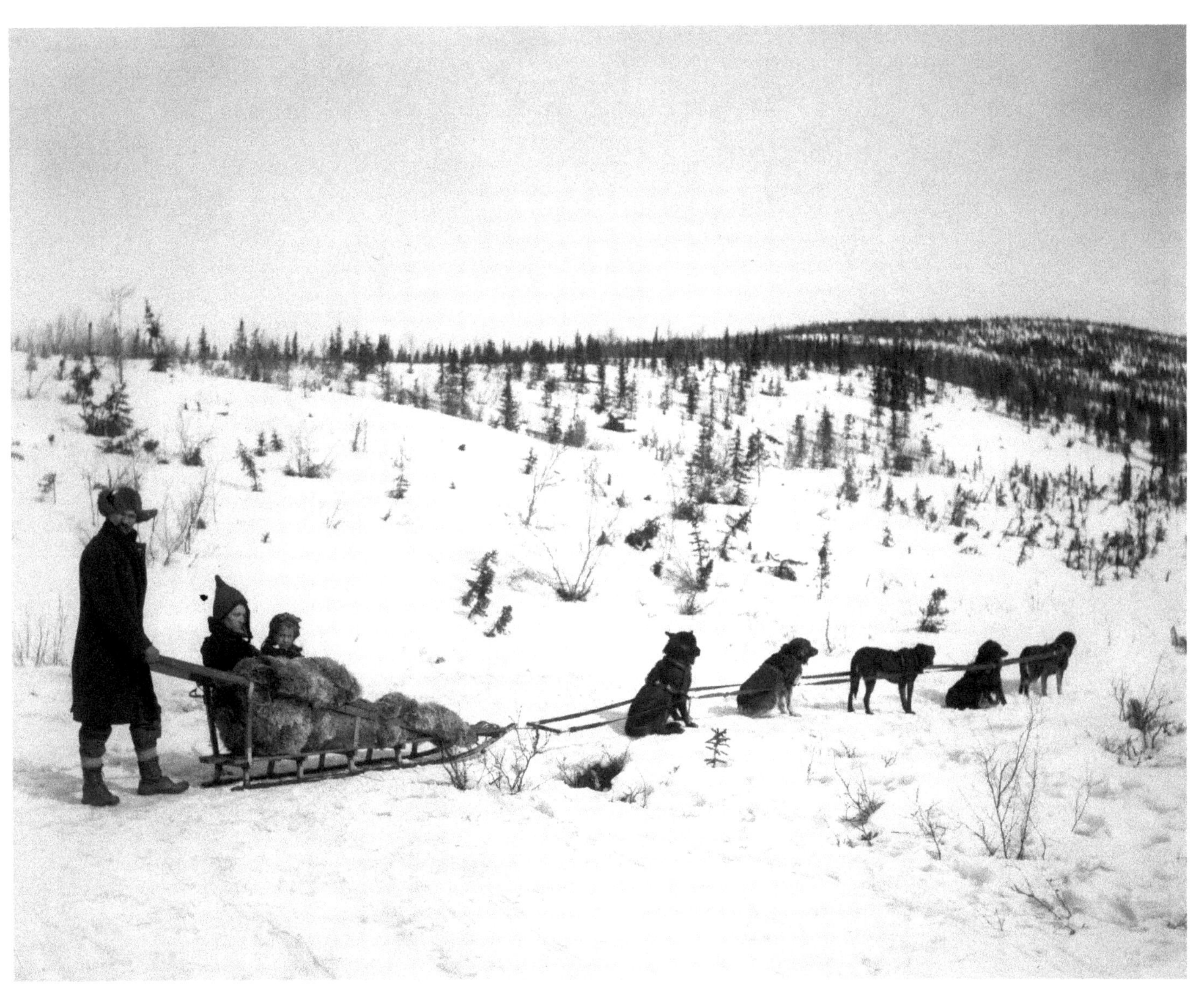

A small dog team provided convenient winter transportation in a land where the roads were few and the trails were frozen.

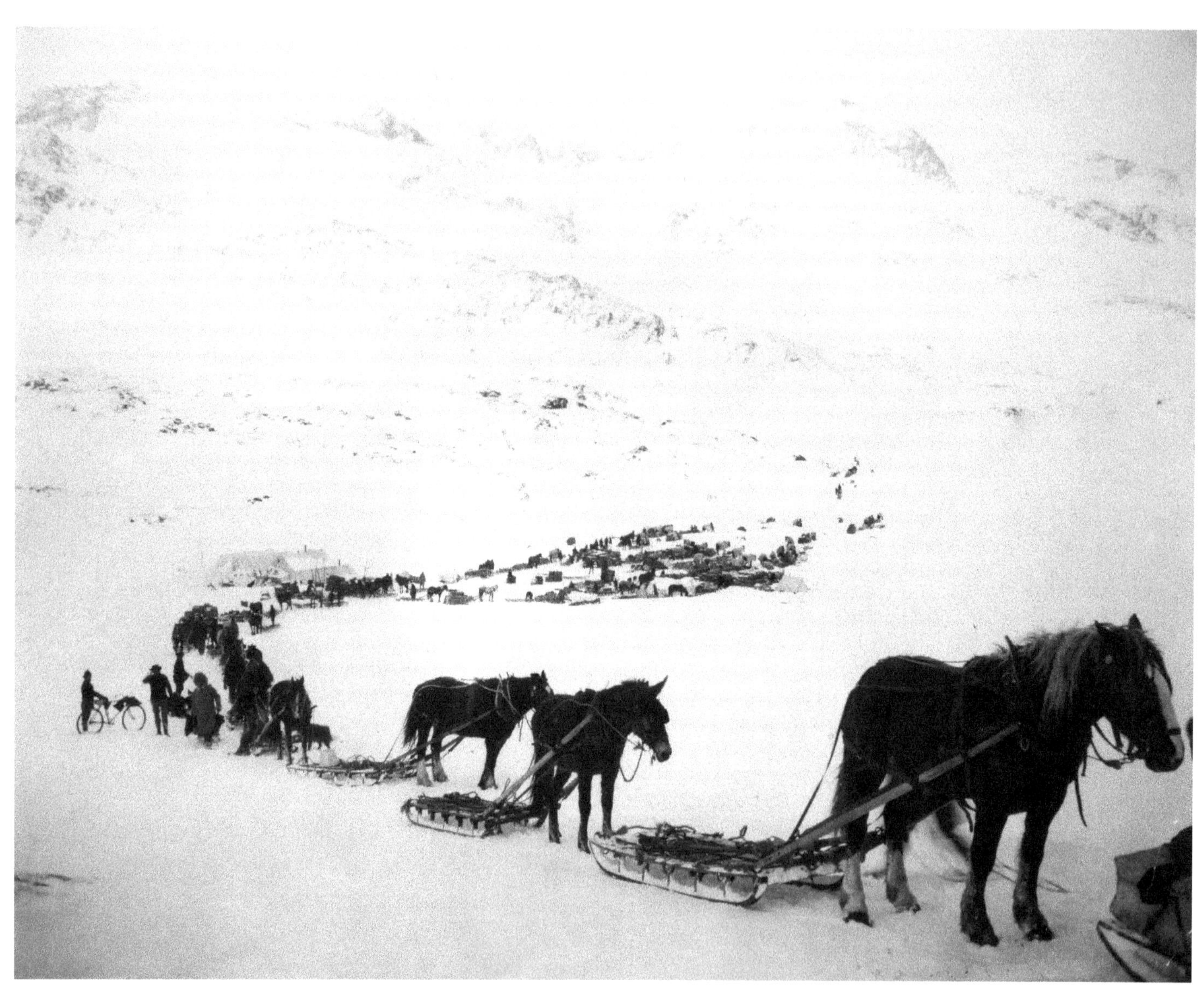

With the mountains in the distance, the route to the summit of the Valdez Trail was like a highway in the early 1900s for a procession of horses, mules, dogs, and one man with a bicycle, visible on the left.

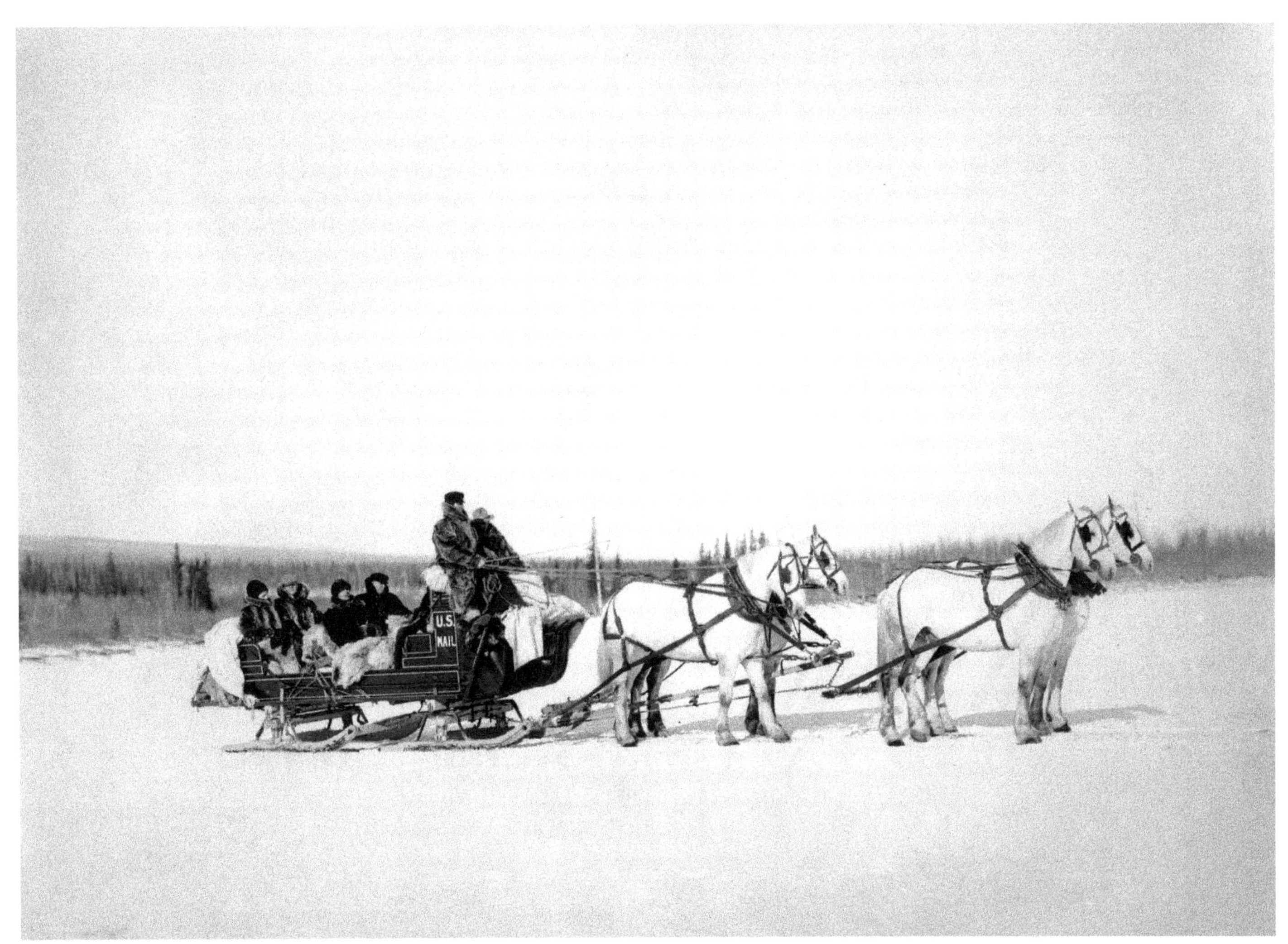

Passengers bundle up in furs and keep large rugs over their laps to stay warm in a horse-drawn sled that was taking them and bags of U.S. Mail to their destination outside of Nome in the early 1900s.

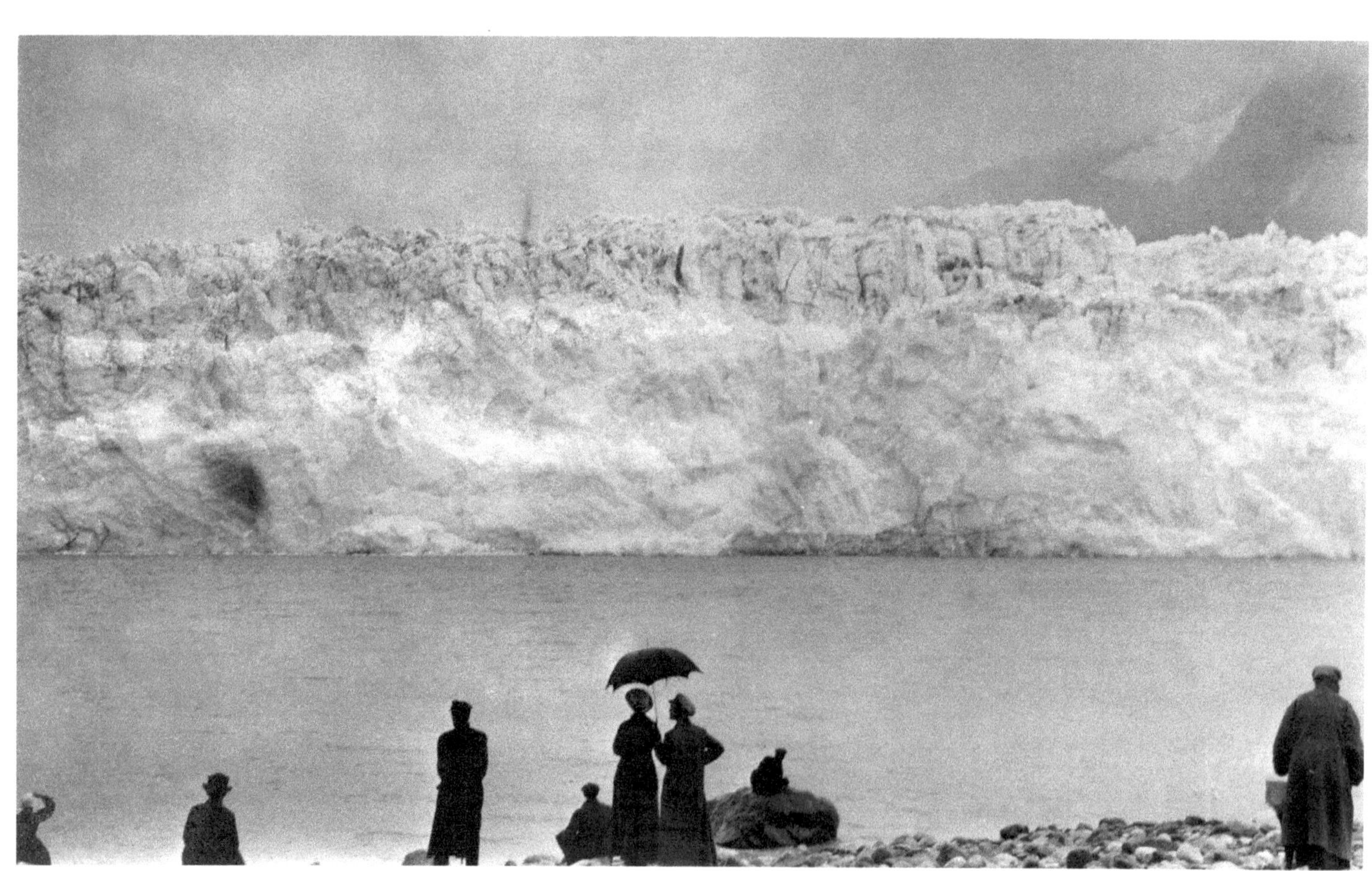

The Childs Glacier, about fifty miles from Cordova, feeds into the Copper River and offers an arresting view for travelers.

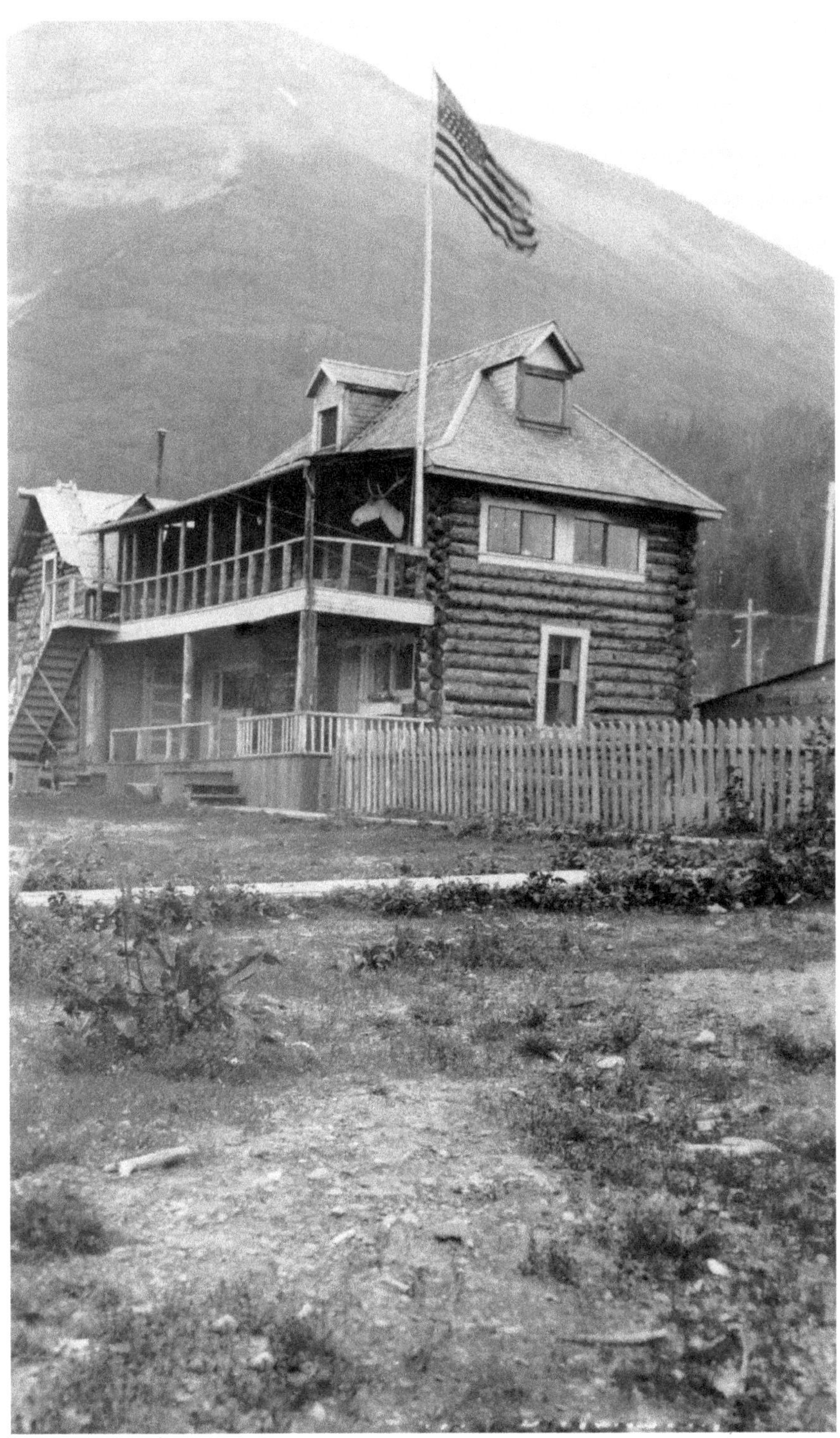

A log cabin served as the U.S. Marshal's office in Seward. The federal marshals provided law enforcement in much of Alaska during the early decades of territorial rule.

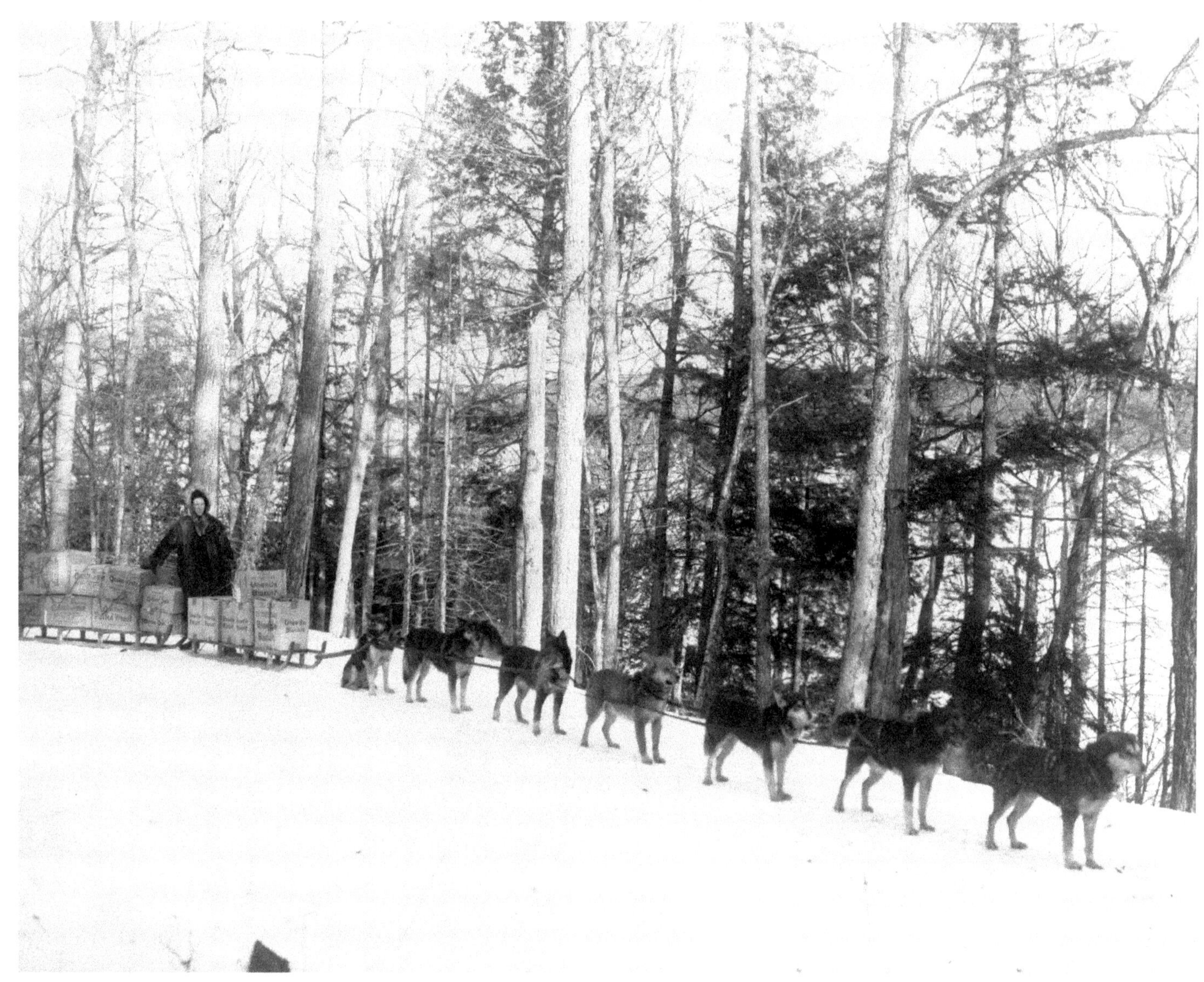

A dog team delivers two sleds loaded with crates of Quaker Oats, Quaker Puffed Wheat, and Uneeda Biscuits in 1911.

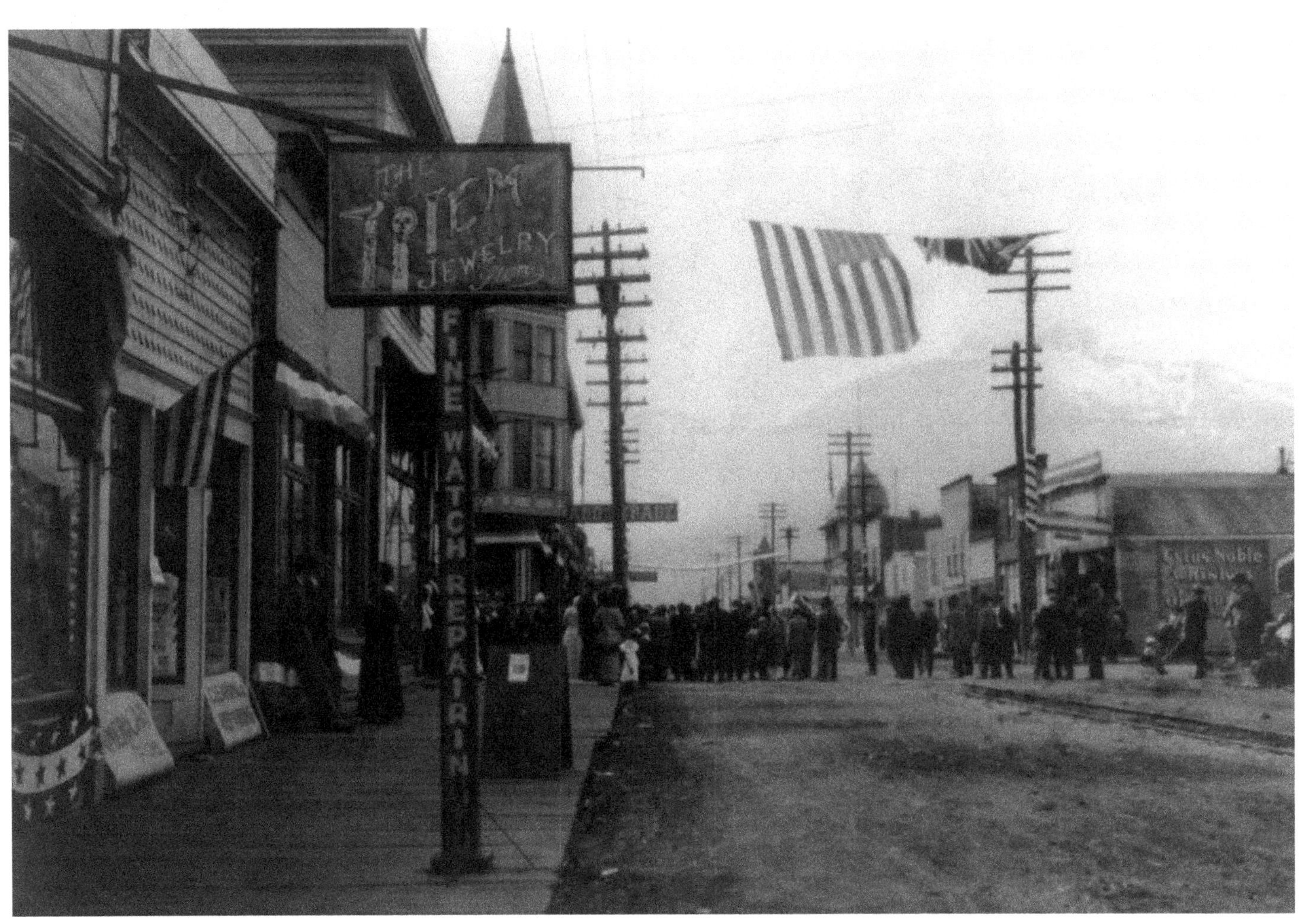

Skagway residents celebrate the Fourth of July with games and other festivities in the center of town.

Strong men of Skagway give their all in a tug-of-war during a Fourth of July celebration, digging their feet in and trying to yank the opposing side over the line.

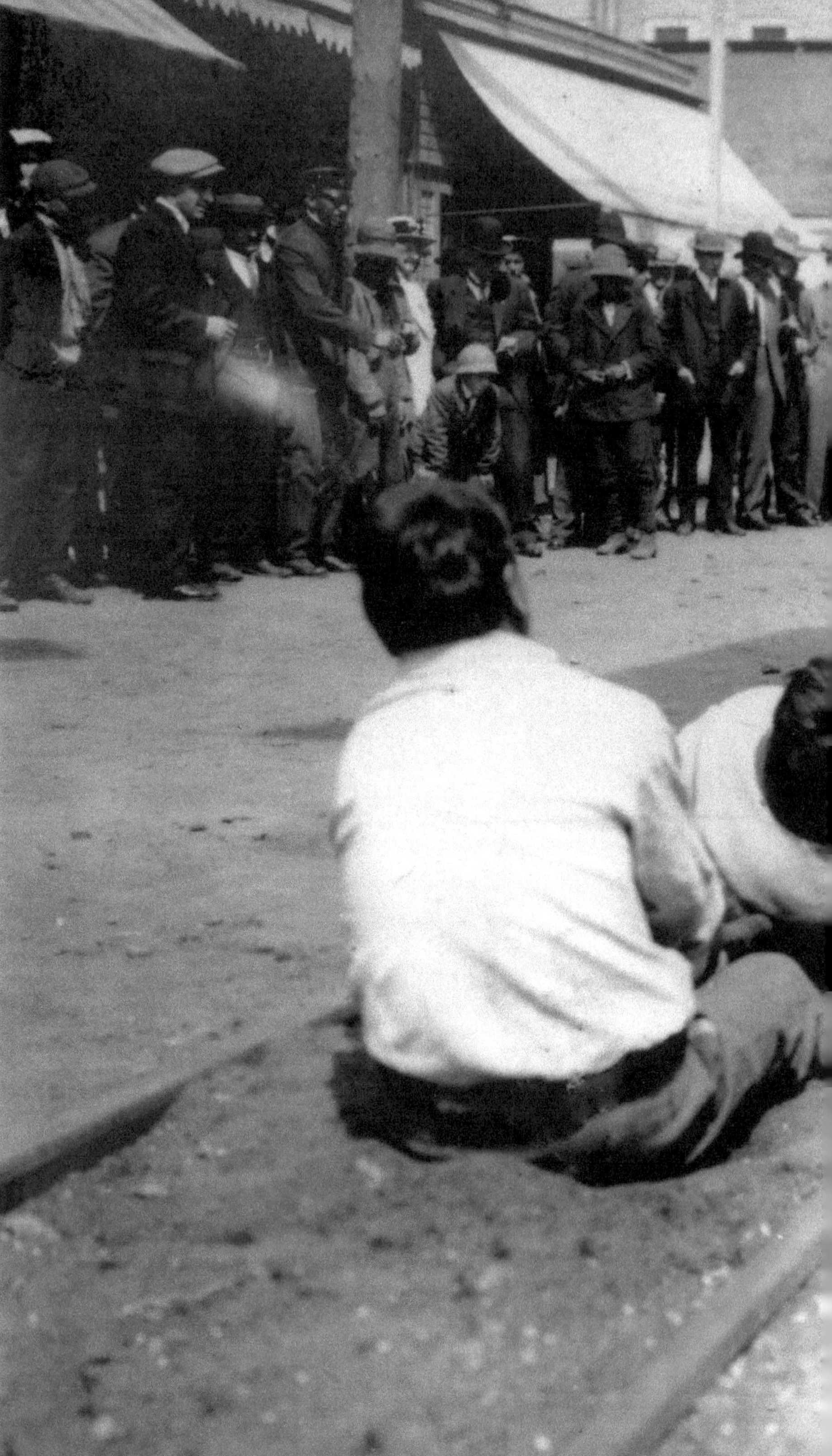

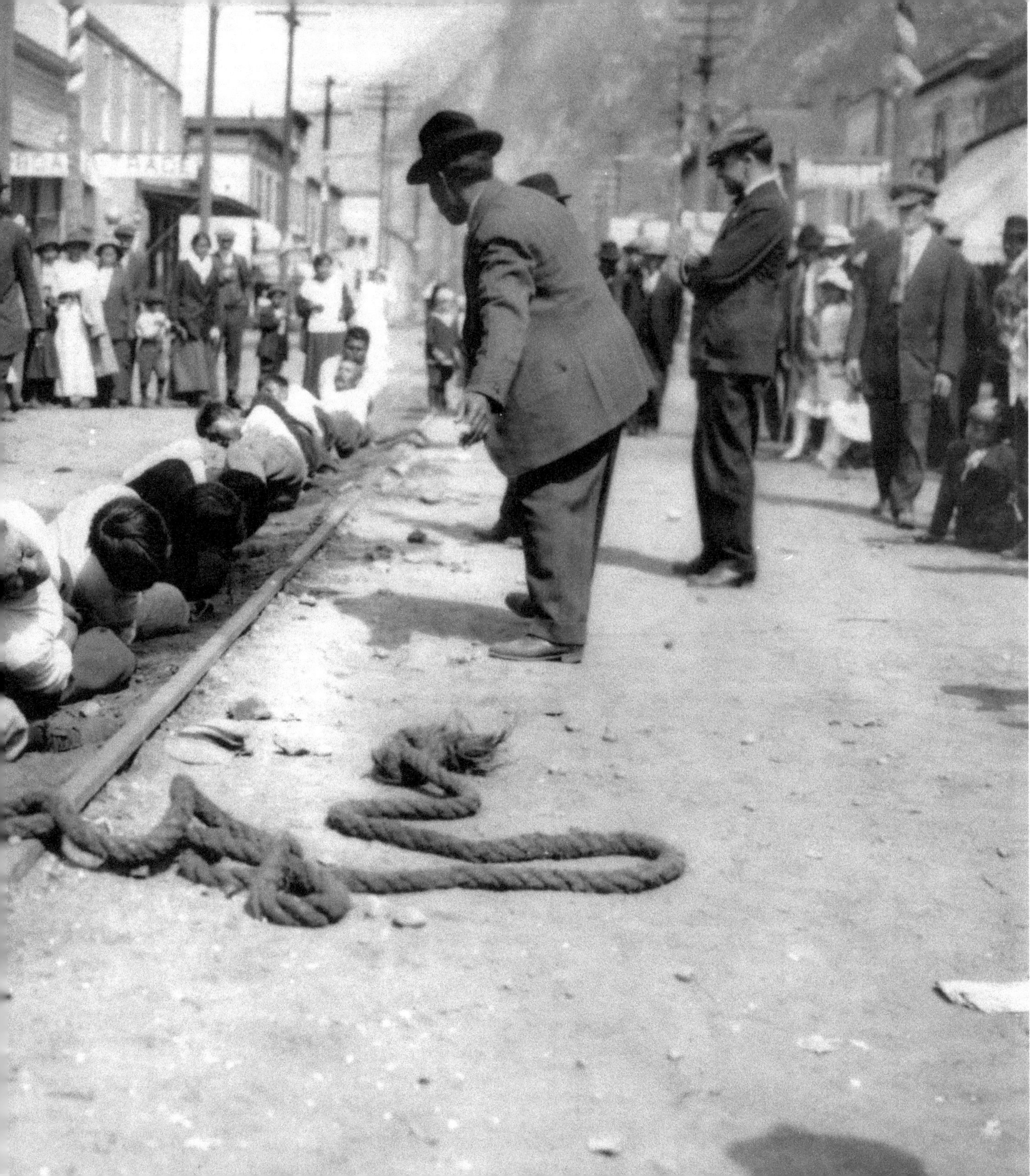

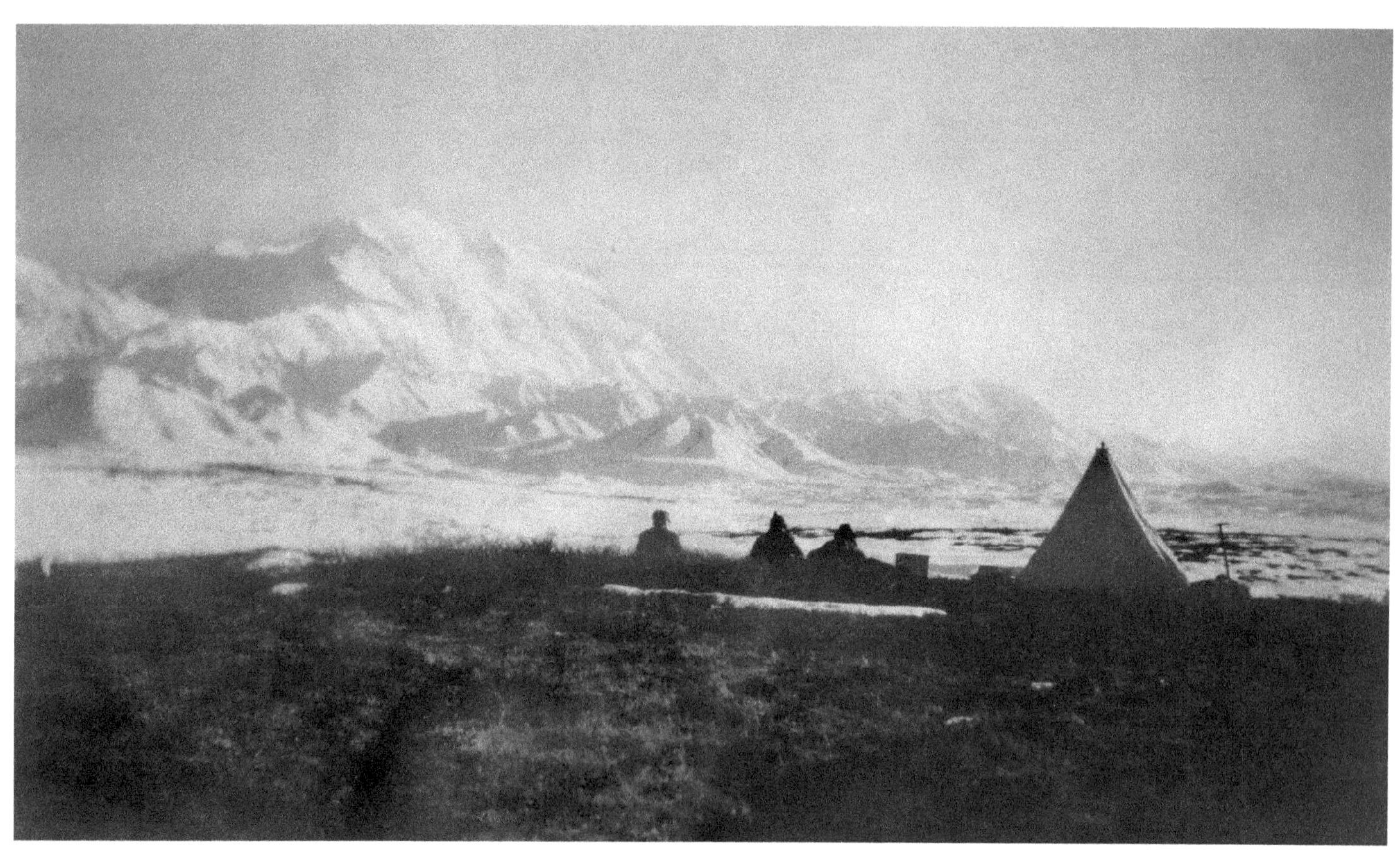

Belmore Brown, a prominent artist and explorer, climbed Mount McKinley in 1912. He photographed this campsite, twenty miles from the peak, on that trip to Alaska.

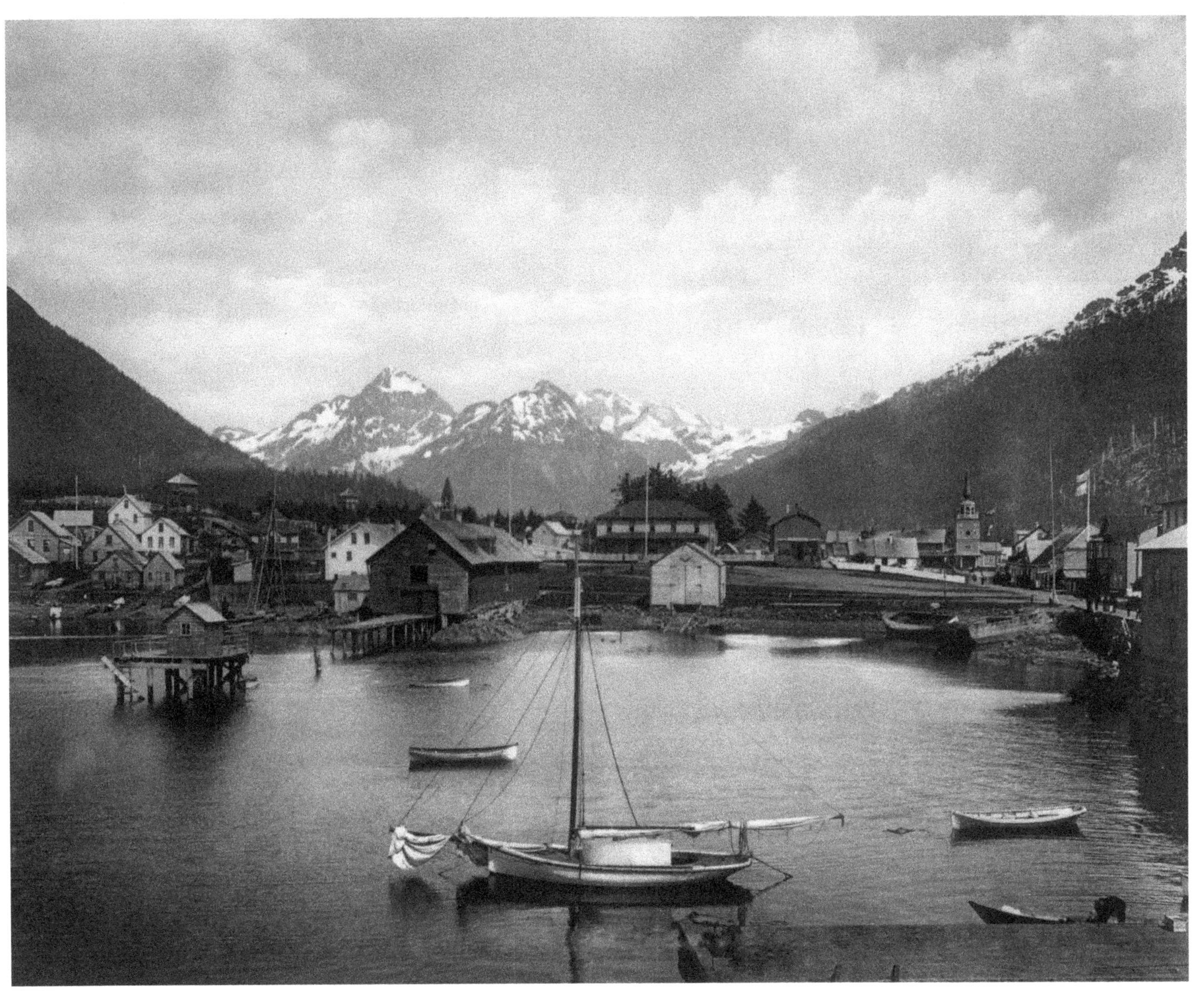

Sitka, as seen from the water, showing boats in the harbor, buildings in the city, and the "Three Sisters Mountains" in the background.

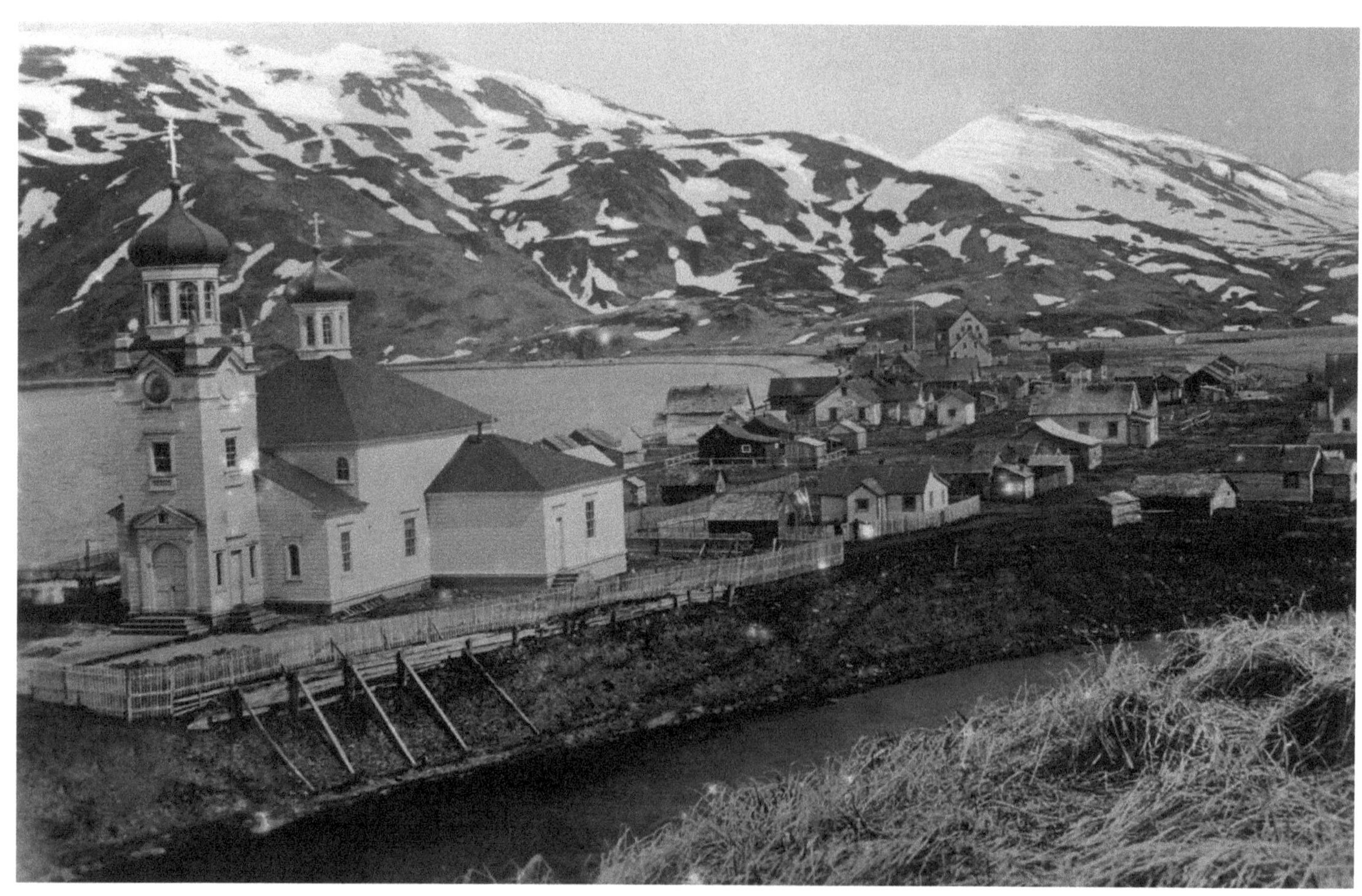

The Russian Orthodox Church of the Holy Ascension in Unalaska, completed in 1826, has long been the preeminent structure in the Aleutian village.

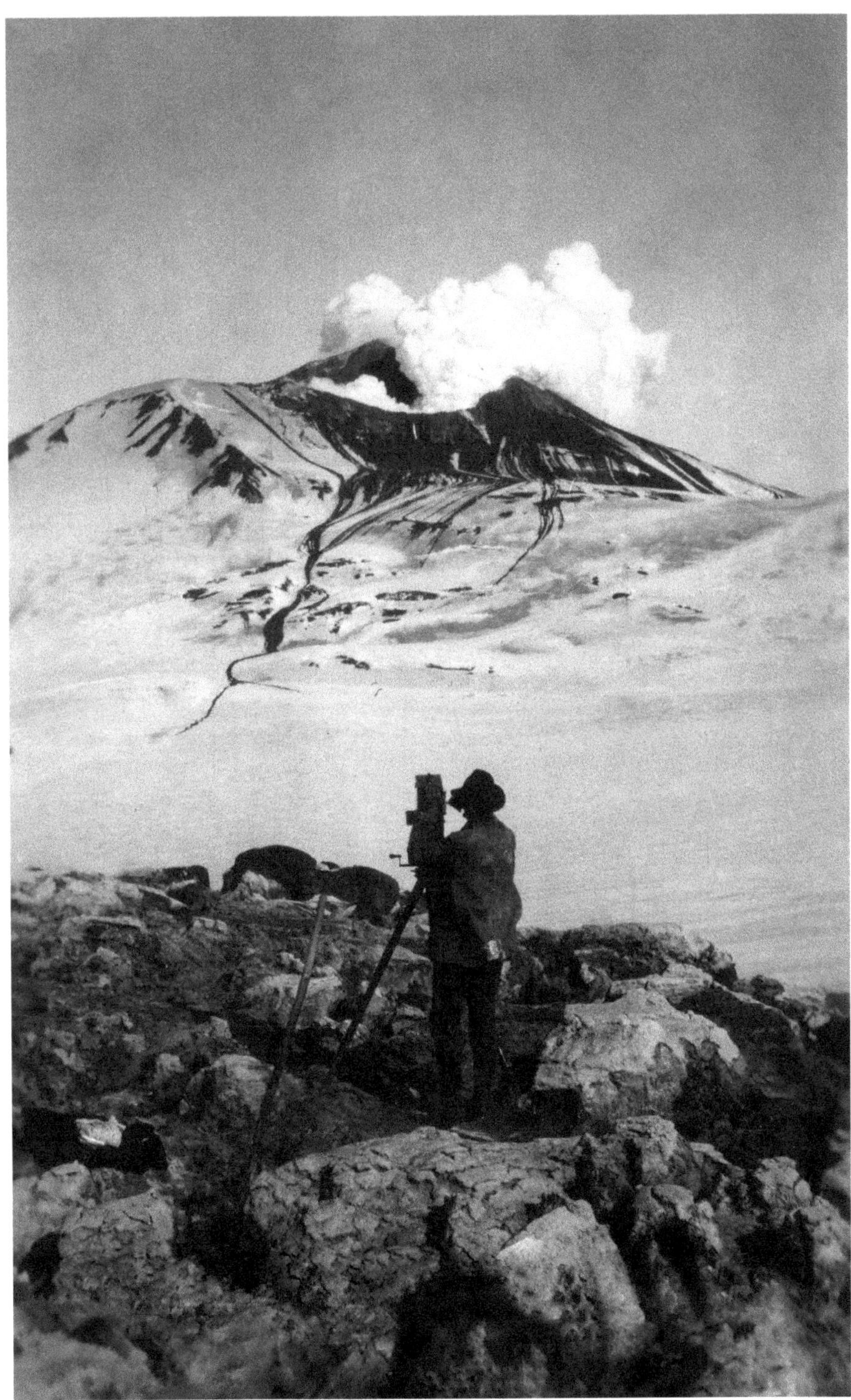

A year after the massive eruption of the Katmai Volcano in 1912, William Hesse hiked through the area and filmed a movie of one of the steaming mountains in the region, Mount Martin.

An anxious crowd awaits the first finishers in the 1913 All-Alaska Sweepstakes in Nome, a four-hundred-mile trek that was the premier mushing event in the territory.

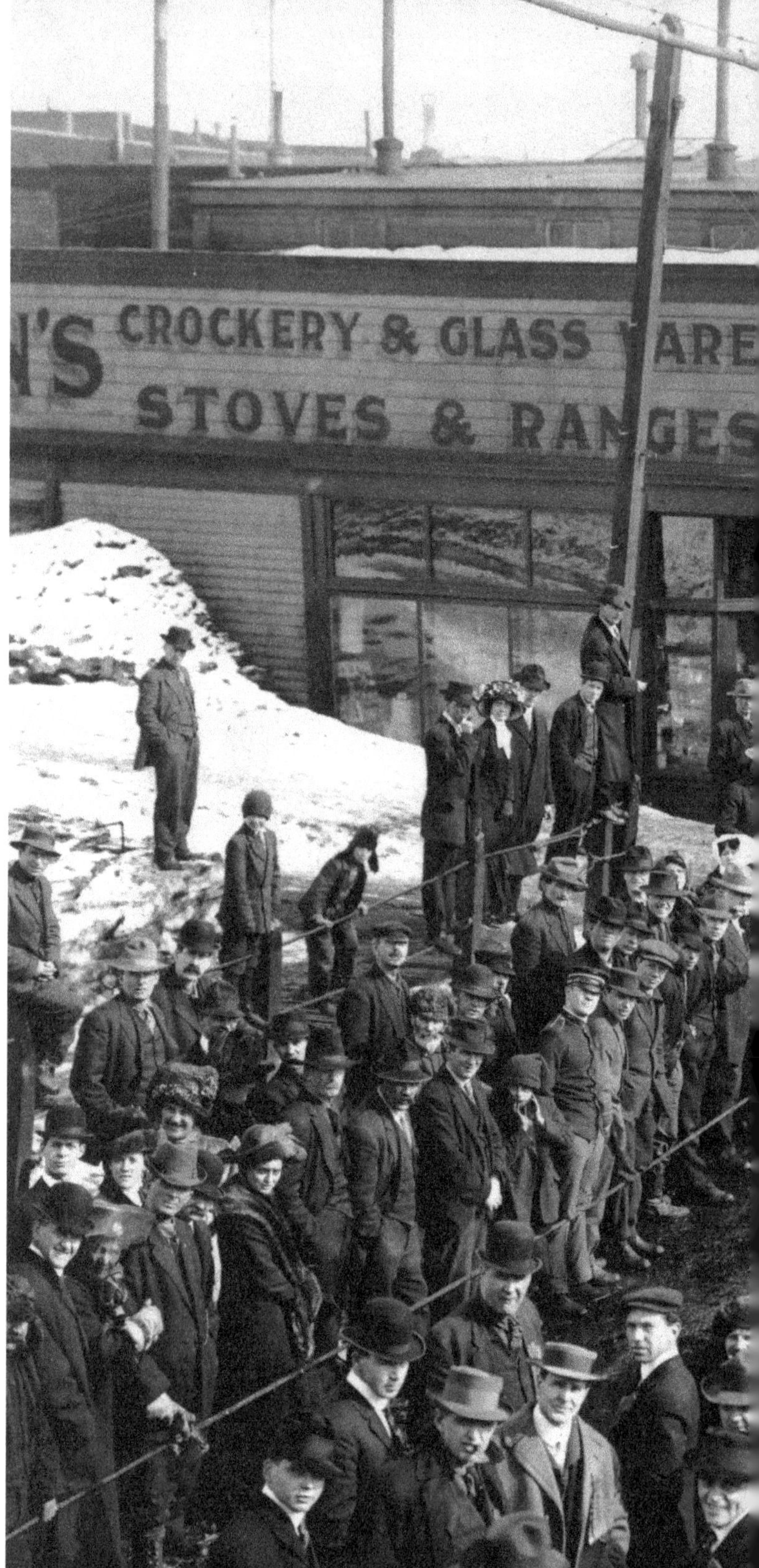

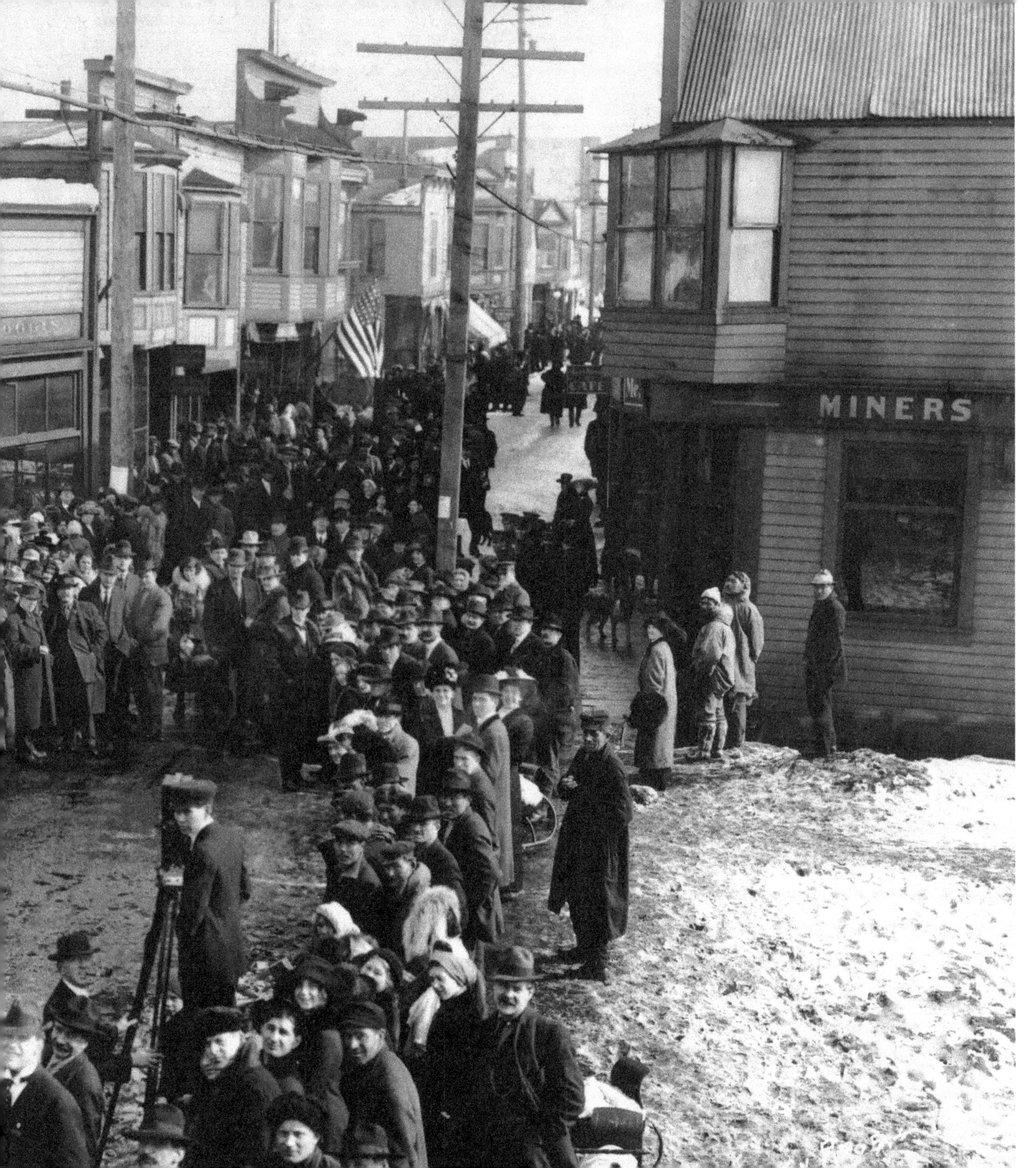
MINERS

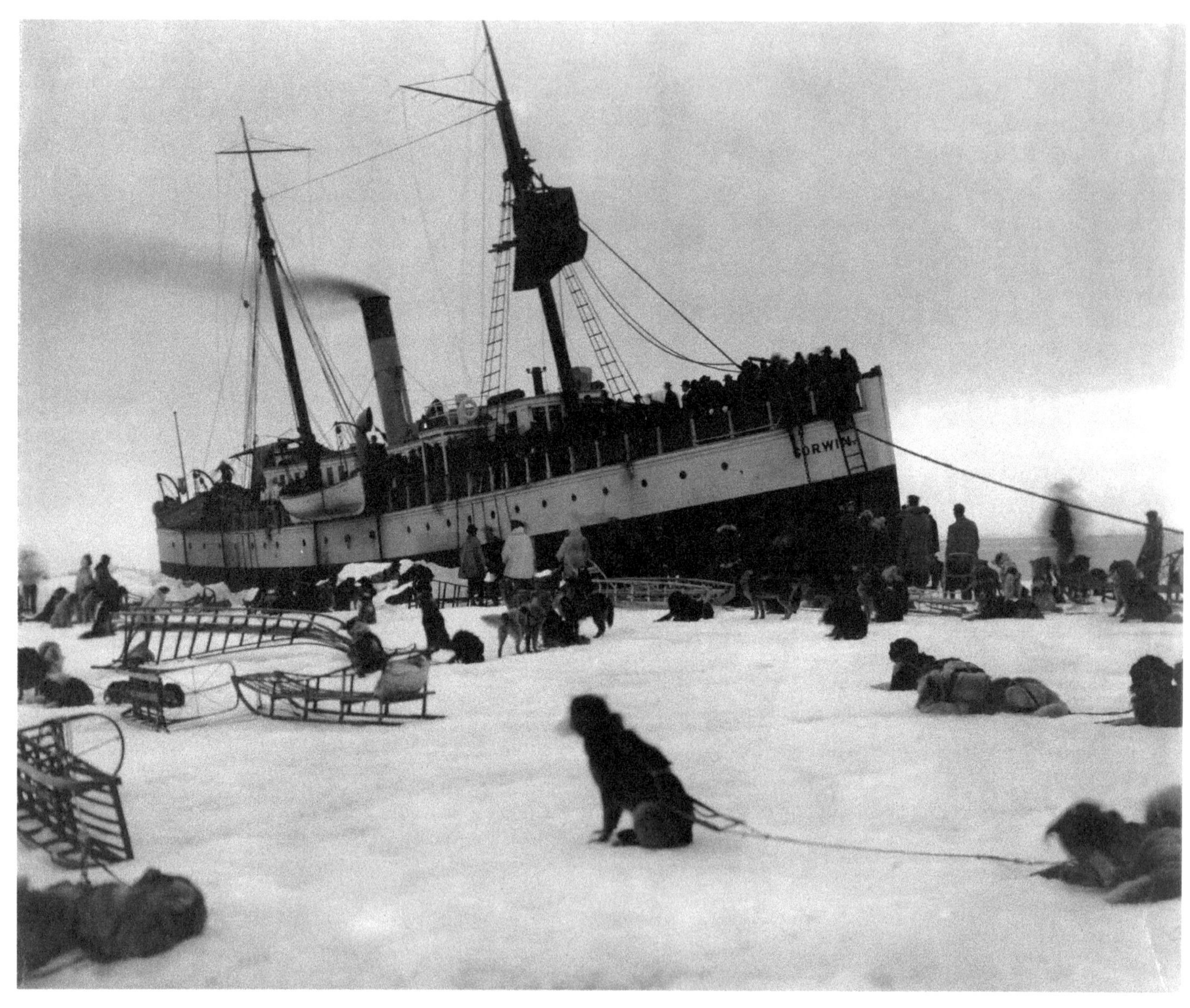

Dog teams meet the S.S. *Corwin* on June 1, 1914, on the coast of Nome.

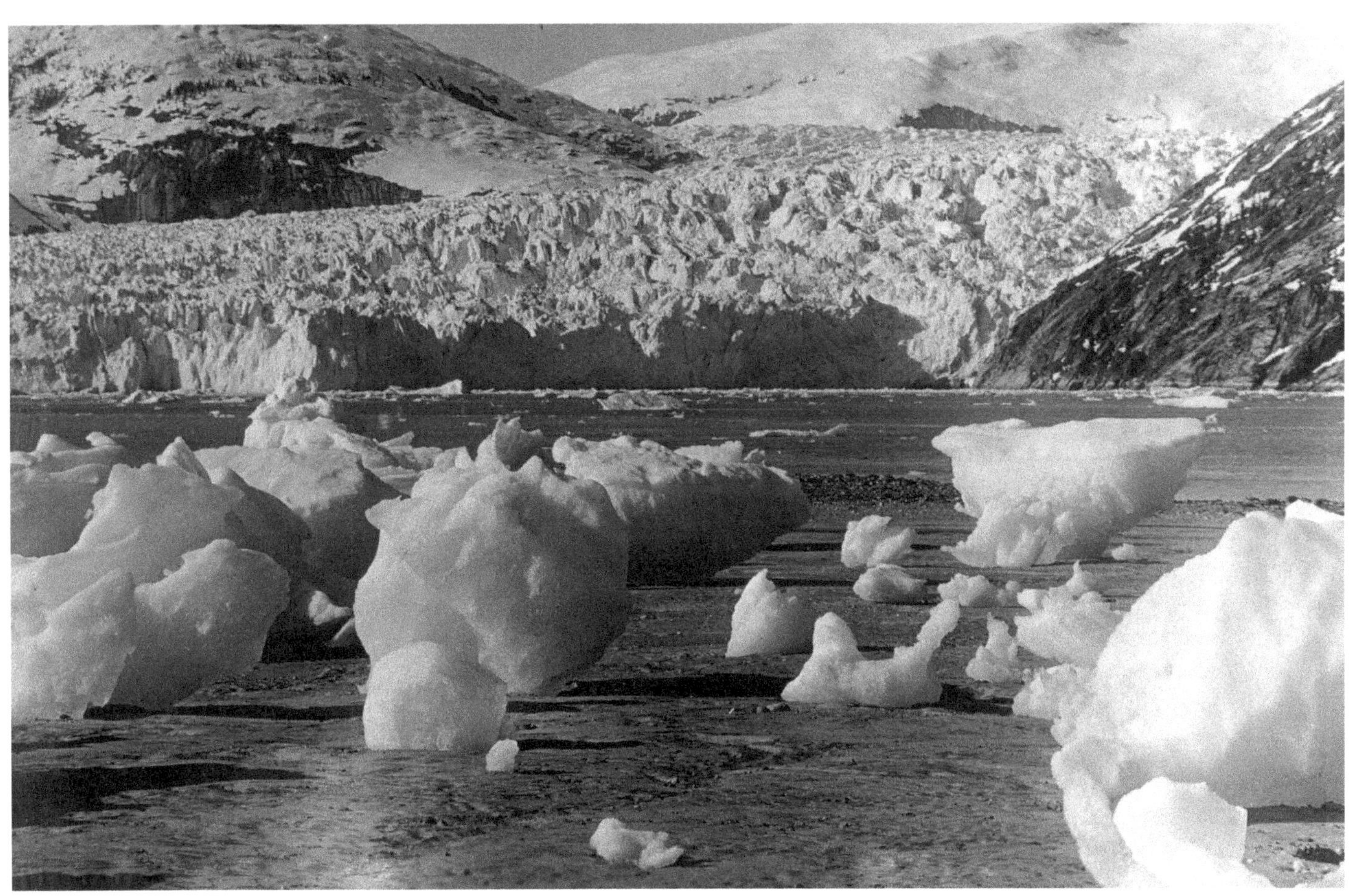

The Taku Glacier near Juneau, with a maximum depth of nearly 1,500 yards, has advanced about 4.5 miles since 1890, which makes it unique in a region of retreating glaciers.

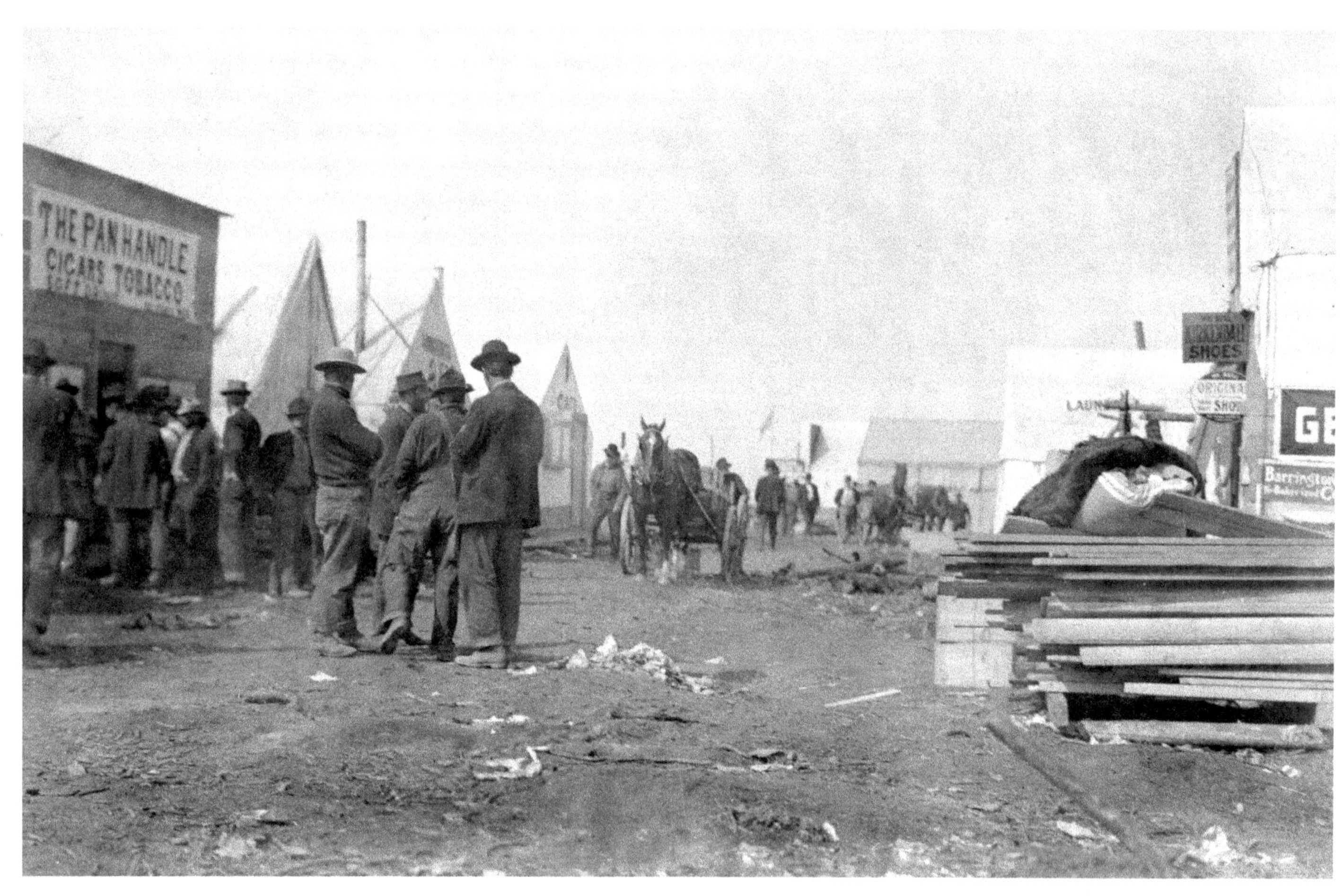

Anchorage began as a tent city in 1915, designated as a construction headquarters for the building of the Alaska Railroad to Fairbanks.

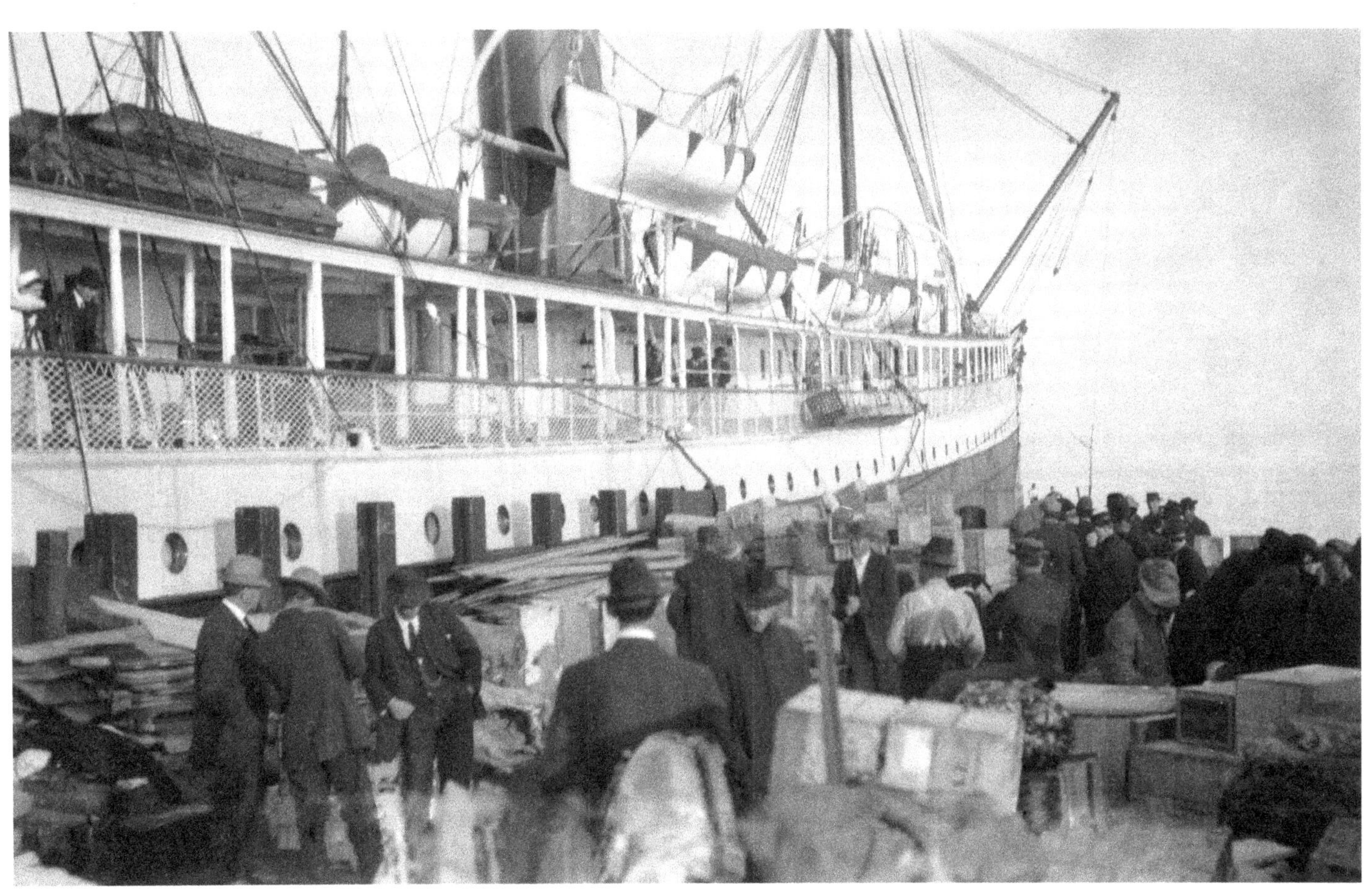

Carrying supplies for the Alaska Railroad construction effort, the S.S. *Alameda* unloads in Anchorage.

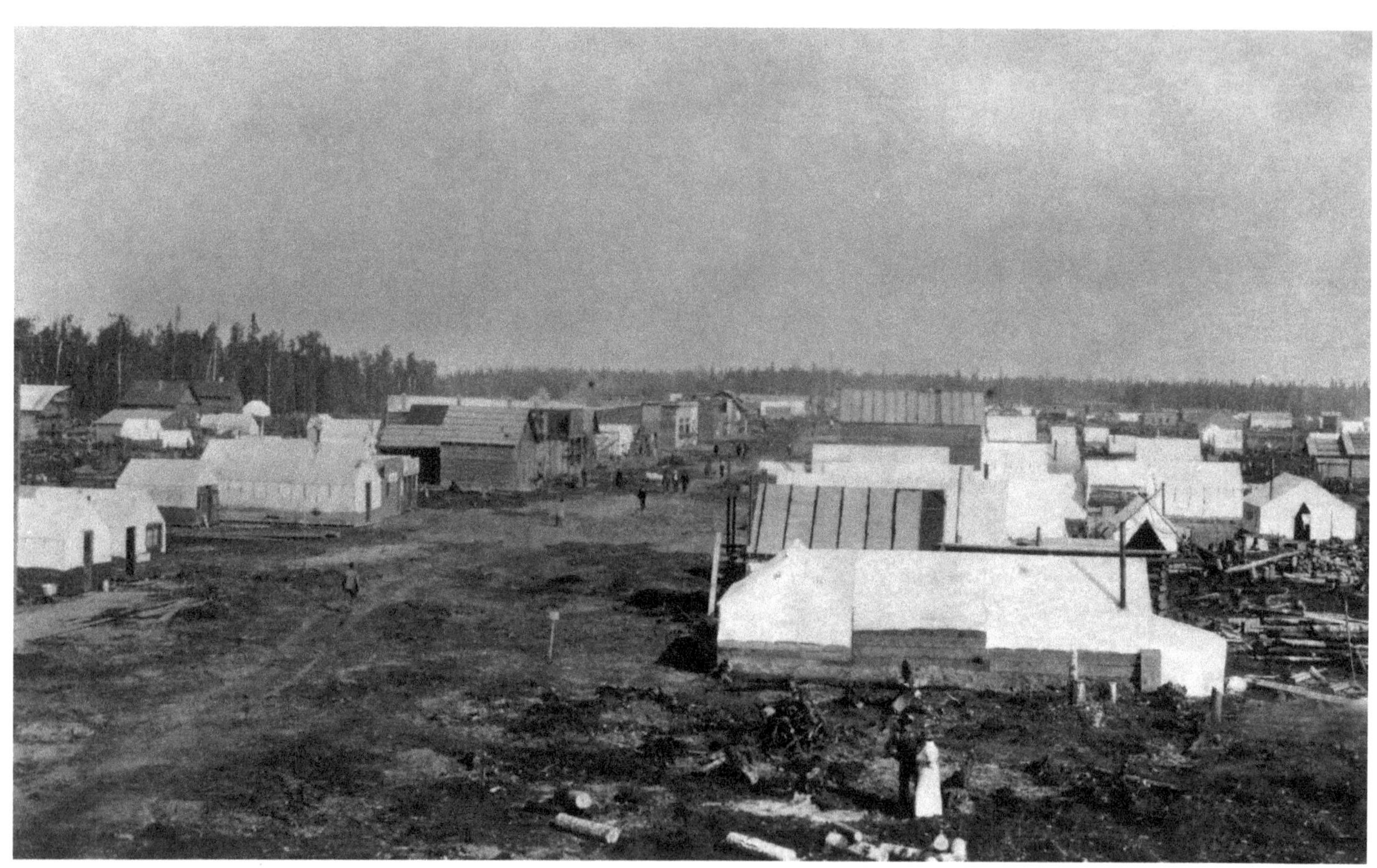

The railroad crews and other construction hands cleared land along Turnagain Arm and built sheds, warehouses, and cabins as fast as they could, with about two thousand people on the scene in 1915.

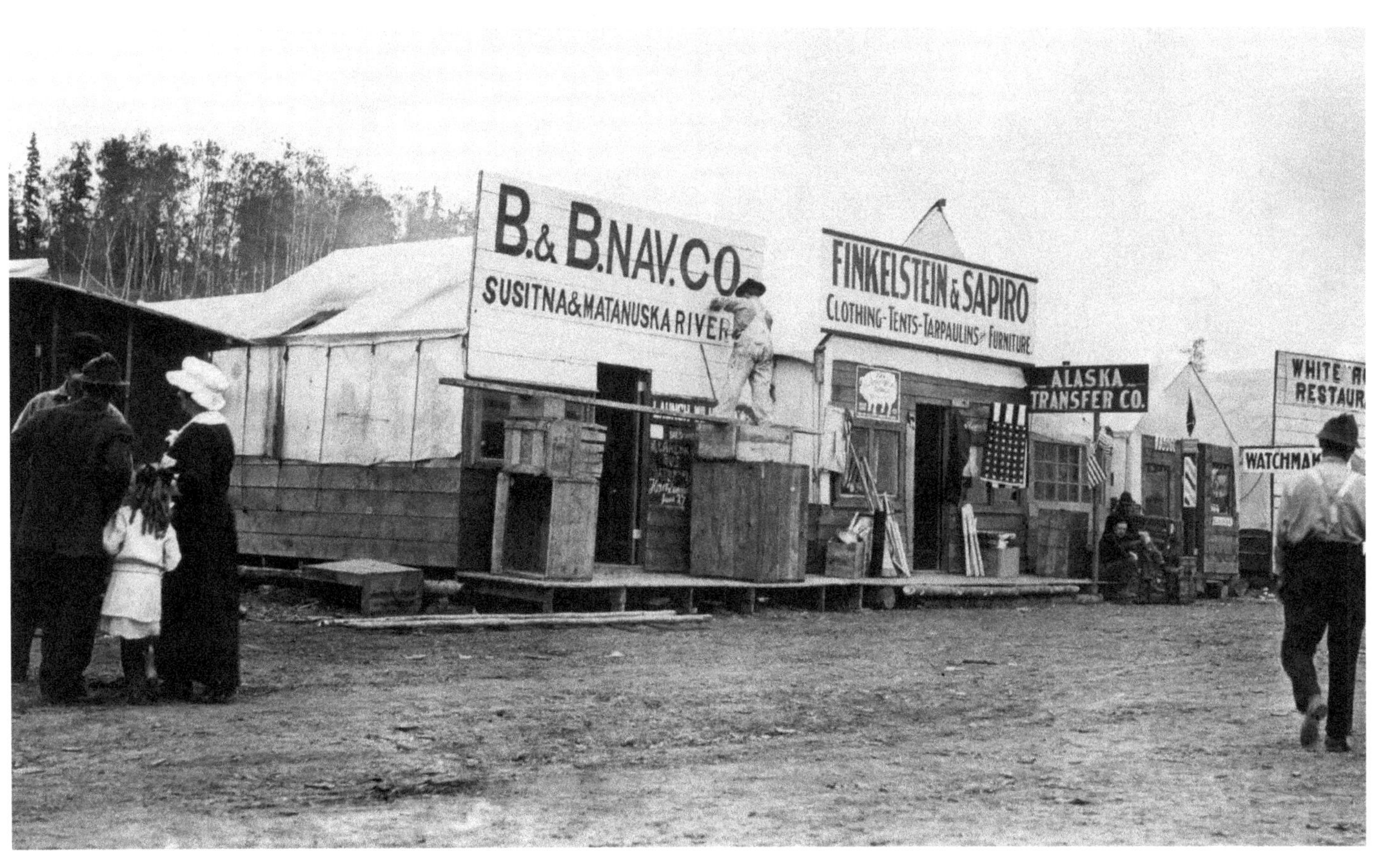

A painter puts the finishing letters on a street sign advertising the services of the B & B Navigation Co. in Anchorage, which provided transportation on the Susitna and Matanuska rivers.

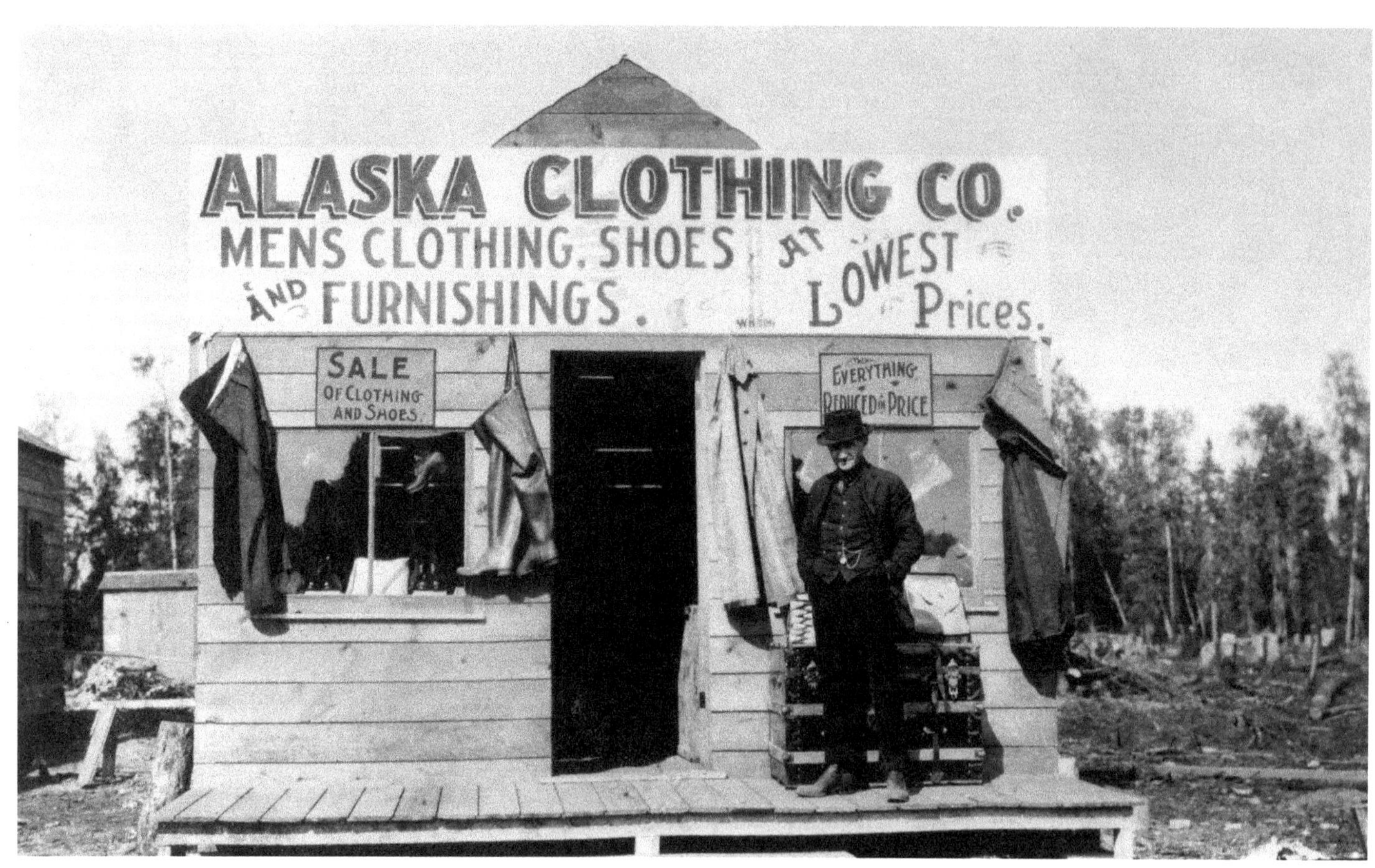

The Alaska Clothing Co., in the fledgling camp of Anchorage, did a big business selling rain boots, work pants, and coats to construction workers in 1916.

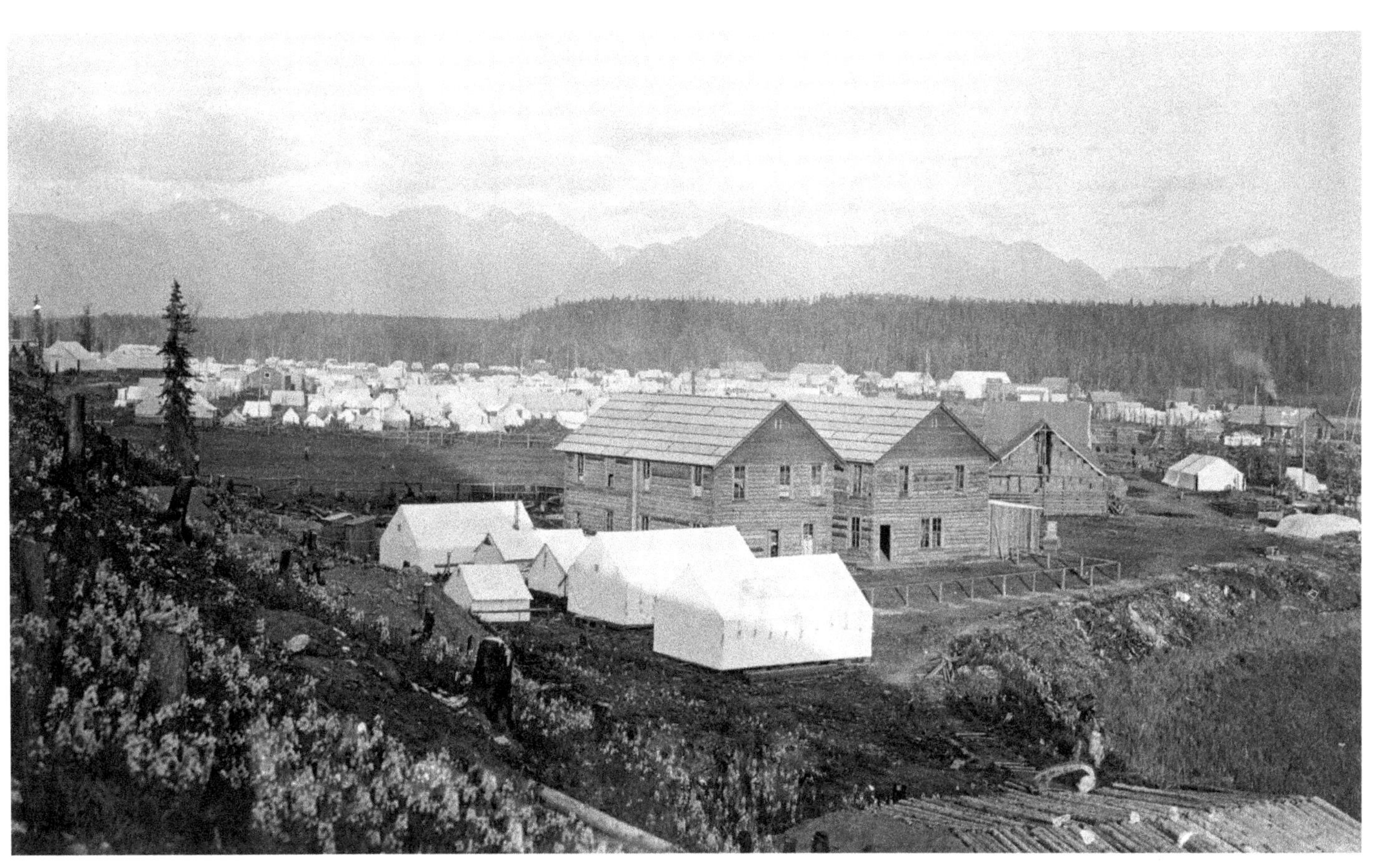

The Alaska Railroad opened an Anchorage hospital in the twin, two-story, log buildings in the foreground, close to Government Hill.

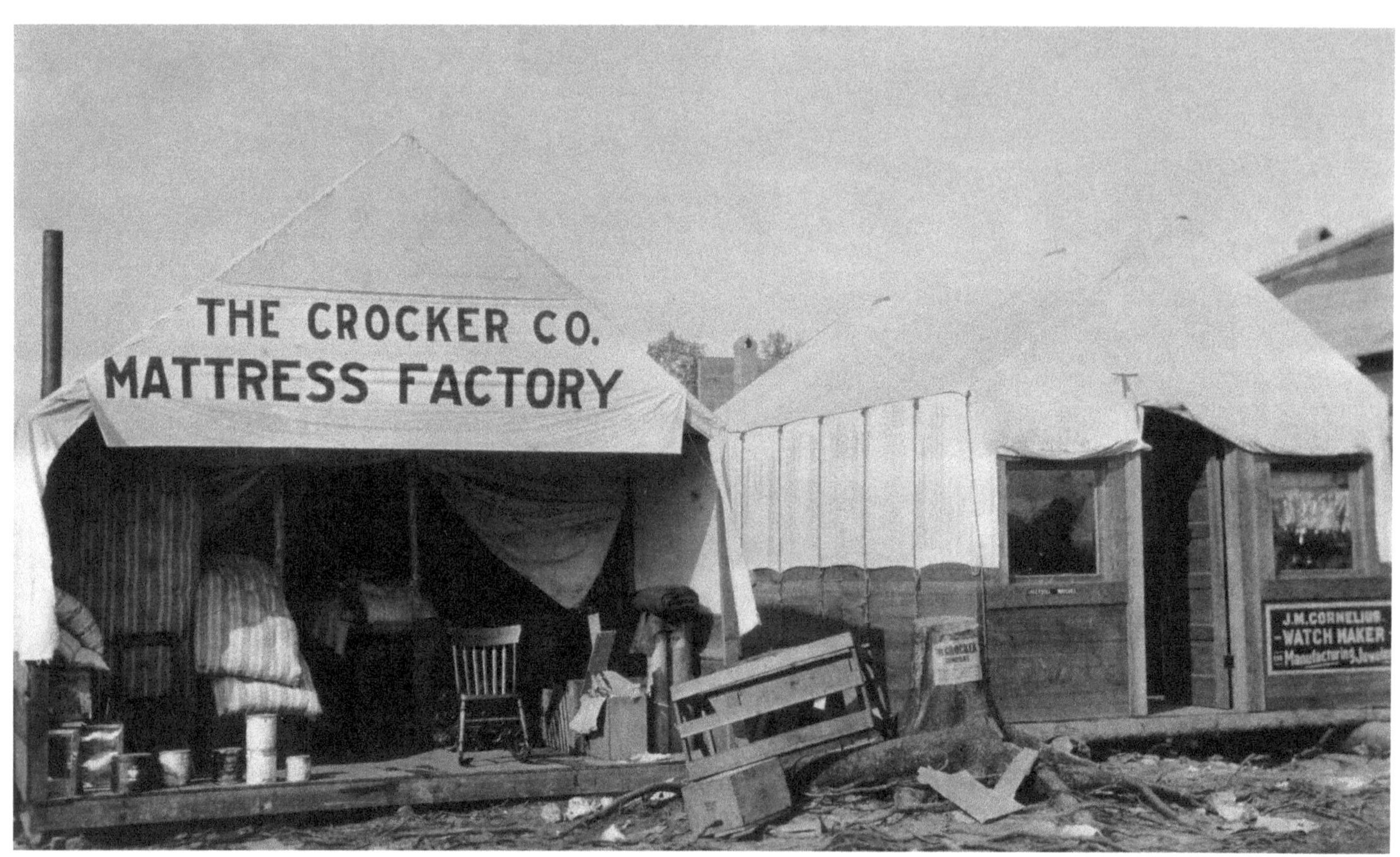

Every town in Alaska had to have a mattress factory, and Anchorage was no exception. A mattress was one of the things that most people didn't bring to Alaska.

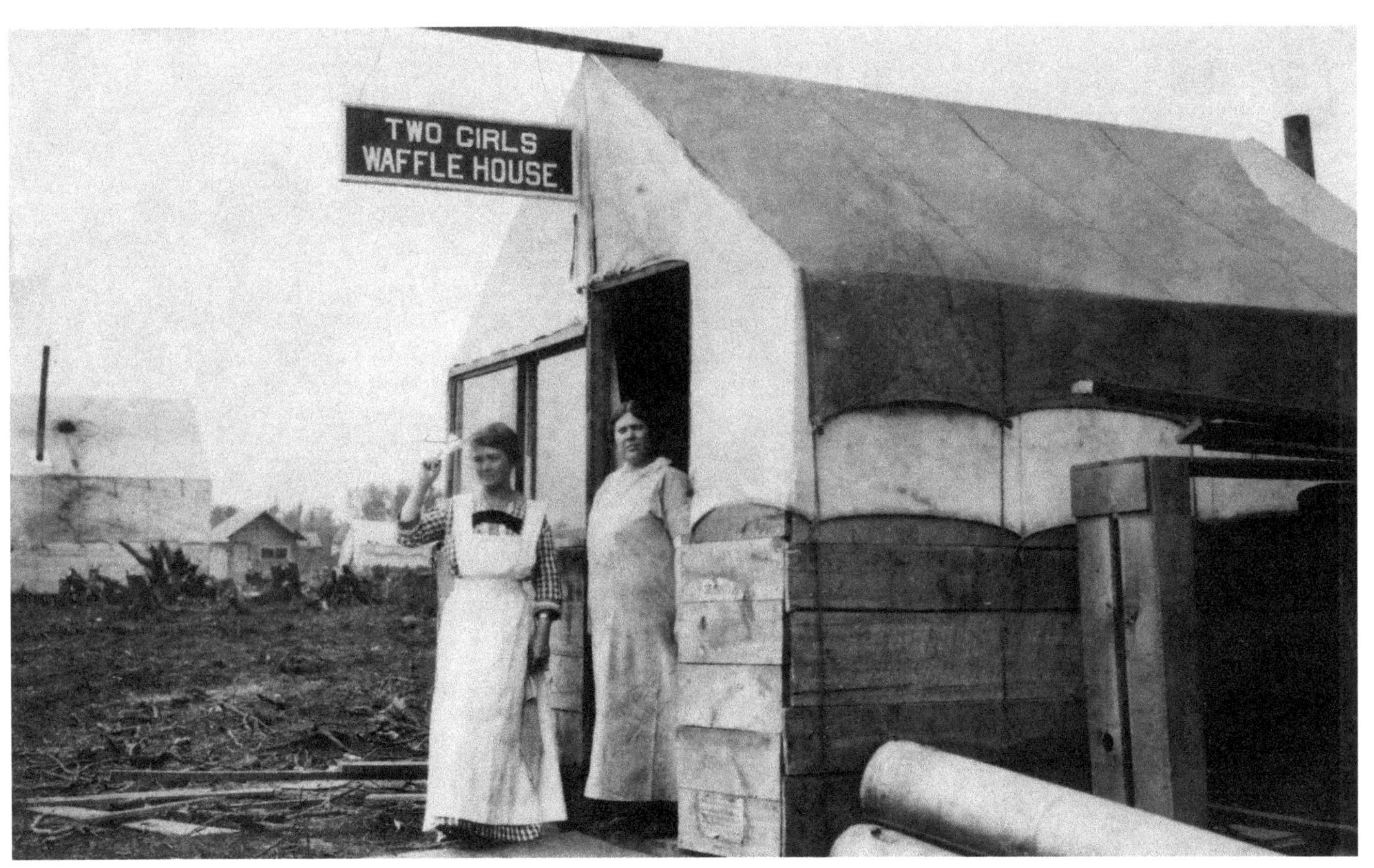

Railroad workers had to eat in Anchorage and where better than the Two Girls Waffle House, a compact eatery in the tent city.

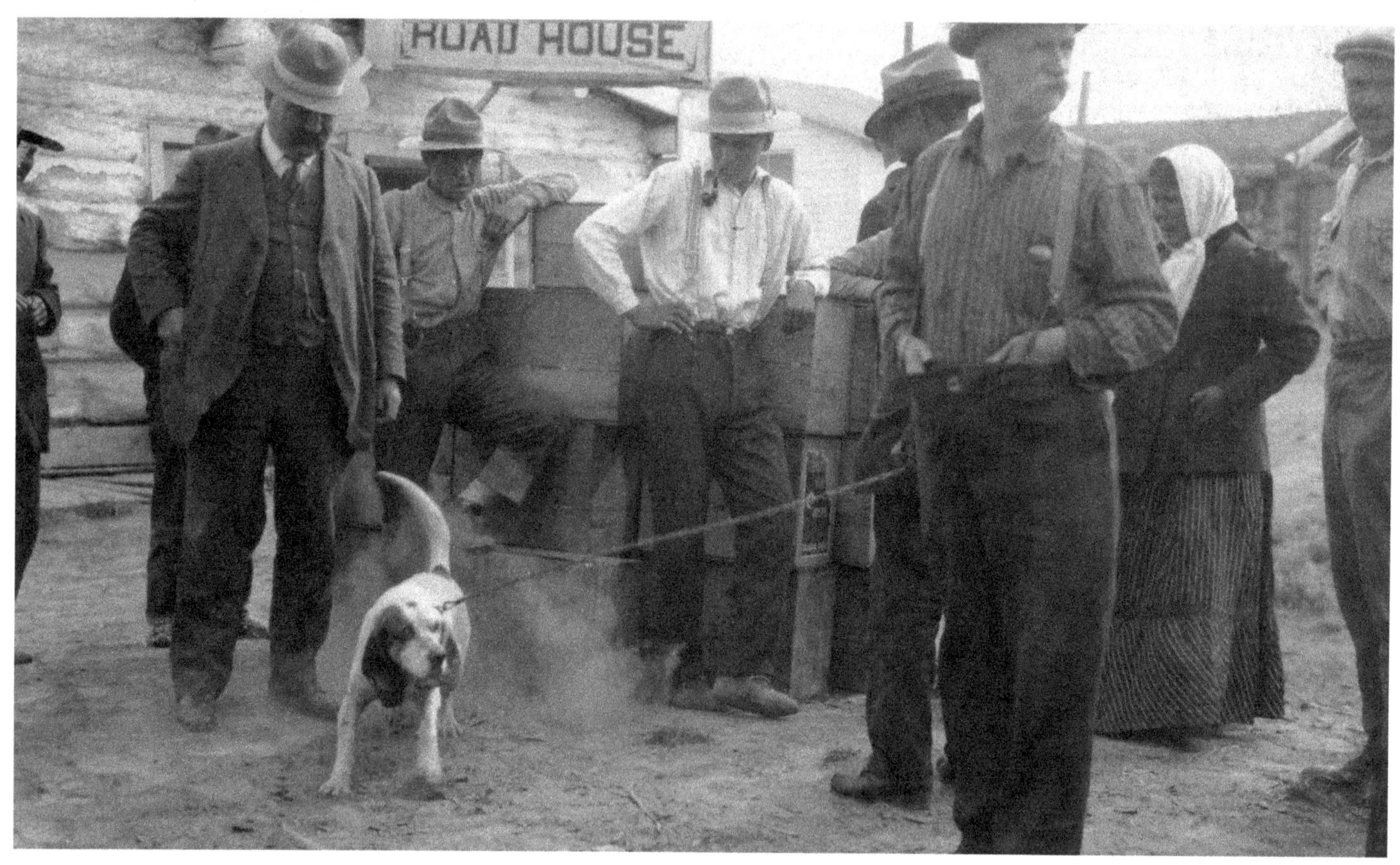

Jim Haly, right, and others gather outside his roadhouse, while Haly and one of his dogs look off into the distance.

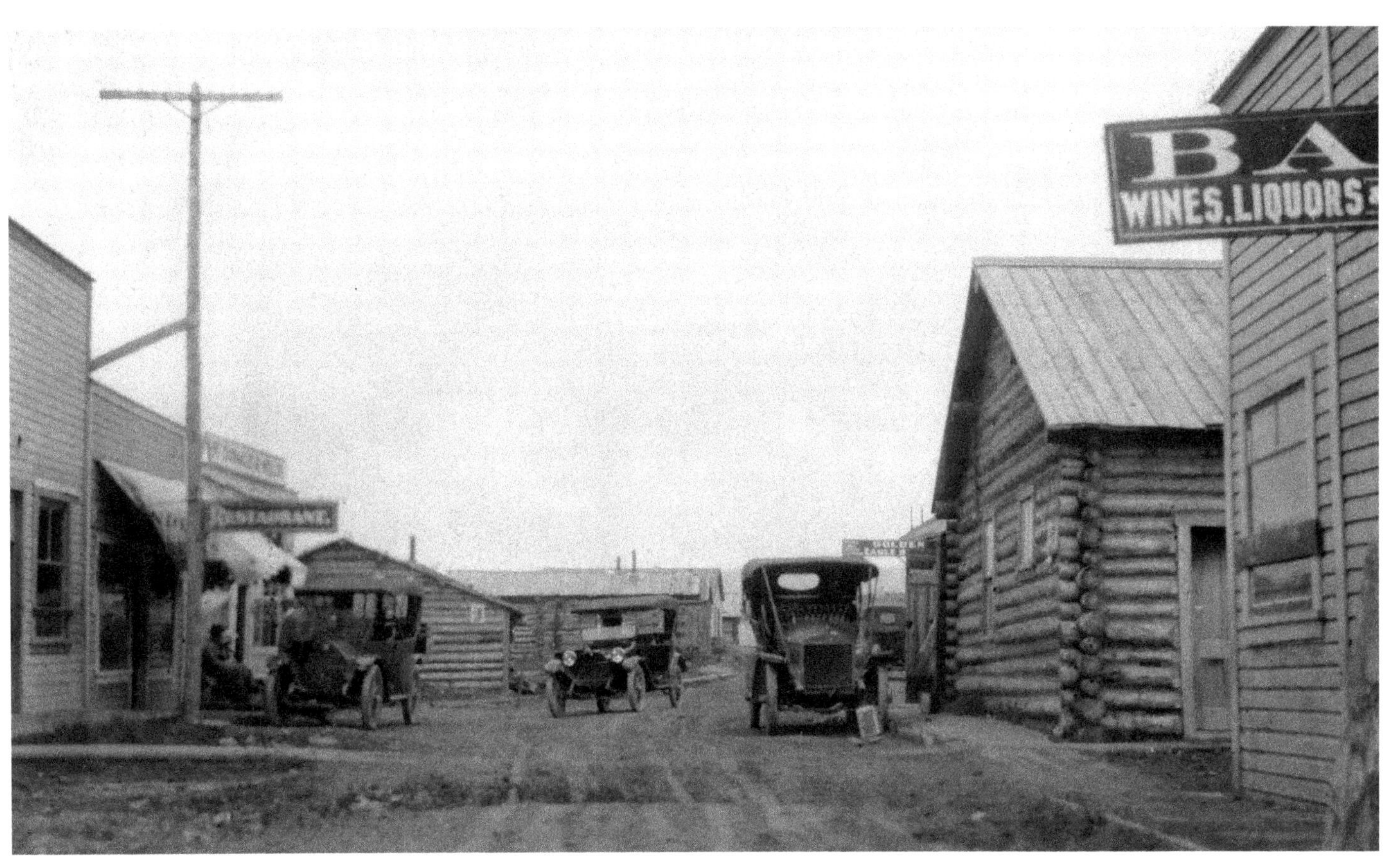

The muddy streets of Ester, a mining camp just west of Fairbanks that thrived in the early years of the century but declined along with the rest of the area during World War I.

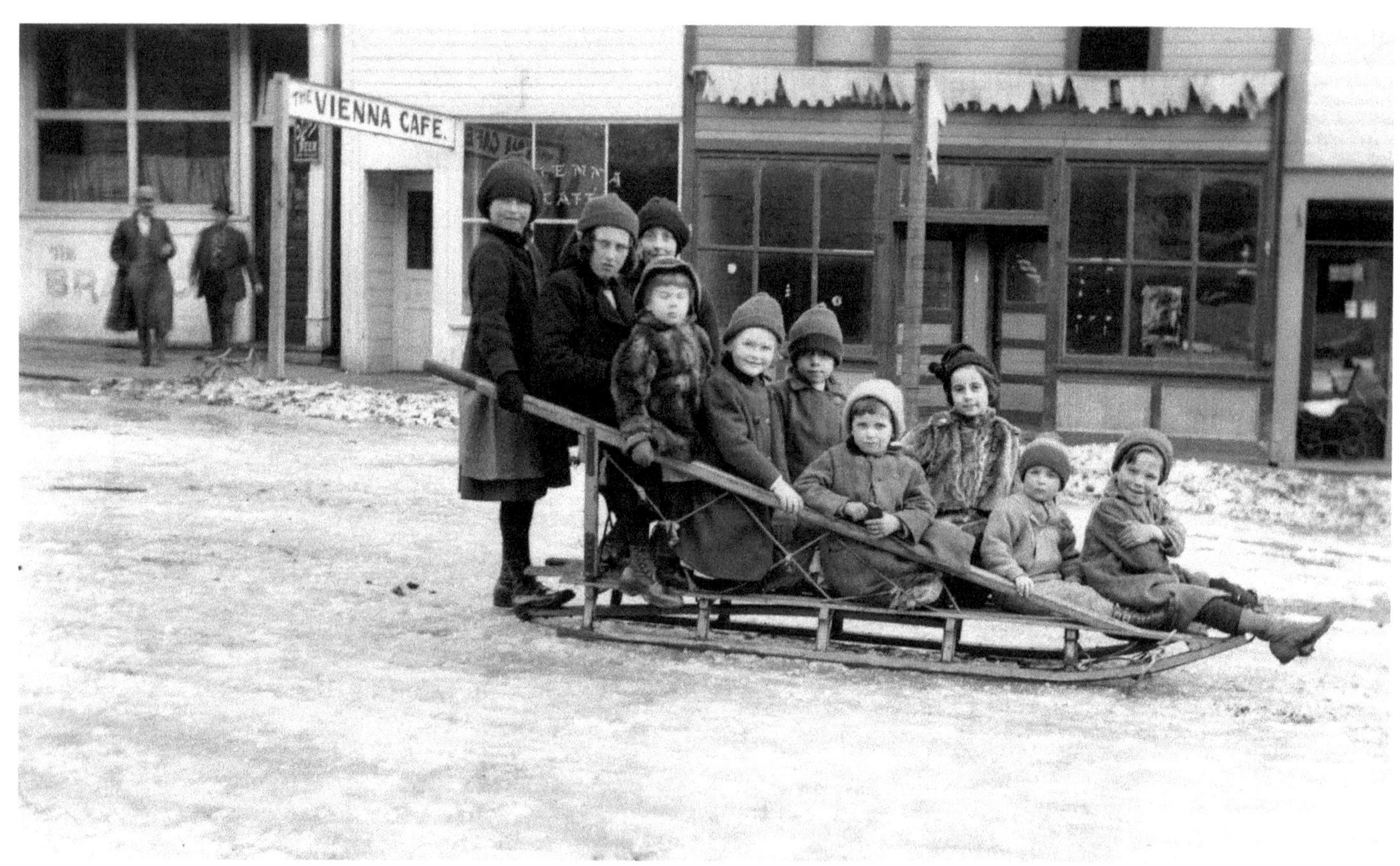

How many kids can fit on a dogsled? Ten, in this case, with room to spare.

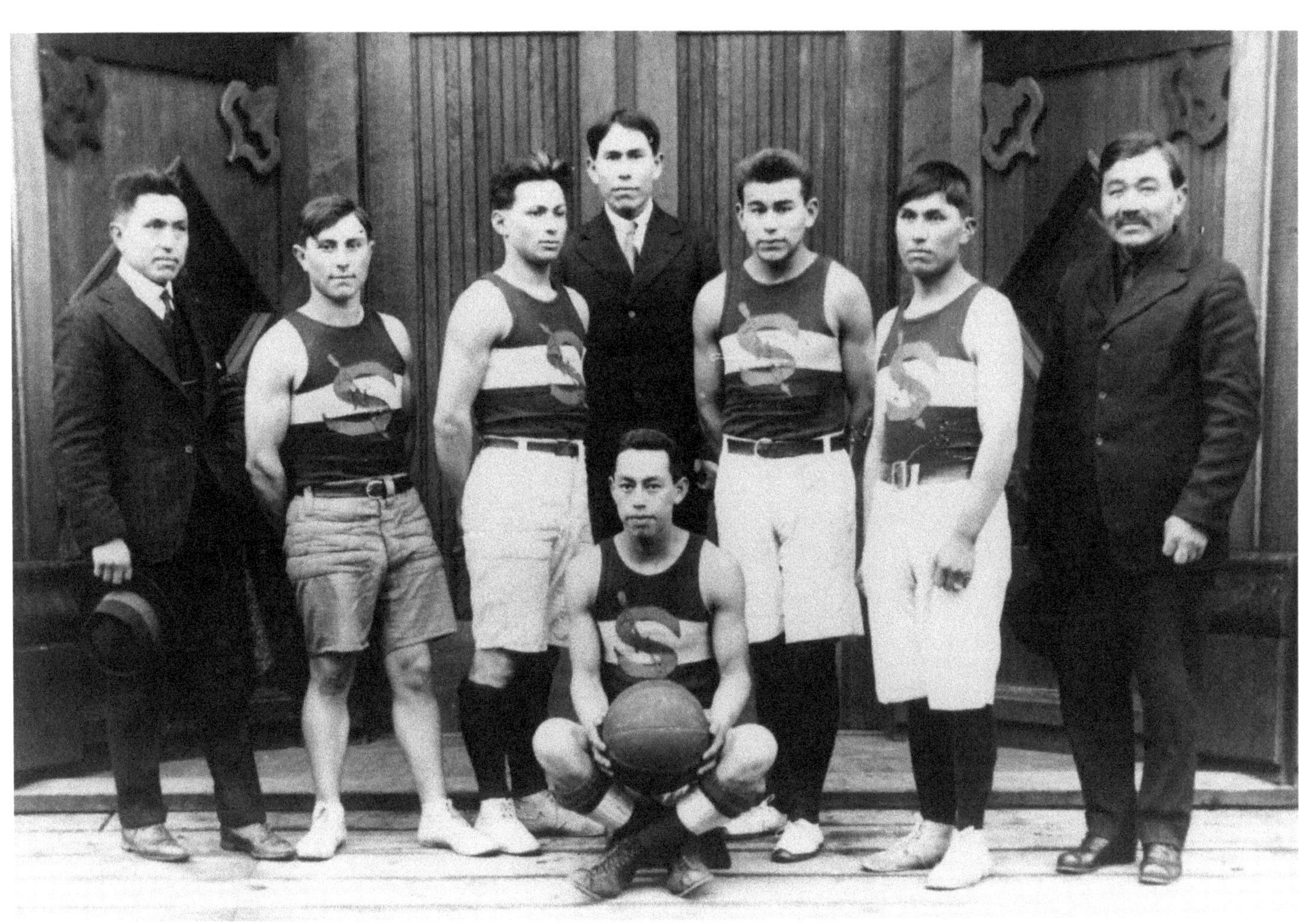

The first basketball team of the Alaska Native Brotherhood played for Sitka in 1917.

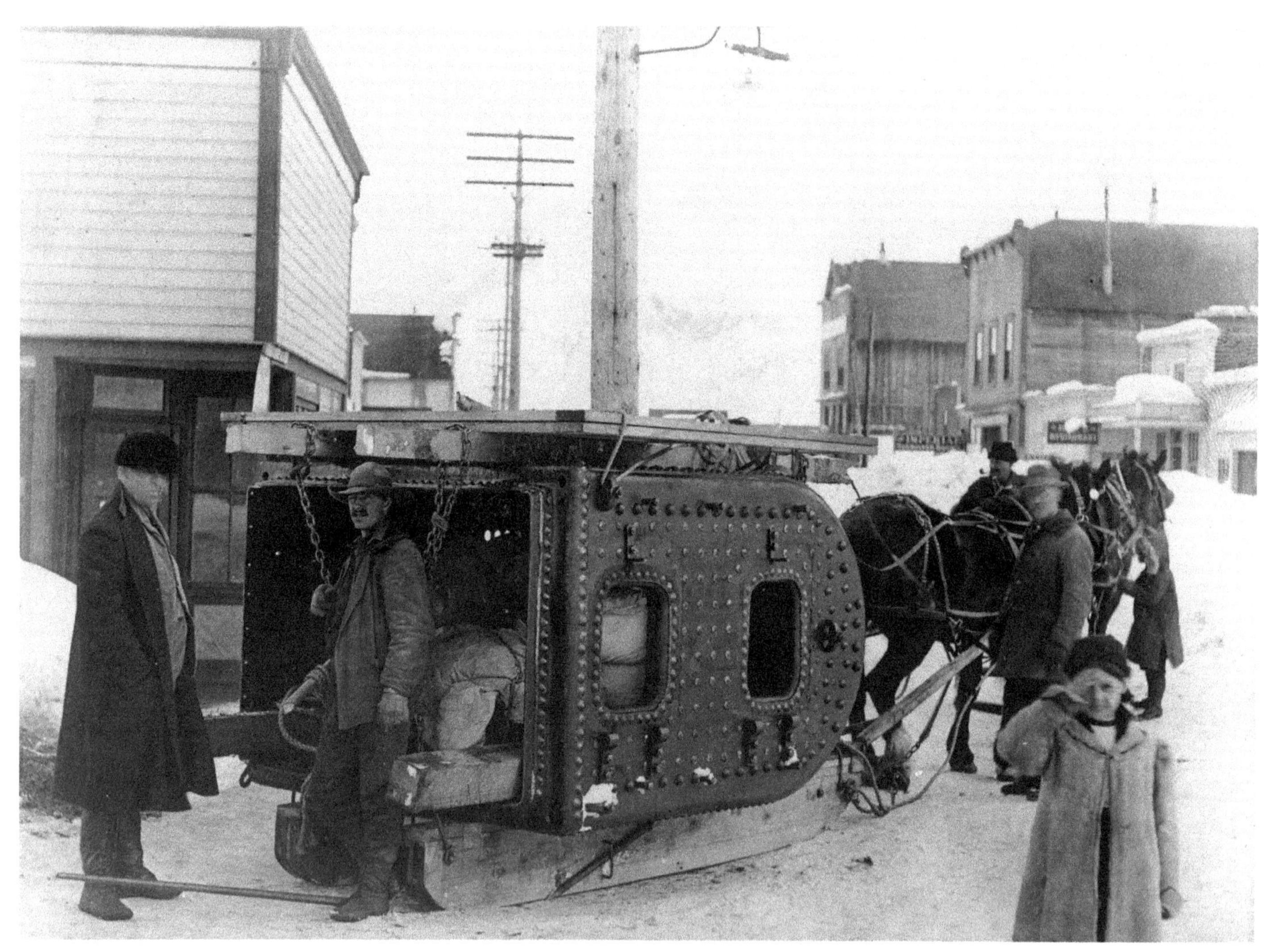

A freighter prepares to leave Valdez with a 5,700-pound firebox for the steamer *Chitina,* a riverboat that operated on the Copper River.

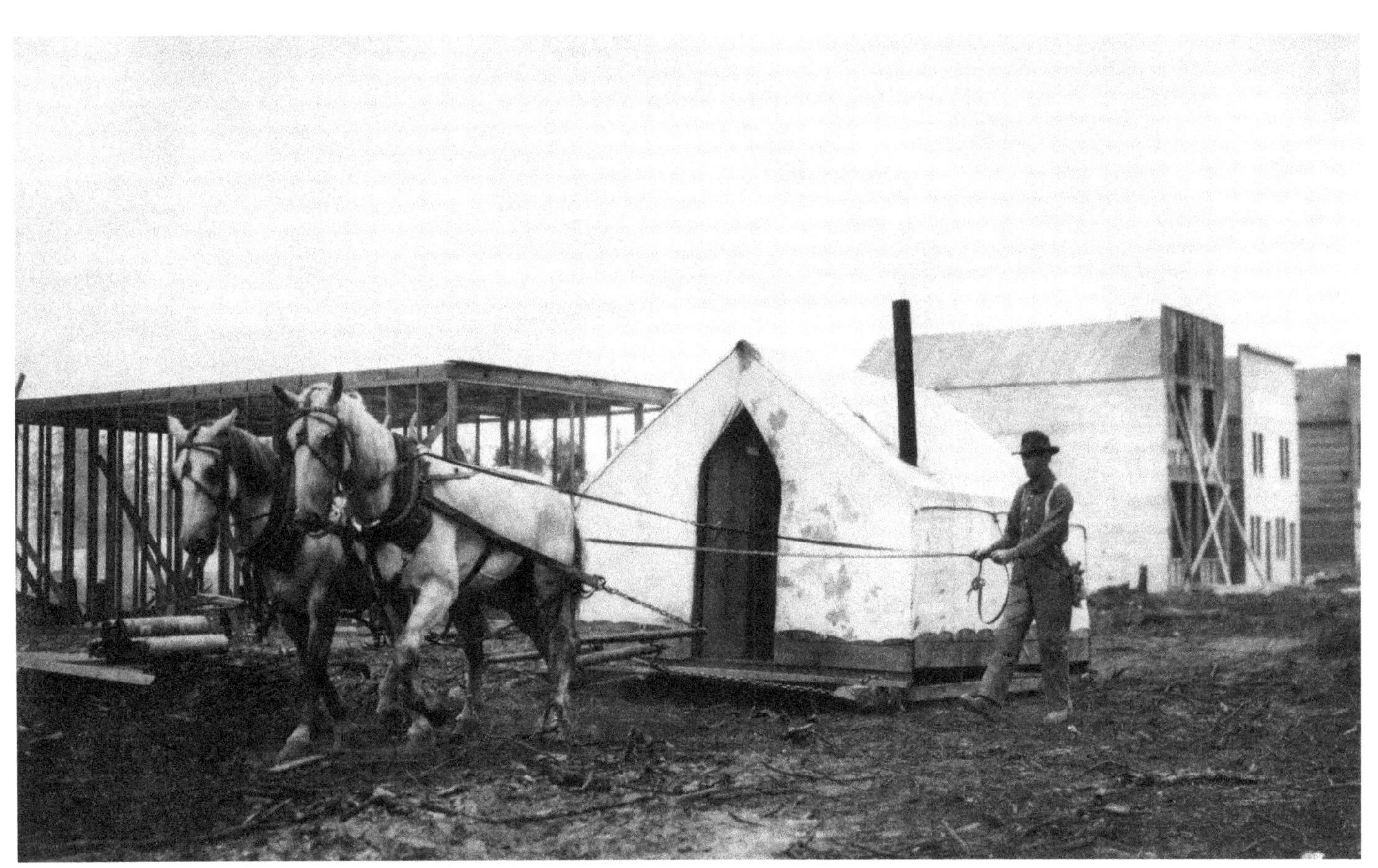

Moving a house in early day Anchorage required, in this case, two horsepower.

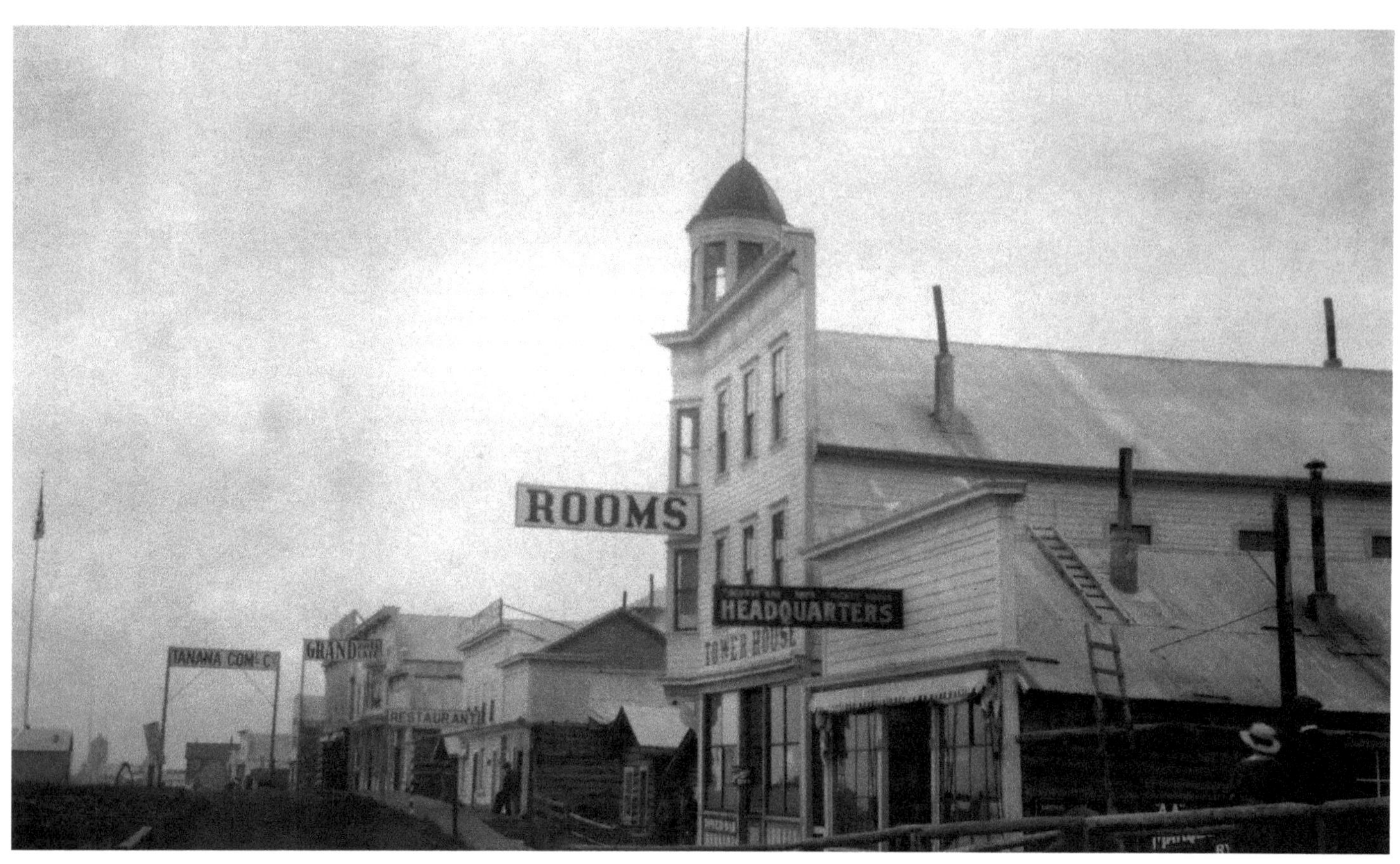

Travelers to Tanana, a village on the Yukon River across from the mouth of the Tanana River, often stayed at the Tower House Hotel on the village's main street.

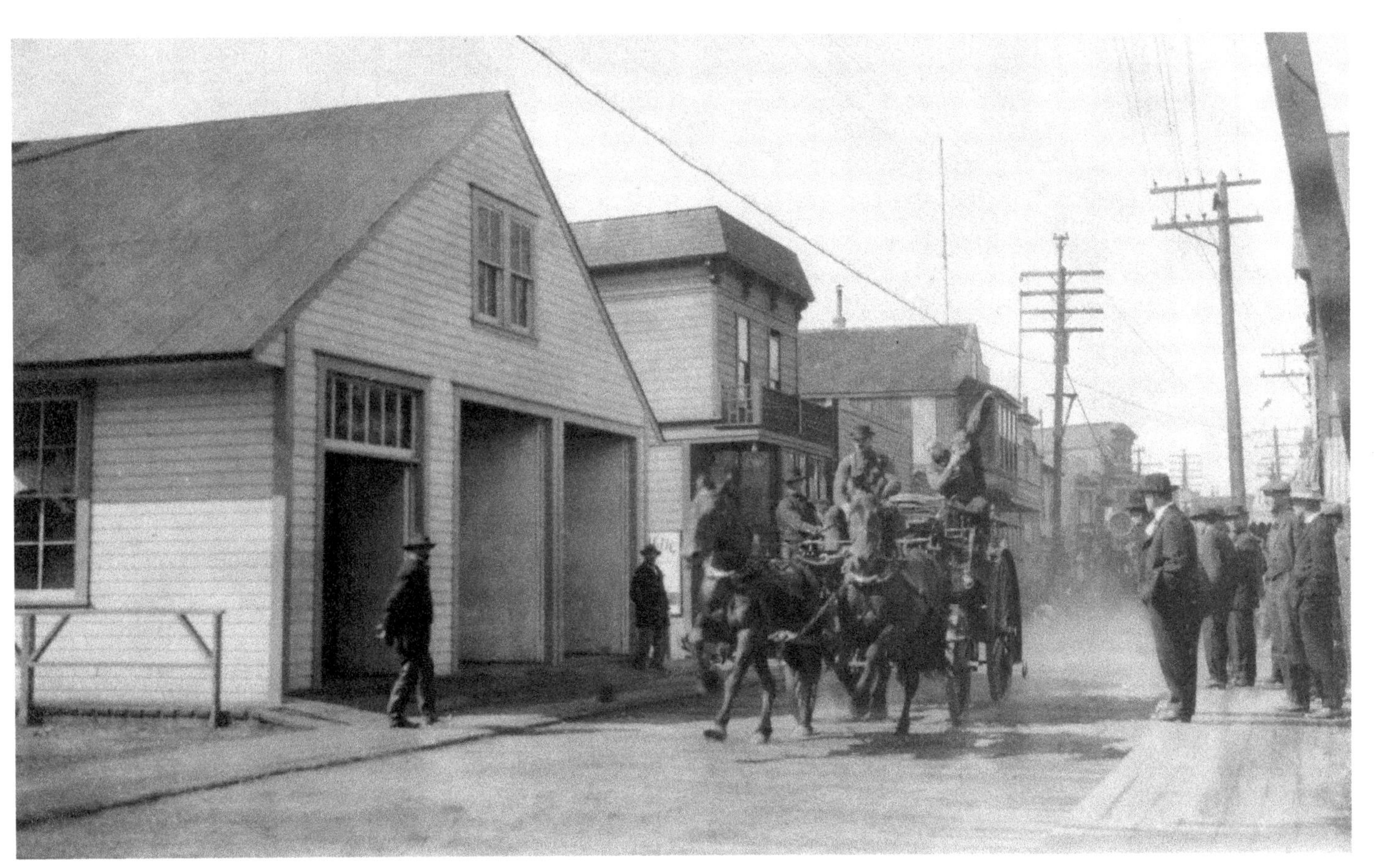

A Nome fire crew tests its response time in a fire drill in the early 1900s.

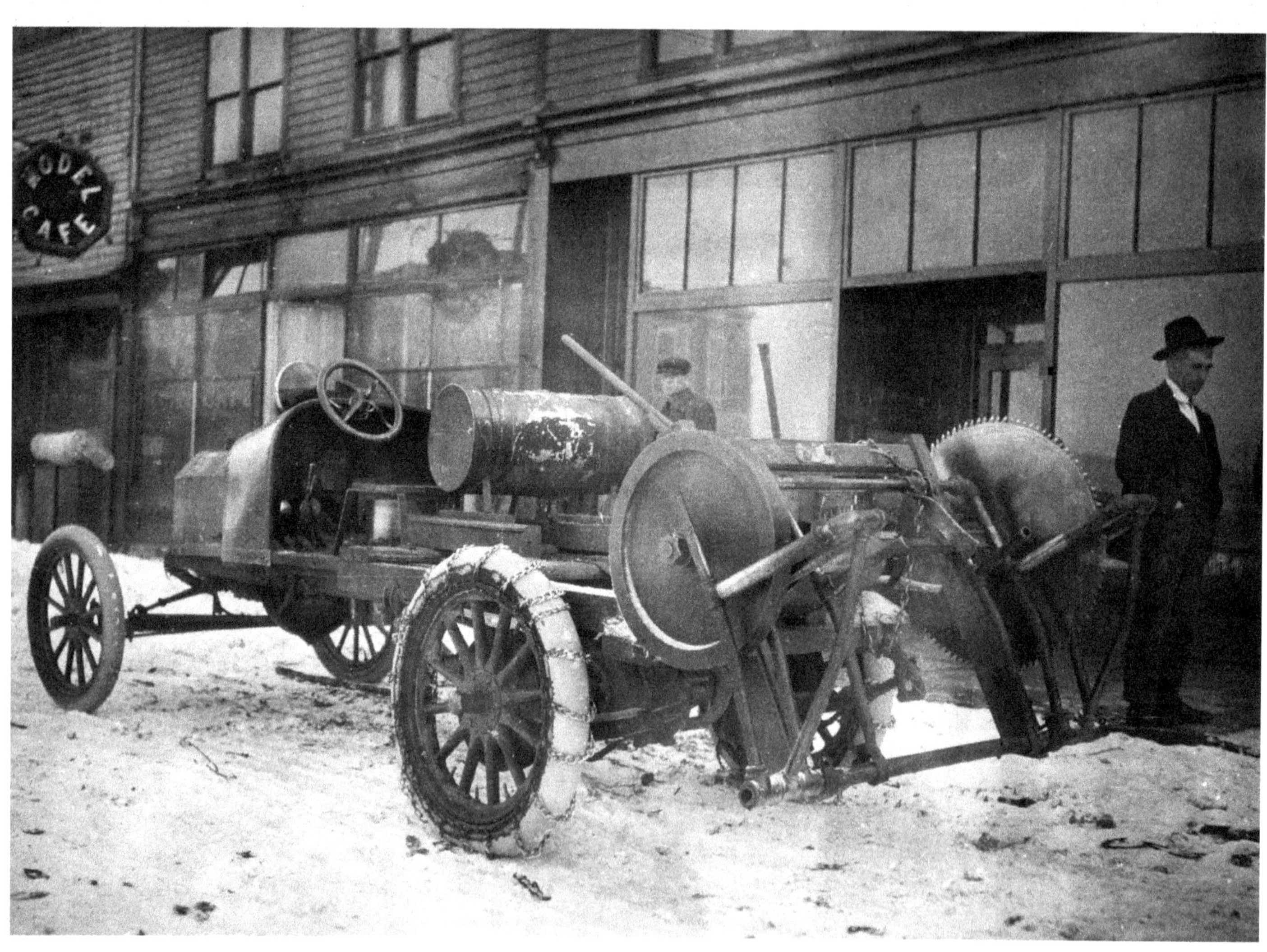

The Model T Ford, as adaptable as any vehicle ever made, provided the power for a heavy-duty saw used to cut firewood and lumber in Fairbanks about 1915.

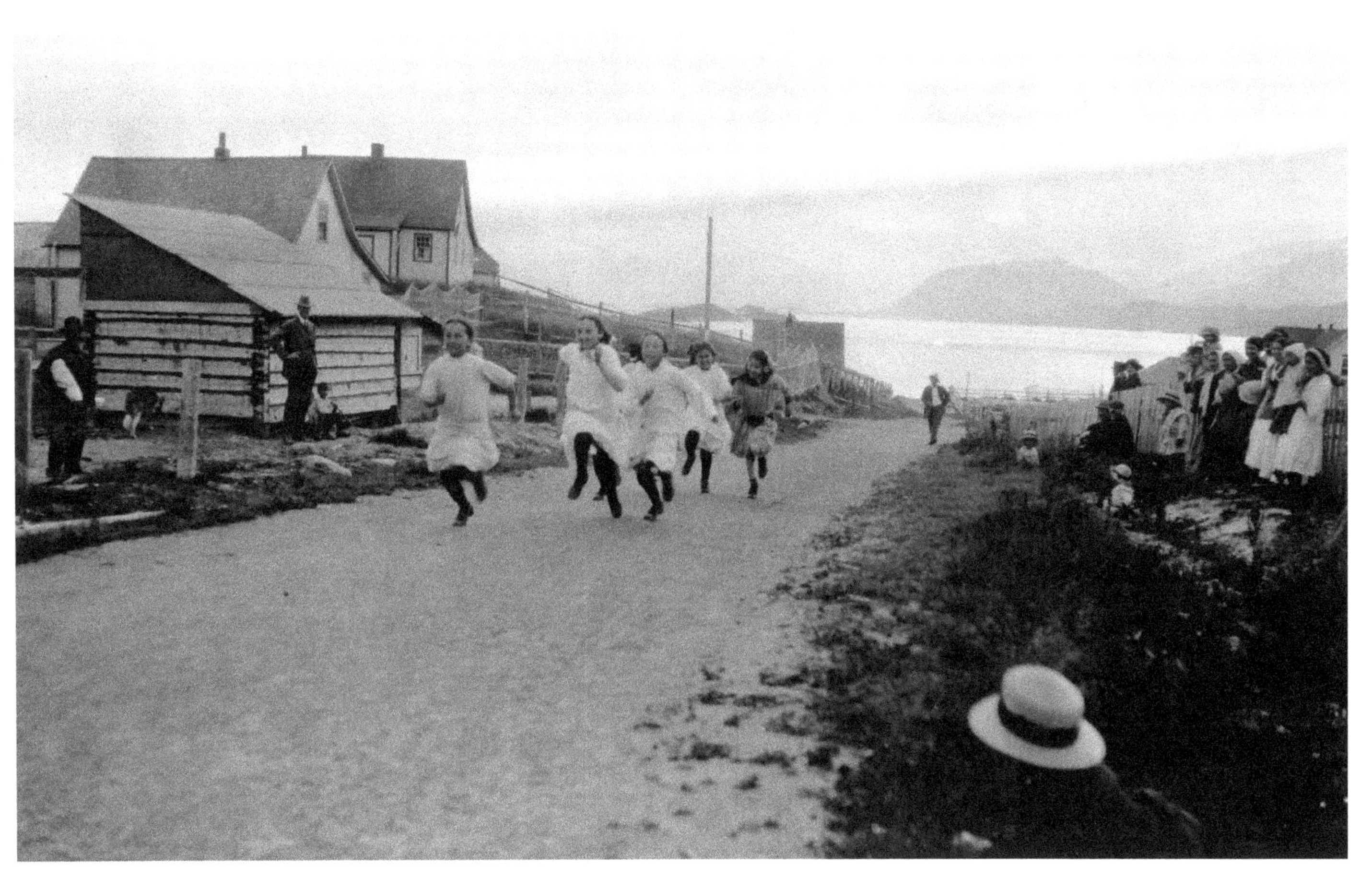

School girls head for the finish line in a Fourth of July race in Kodiak in 1915.

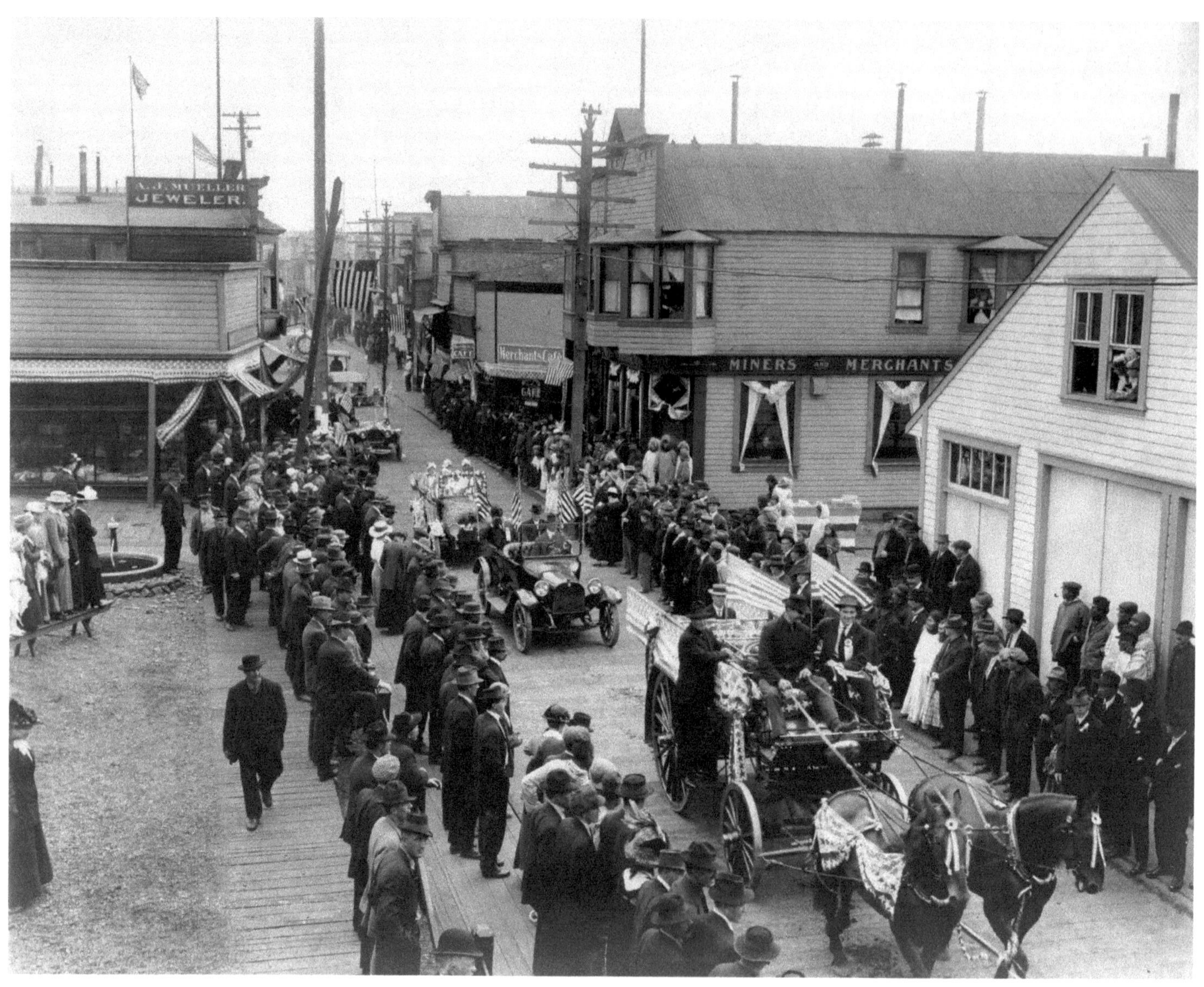

Automobiles had made their way to the western edge of the continent in sufficient numbers by 1915 to be a regular part of the Fourth of July celebration in Nome, but horses were not gone from the scene.

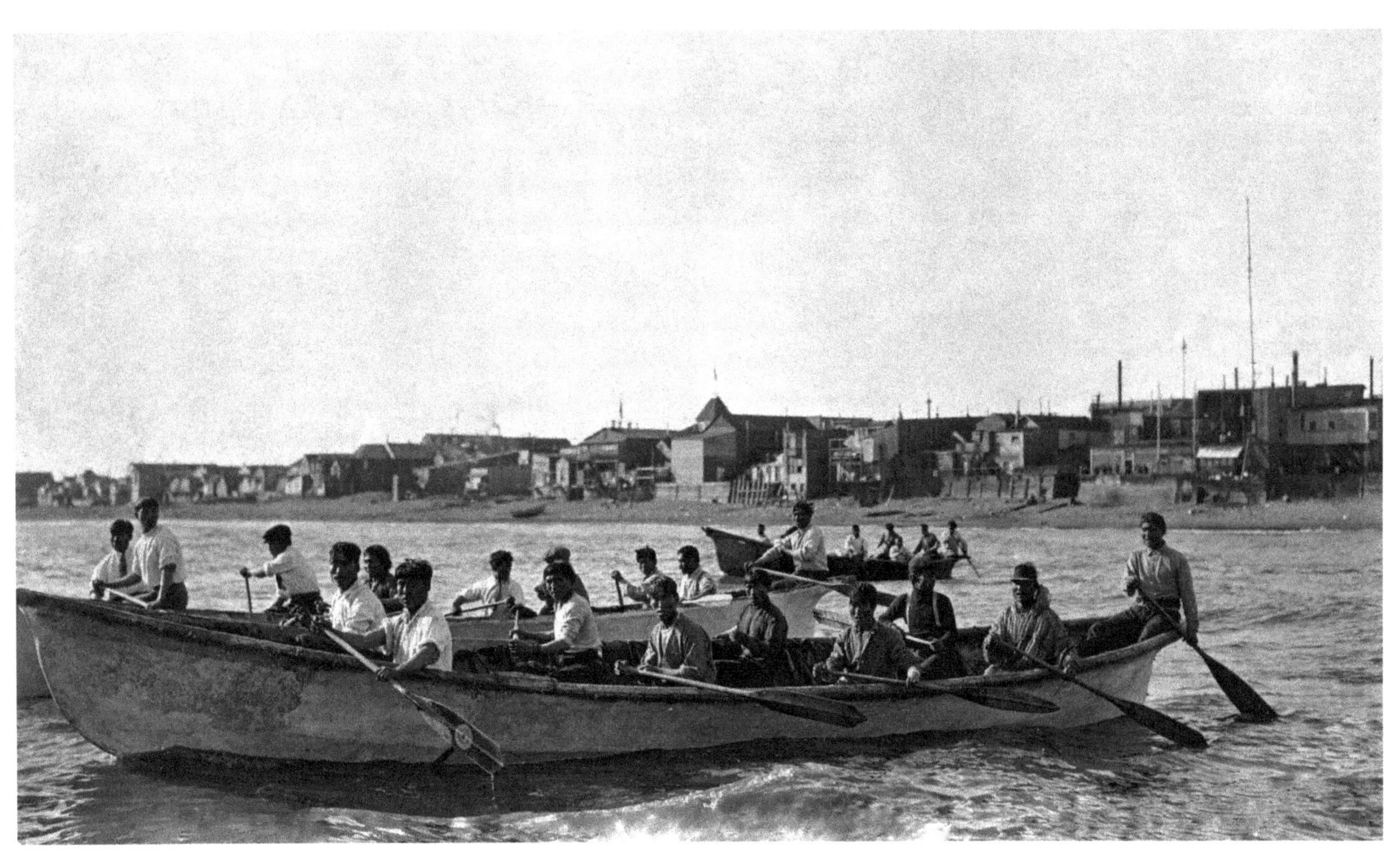

The large, skin-covered boats known as umiaks, utilized for hunting whales and other animals, were also used in races off the Nome coast on July 4, 1915.

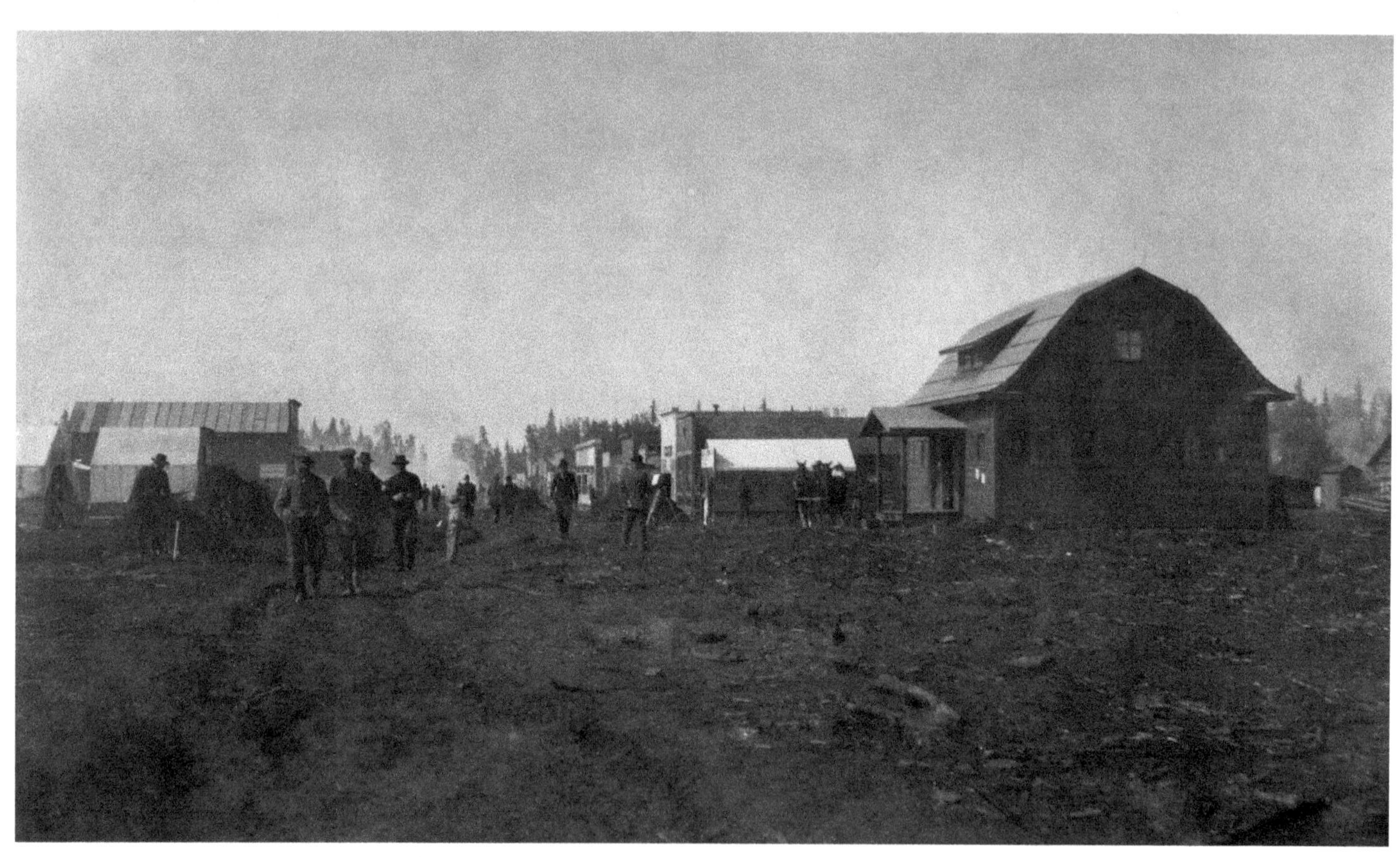

By the summer of 1915, Fourth Street in Anchorage already had a name, though there were still stumps sticking out of the ground on the routes designated as streets, which were laid out in a logical grid pattern befitting government engineers.

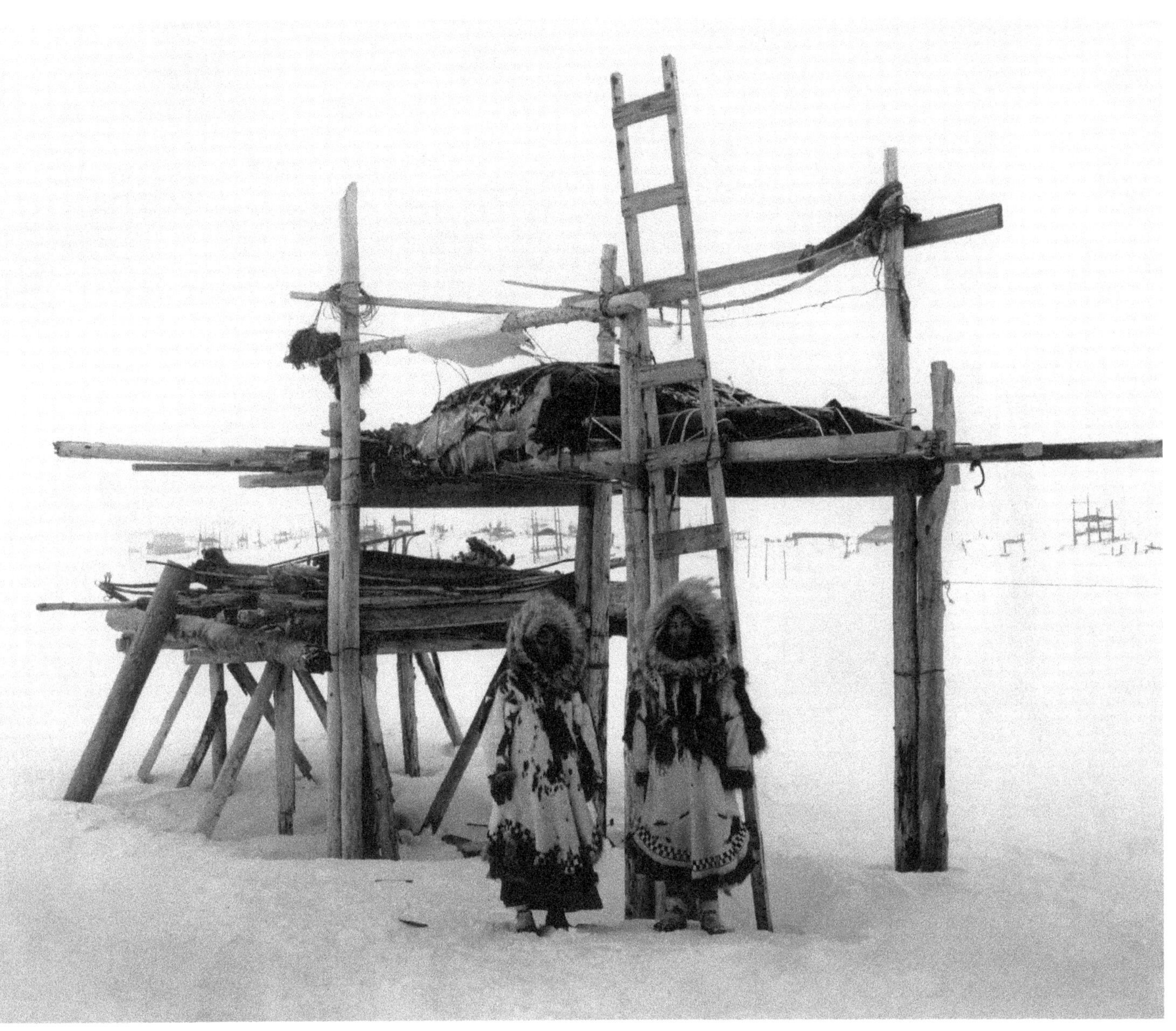

Whale meat and other staples of the Eskimo diet are stored in an elevated cache at Cape Prince of Wales. These elevated platforms were set up to keep polar bears and other animals away from supplies.

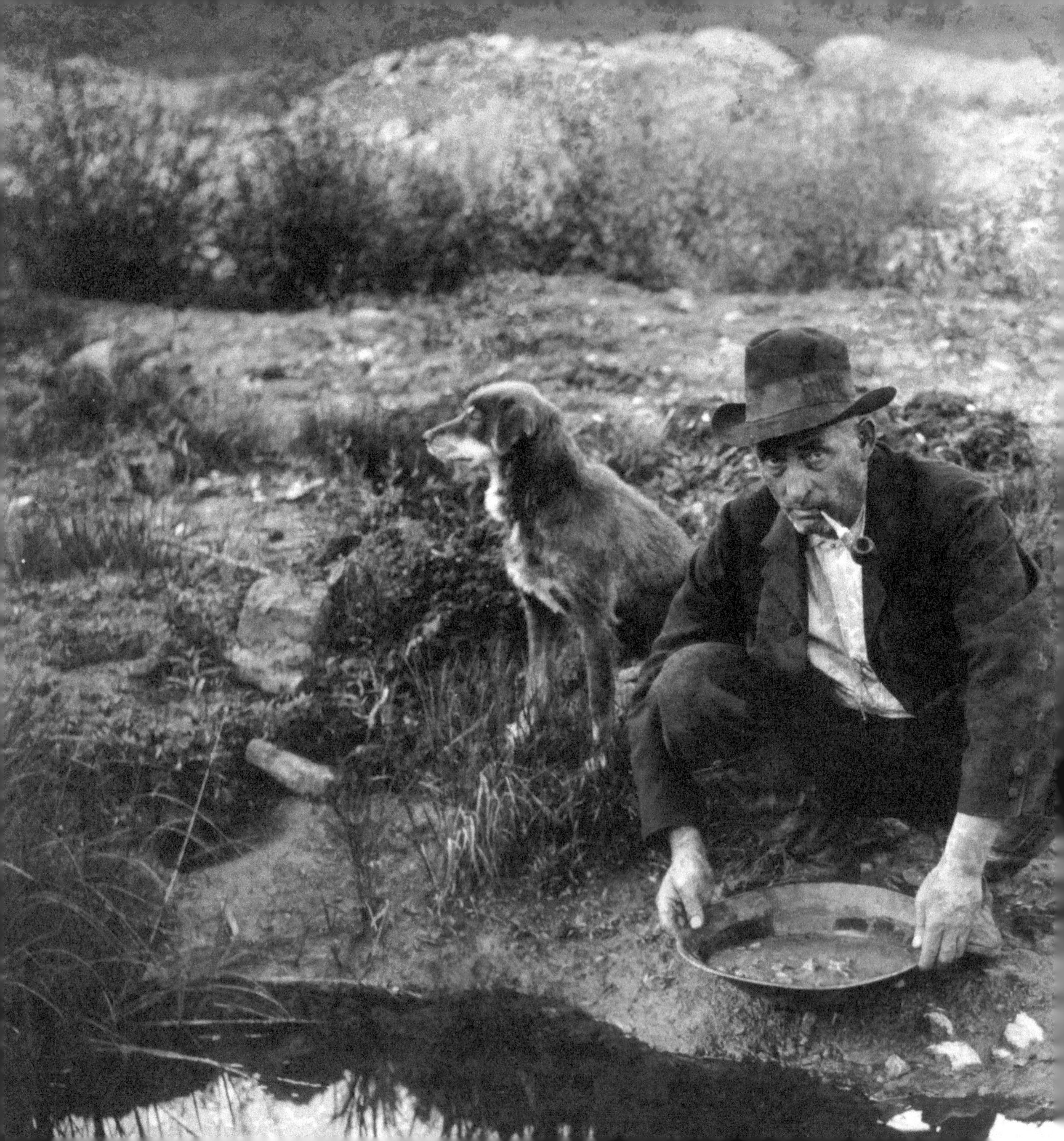

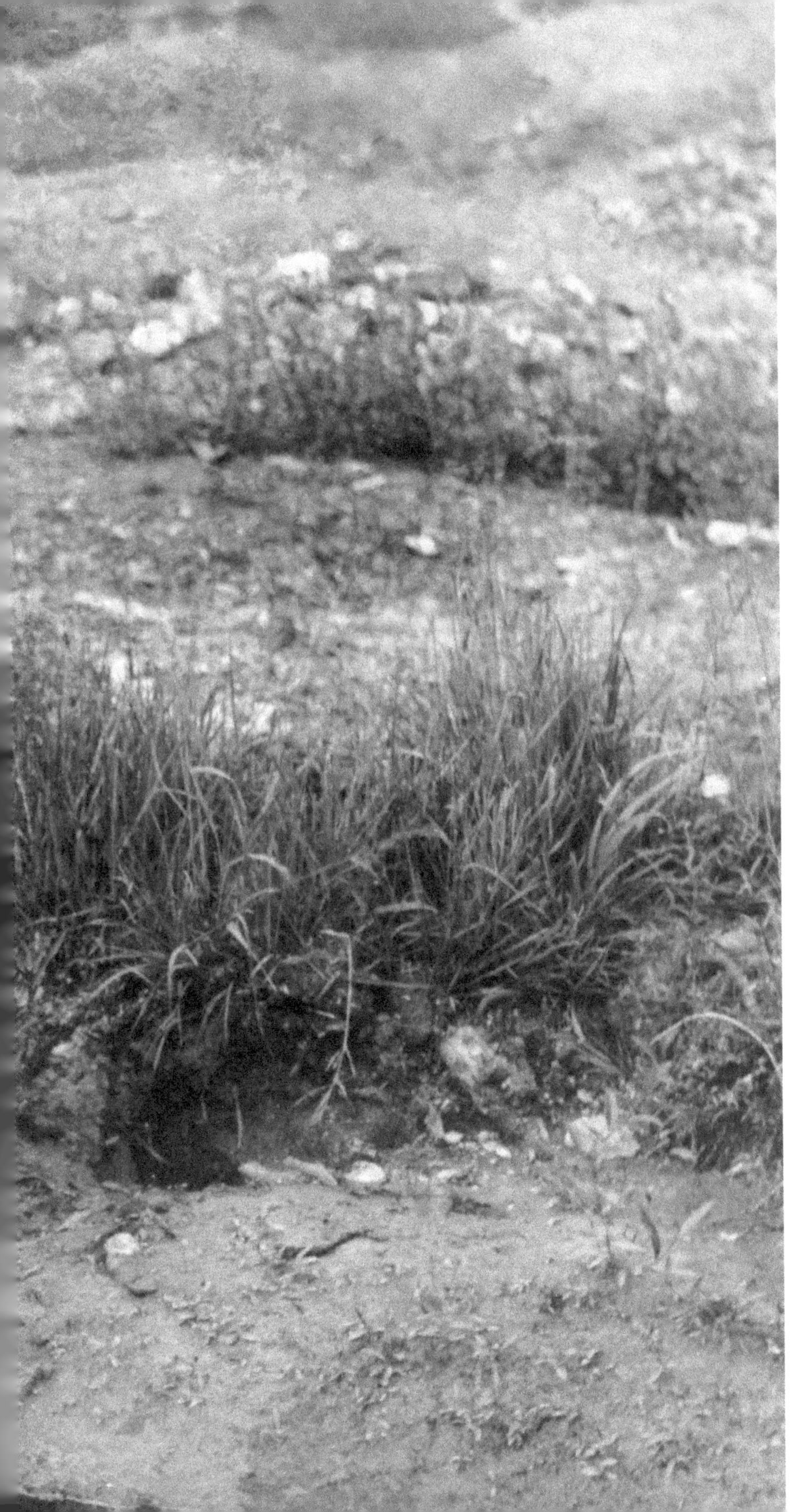

An Alaska miner in 1916 looks for gold-bearing gravel from a creek.

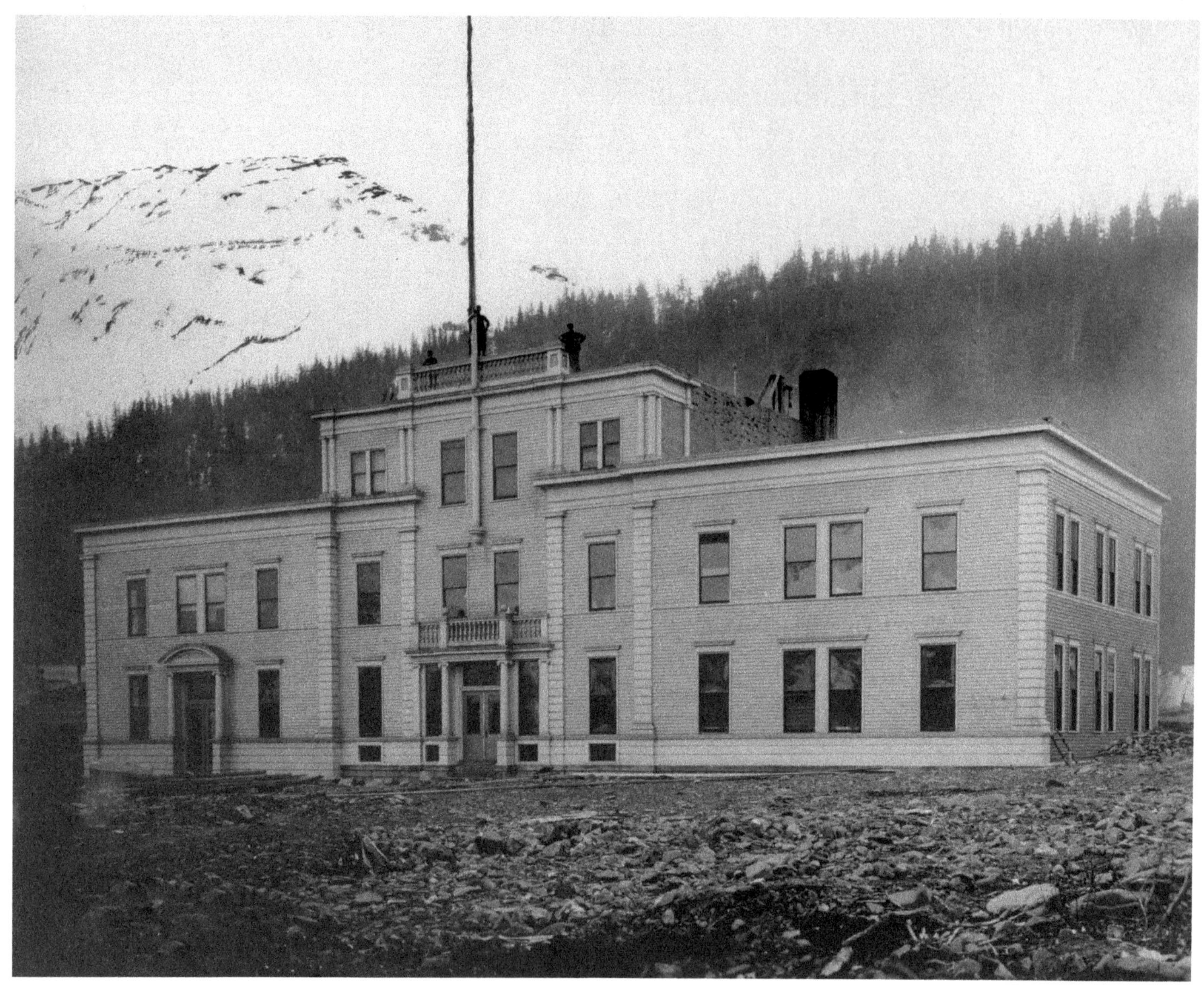

The newly built offices of the Alaska Railroad in Seward in 1916, the southern terminus of the rail line.

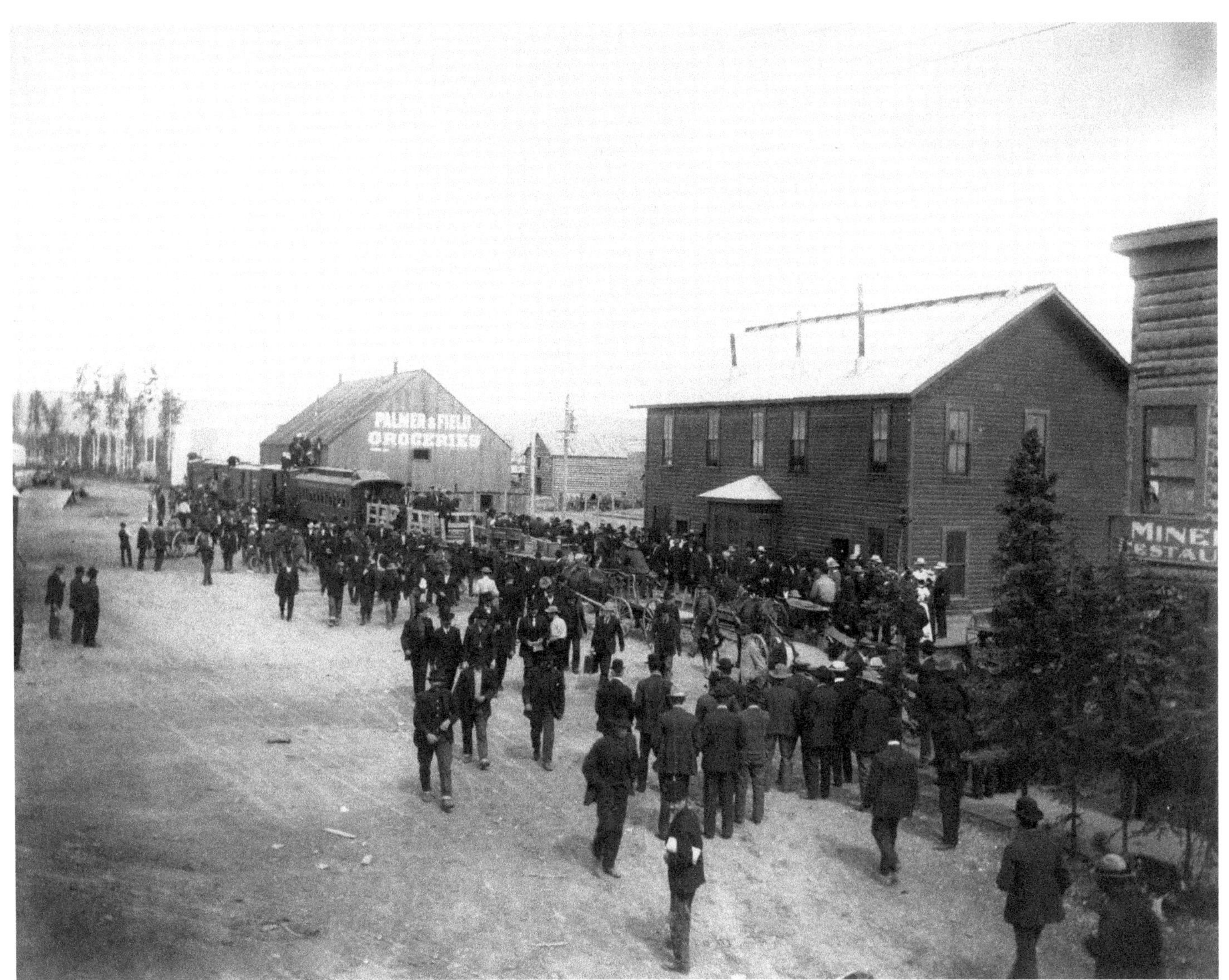

Visitors arrive in Fairbanks on the Tanana Valley Railroad for the Fourth of July celebration in 1916.

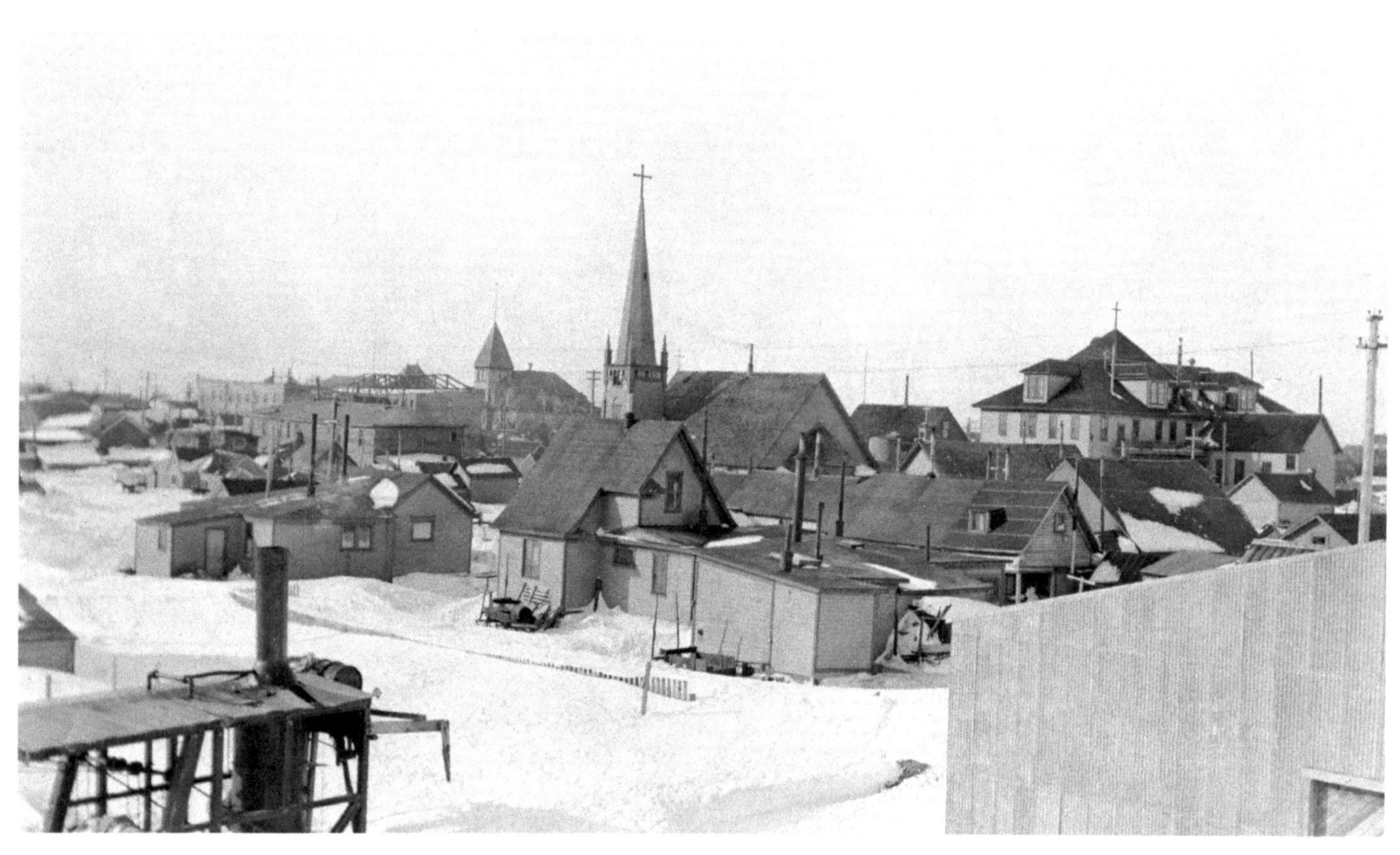

Winter in Alaska brought with it cold, snow, and a slower pace of life in Nome, pictured in 1916.

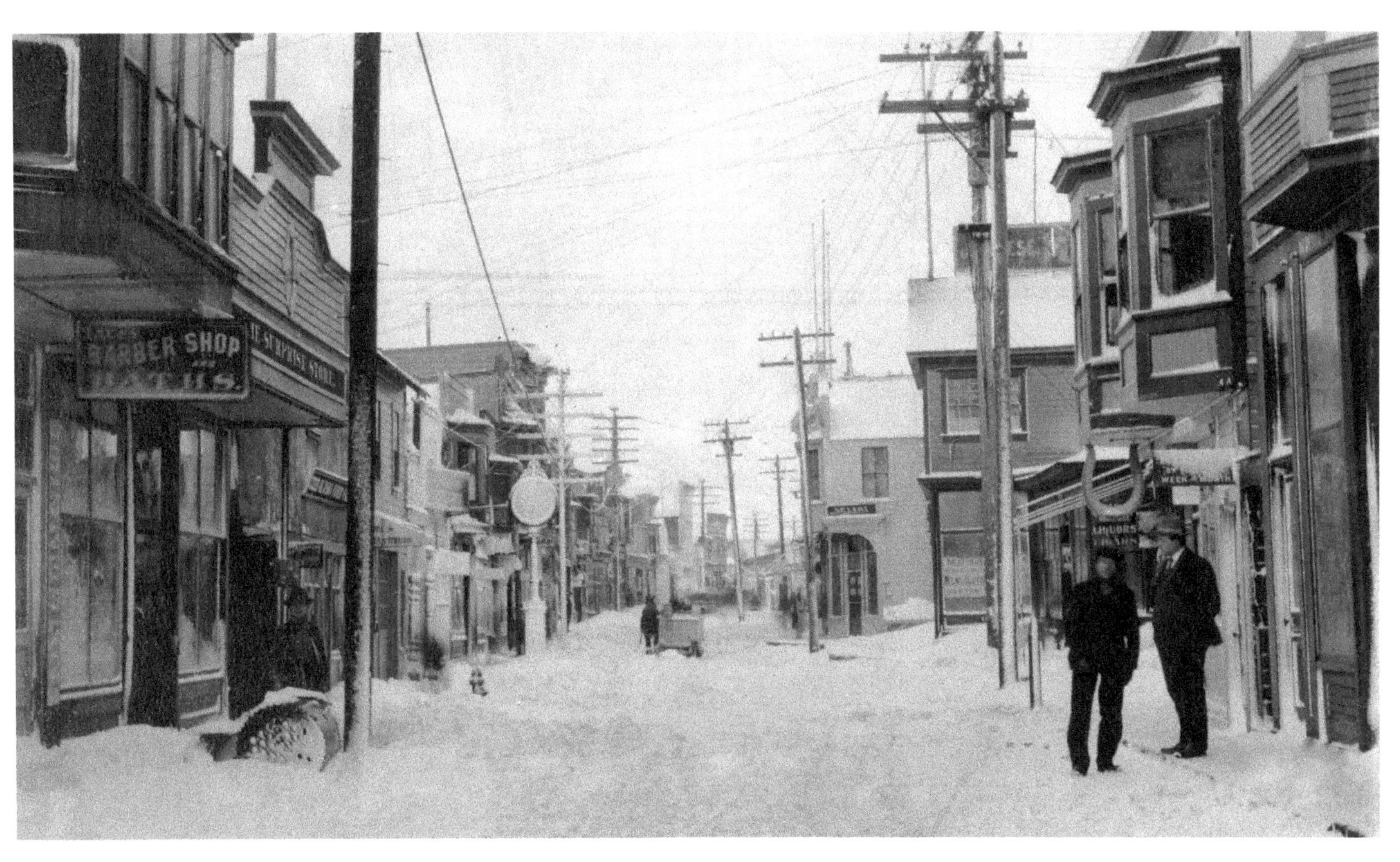

A quiet winter day on Front Street in Nome.

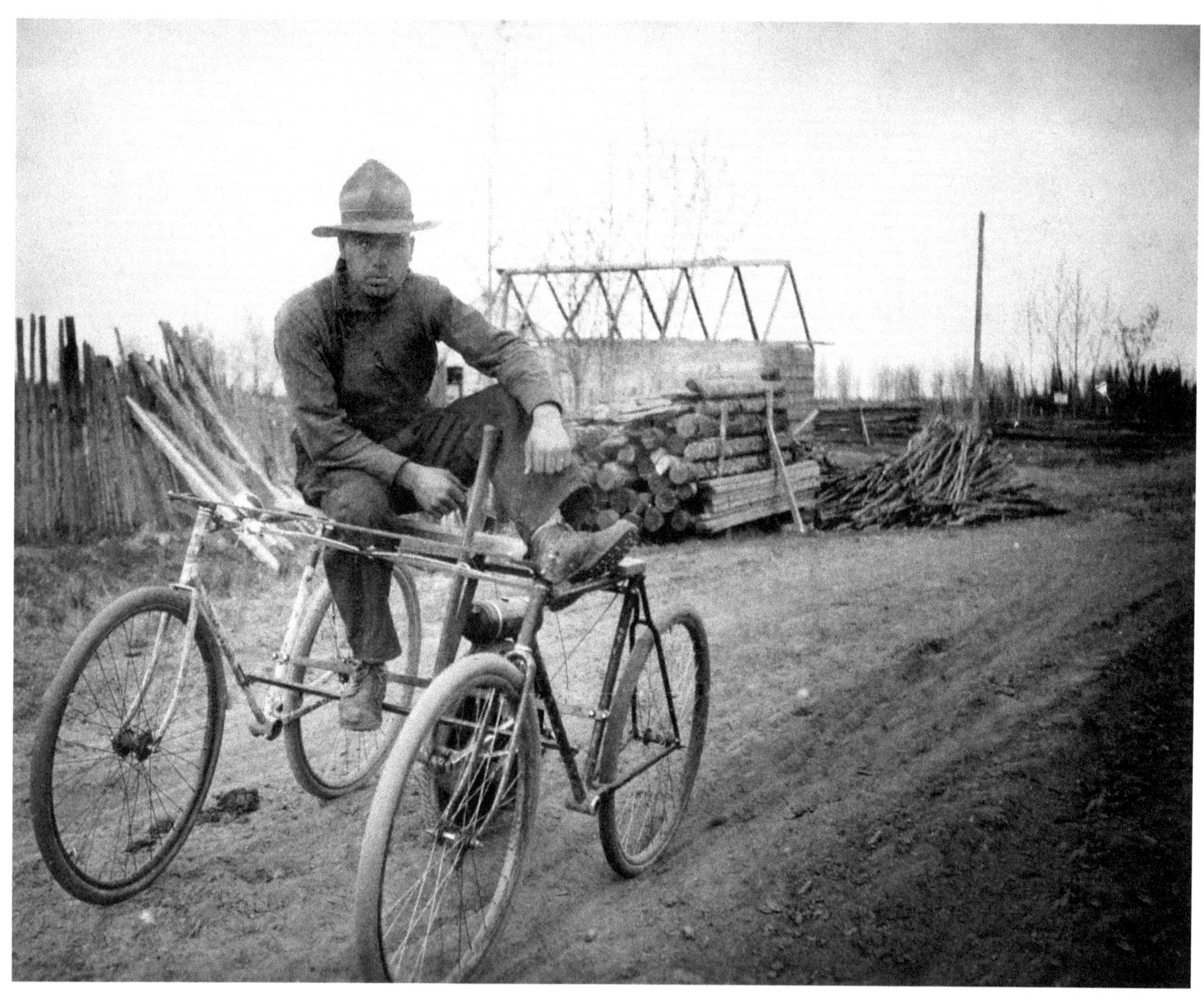

Ingenuity was a prized trait among Alaskans, whether that meant building a better cabin or stringing two bikes together, adding a motor of some kind, and calling it a 110-pound auto.

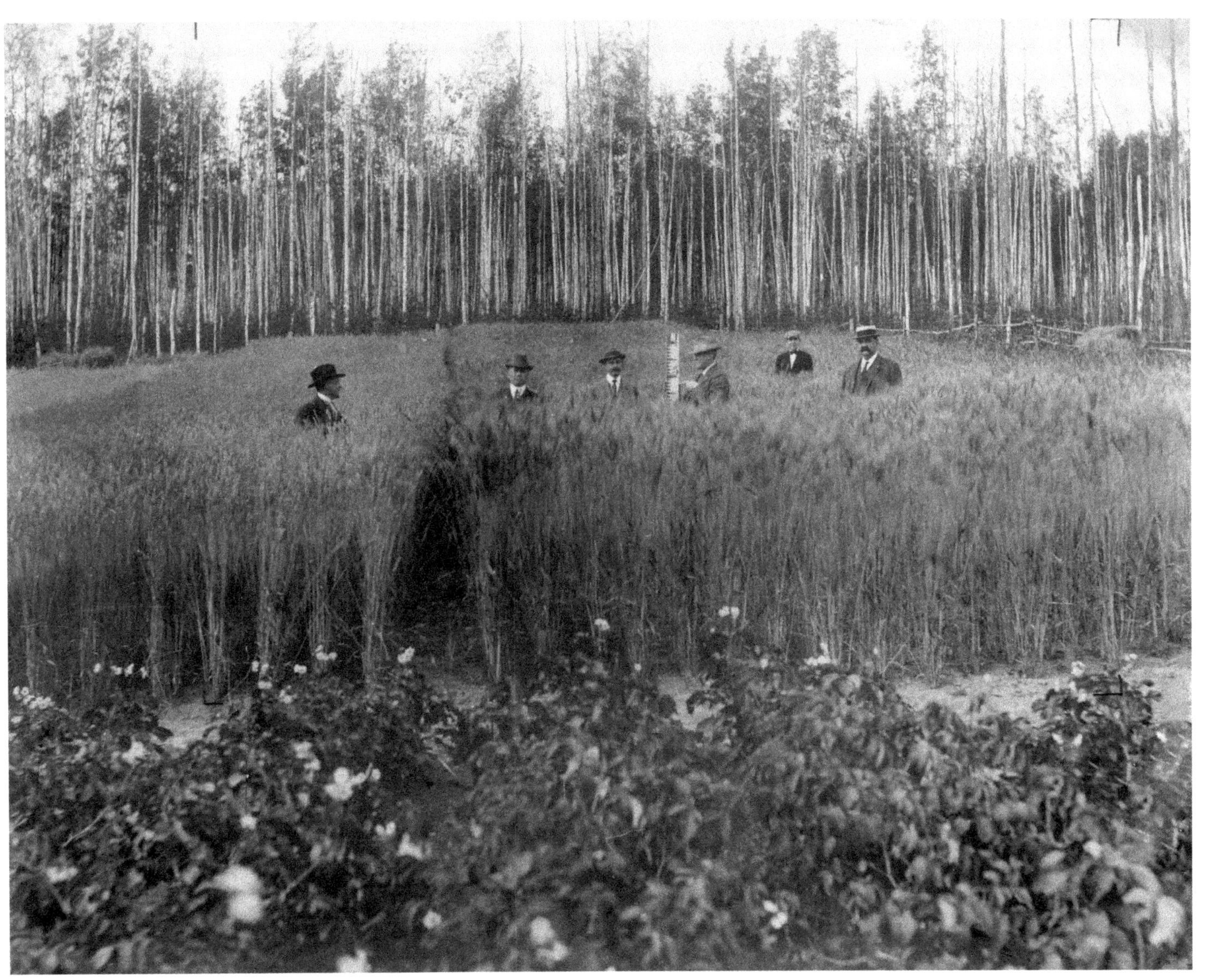

A grain field outside of Fairbanks, with plants pushing the five-foot mark, shows the results of good growing conditions aided by round-the-clock summer daylight.

The sun brightens a snow-covered trail outside of Seward in 1916.

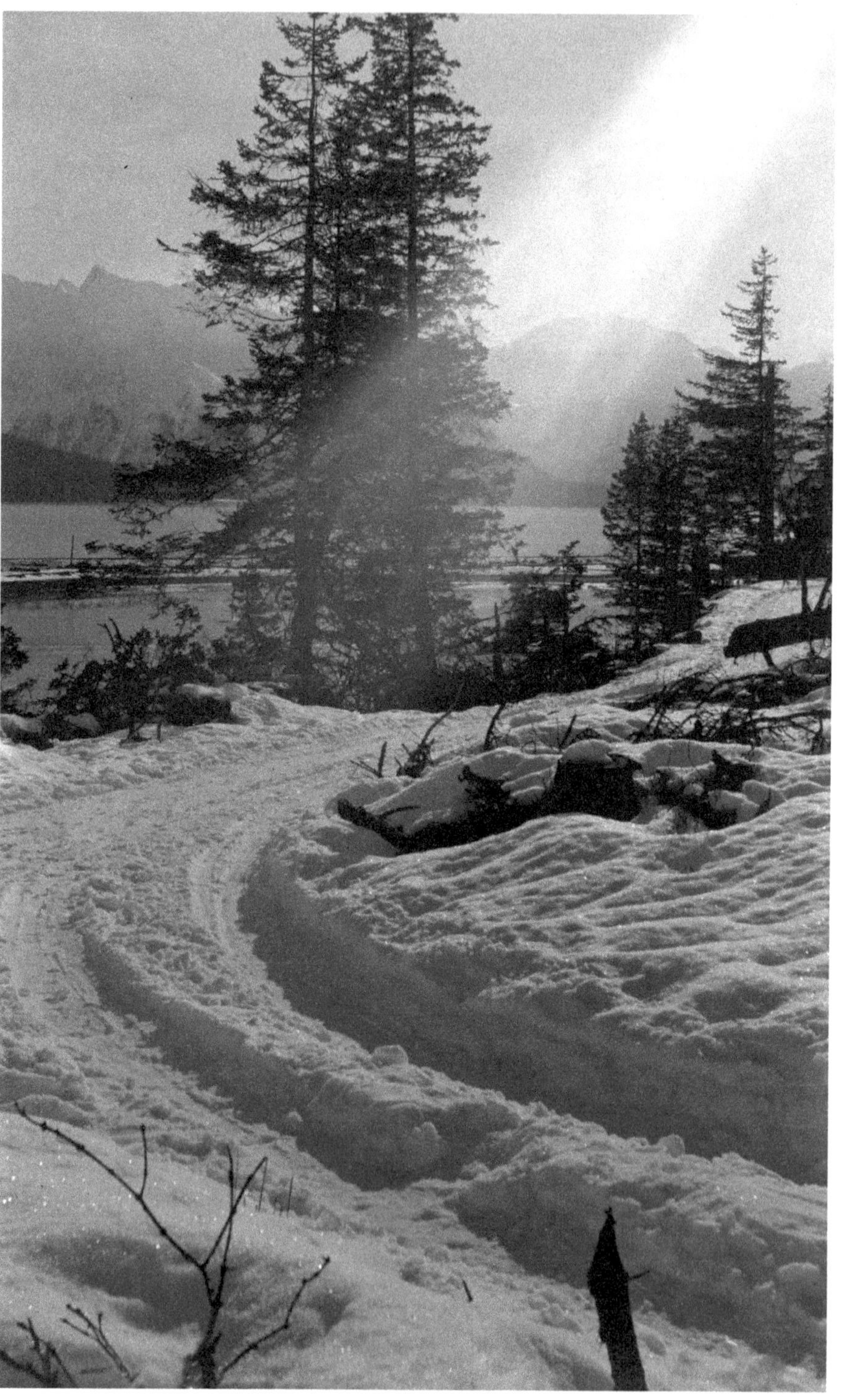

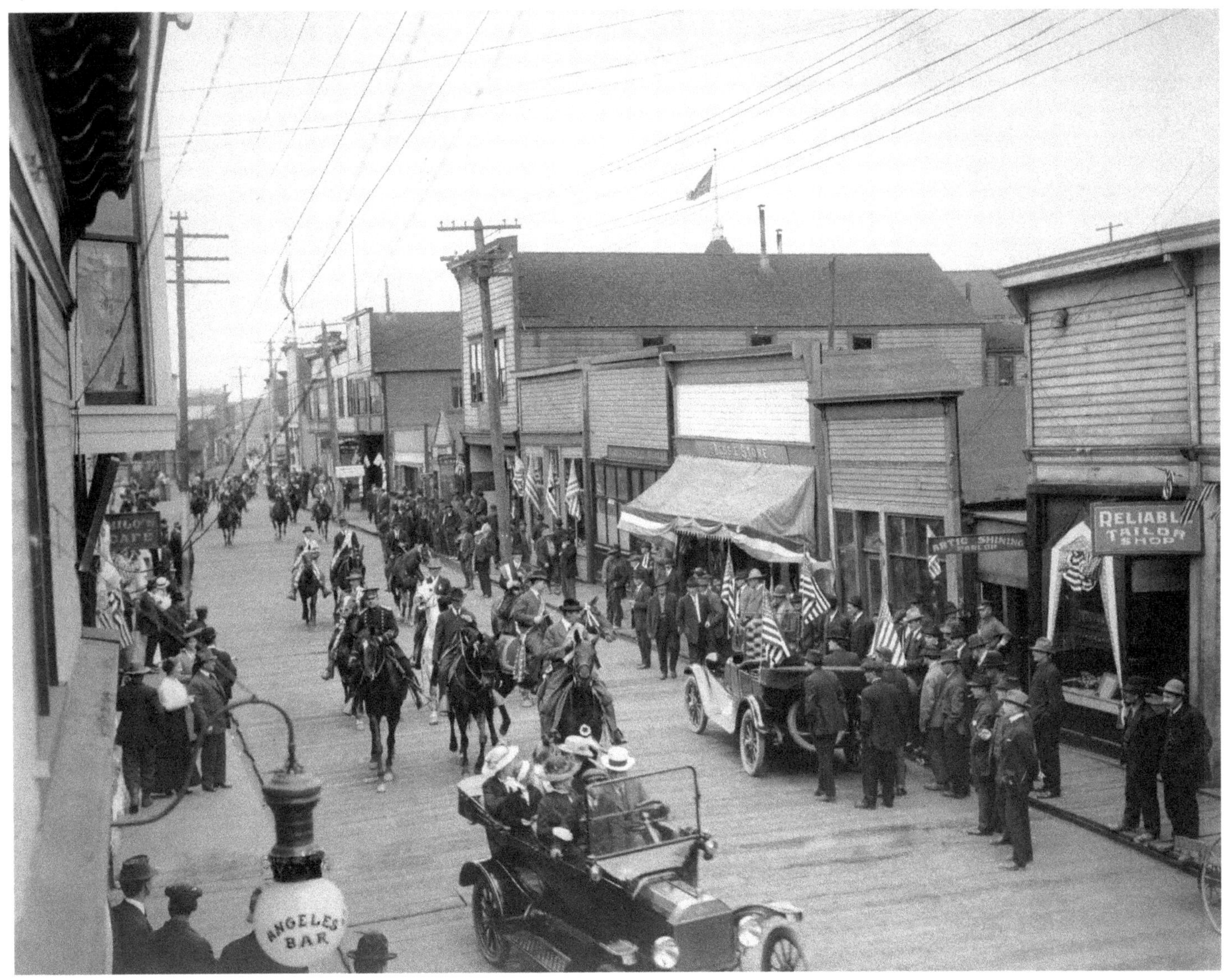

Nome citizens celebrate the Fourth of July along Front Street in 1916.

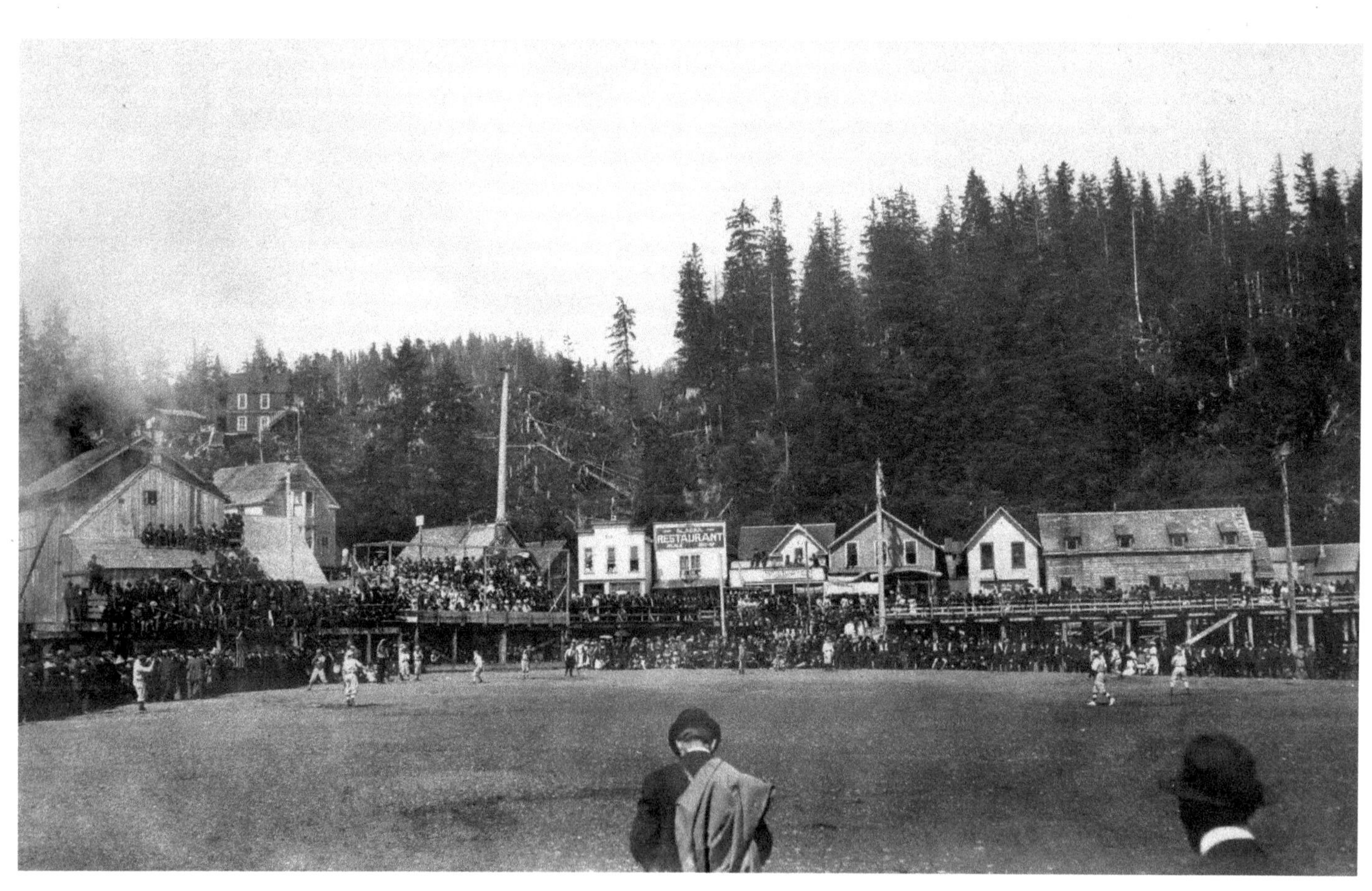

The Ketchikan baseball team battles Prince Rupert in 1916, edging the Canadians 1–0 in twelve innings.

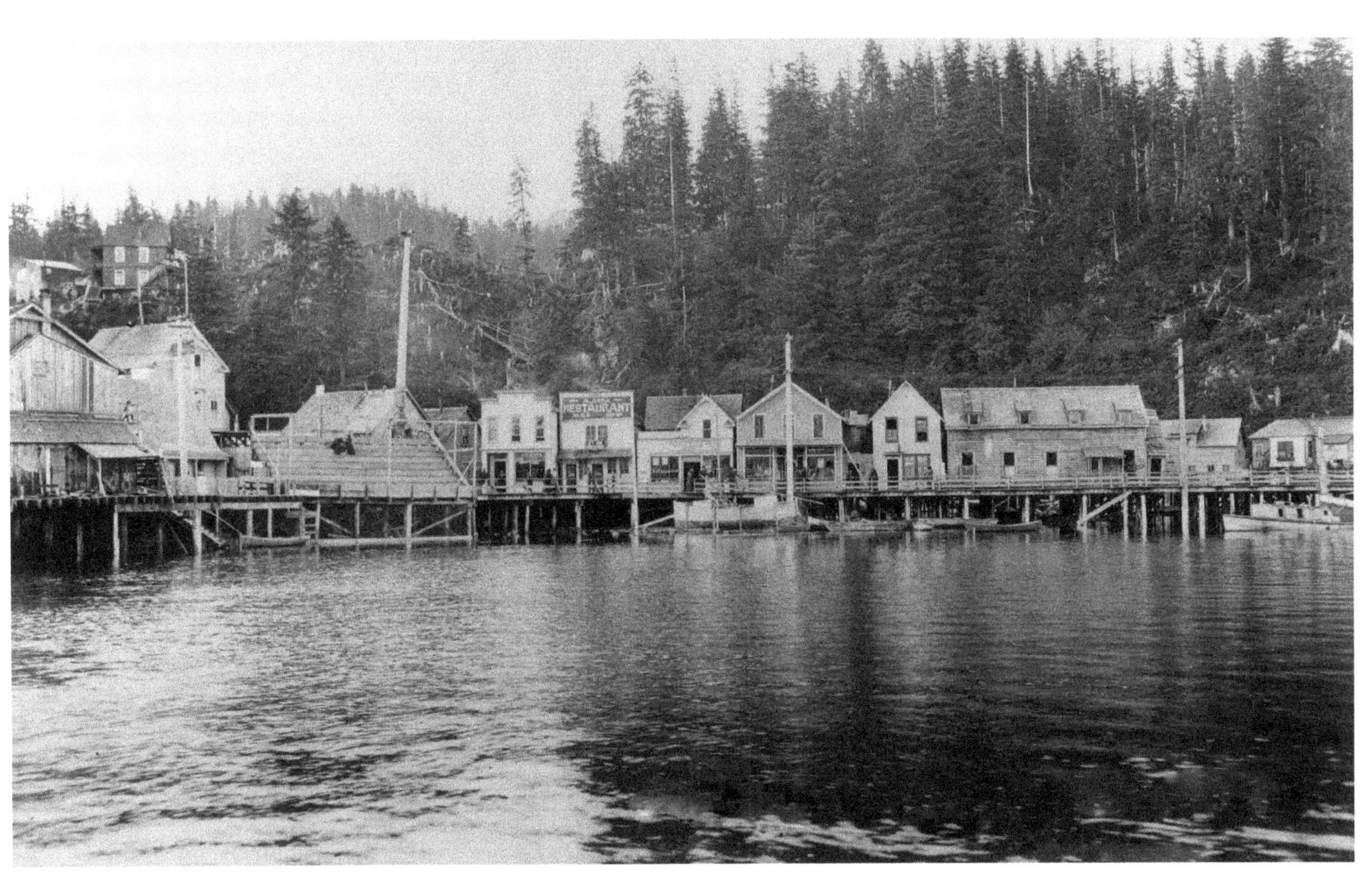

The tide rolls in and the Ketchikan baseball field is under water in the summer of 1916.

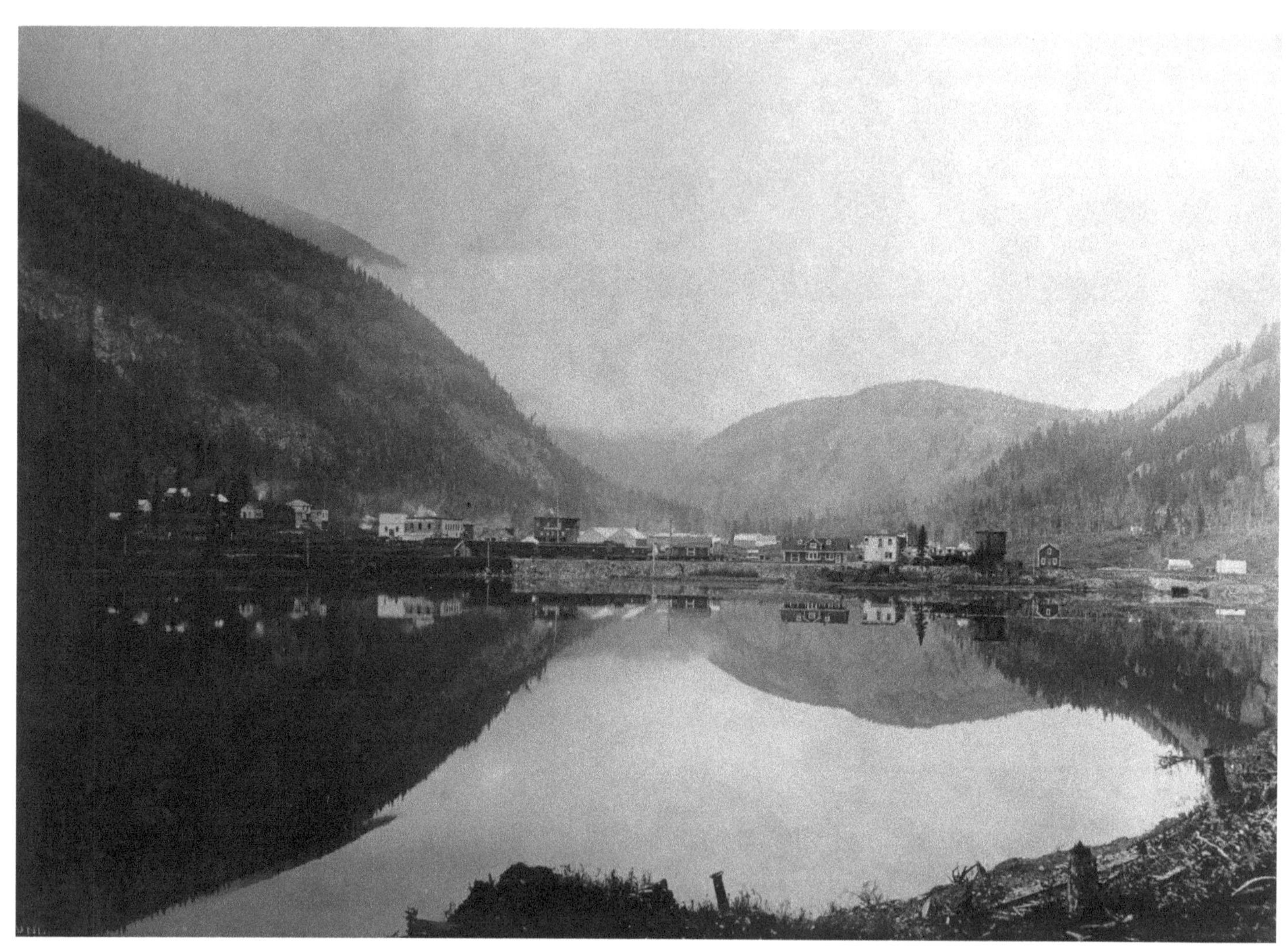

Chitina, a town on the Copper River, developed along the route of the river and the Northwestern Railway.

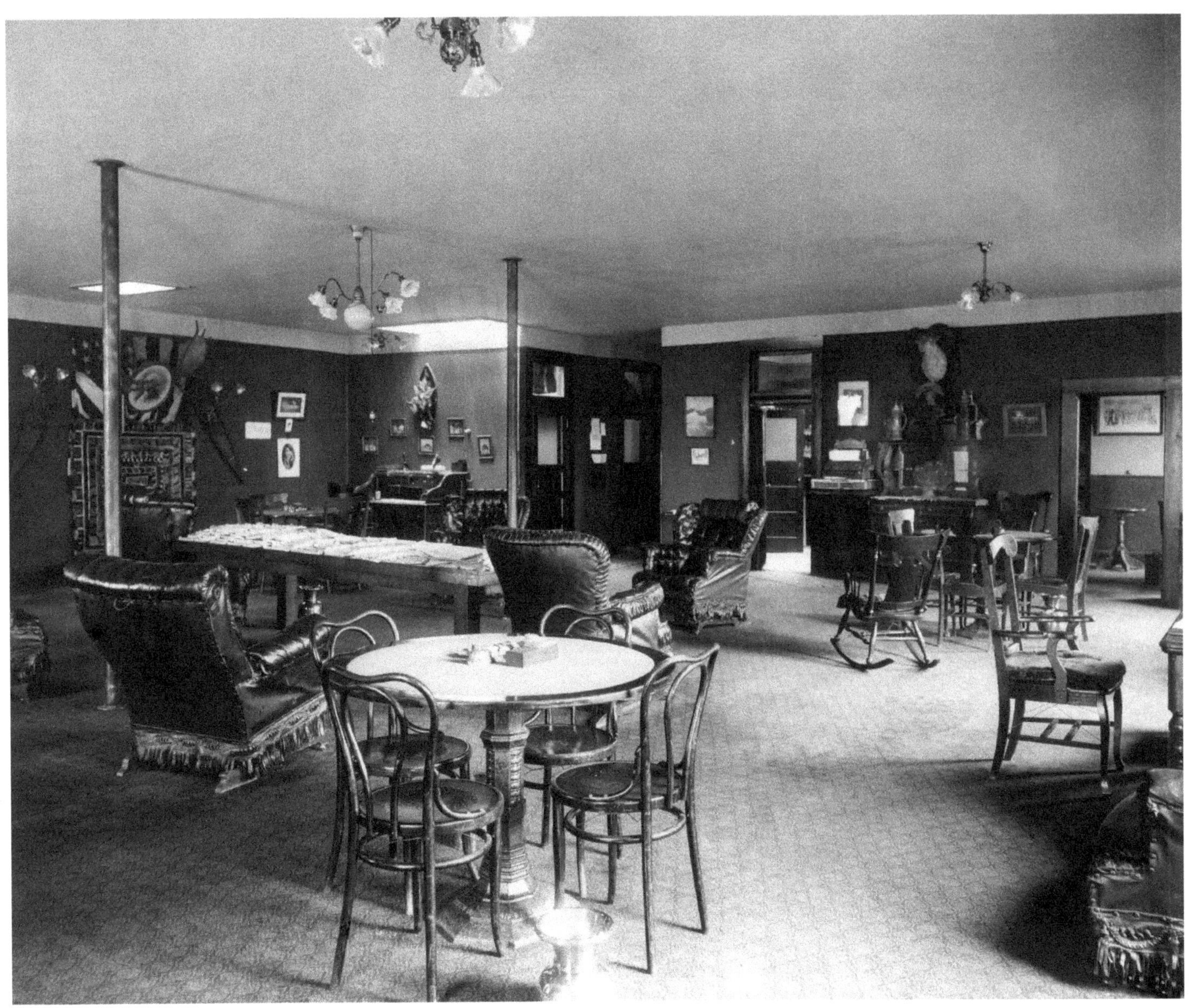

The Tanana Club in downtown Fairbanks provided a place for men to relax, play cards, have a drink, smoke cigars, and socialize in the early years of the gold-rush town.

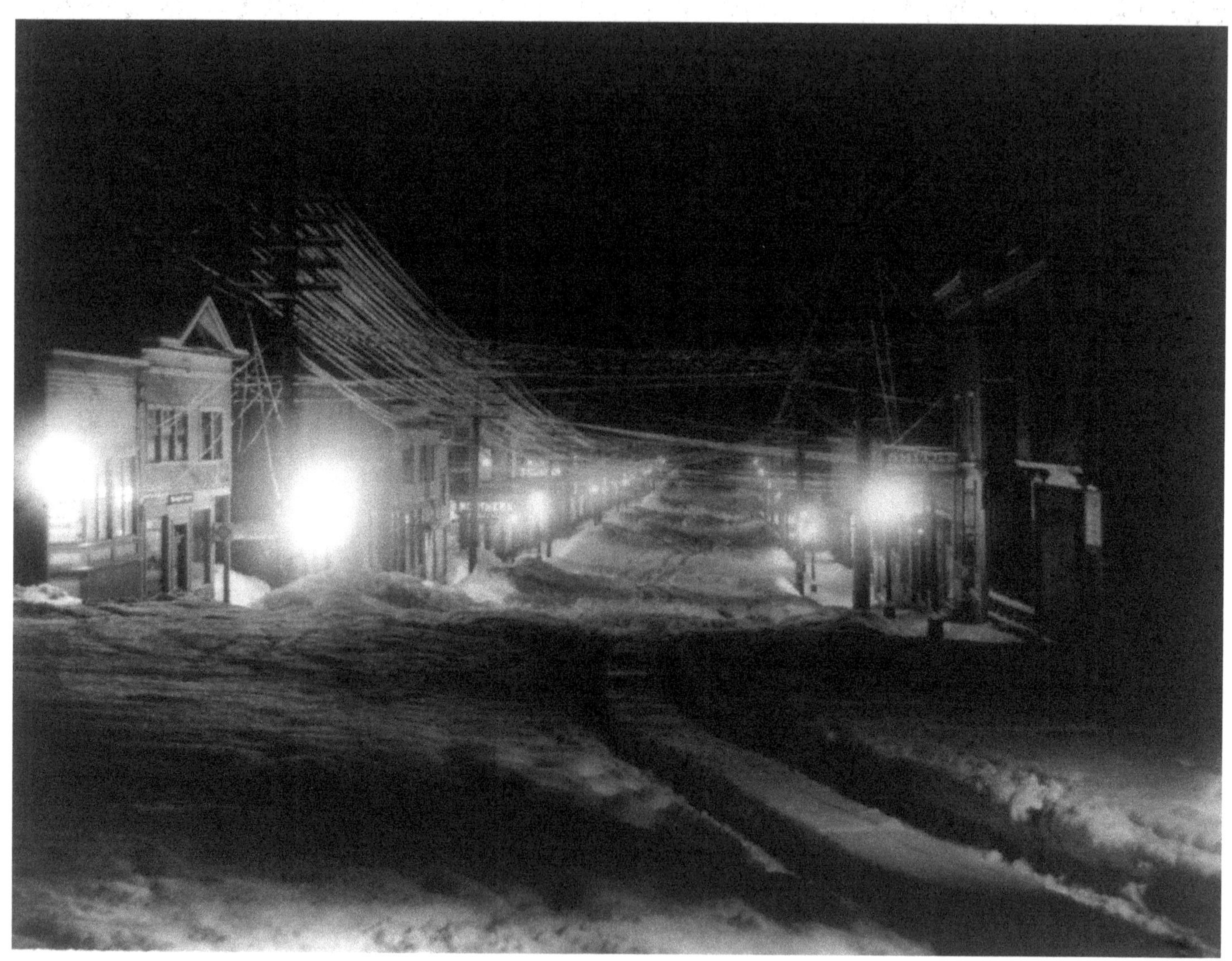

A winter night in Cordova, in the era before motor vehicles ruled the roads.

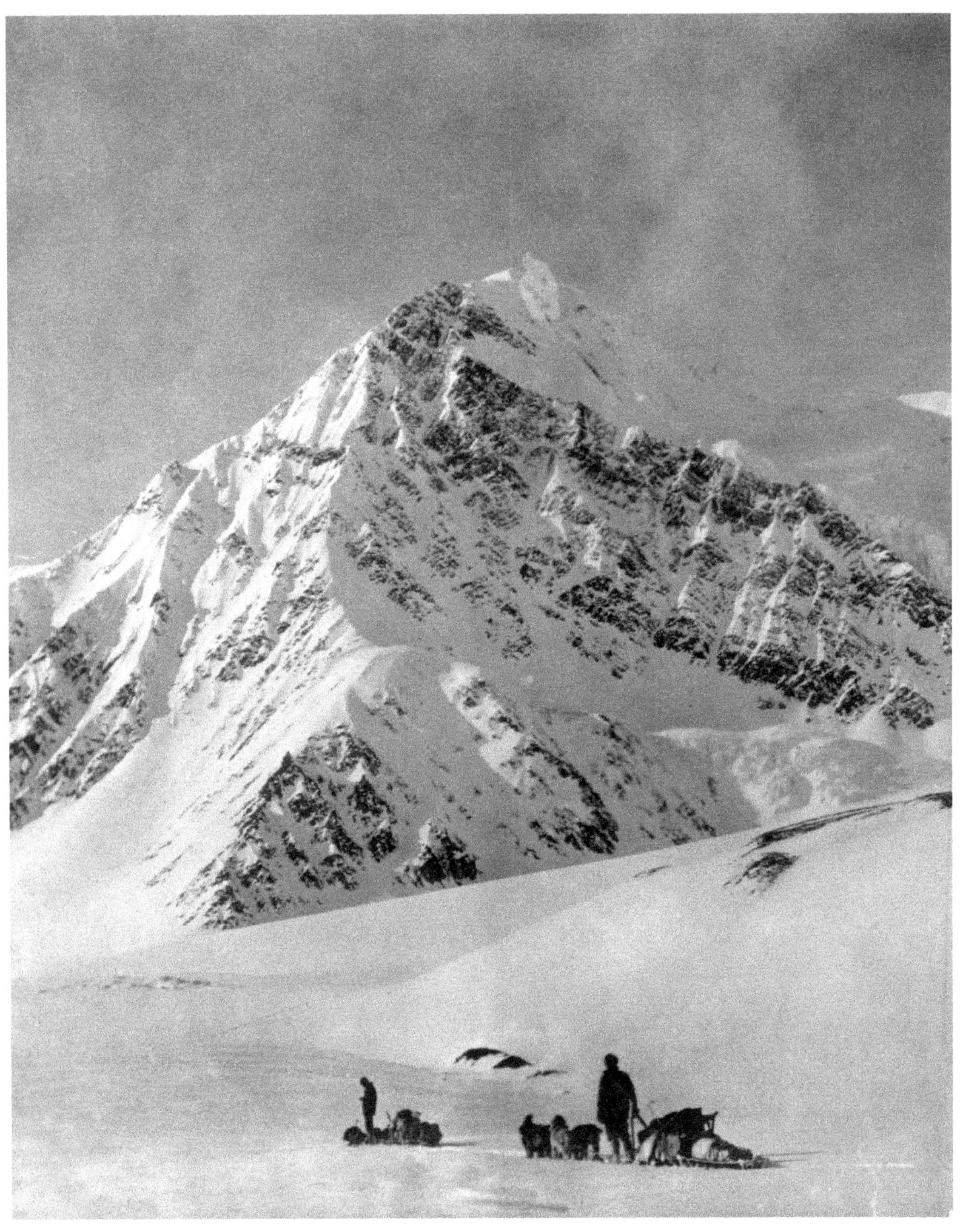

Dog teams travel in the Alaska Range in the shadow of Mount McKinley.

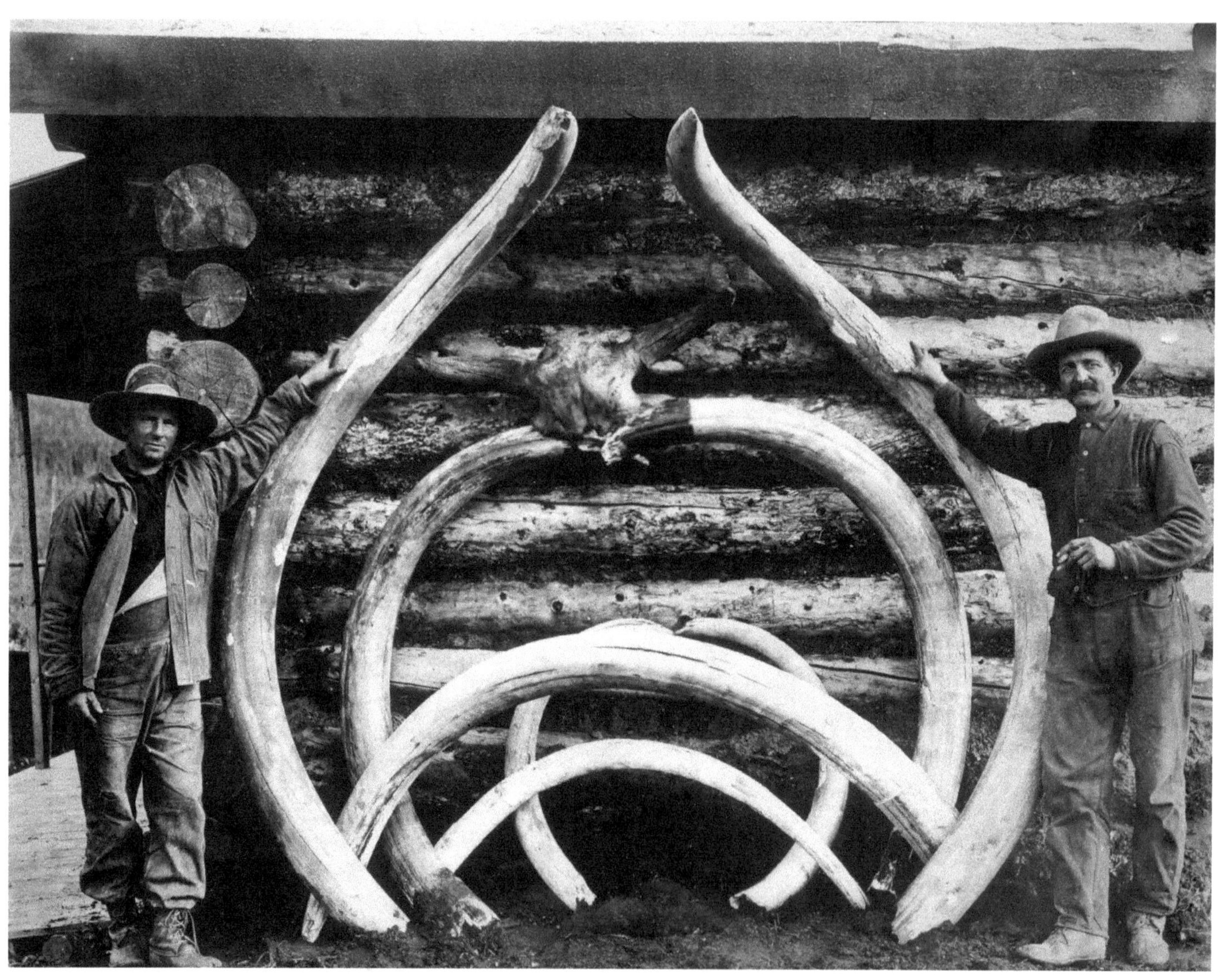

Miners digging through ancient creek beds occasionally discovered prehistoric tusks of the mastodons and mammoths that roamed Alaska thousands of years ago.

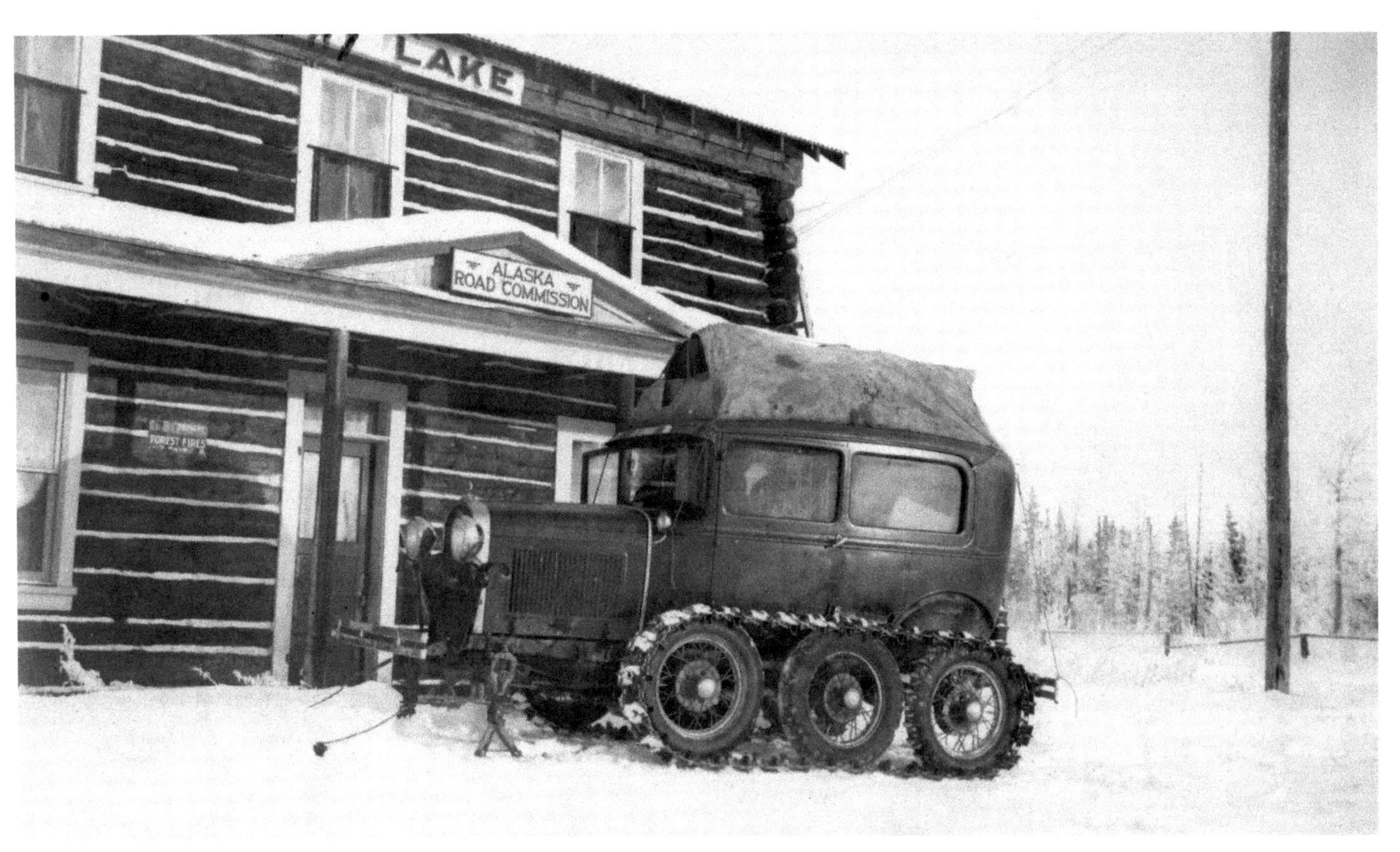

Carlson's mail truck stops at an Alaska Road Commission office on a regular winter delivery.

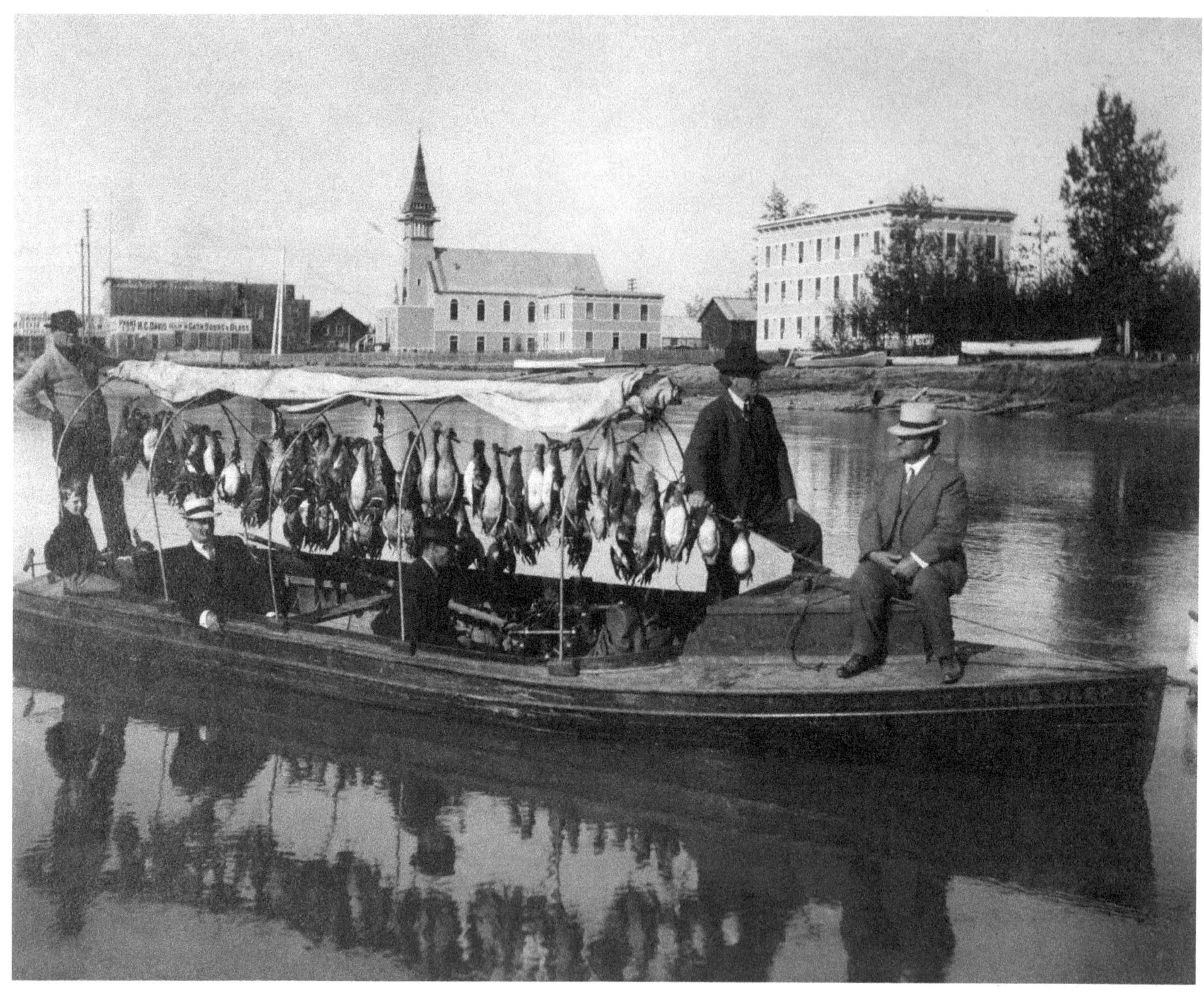

Federal Marshal L. T. Erwin and other hunters return to downtown Fairbanks on the Chena River with a couple of dozen ducks about 1915.

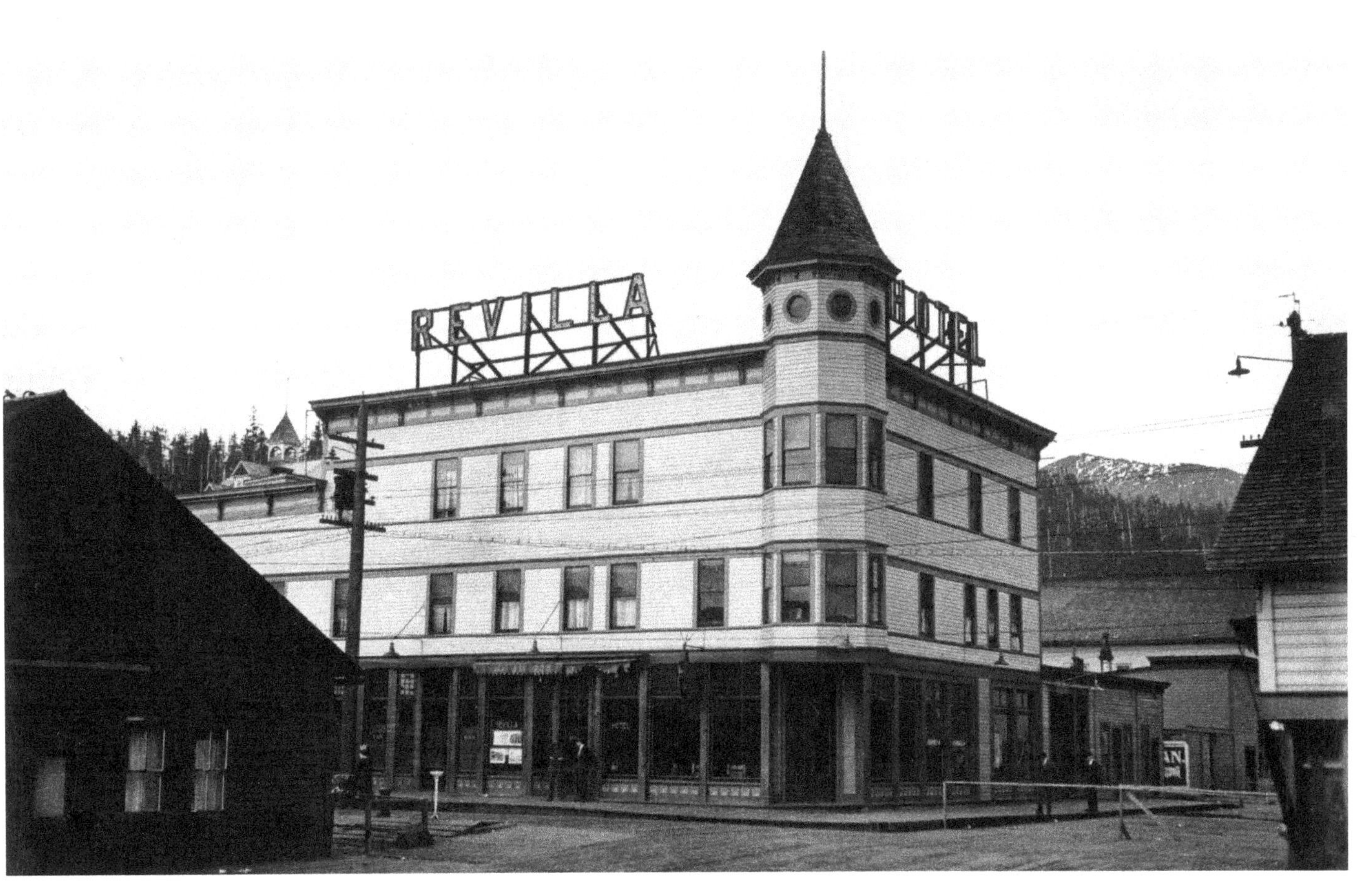

The Revilla Hotel provided rooms in downtown Ketchikan from the early 1900s until it was destroyed by fire in 1924.

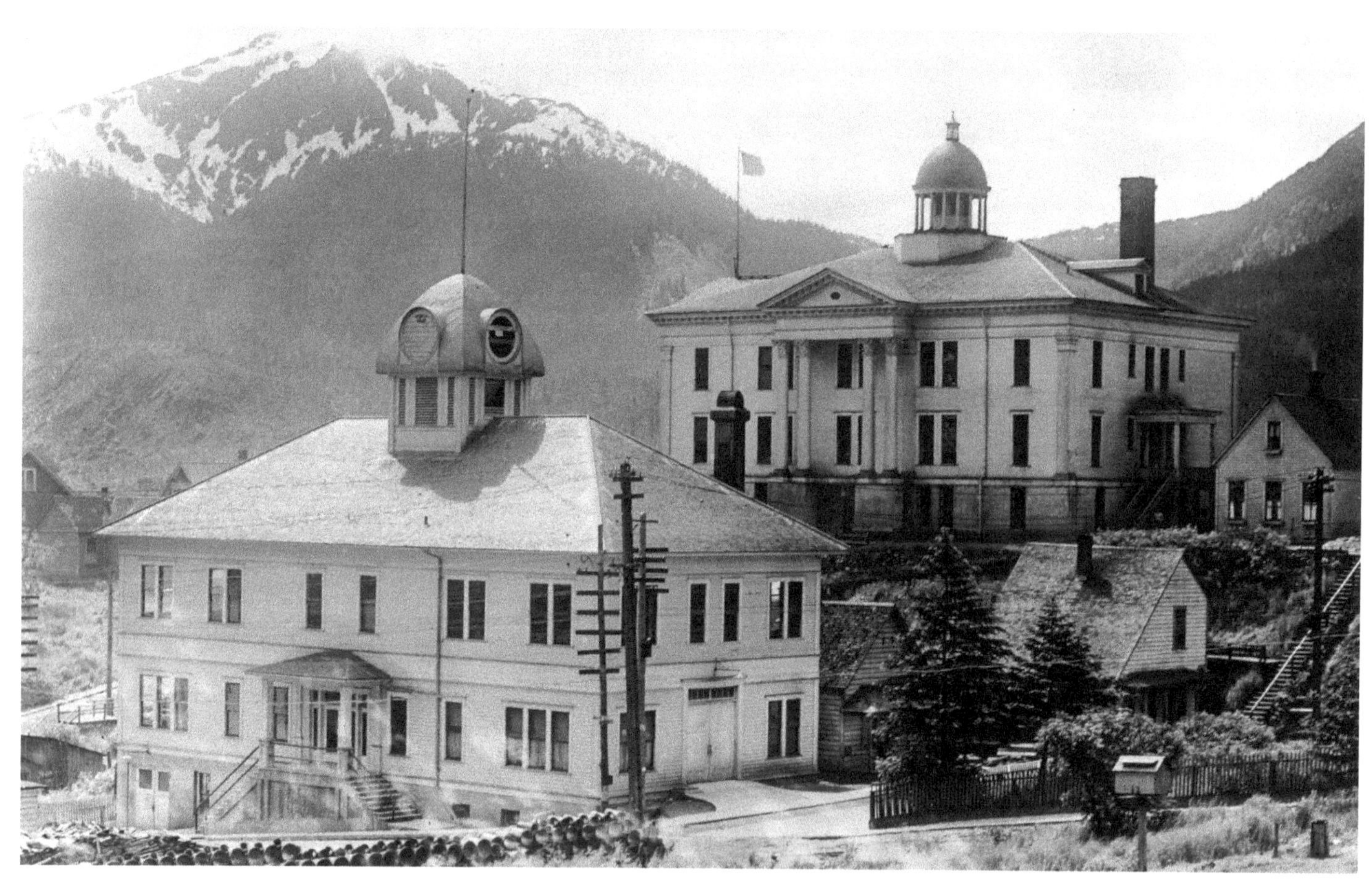

The Juneau City Hall and courthouse in the capital city of Alaska about 1920.

Dredging through the Depression

(1920–1940)

People on the ground quickly grasped that in a flight of a few hours it was possible to go farther than a dog team could travel in a month. By 1937 there were nearly one hundred civilian airfields.

The airplane and the railroad helped spur the development of gold dredging in the late 1920s in major gold fields at Fairbanks and Nome, areas that had declined once the richest deposits had been worked by hand.

The gold dredges were massive machines that scooped up gravel by the ton and removed the precious metal before depositing the gravel tailings in the rear. It was said by some that "Alaska never knew the Depression," an overstatement to be sure, but a comment rooted in the relative prosperity that continued through the 1930s because of gold dredging.

Along the coast, fishing was the lifeblood of the economy, an industry dominated by Seattle-based interests that operated large canneries and shipped fish all over the country.

One of the most publicized parts of the New Deal in Alaska was the establishment of the Matanuska Colony northeast of Anchorage. The colony was conceived as a means of helping two hundred impoverished families from the Upper Midwest start over by building a new community in the wilderness.

During those same years a new concern began to develop in Alaska that the territory was woefully lacking in defenses, especially given a growing militaristic spirit in Japan. Alaska's delegate to Congress repeatedly warned his colleagues that money was being spent to fortify Pearl Harbor in Hawaii, but Alaska had no modern military installations. It was like locking the front door of a house and leaving the back door wide open, he said.

The cajoling didn't work, but the support of men like Lieutenant Colonel Henry "Hap" Arnold, coupled with the realization that war in Europe posed a real threat to U.S. security, finally led to a military buildup that began in 1940.

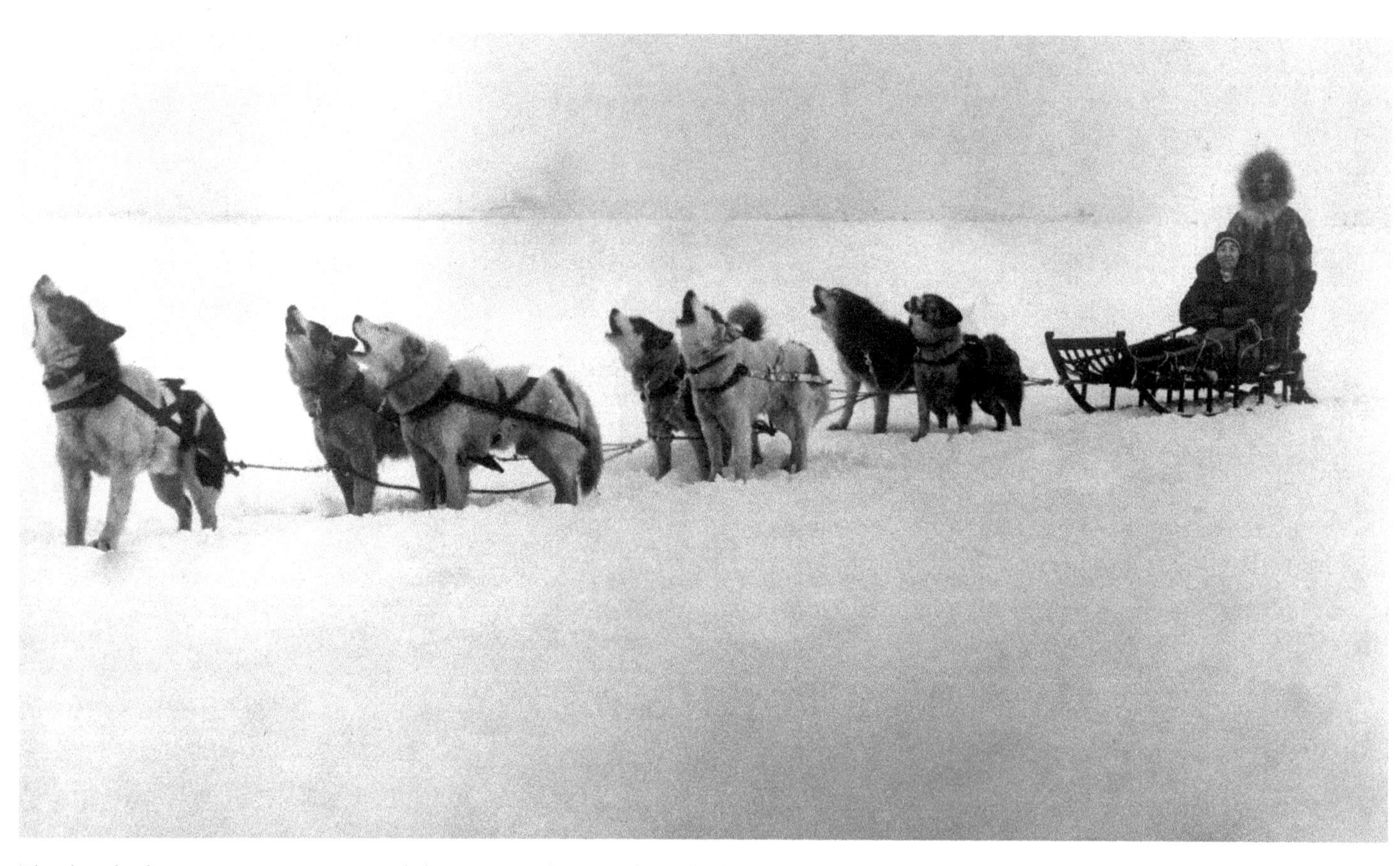

The dogs bark in unison, creating a wail that a 1920 photographer called the "Malamute Chorus."

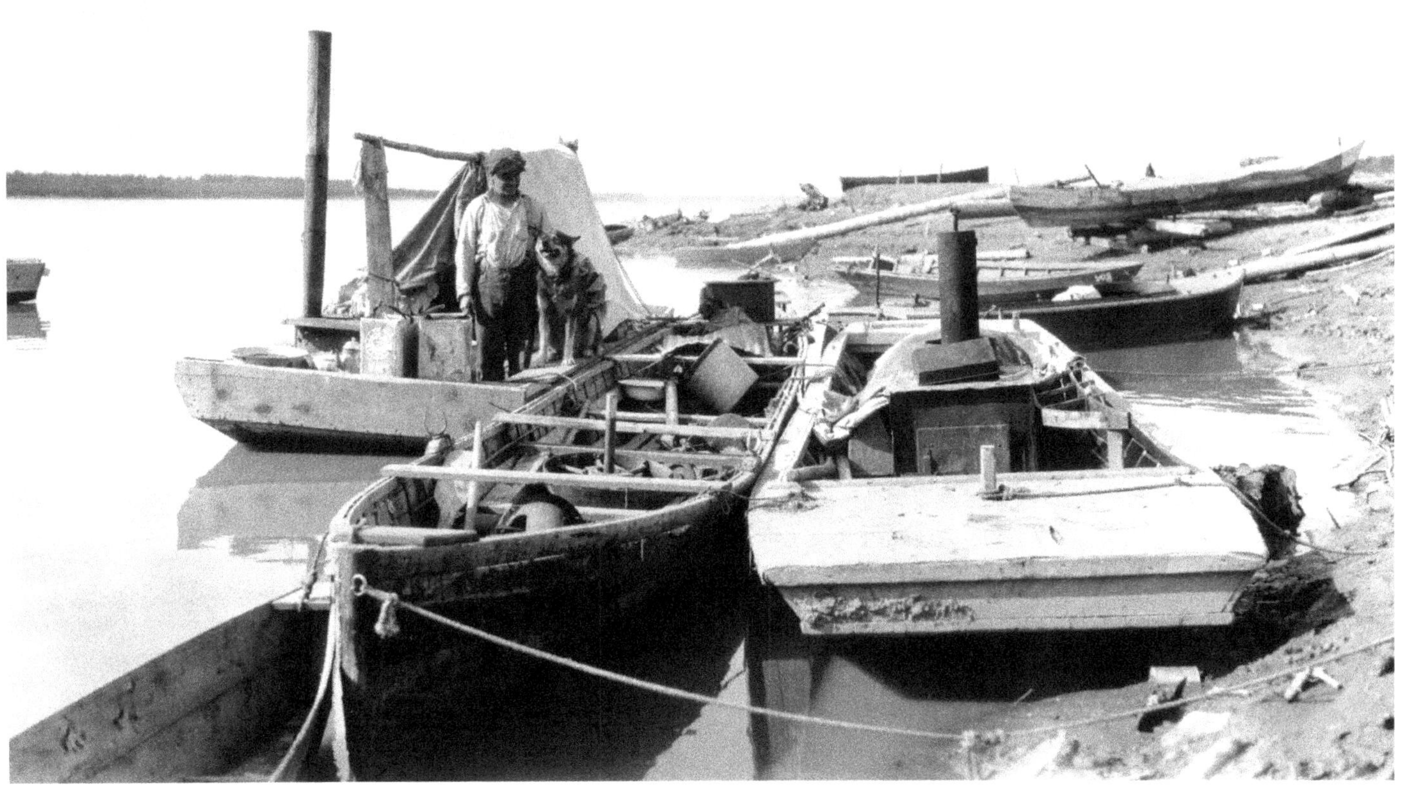

A man and his dog stand in a riverboat that doubled as a campsite when he left the village of Nulato on the Yukon River in 1926.

Eddystone Rock, a 237-foot pillar of basalt, stands like a sentinel outside Misty Fjords, now part of a national monument in Southeast Alaska.

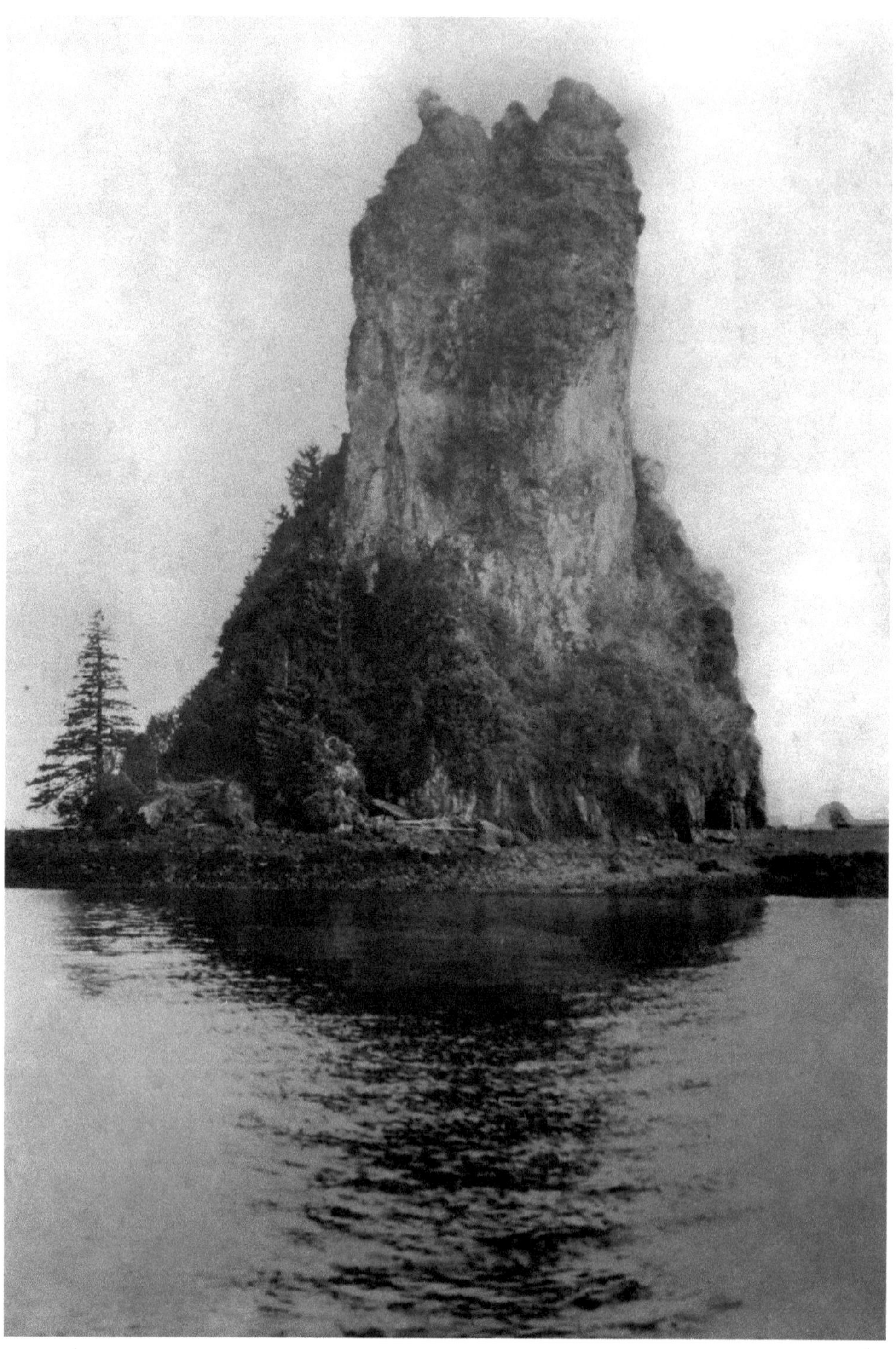

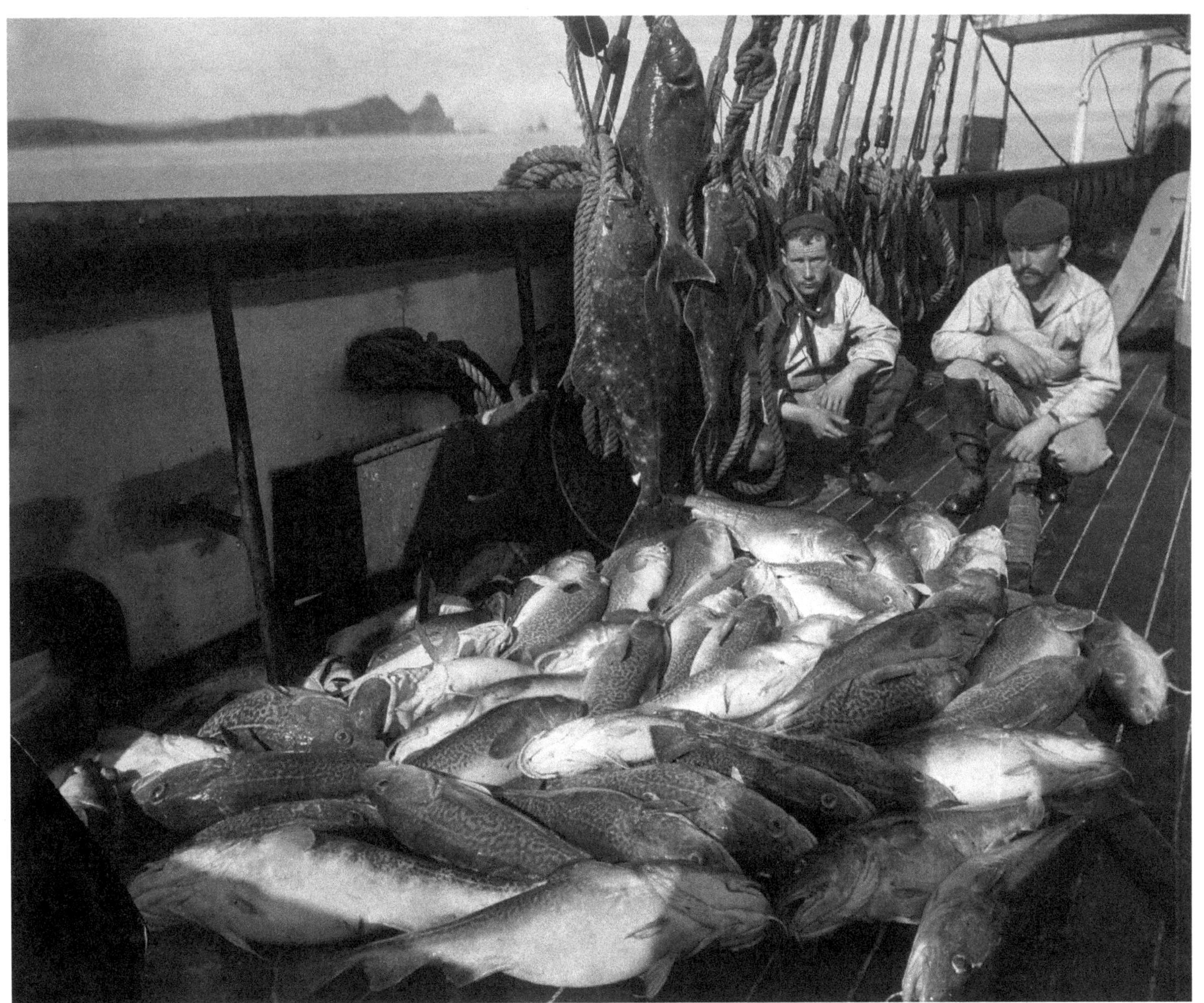

Fishermen with a portion of a catch of halibut and cod in the 1920s.

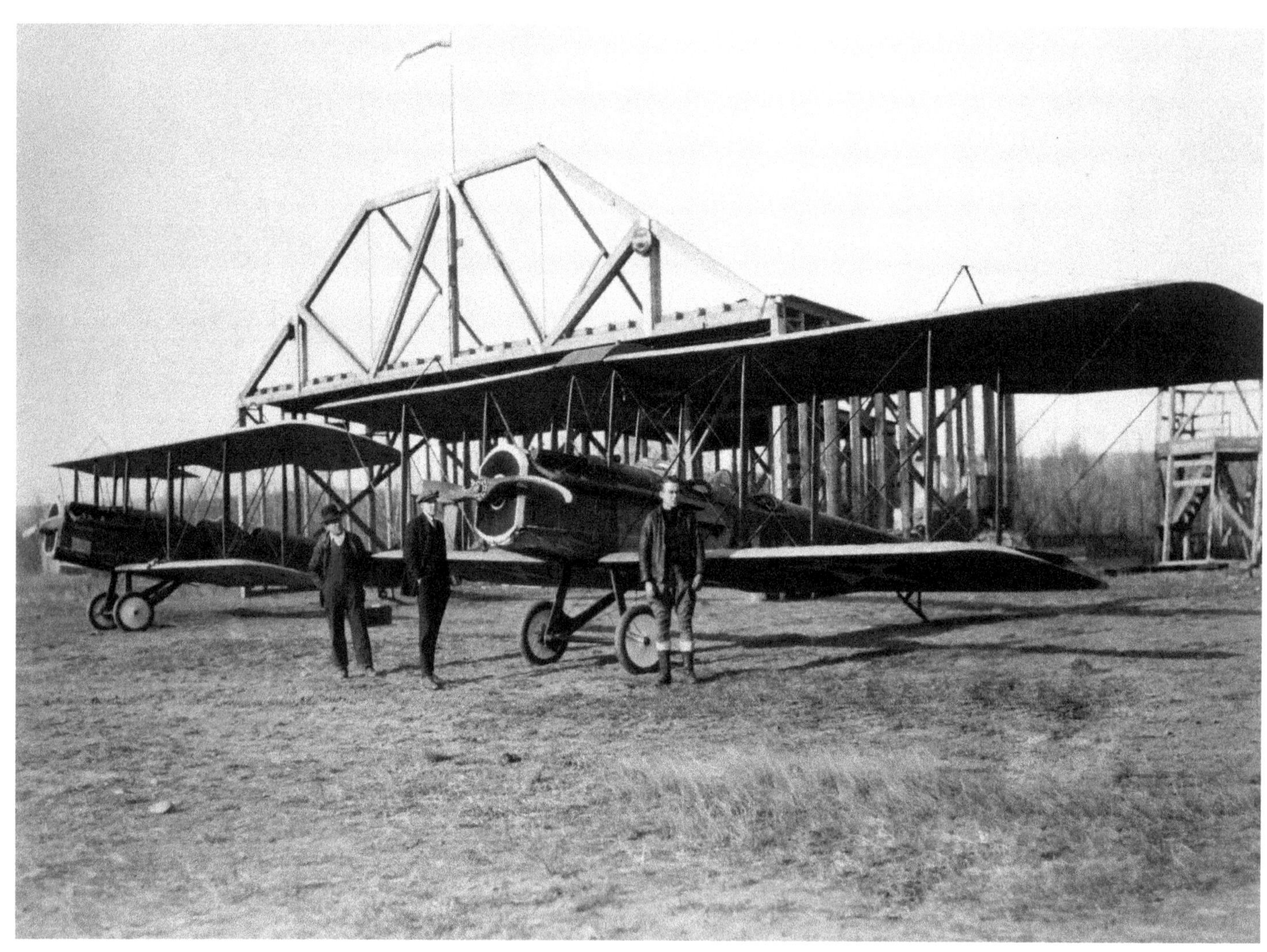

Noel Wien, right, followed the trail of Carl "Ben" Eielson and helped establish flying as a practical enterprise in Alaska. These two Hisso Standard biplanes, owned by James Rodebaugh, left, were the only planes flying in the territory in 1925. The man in the middle is Eddie Hudson of Fairbanks, who was taking flying lessons.

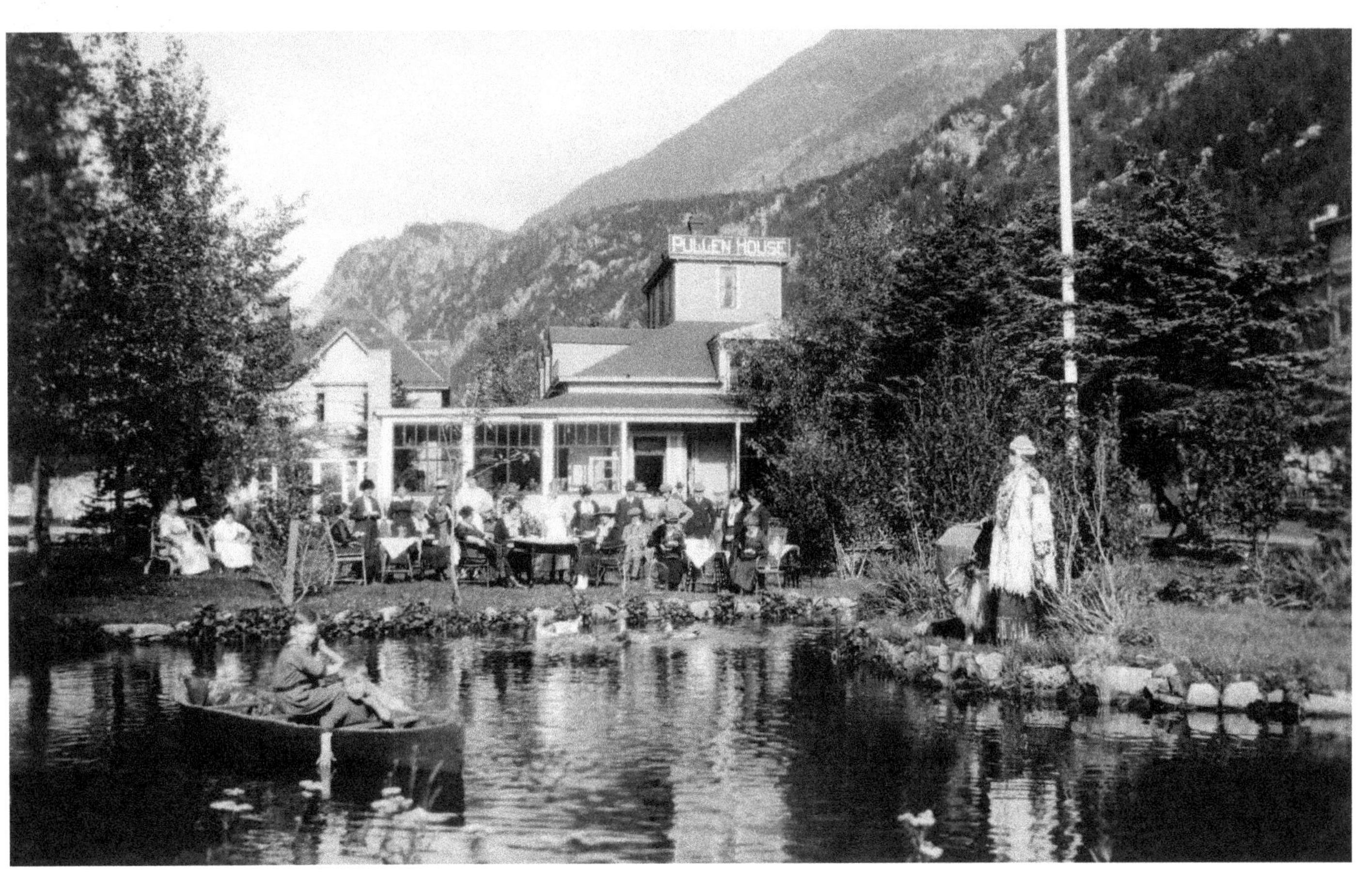

Two boys play in a rowboat, while on shore the guests enjoy a lawn party outside the Pullen House in Skagway in the early 1920s.

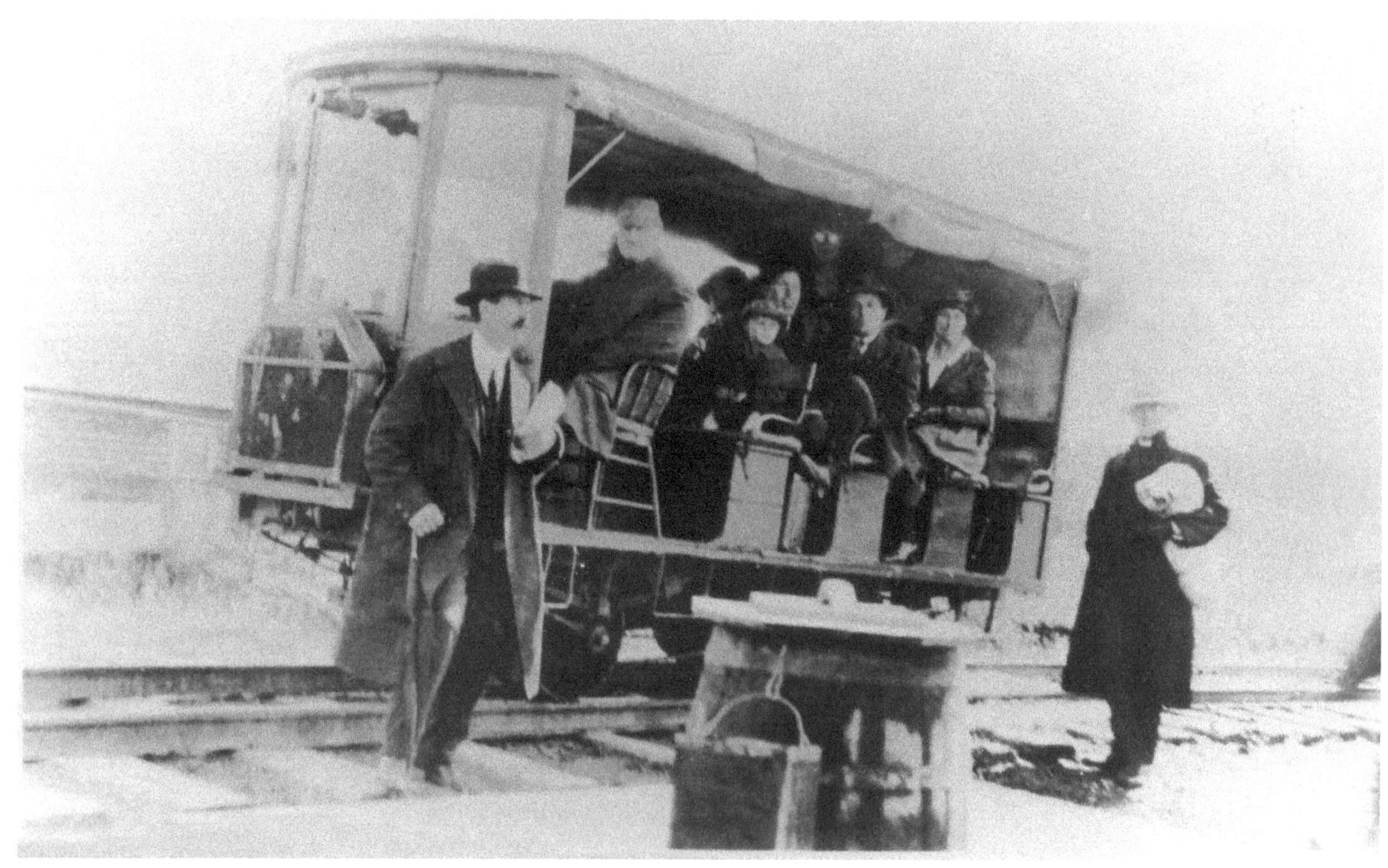

The "Toonerville Trolley" from Fairbanks to the University of Alaska campus provided regular transportation for students and faculty members in 1922 before there were many automobiles in Fairbanks. The name came from a wildly careening trolley in the popular comic strip "Toonerville Folks."

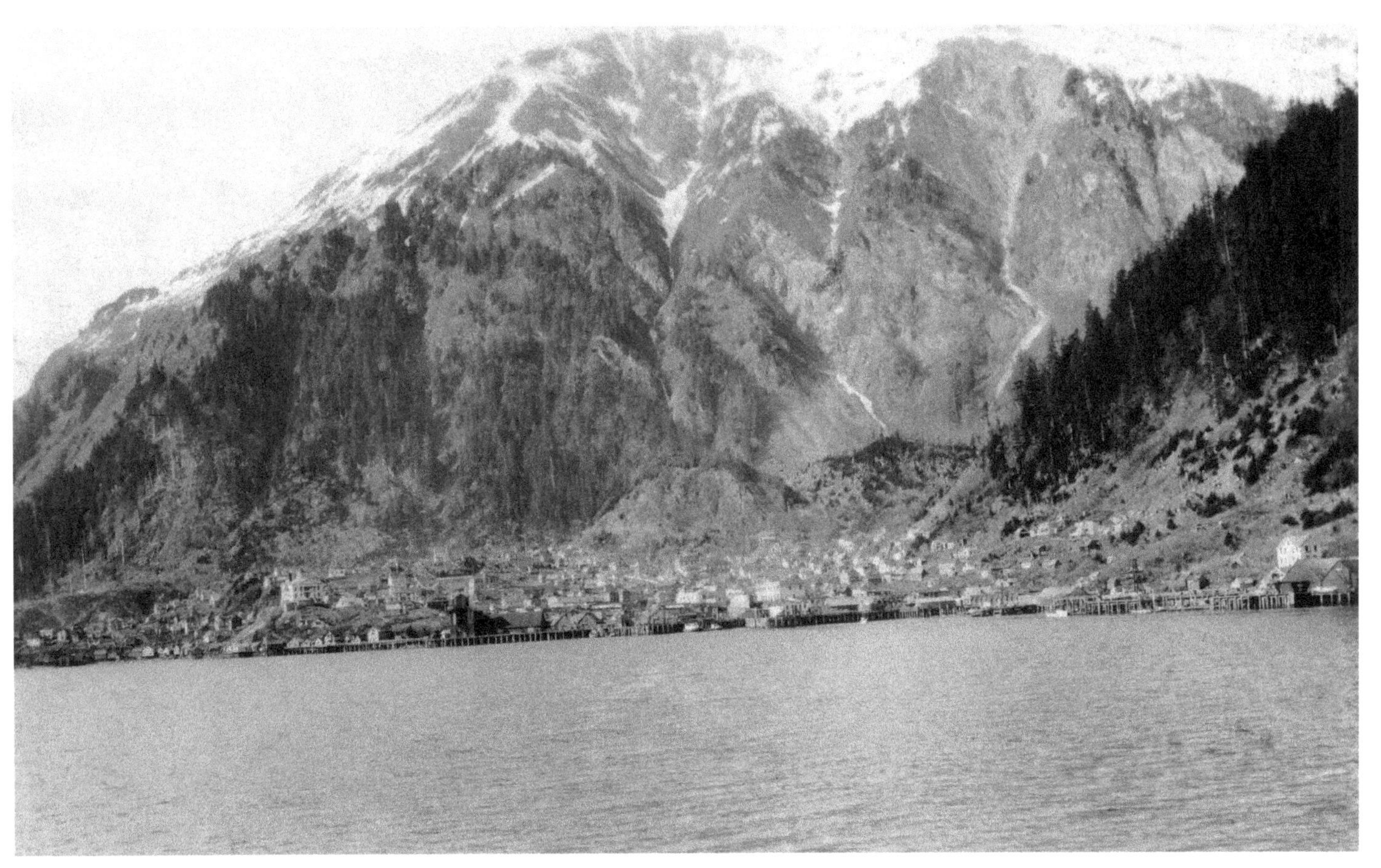

With Mount Juneau in the background creating a dramatic backdrop for the capital city of Alaska, Juneau is a compact city along the shores of Gastineau Channel.

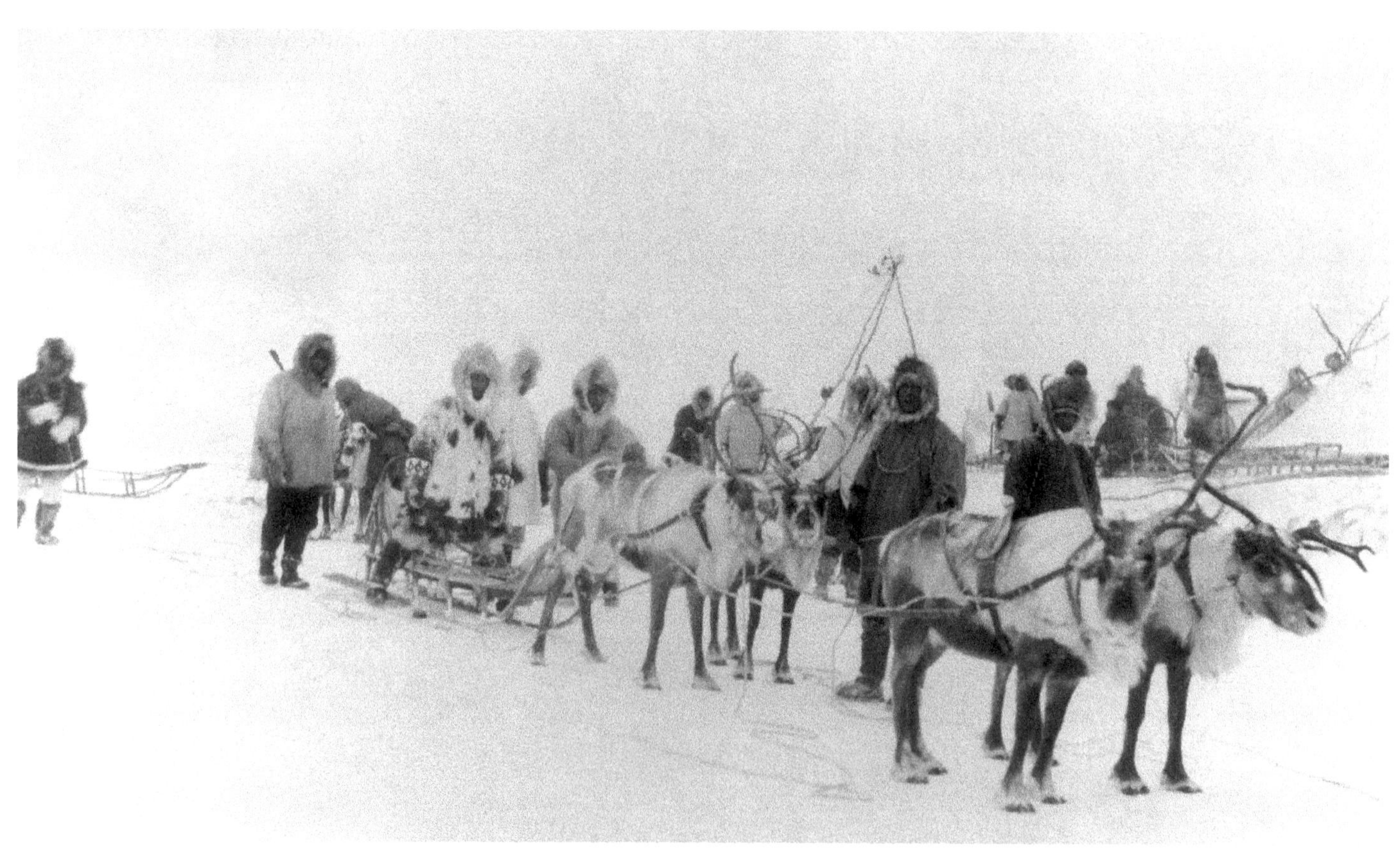

In the early 1900s, some Alaskans promoted the idea of harnessing reindeer for transportation, saying that they were better suited than dogs, easier to keep, and a single animal could haul as much as six dogs could. The photo of this team was taken in 1922.

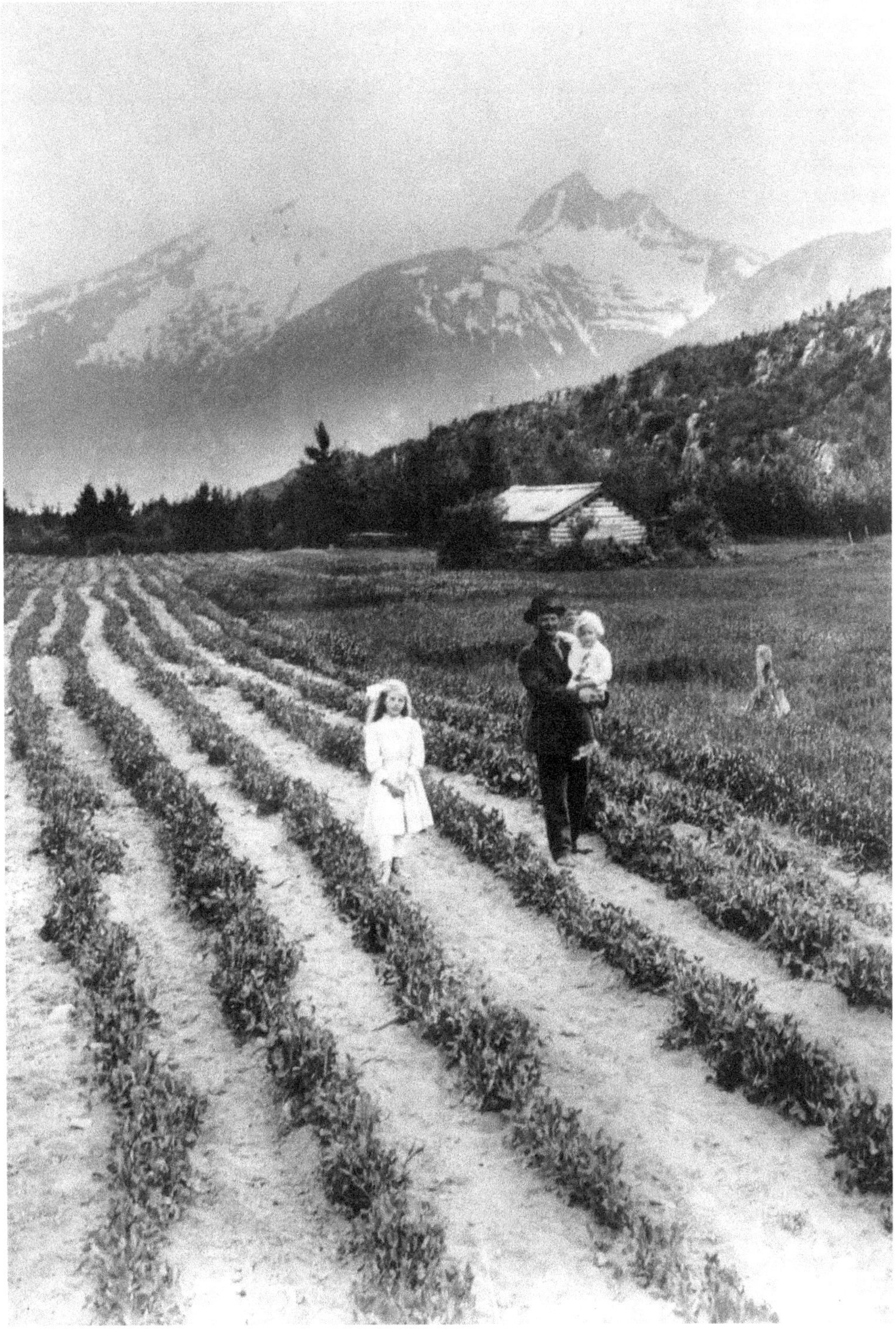

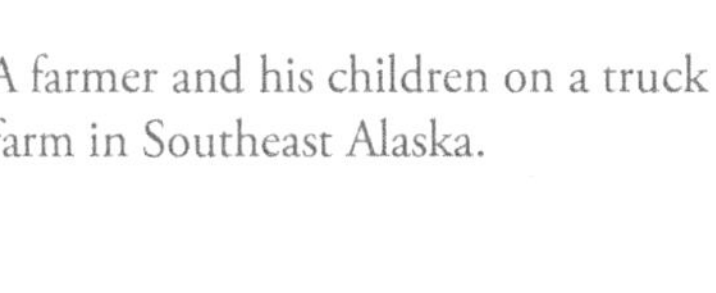

A farmer and his children on a truck farm in Southeast Alaska.

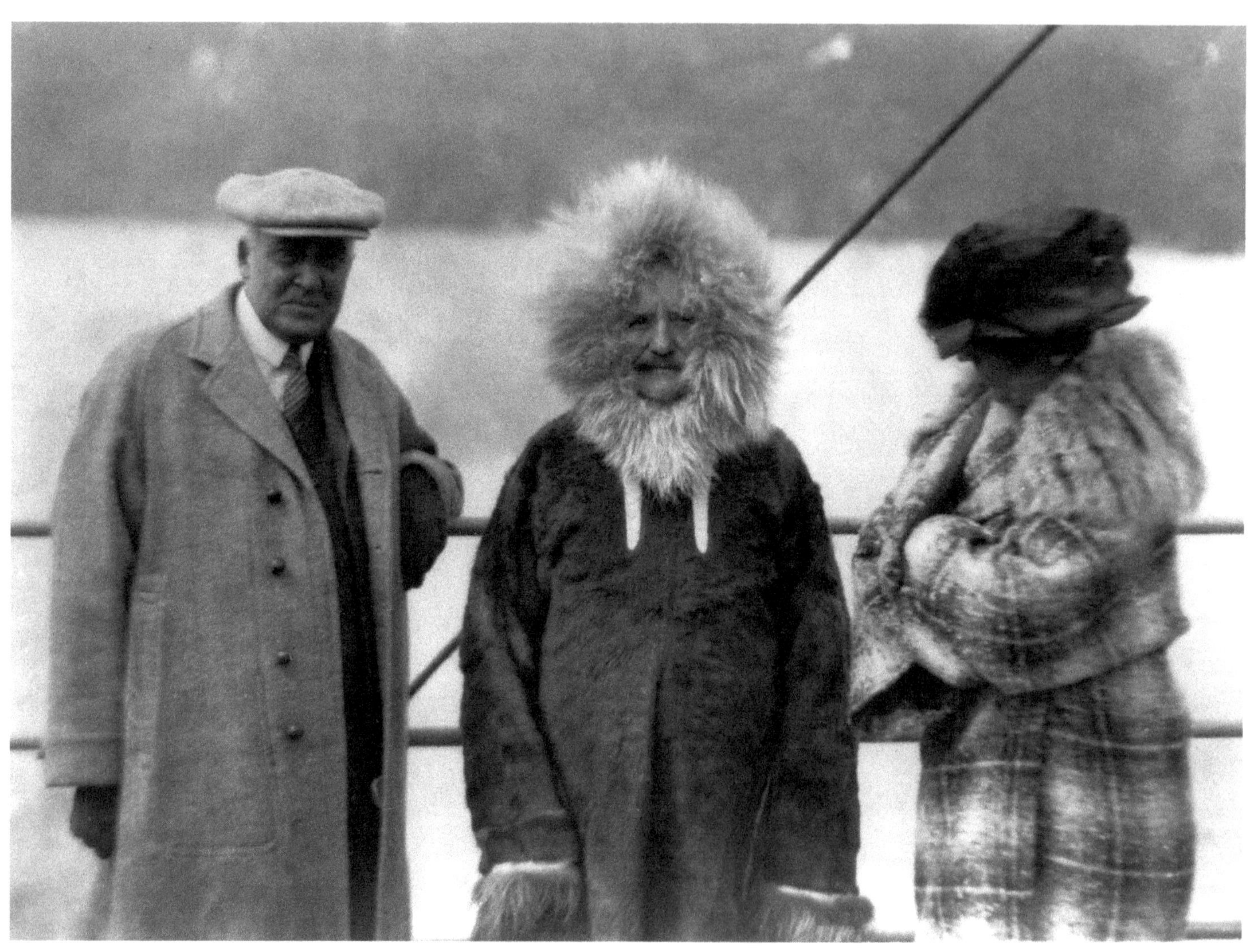

President Warren G. Harding and his wife, Florence, stop in Seward on their trip to Alaska, while Alaska Governor Scott Bone models the latest in fur fashion. Harding died in San Francisco on his way back, just days after this photo was taken.

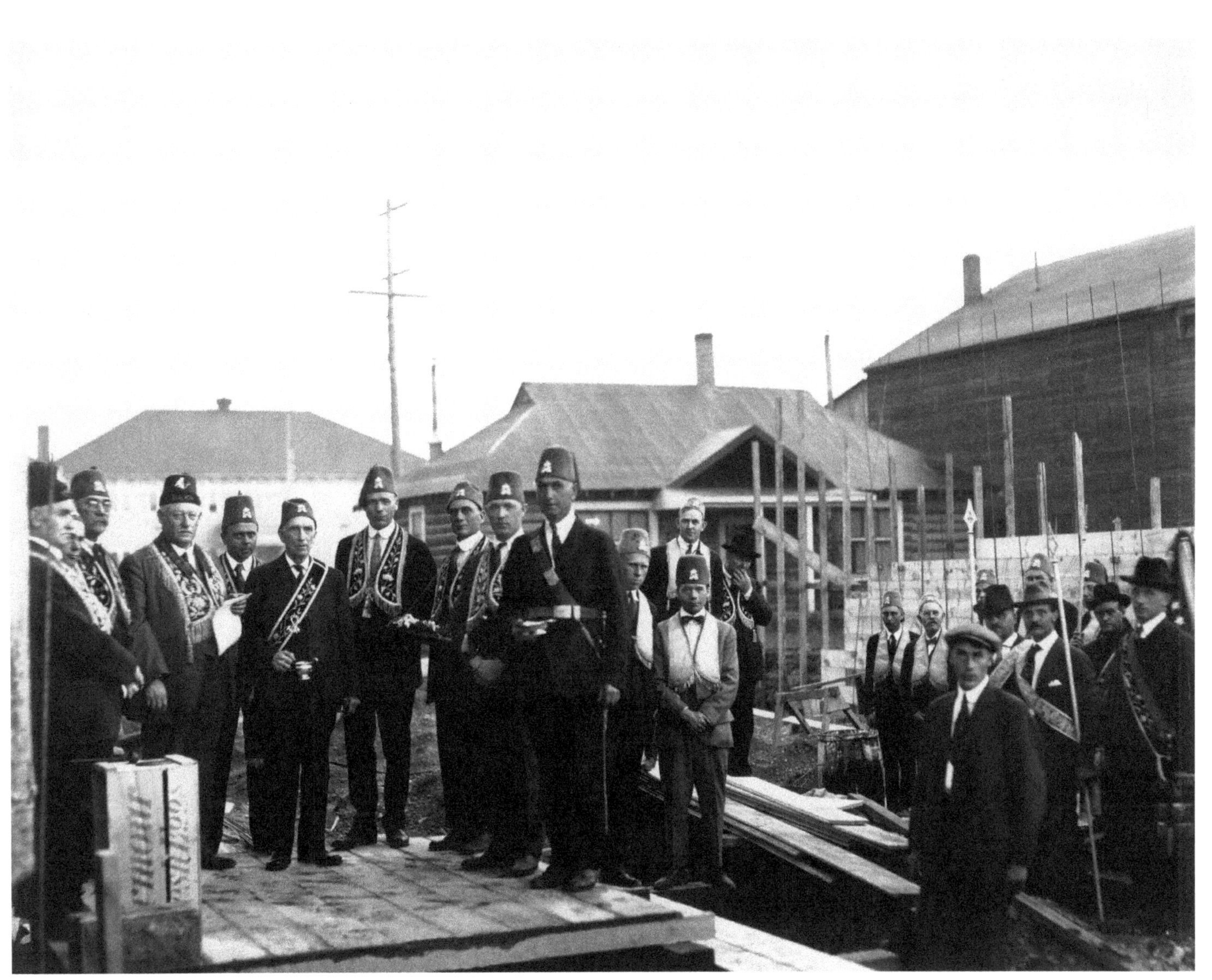

Members of the Odd Fellows fraternal organization lay the cornerstone for their new temple in Anchorage on August 20, 1923.

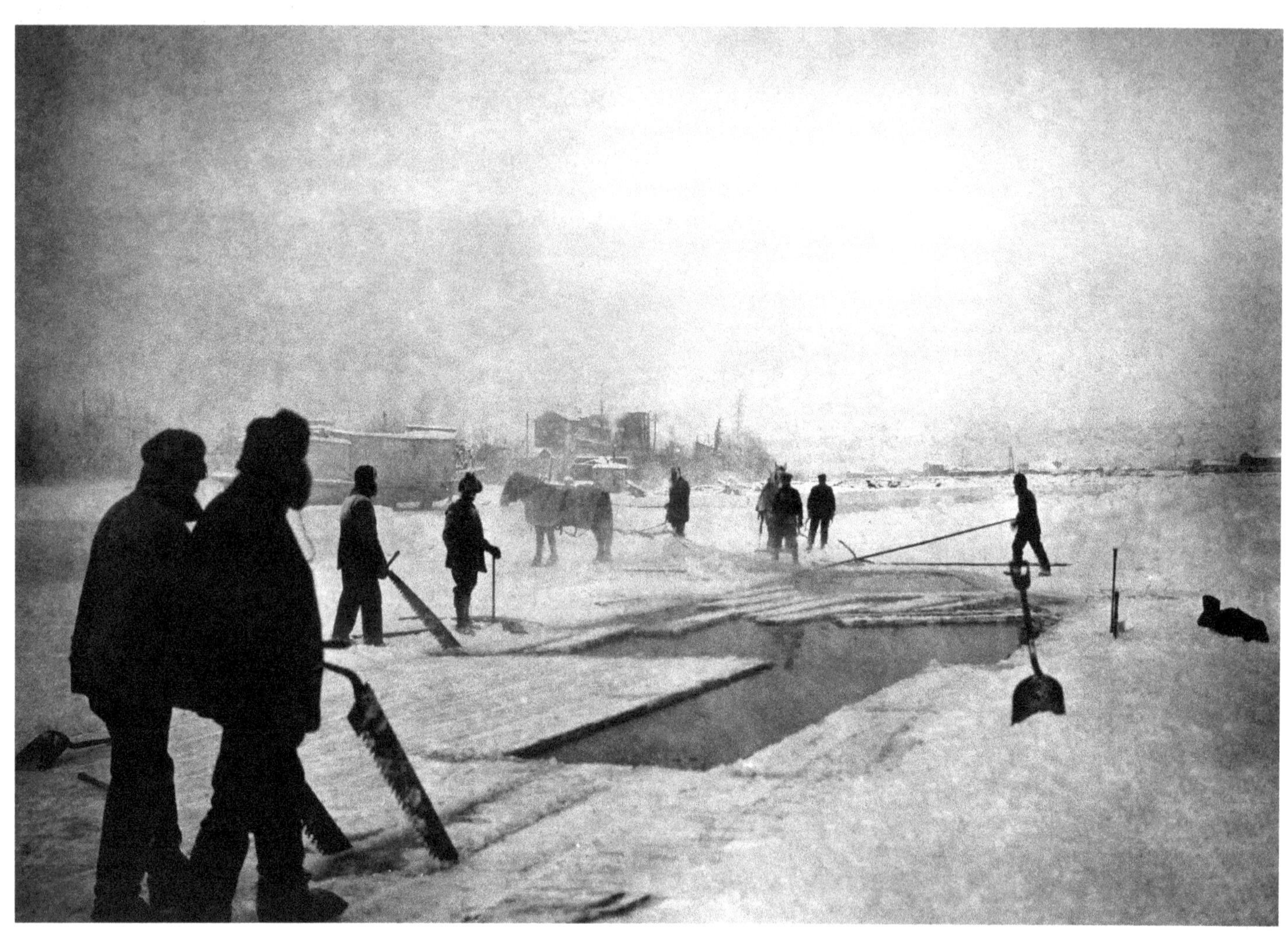

In the years before artificial refrigeration became available, ice cutting was a thriving industry in Alaska communities. Here, an ice company cuts blocks with long handsaws. The blocks were preserved in sawdust when winter ended.

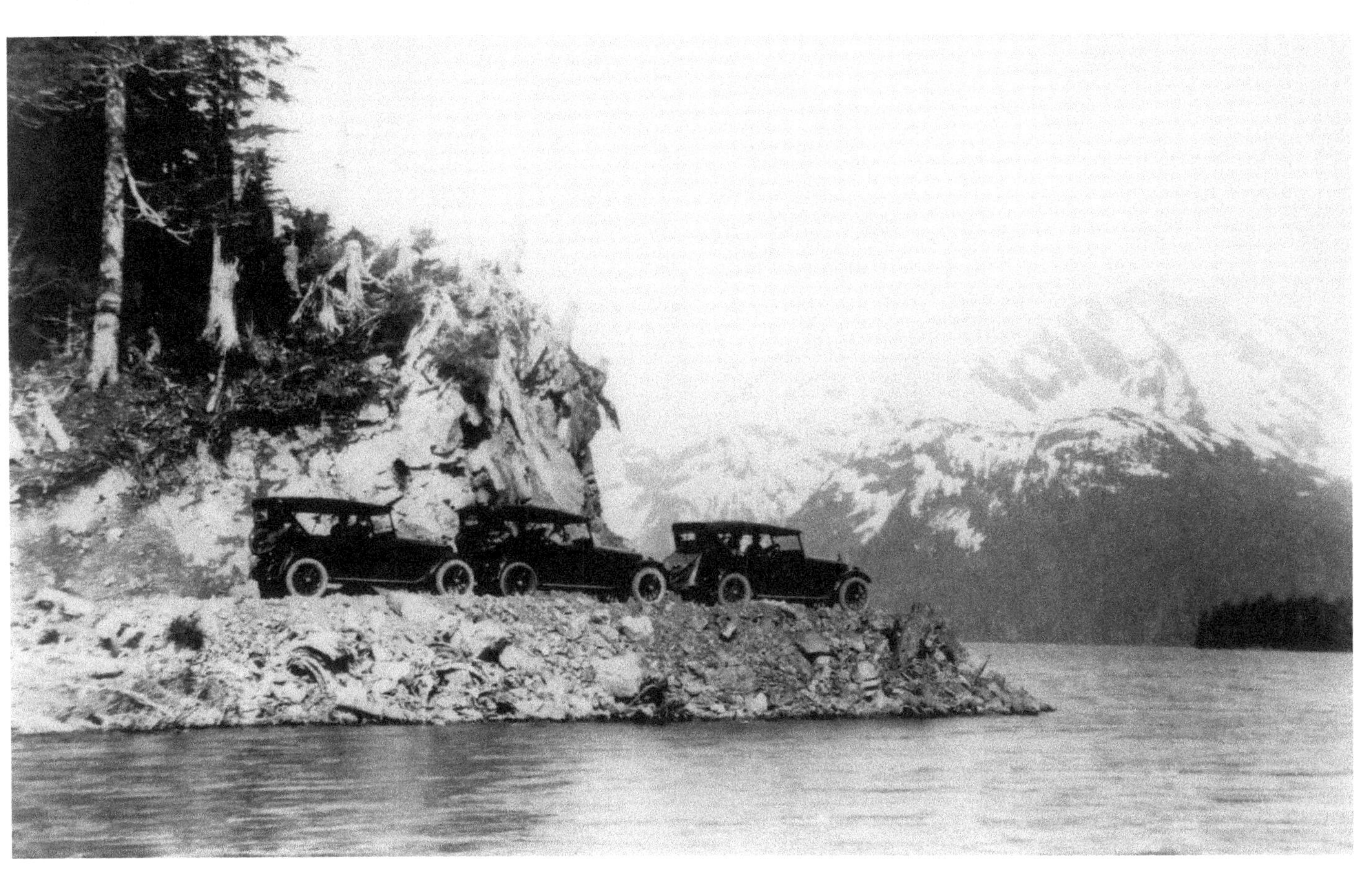

What began as a trail from Valdez to Fairbanks for horse-drawn sleighs and dog teams evolved into the Richardson Highway by the 1920s, with automobiles slowly making their way through the mountains and valleys.

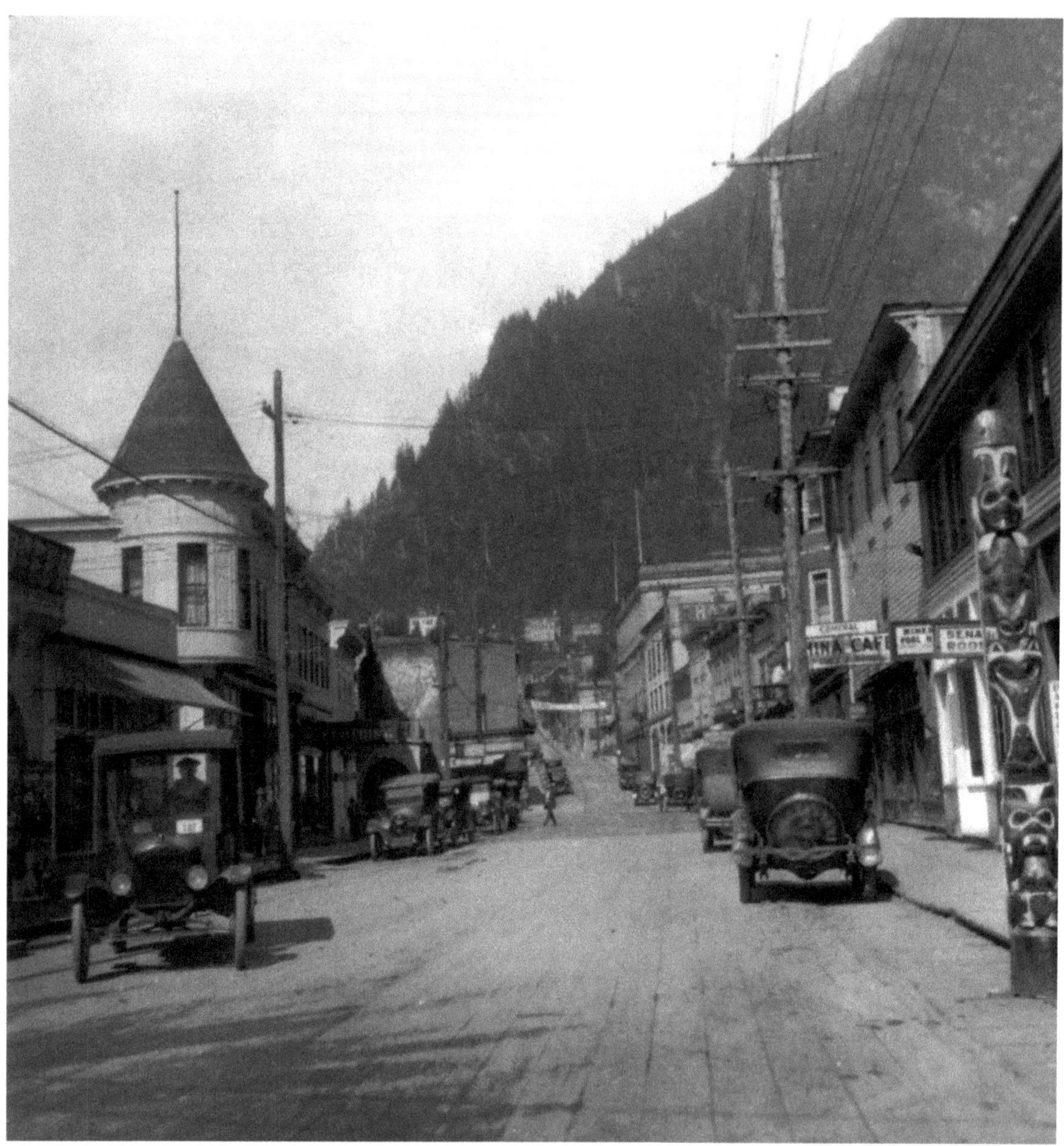

The main street of Juneau's business district in 1926.

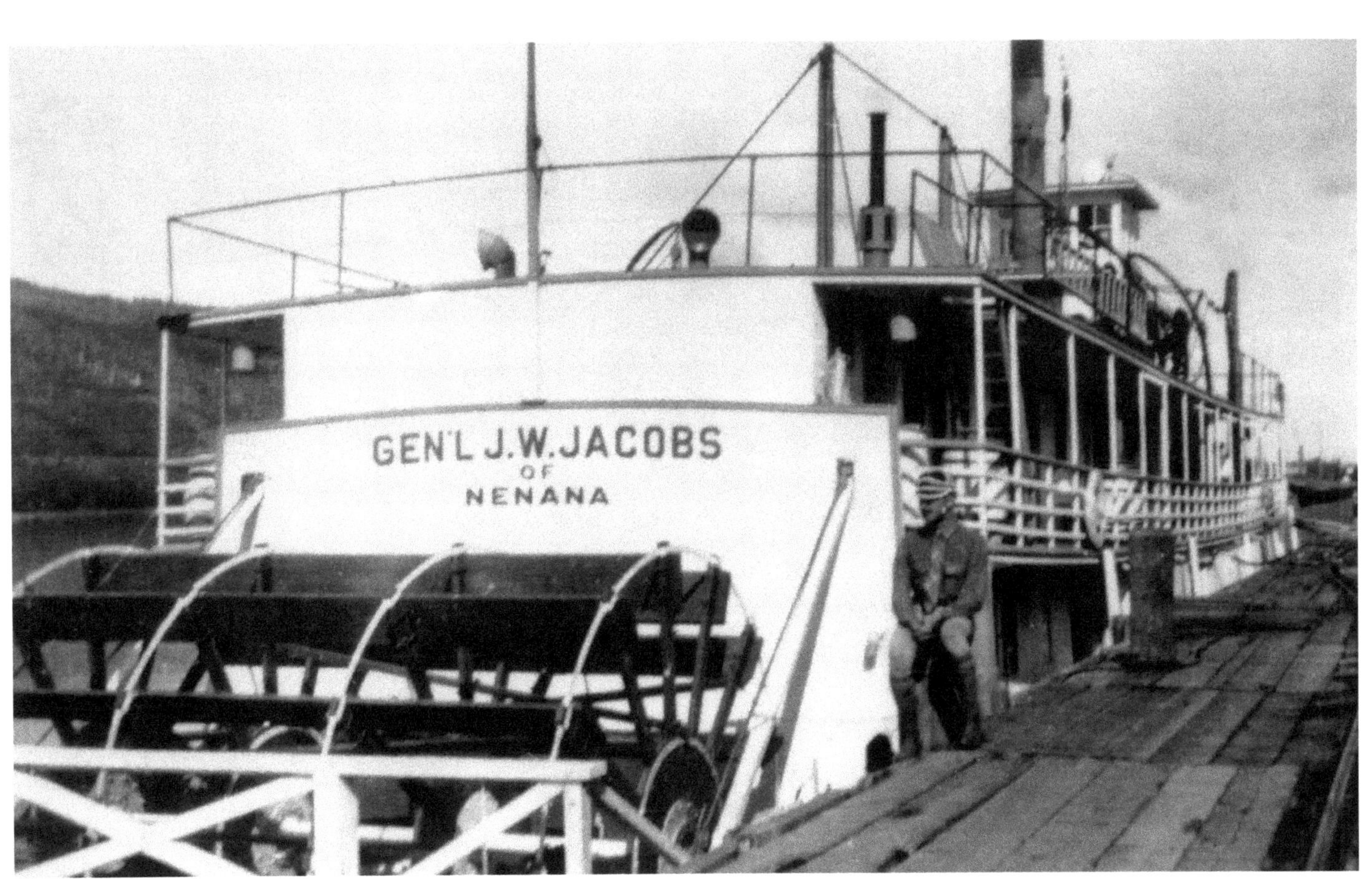

The stern-wheeler *Gen'l J. W. Jacobs,* owned by the Alaska Railroad and pictured here in 1928, carried passengers and freight along Interior rivers from its home port of Nenana.

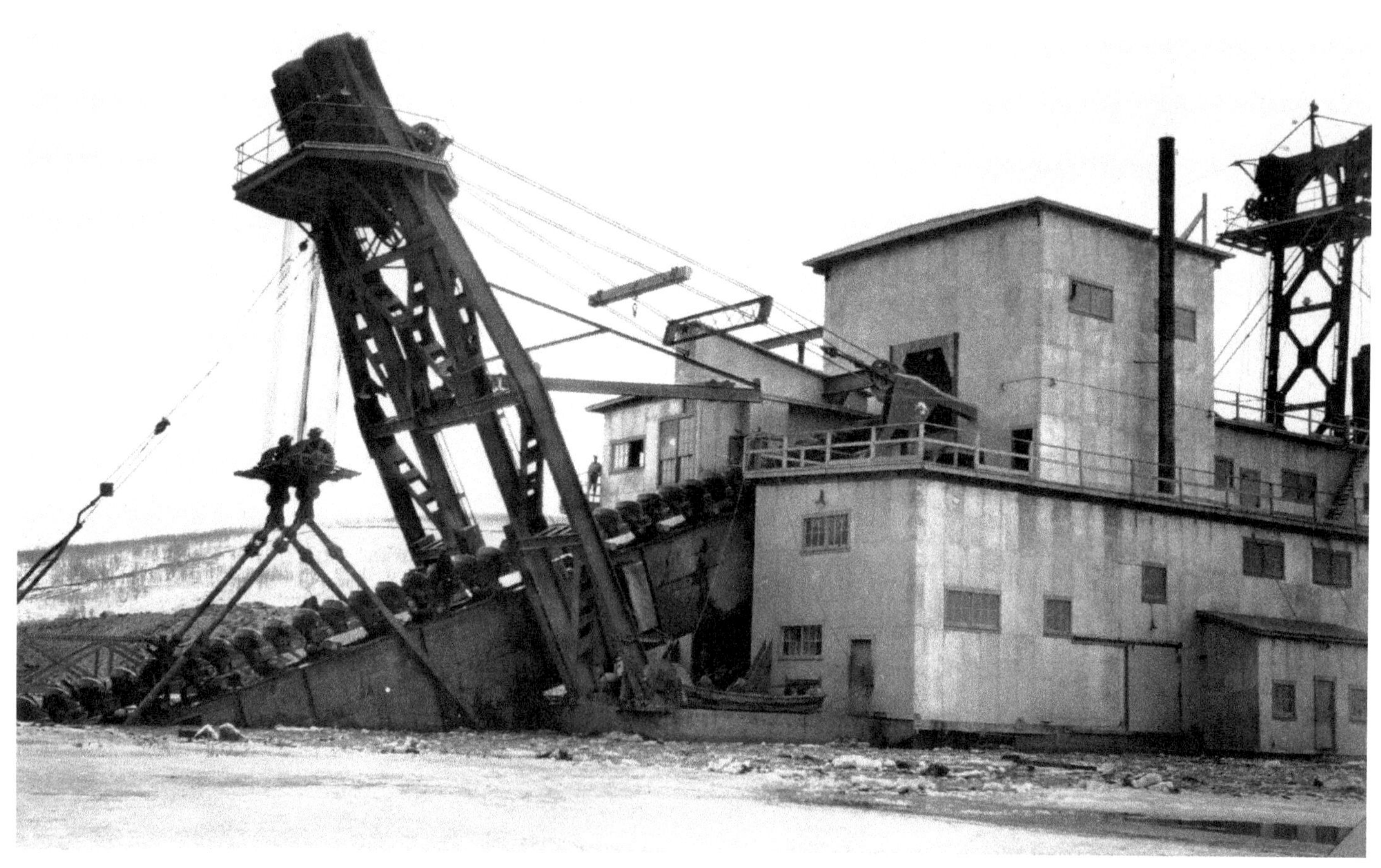

The dredge buckets on a gold dredge dig into the gravel surface below the water, scooping up rocks by the ton. Large gold-dredging operations were a mainstay of the Alaska economy from the late 1920s until World War II.

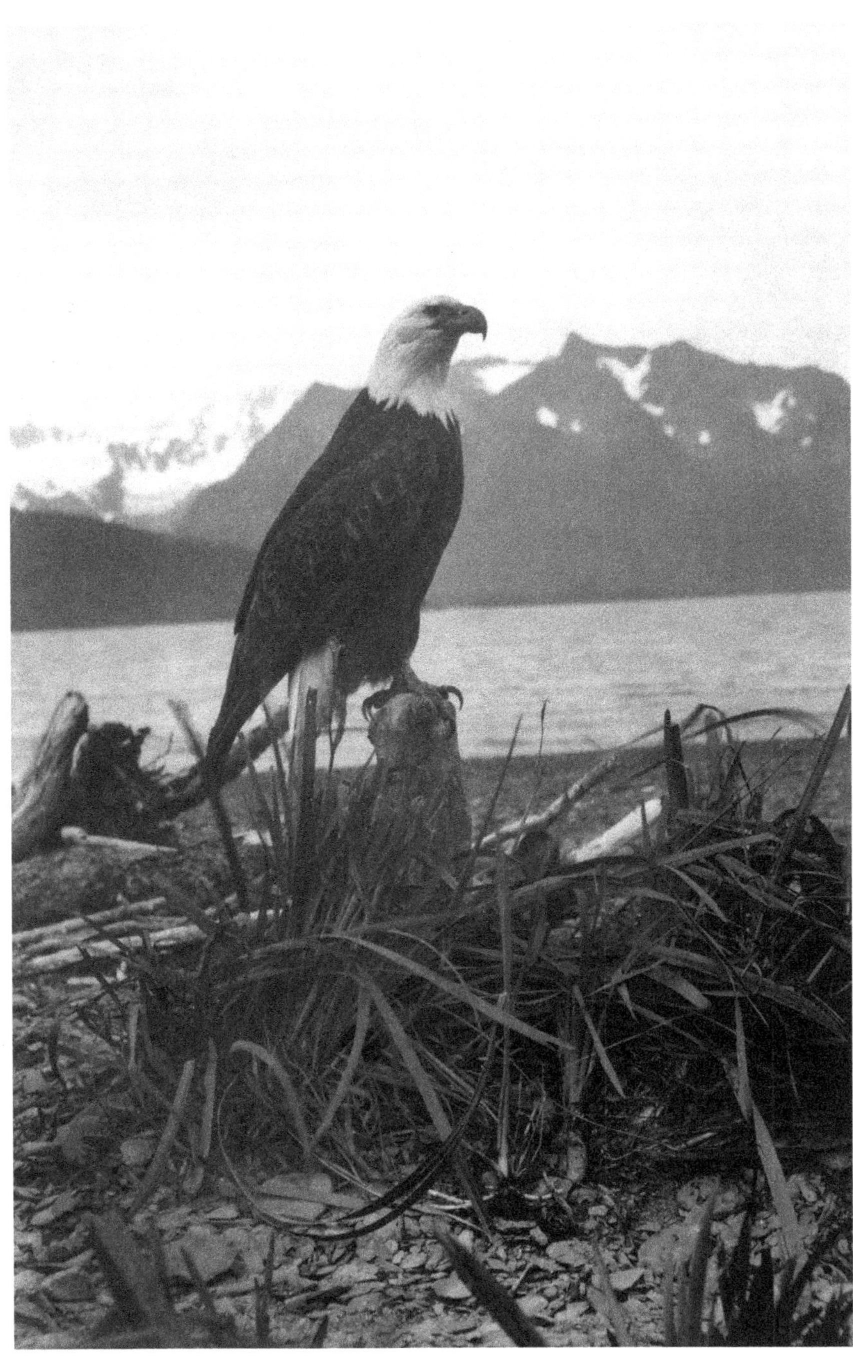

The bald eagle, the symbol of the United States, is a common sight in many parts of Alaska, especially along the coast in Southeast and Southcentral.

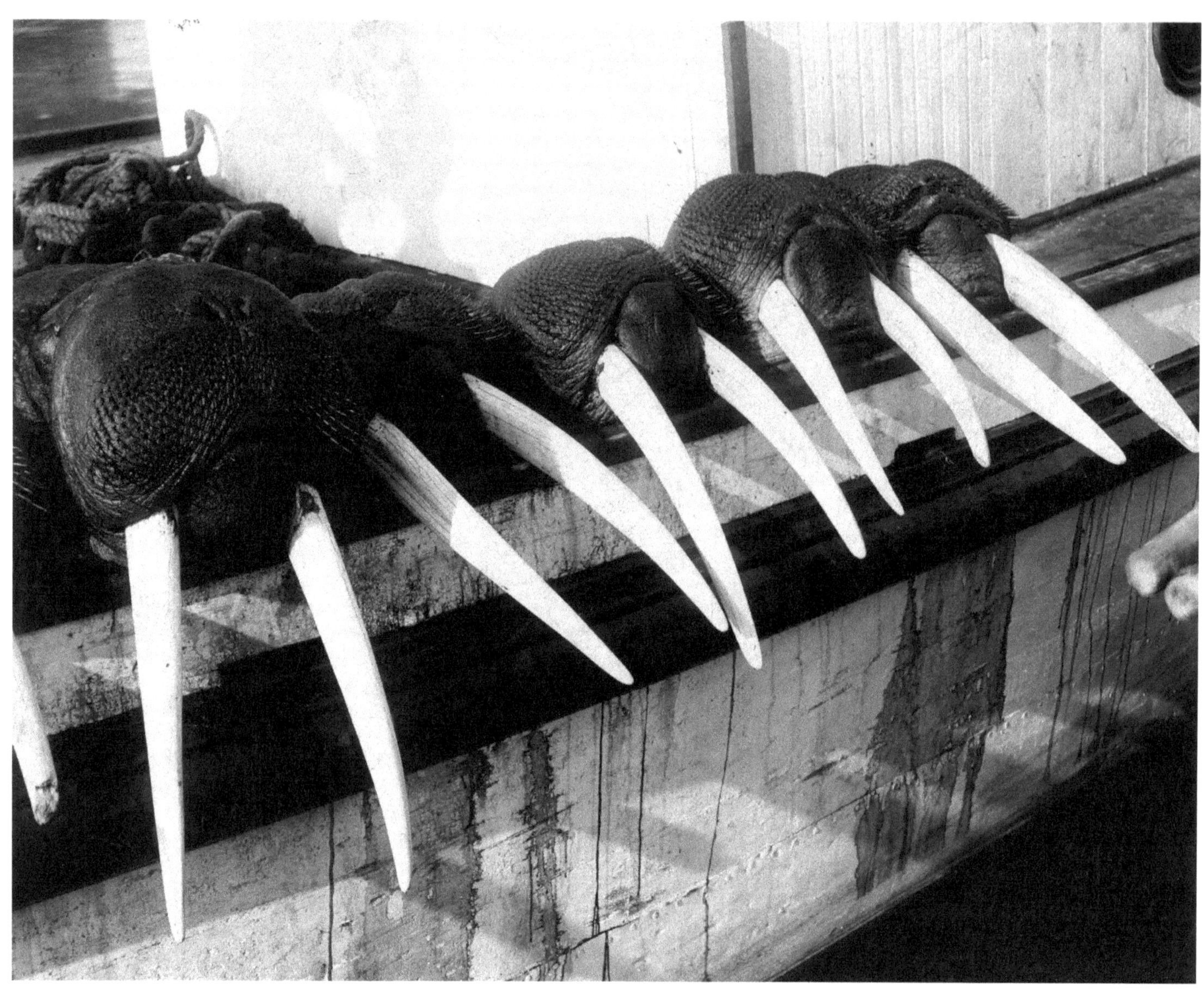

Walruses hunted in 1931 in the Bering Sea were valued for their tusks.

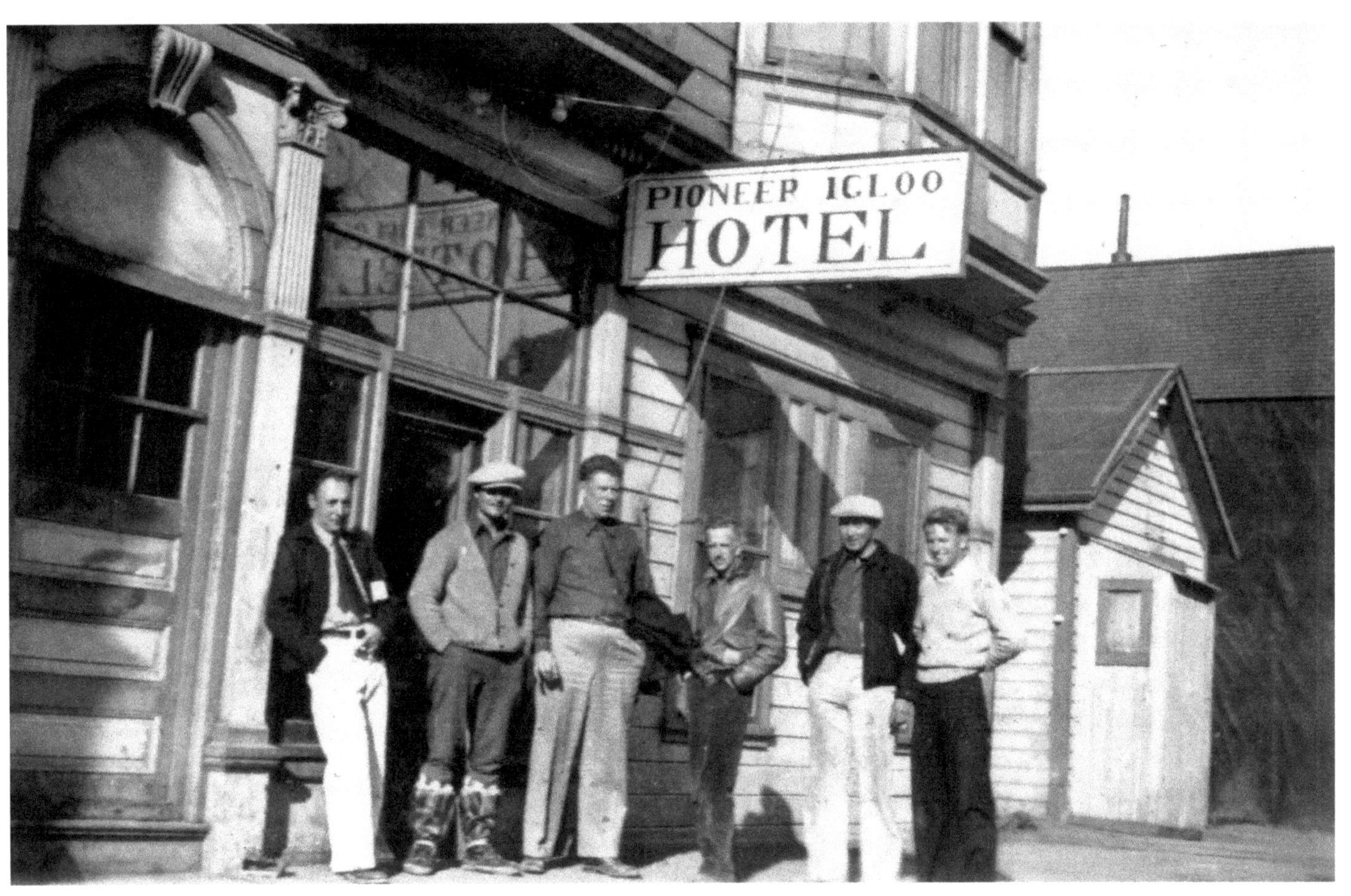

A film crew from the movie *Eskimo,* a docudrama mostly shot on location in Alaska during 1932–1933, poses outside a hotel. The MGM production starred Ray Wise, the son of an Anglo trader and an Eskimo mother, as Mala the Eskimo. He later acted under the screen name Ray Mala.

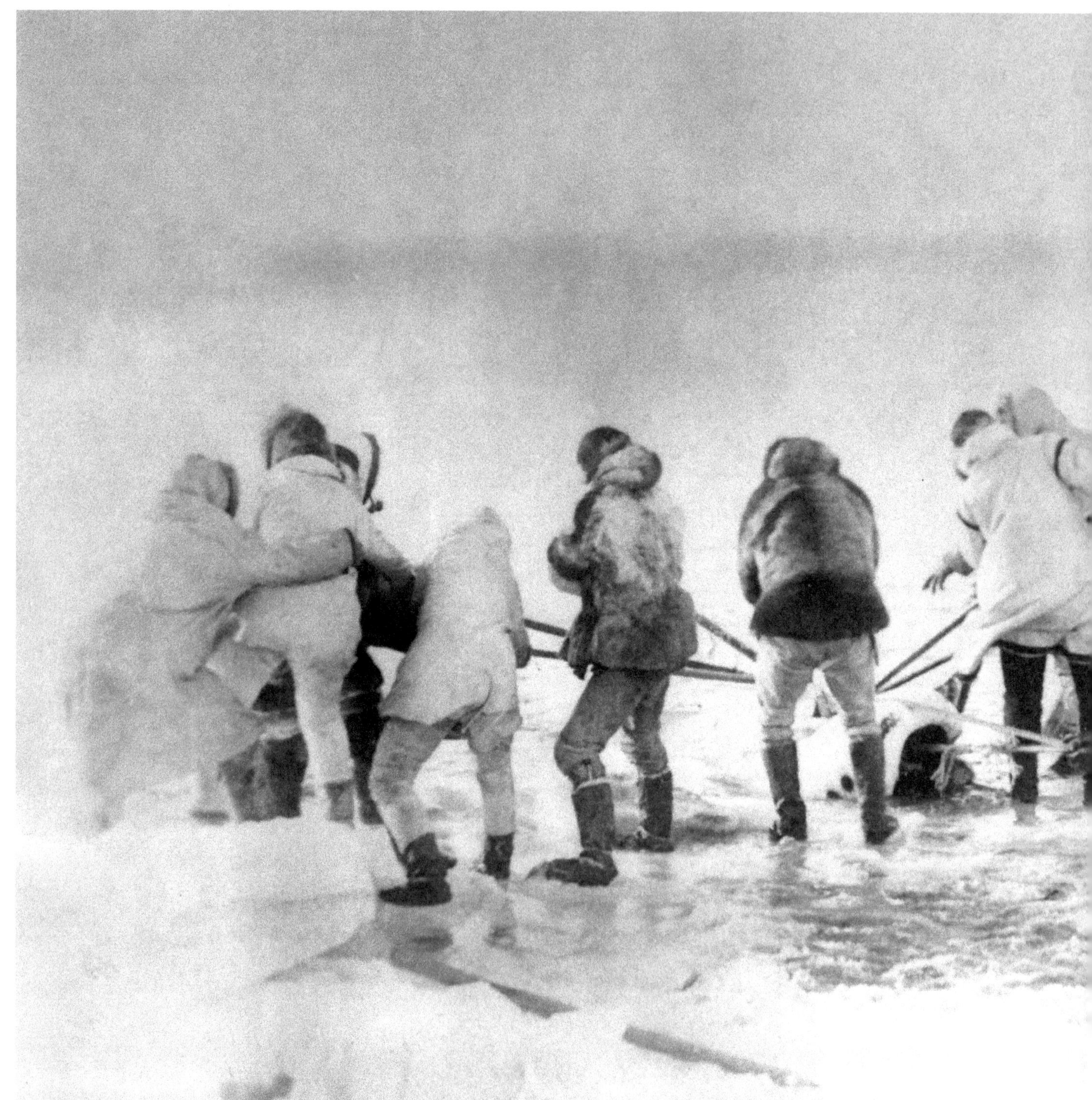

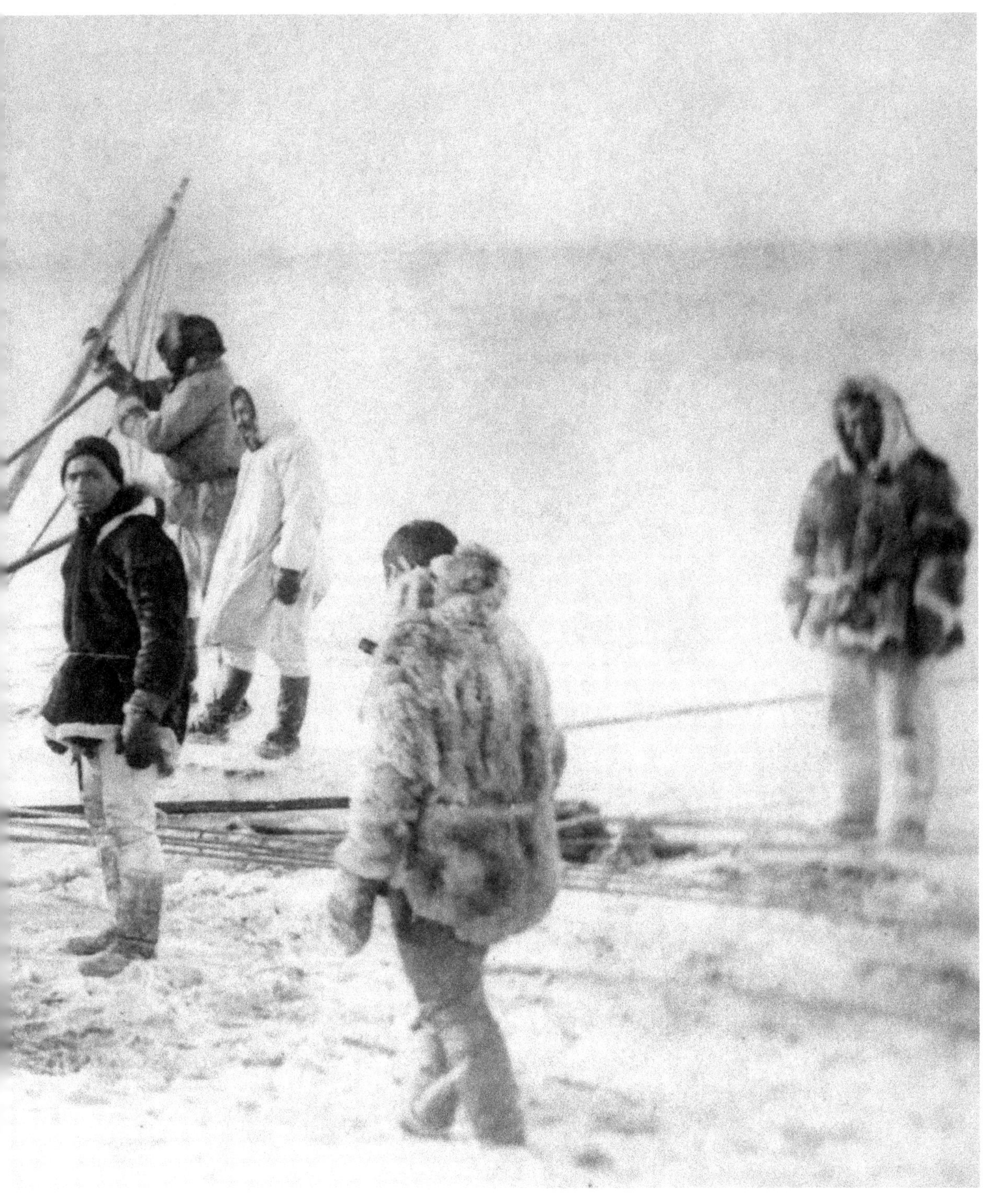

Frank Yasuda, facing the camera, was among the most prominent Japanese in Alaska. He won acclaim for his endurance and strength on long-distance journeys and for leading a cross-country trek and founding the village of Beaver. Here, he works with hunters who are landing and butchering a seal or small whale.

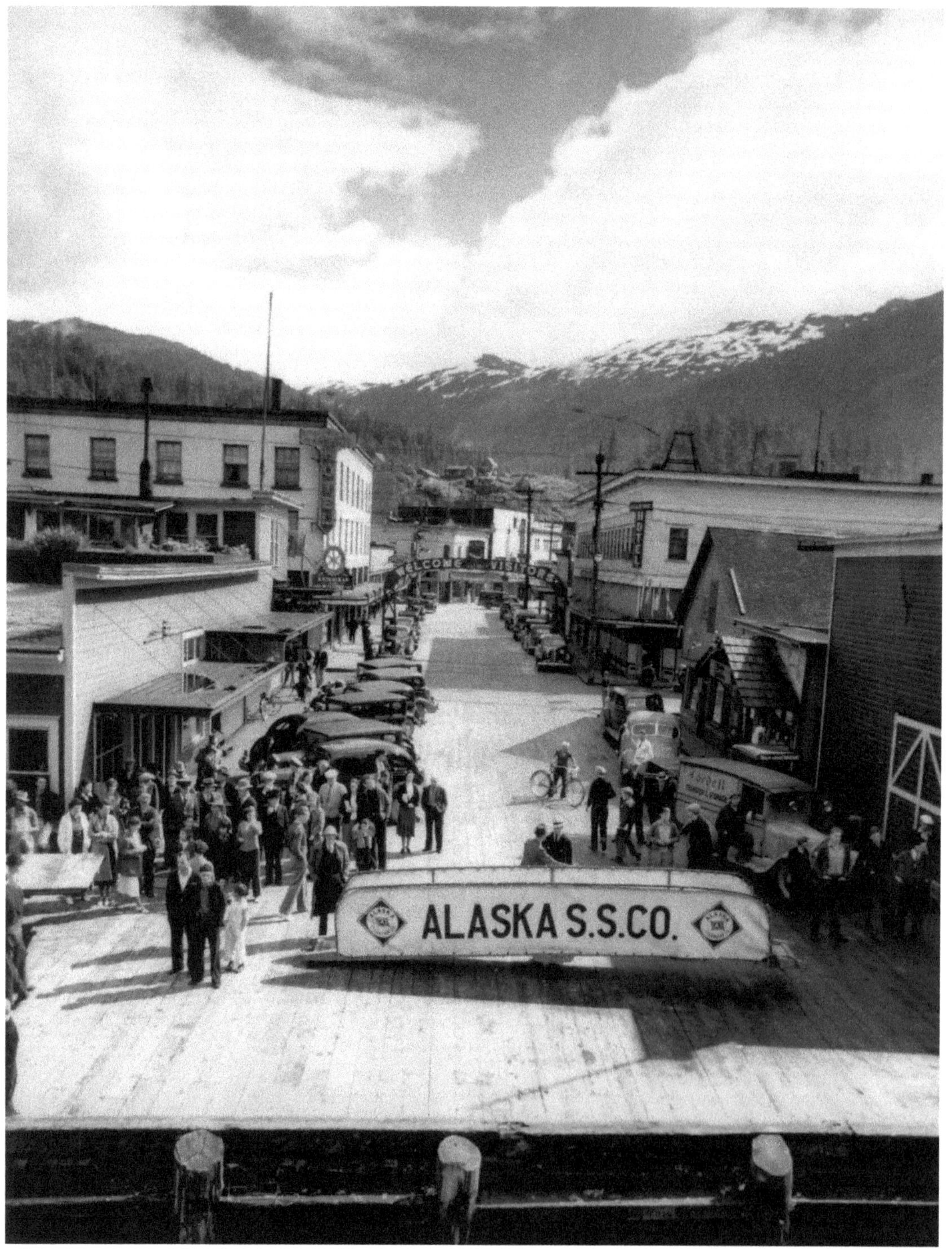

Ketchikan was the first steamship stop in Alaska for tourists and for residents returning home in this era.

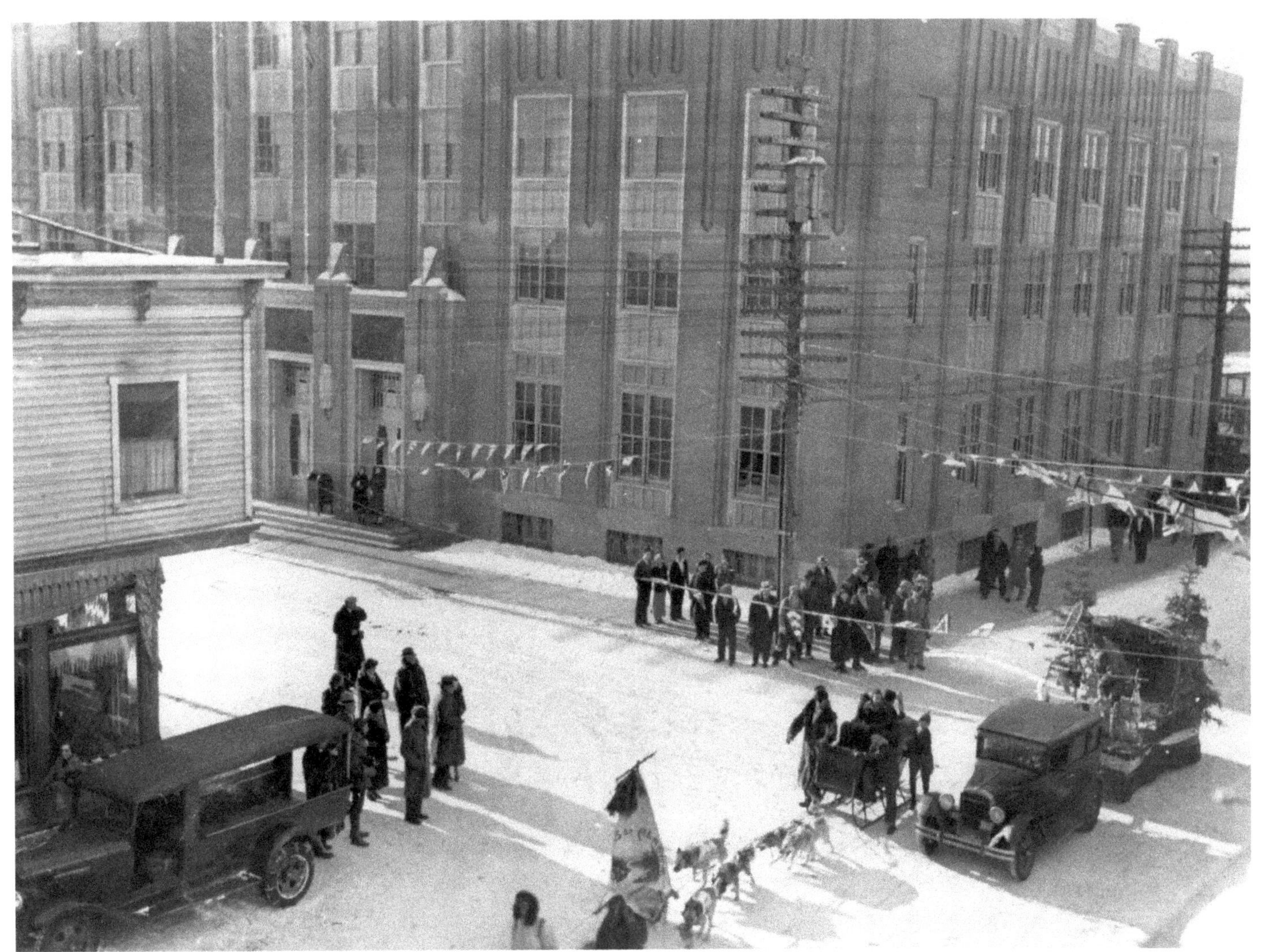

The Fairbanks Ice Carnival parade in 1935 crosses Cushman Street along Second Avenue. The new federal courthouse and post office is in the background.

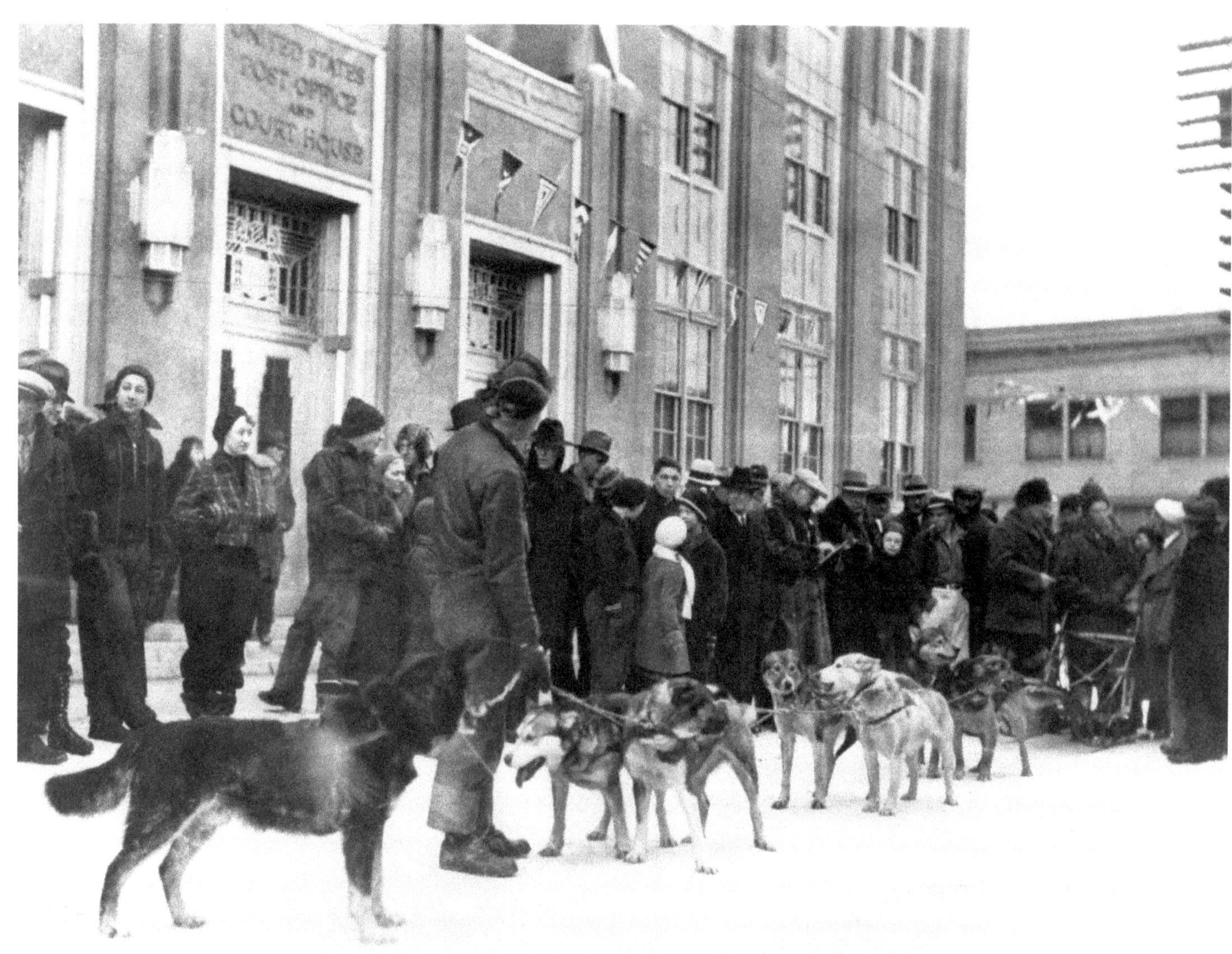

Spectators, along with a musher and dog team, gather outside the new Fairbanks federal building during the 1935 Fairbanks Dog Derby.

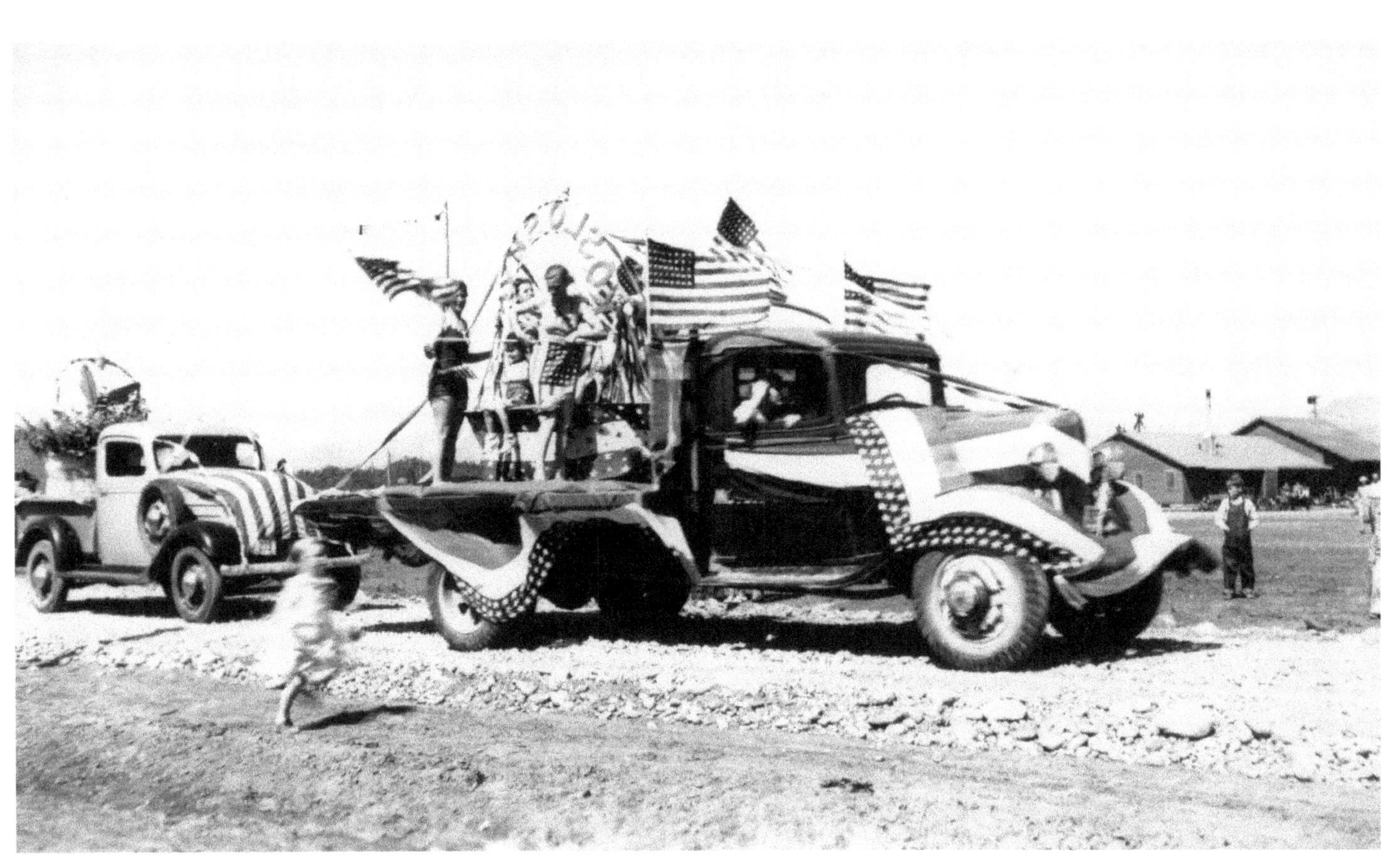

The Grange float in the Palmer Fourth of July parade in 1936 strikes a patriotic note. The preceding year, the Matanuska Valley colonists had arrived as part of a New Deal initiative to deal with the Depression.

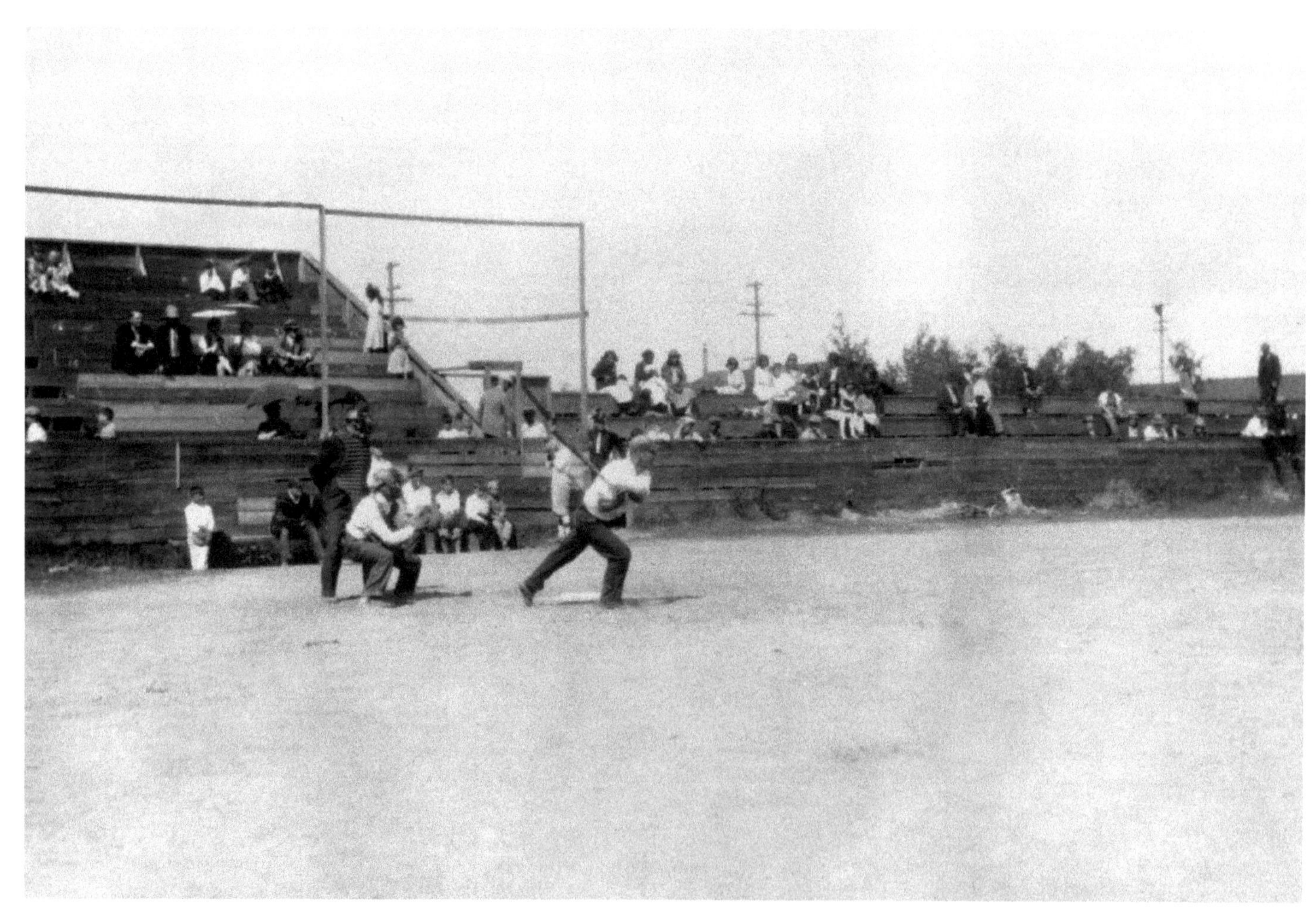

A small Anchorage crowd watches a baseball game in the late 1930s.

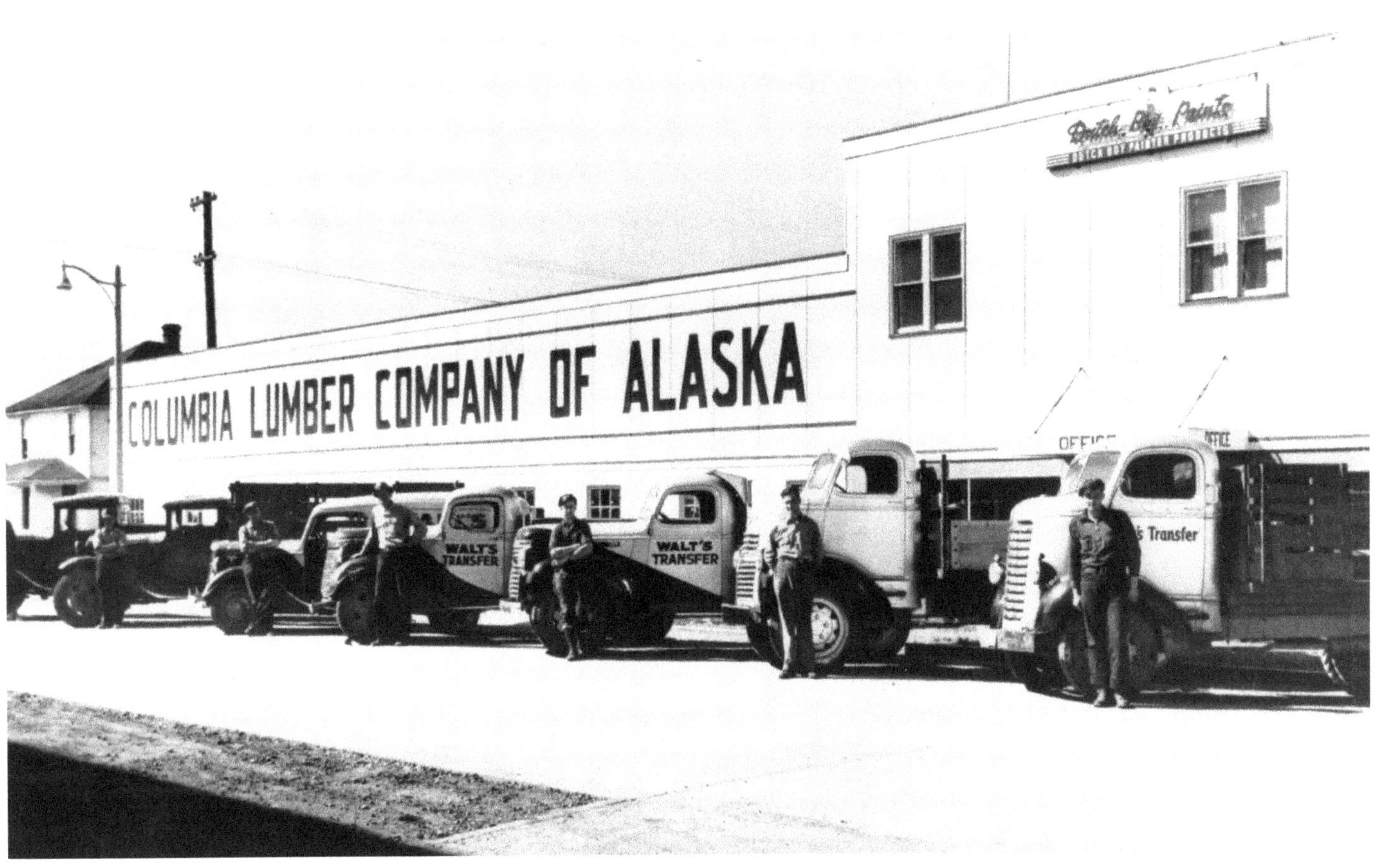

The drivers of Walt's Transfer Co. in Anchorage stand with their trucks for a company publicity shot.

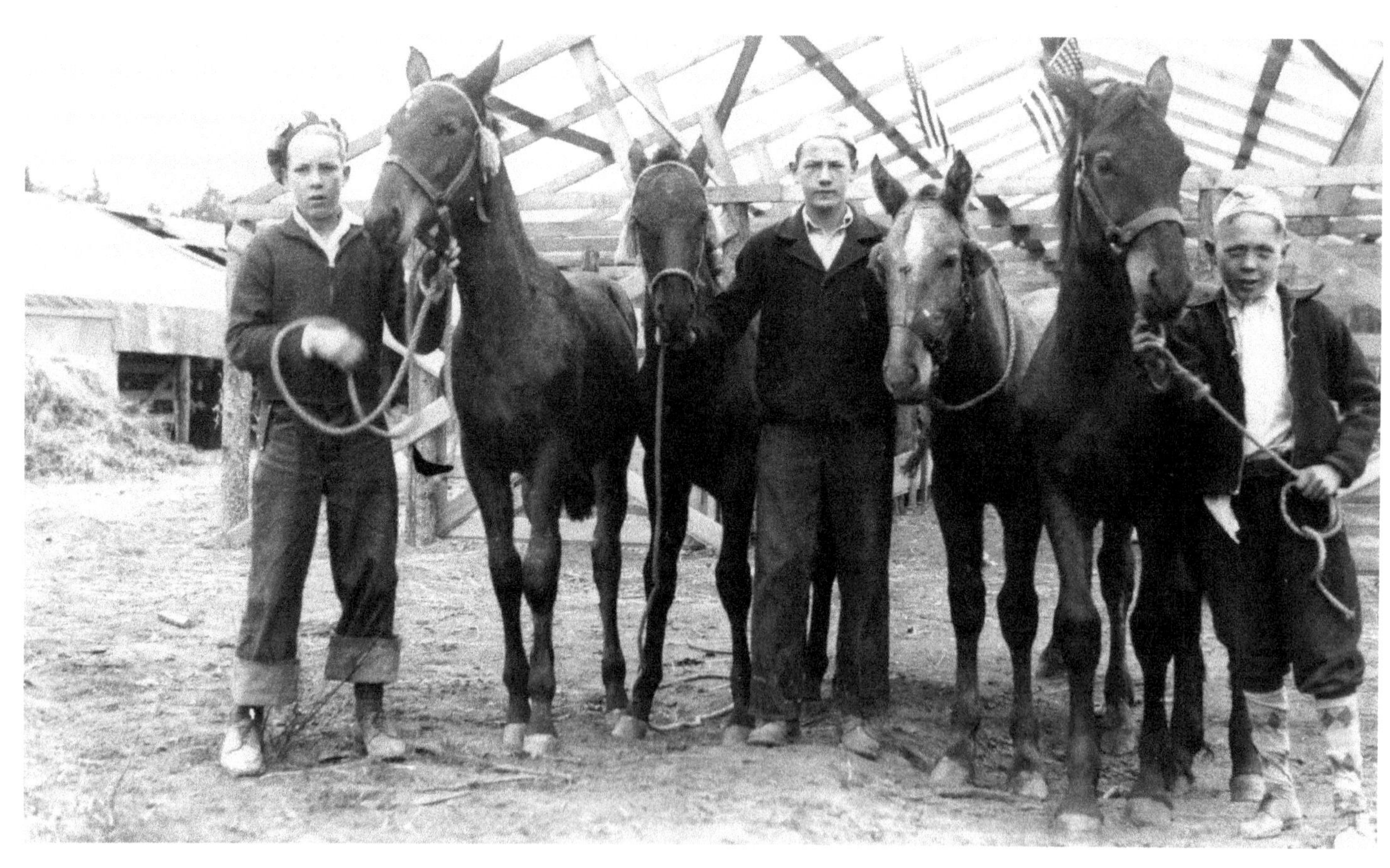

Members of the 4-H club in Palmer exhibited their horses at the annual fair there in 1936.

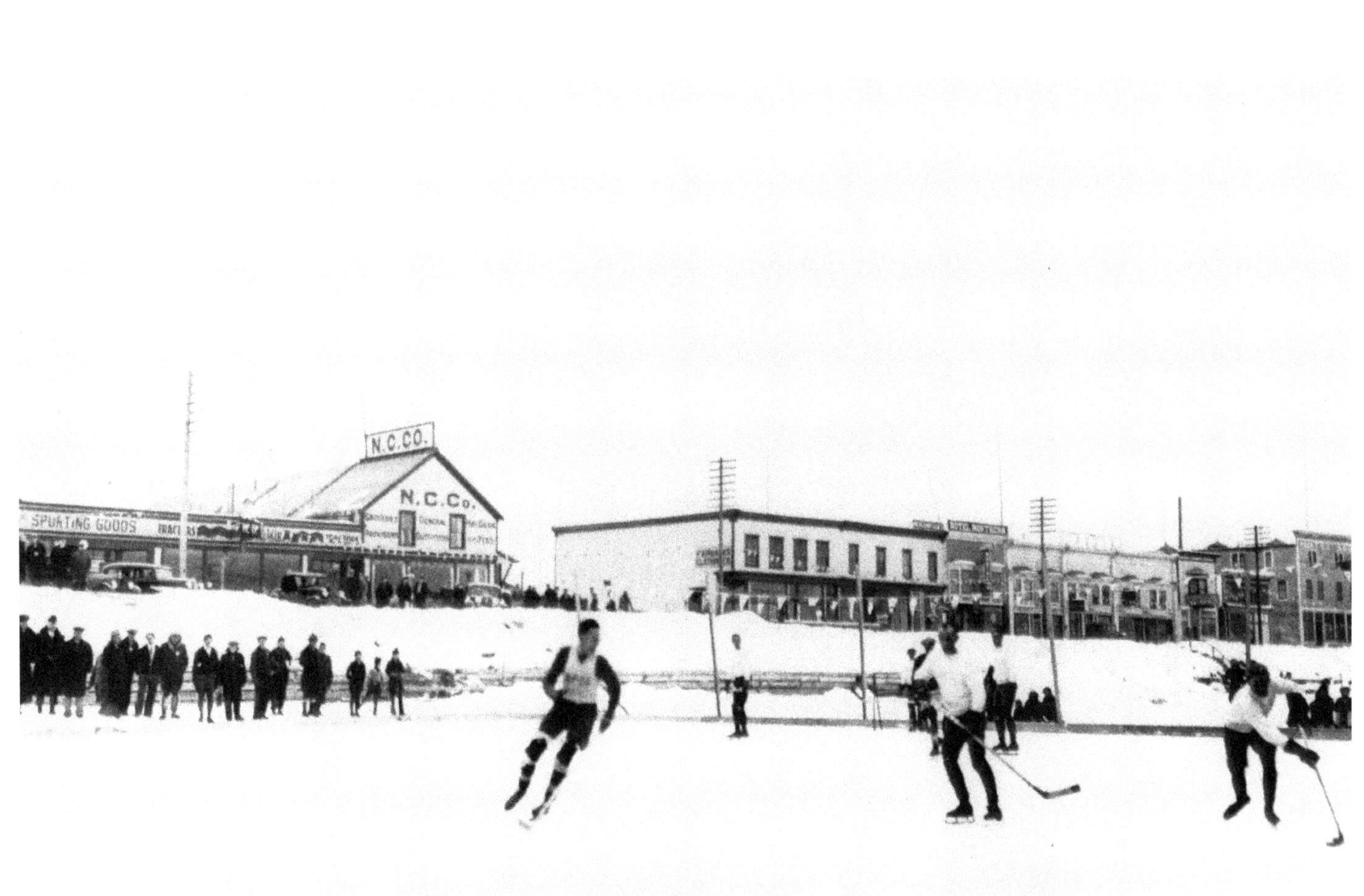

The frozen Chena River in Fairbanks made for an ideal outdoor rink in the late 1930s, and the fledgling local hockey program had no problem finding players to lace up their skates.

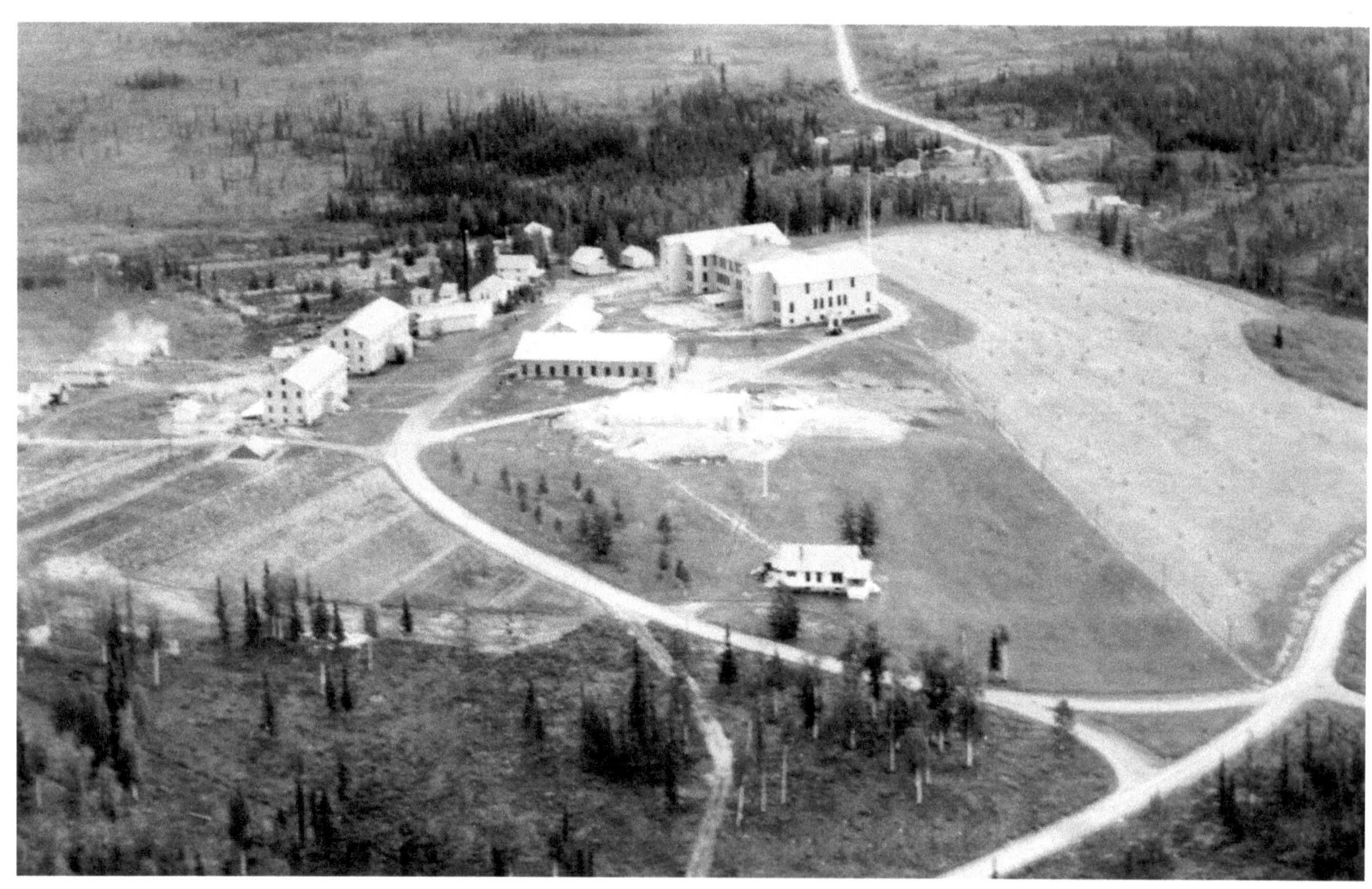

The Alaska Agricultural College and School of Mines in Fairbanks, which became the University of Alaska in 1935, grew into a cultural and educational center on a hill four miles west of town.

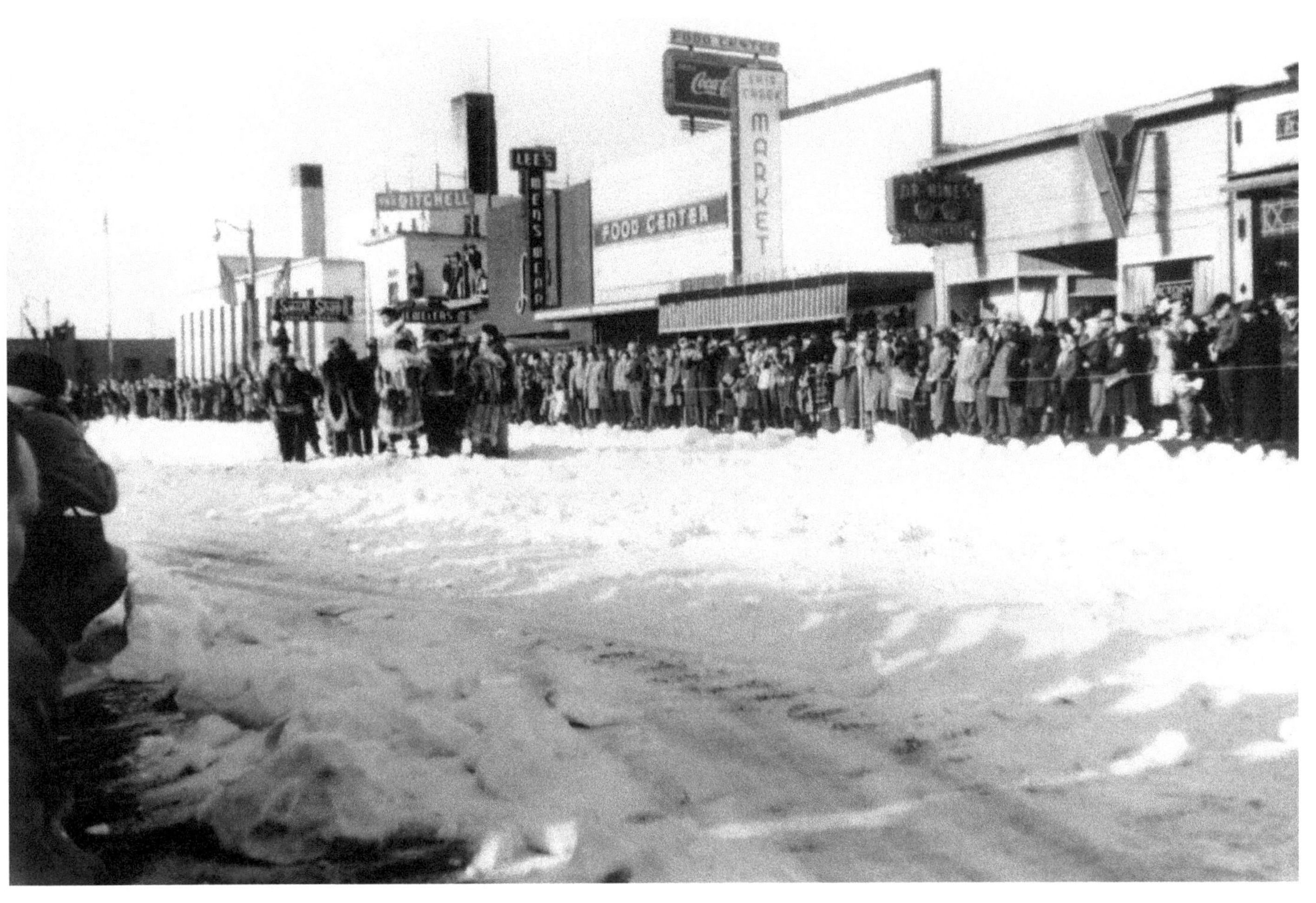

The Fur Rendezvous Parade on Fourth Avenue in Anchorage was a chance to celebrate the approach of spring and to get people out and about after a long winter.

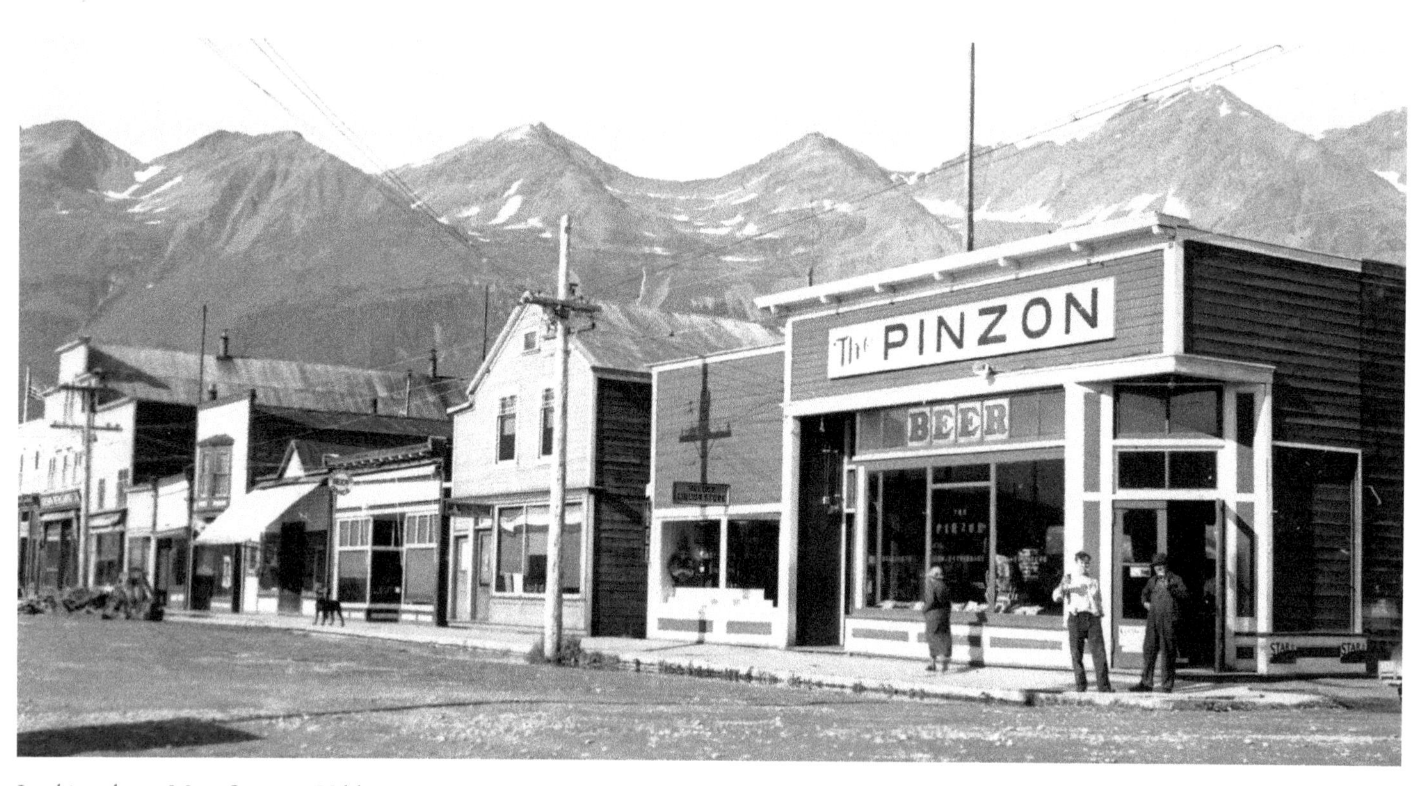

Looking down Main Street in Valdez in 1937. It was no longer a boom town, but as one visitor put it, "Civic pride has by no means died out in this town out on the toes of a glacier."

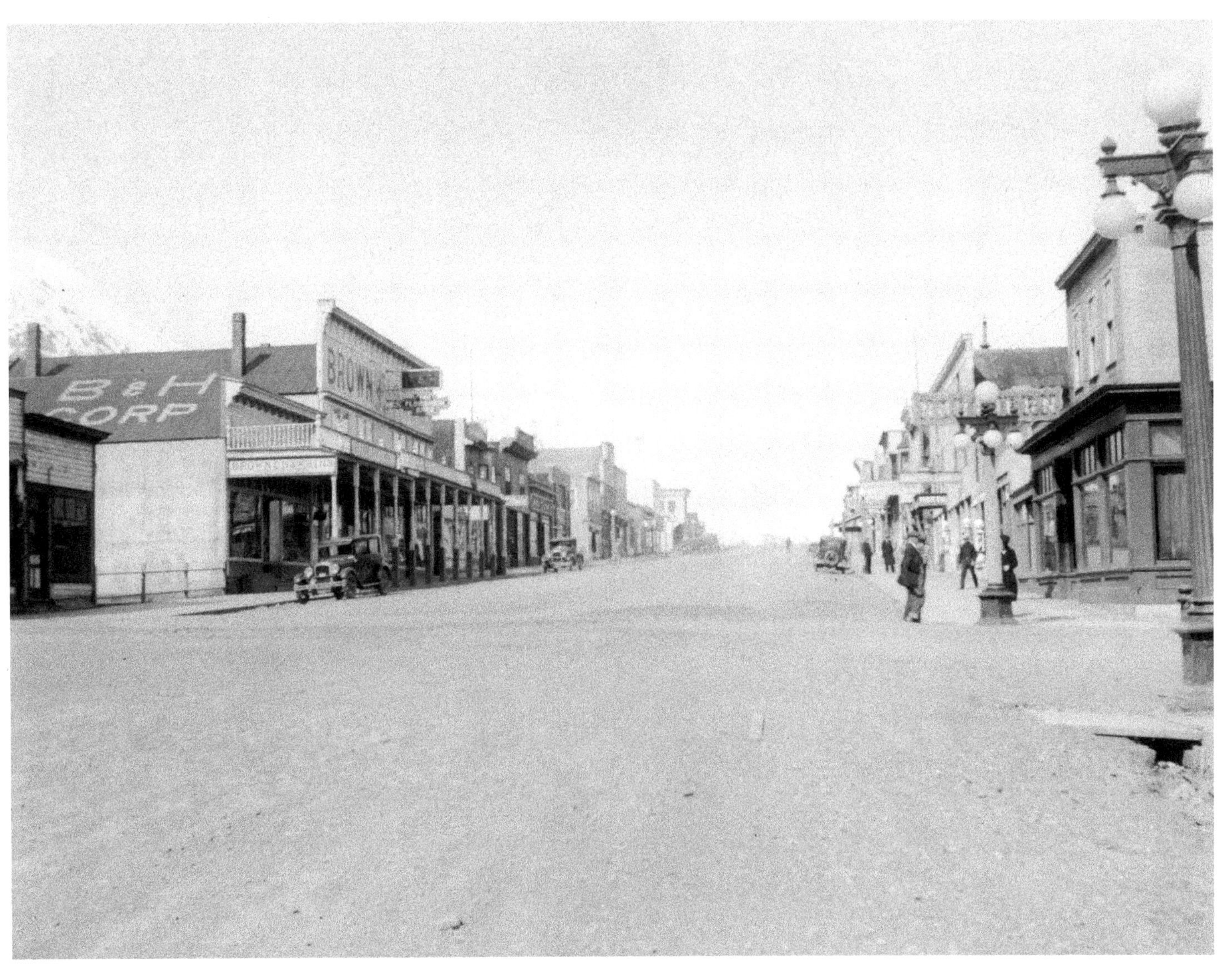

Nome in the summer of 1937, two years after a disastrous fire wiped out much of downtown.

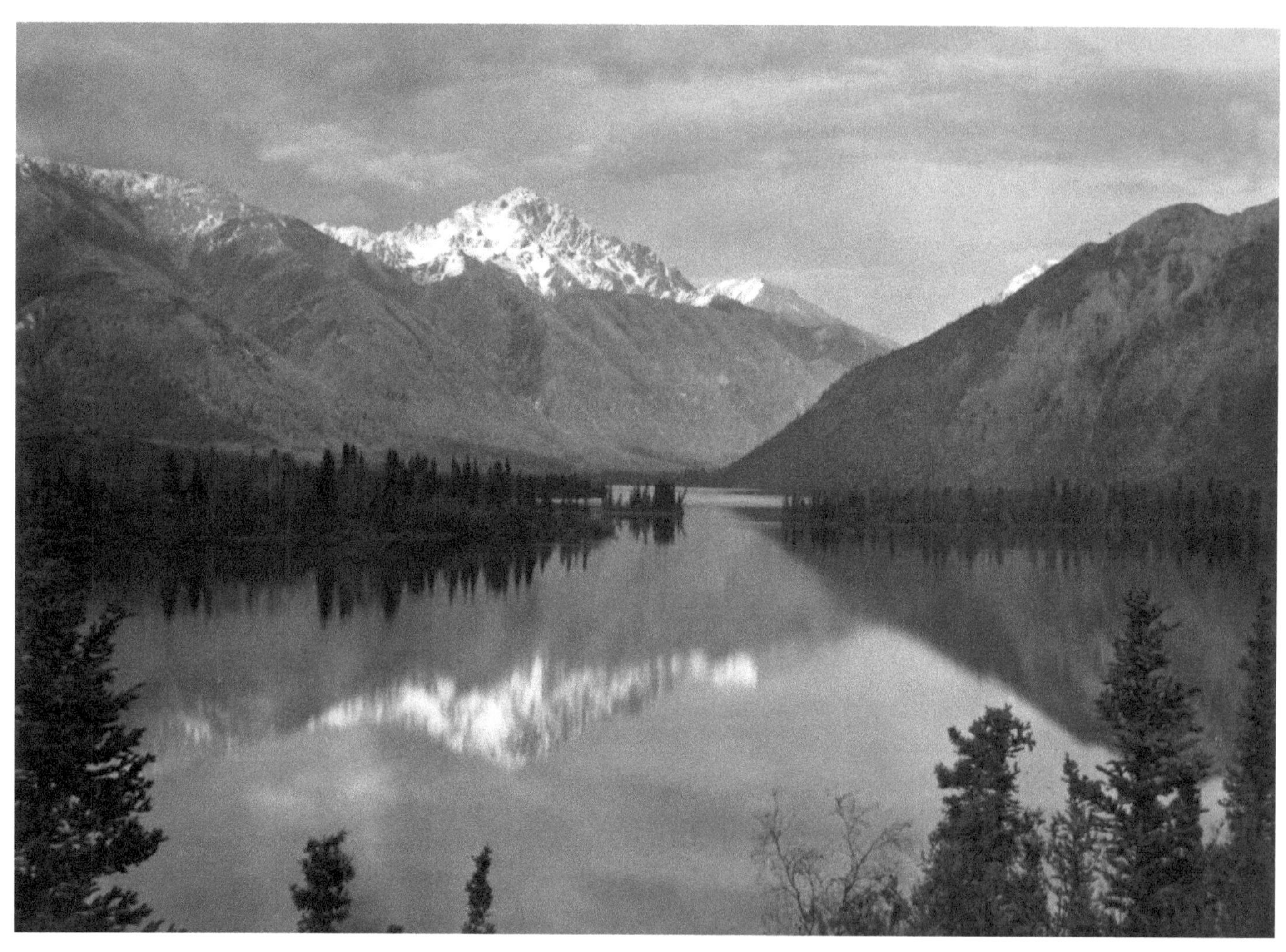

A view of Mentasta Lake, with trees and snow-covered mountains reflected on the water. Views such as this would draw tens of thousands of visitors annually as access to the state improved.

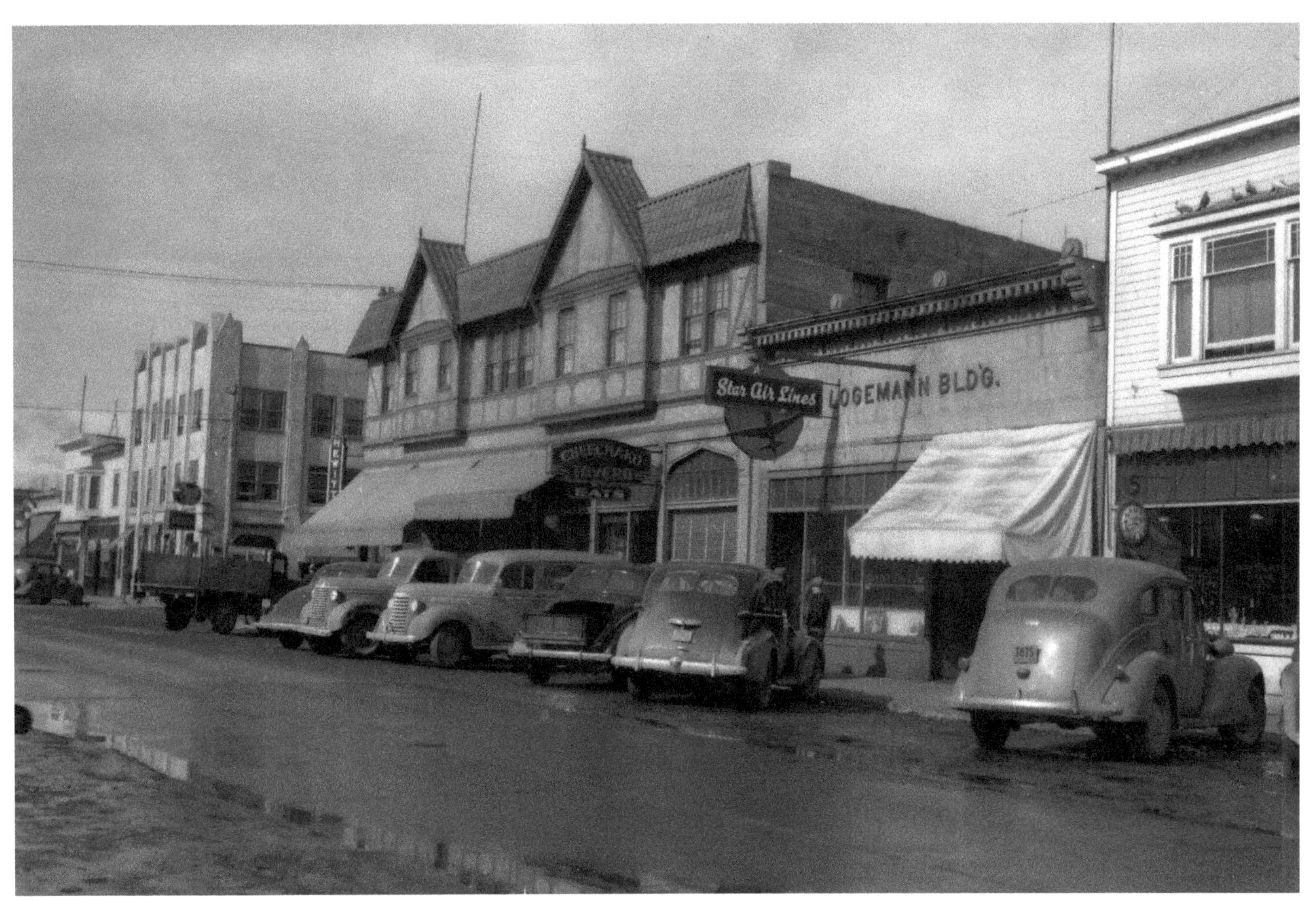

The main commercial district of Anchorage in 1937, marked by continued growth along Fourth Avenue.

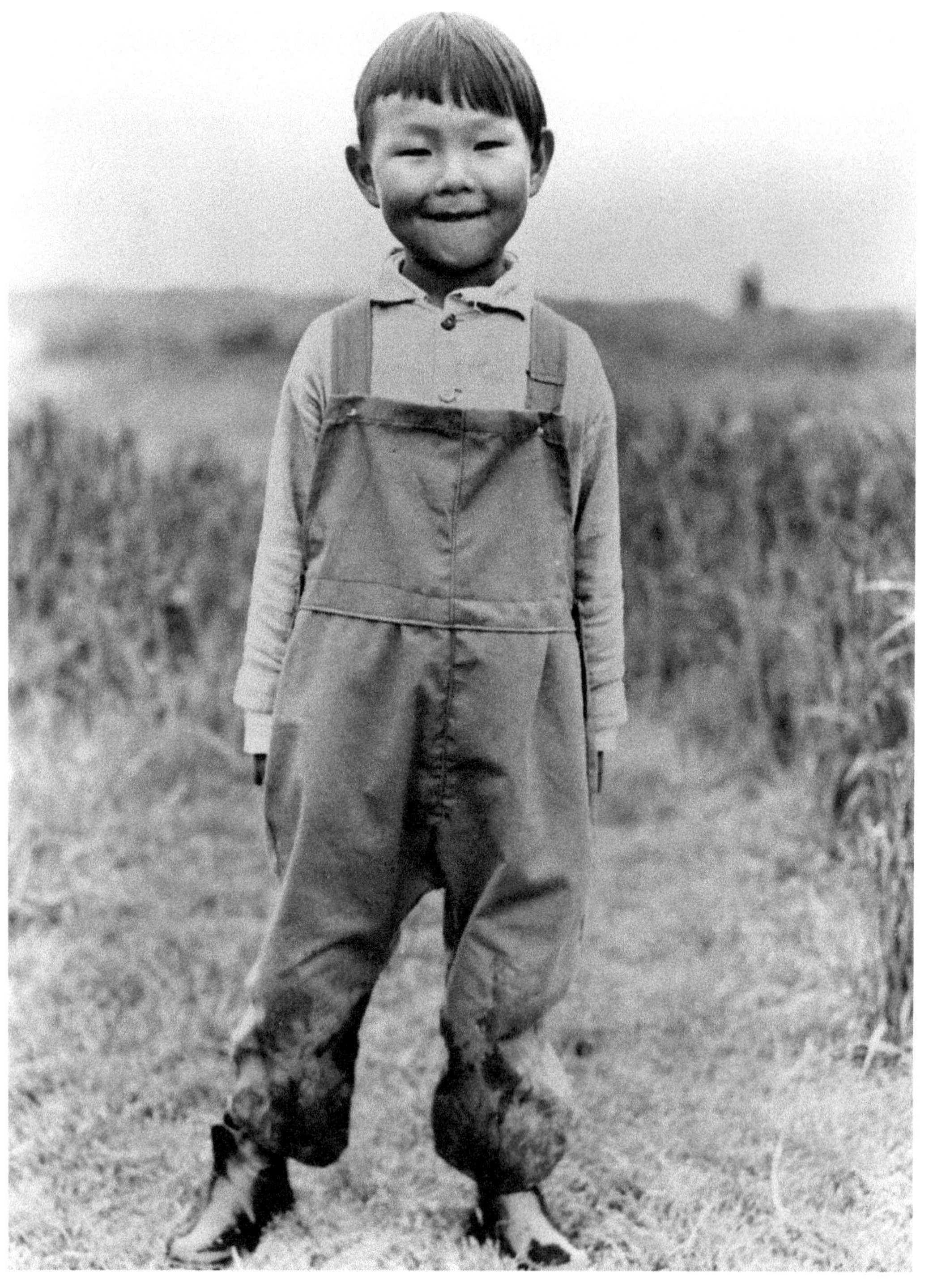

An Aleut boy in his overalls smiles for the camera during a 1938 encounter with a photographer.

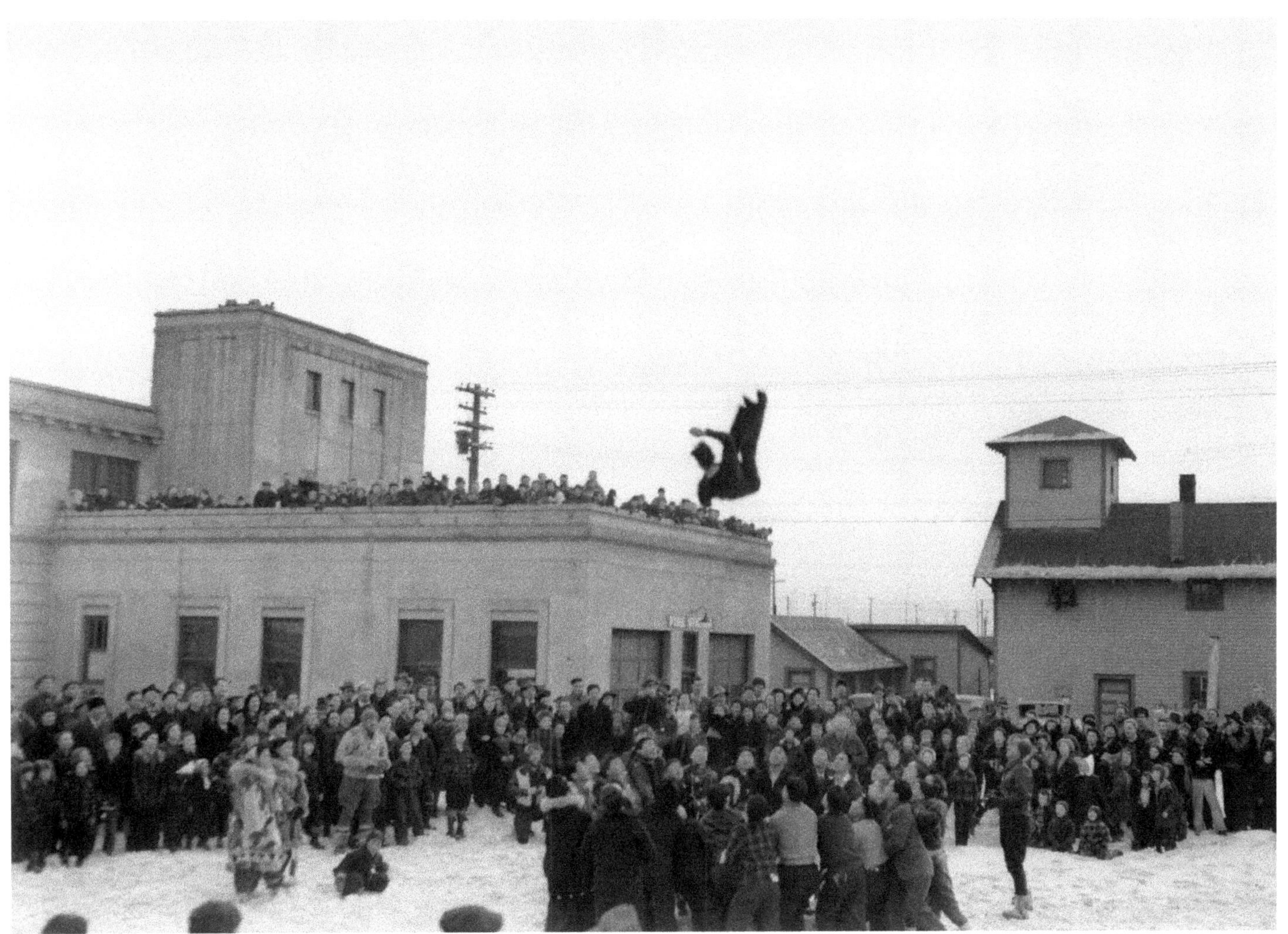

Everyone on the blanket-toss crew during the 1940 Anchorage Fur Rendezvous looks skyward, both to stay under the man being tossed and to prepare to propel him even higher.

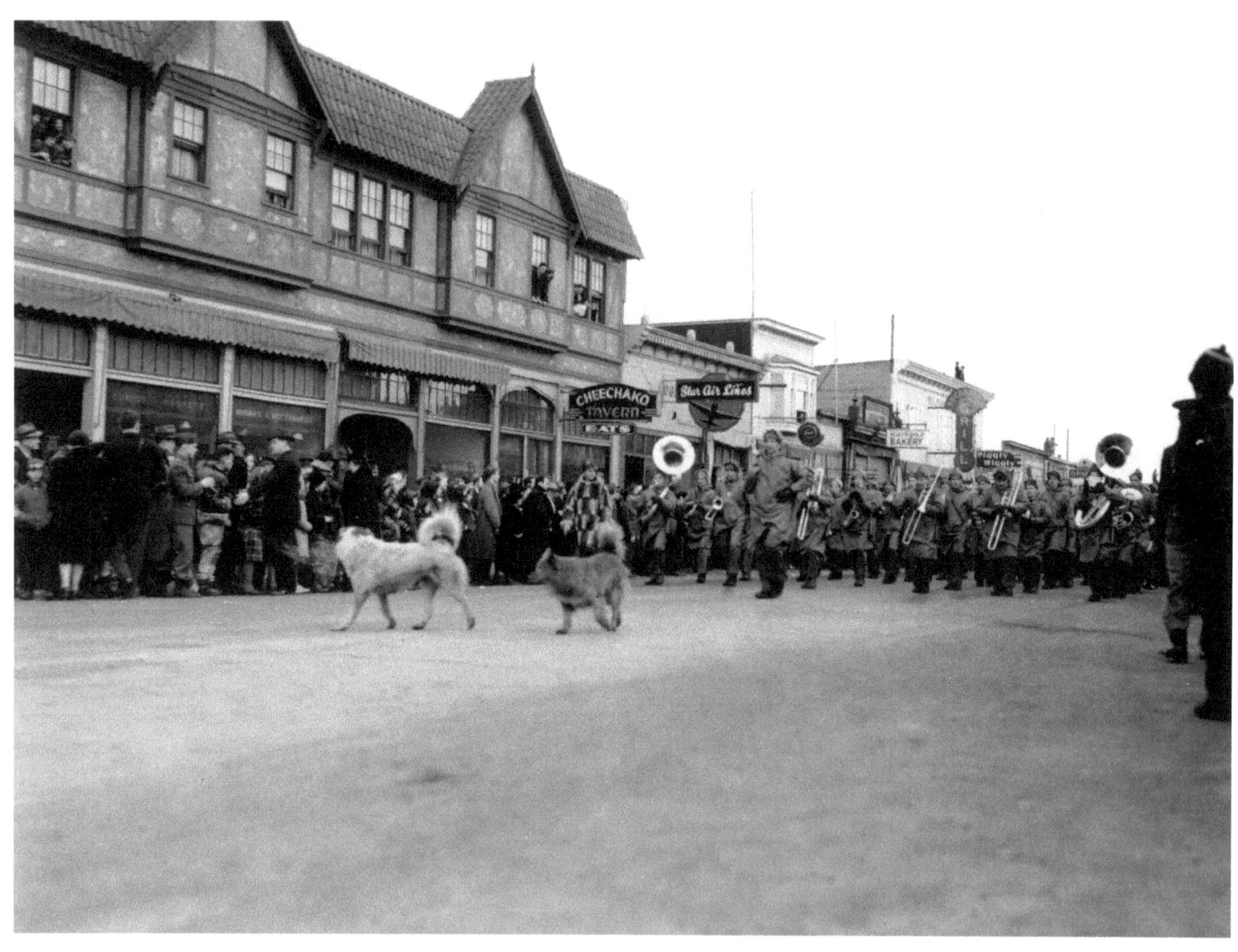

In the 1941 Fur Rendezvous parade, the Army band takes to the streets in Anchorage, along with a couple of loose dogs, passing by the Cheechako Tavern, Star Air Lines, and the North Pole Bakery.

The Long Road to Statehood

(1941–1979)

The drive for self-government has been one of the enduring themes during Alaska's entire history under the American flag. The first bill to grant statehood was introduced in 1916 by Alaska Delegate James Wickersham, who argued that the territory was destined to represent the forty-ninth star on the flag.

The country wasn't ready to act on Wickersham's plan, however, and several decades would pass before the political climate warmed enough to allow statehood for Alaska.

During World War II and in the years that followed, hundreds of millions of dollars were spent to build up military installations, and thousands of people migrated north. They soon began to consider themselves second-class citizens, recognizing that as Alaskans they could not vote for president and had no voting representation in Congress.

The statehood campaign gathered strength in the late 1940s and throughout the 1950s, culminating with action by Congress in the summer of 1958. On January 3, 1959, President Dwight D. Eisenhower signed the proclamation admitting Alaska as the forty-ninth state.

The statehood agreement allowed Alaska to select 103 million acres of land for state ownership, an entitlement the size of California. The land grant was a generous one because it was expected that otherwise Alaska would never be able to stand on its own.

For the first decade of statehood, it appeared that the critics were right and that Alaska could not afford to be a state. The government struggled to keep afloat and matters were made worse by the devastation of the Good Friday earthquake in 1964, among the largest quakes ever recorded.

It turned out that those who believed the financial future of the state was in its land holdings were right, however. Among the lands selected for state ownership were those on the North Slope of Alaska near Prudhoe Bay.

In 1968, after a long search, the oil industry discovered the biggest oil field ever found in North America. The oil strike revolutionized Alaska the way the gold strikes did nearly 70 years earlier.

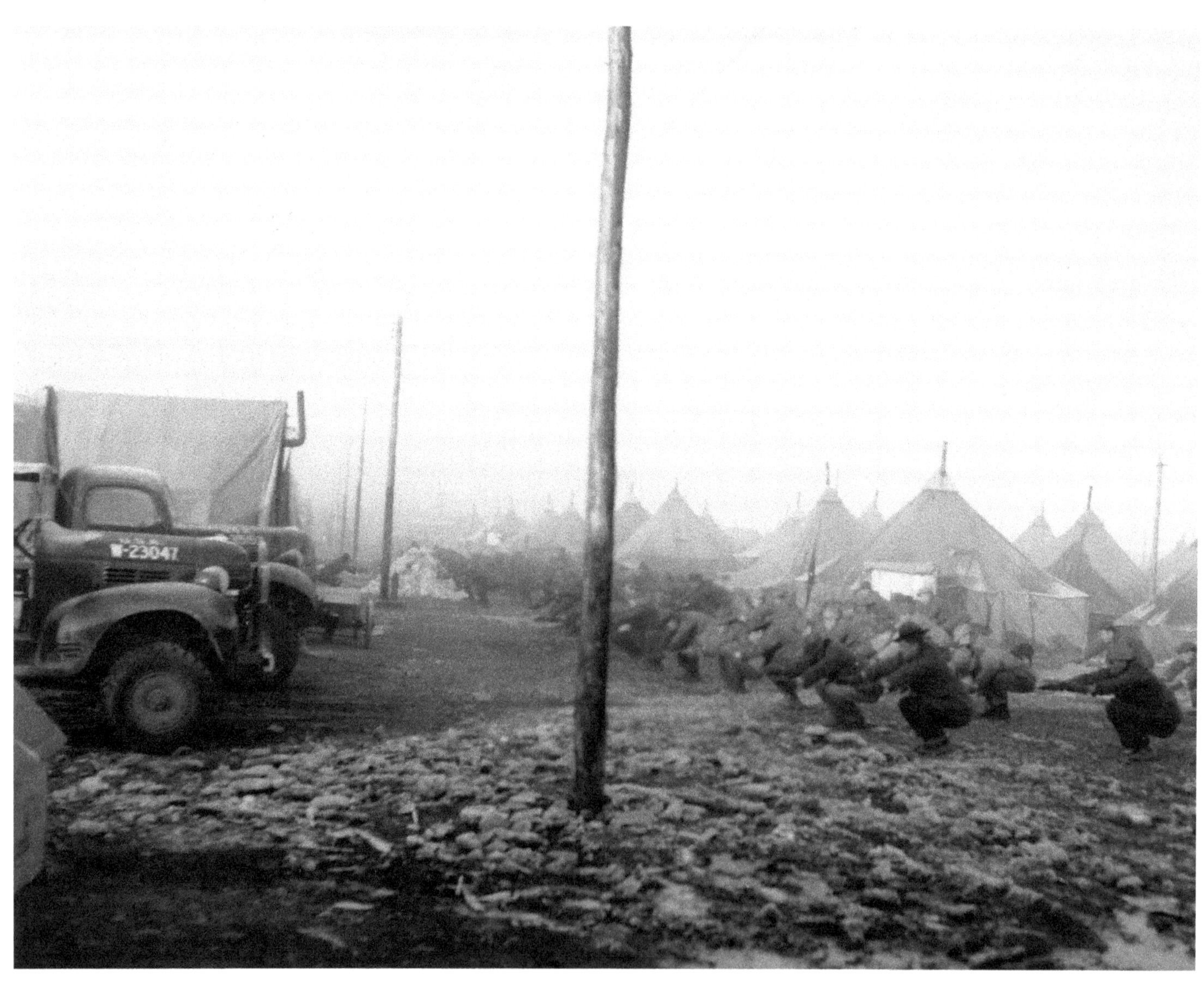

Soldiers bend and stretch to get limbered up at Fort Richardson in Anchorage, one of the first major military installations in the territory.

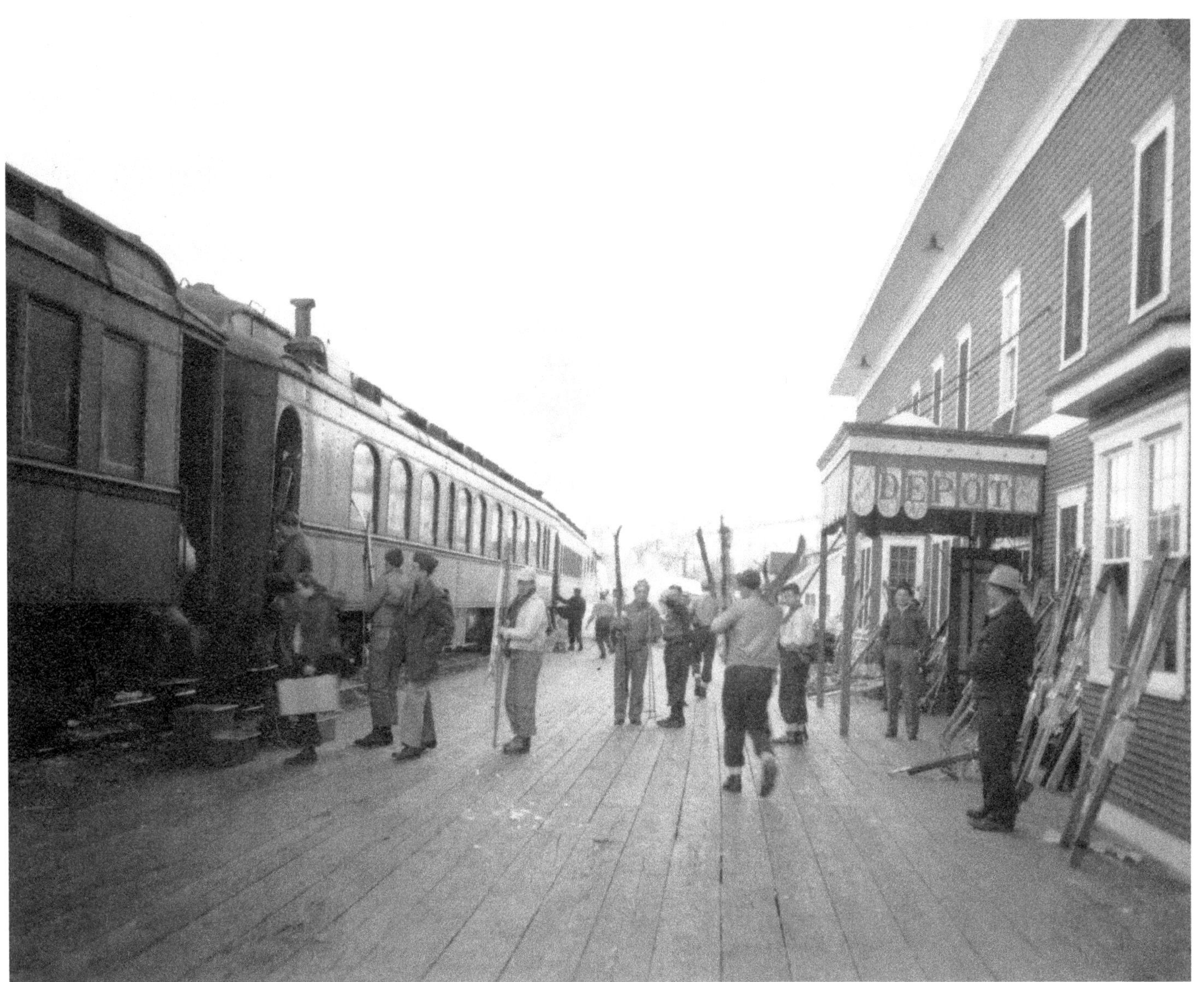

With their skis in hand, passengers board the Alaska Railroad ski train in Curry, preparing to return to Anchorage after trying out the snow, followed by an overnight stop near Talkeetna.

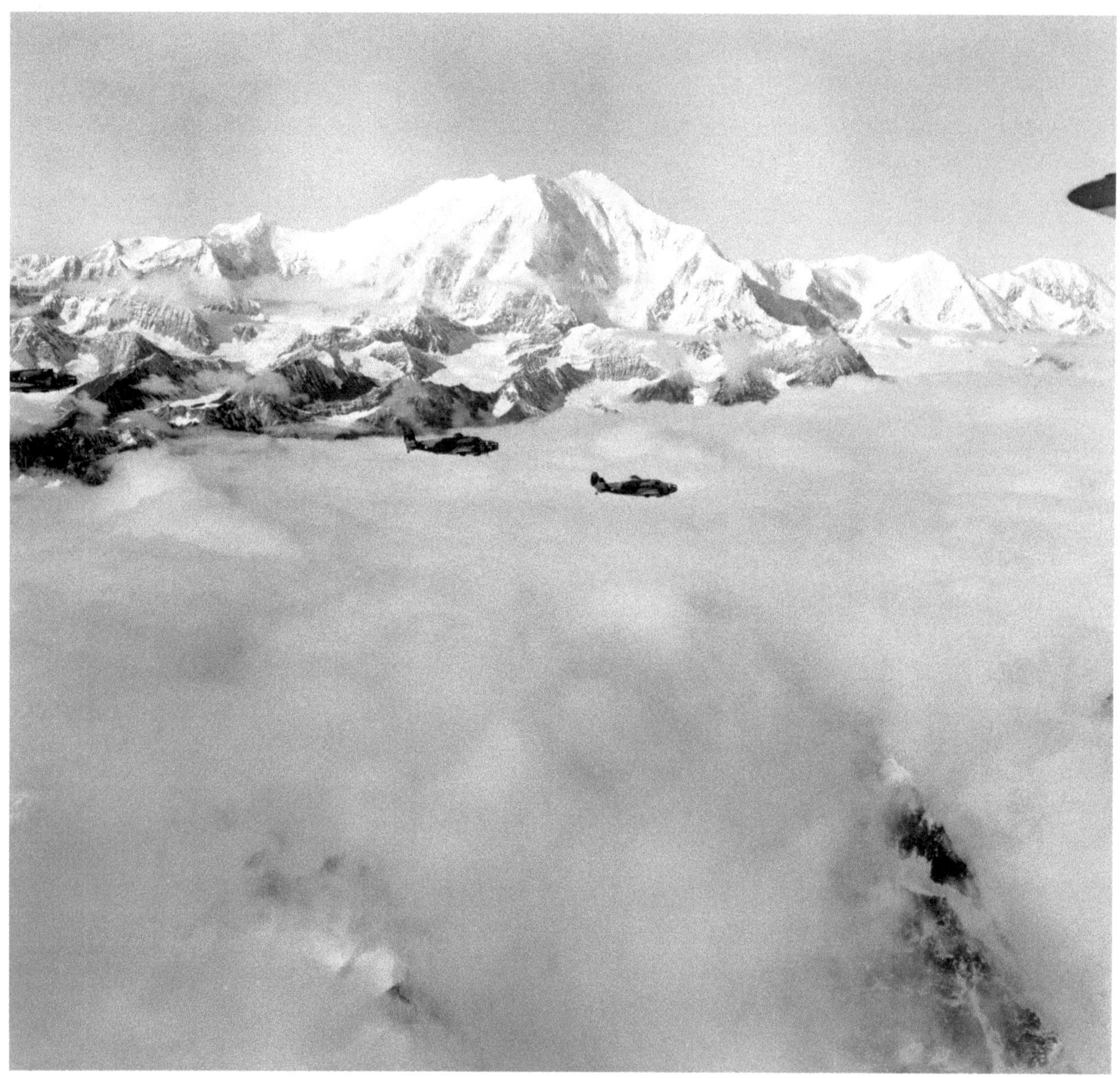

American Lockheed A-29s fly near Mount McKinley in February 1942. After the attack on Pearl Harbor, concerns that Alaska might be next gave new urgency to a military buildup that had started a couple of years earlier.

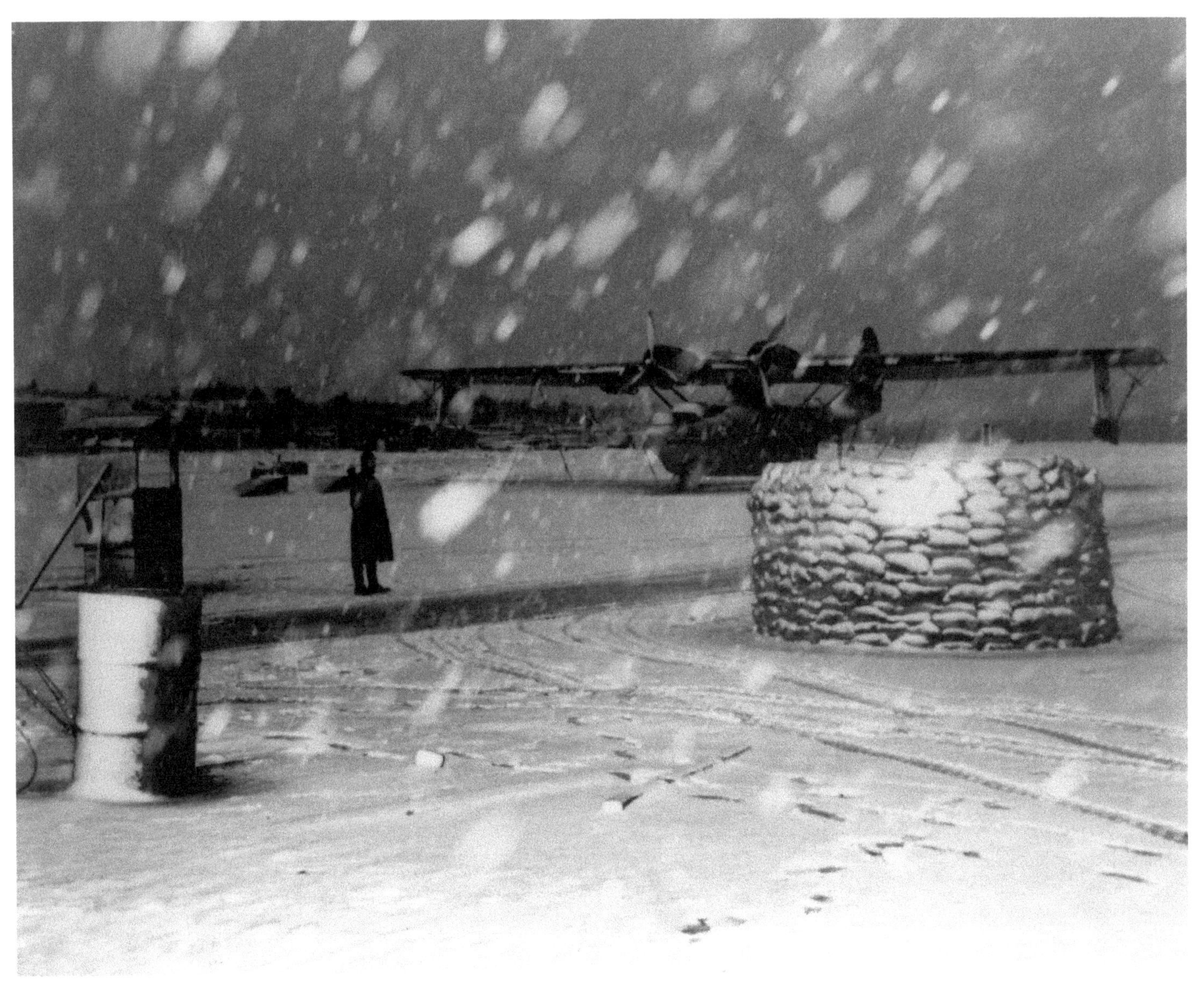

A Navy plane on the ground during a snowstorm in Kodiak on March 20, 1942.

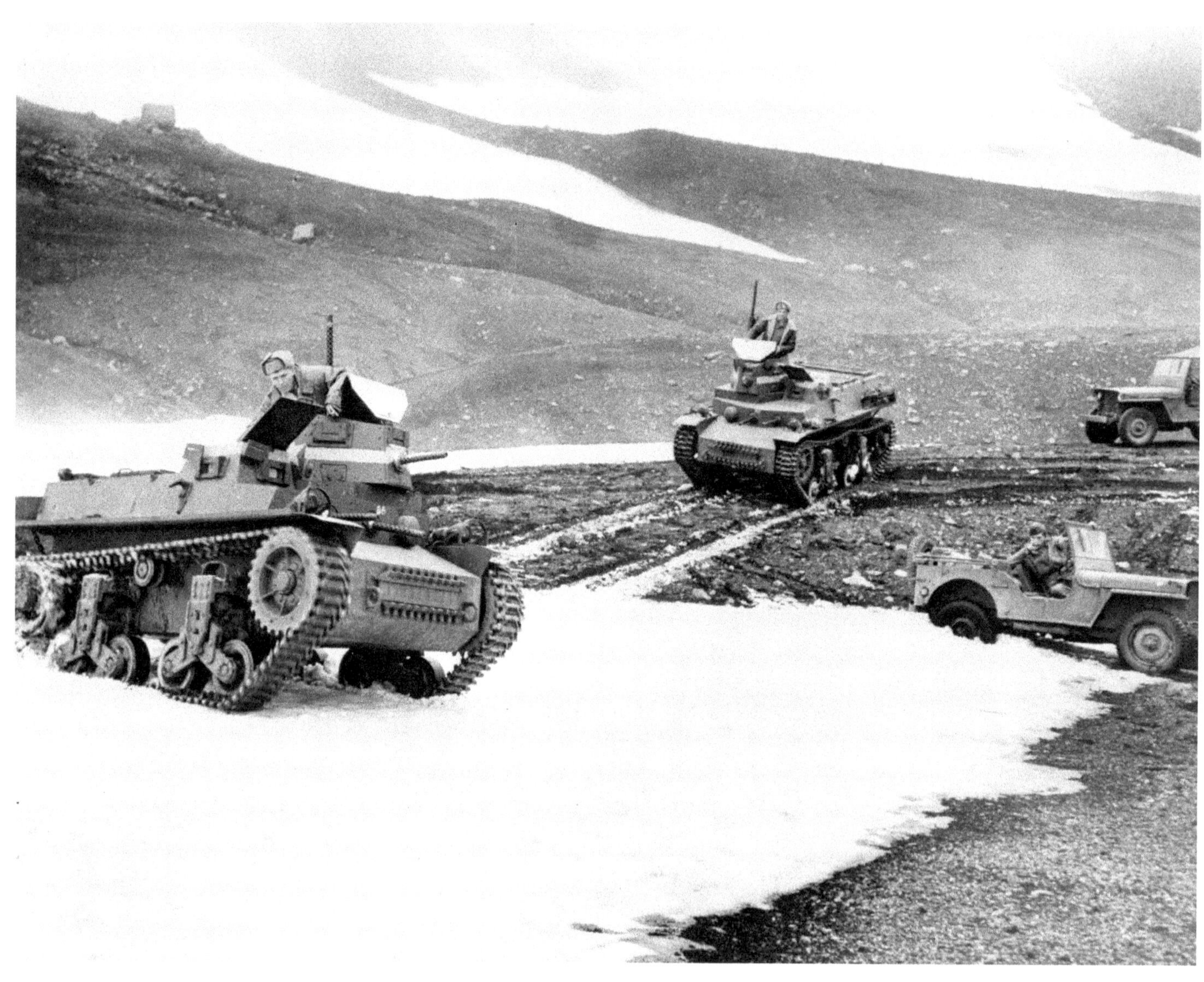

Two-man T16 light tanks maneuver in a mountain pass in Alaska in the summer of 1942. Only 240 of these four-ton vehicles were manufactured, primarily for use by America's allies China and the Netherlands East Indies. Very few were used by the U.S. Army.

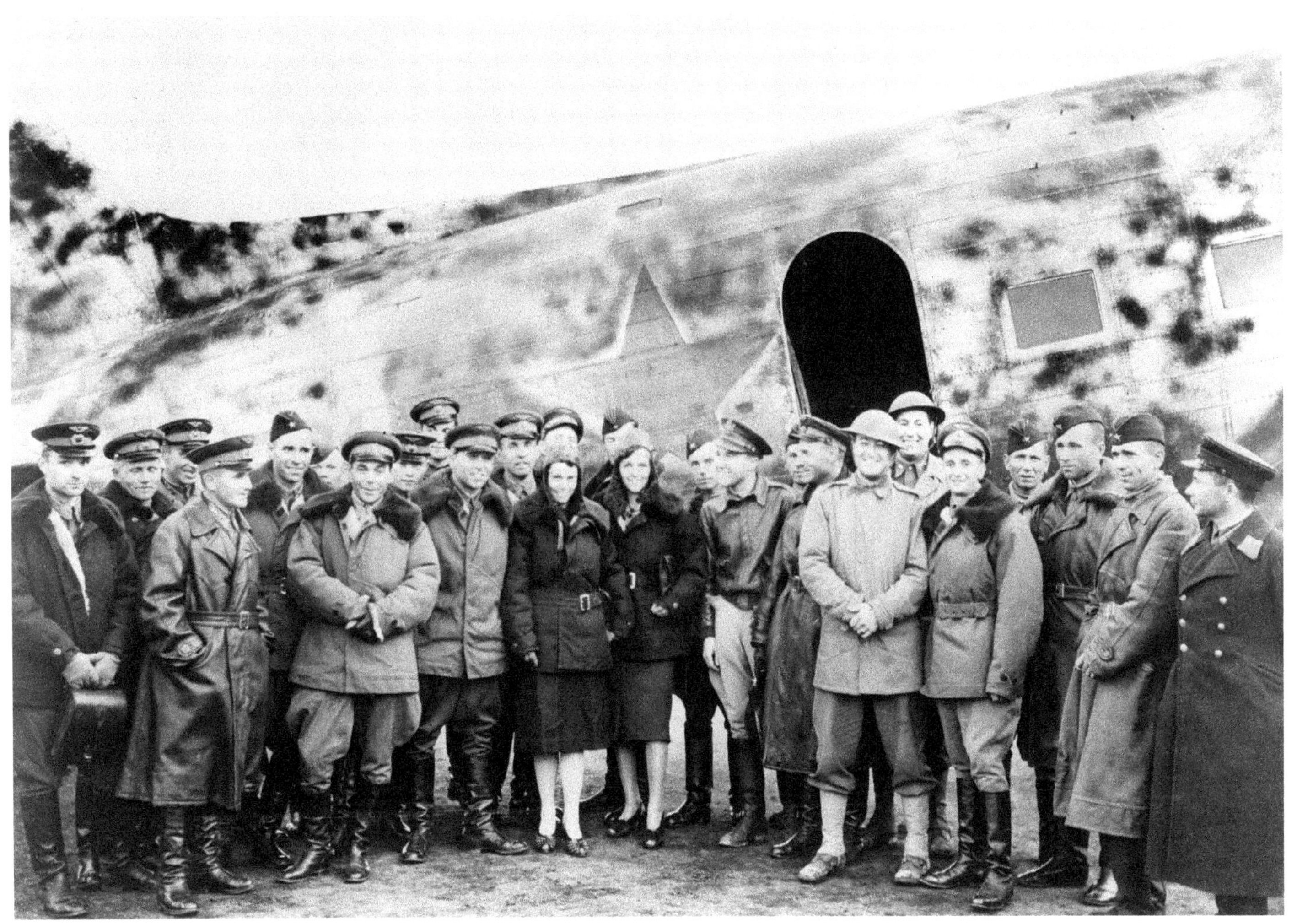

The first Russian military mission to Alaska is greeted by American service personnel at Nome in 1942. Through the Lend-Lease program, nearly eight thousand military aircraft were delivered to the Russians at Ladd Field in Fairbanks during the war, flown to Nome, and then on to Russia.

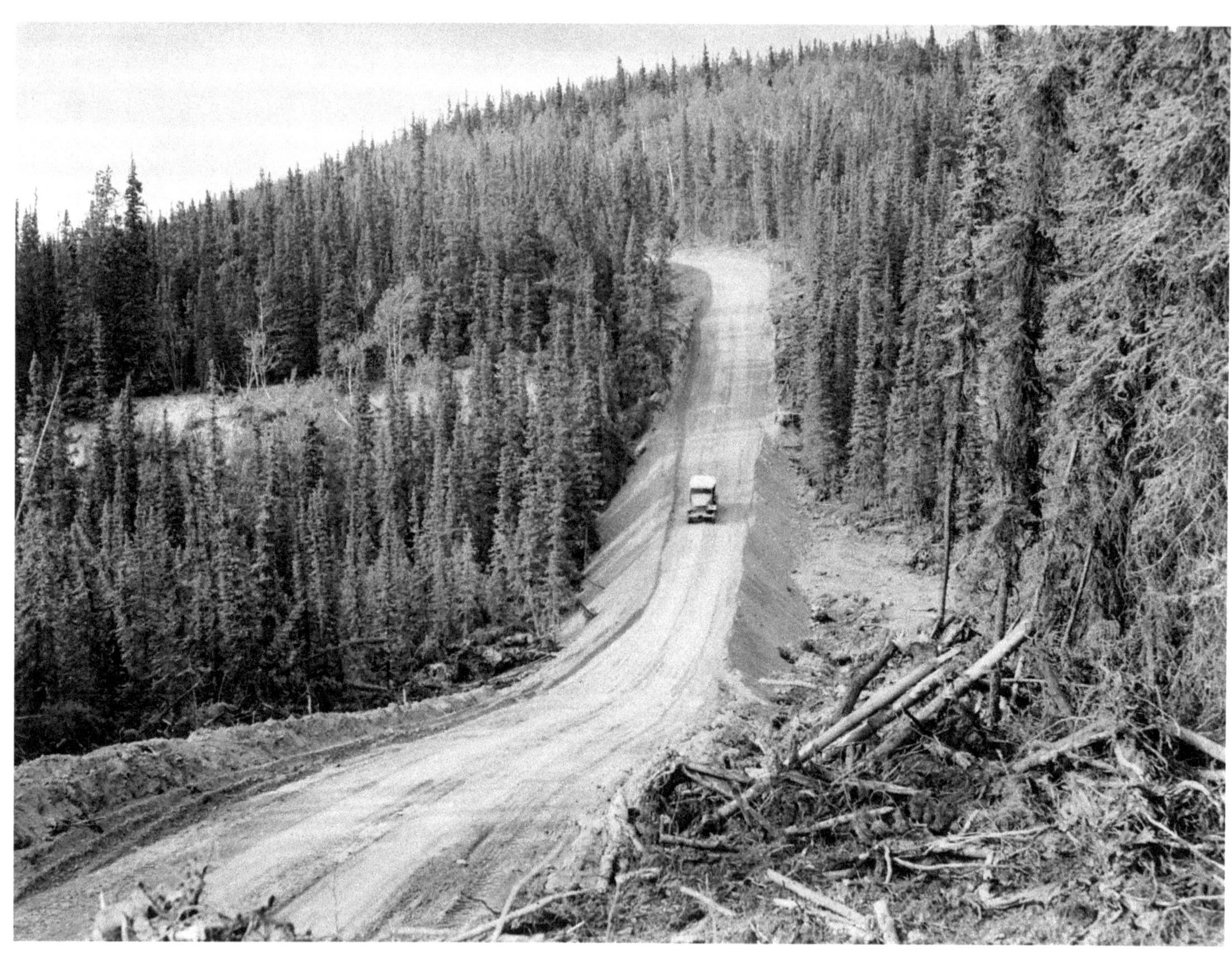

Built in a rush during World War II, the Alaska Highway cut a new path through the wilderness to connect Alaska with the Canadian highway system. One solider said the scenery consisted of "miles and miles of miles and miles."

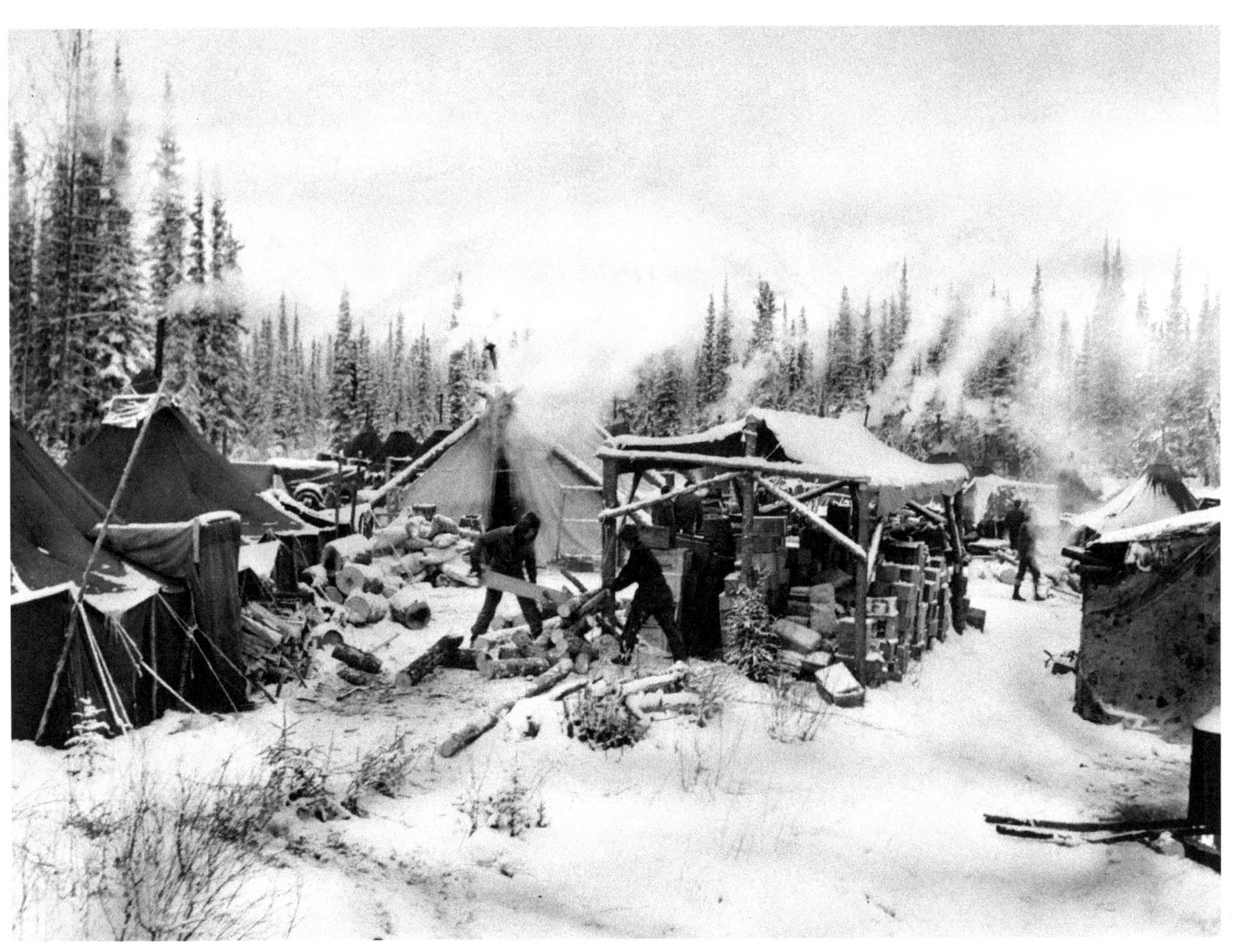

Two workers on the Alaska highway in the winter of 1942 cut firewood in one of the first remote camps on the 1,680-mile project. Staying warm was as much of a challenge as staying on schedule. The pioneer road was opened to Alaska in a little more than seven months.

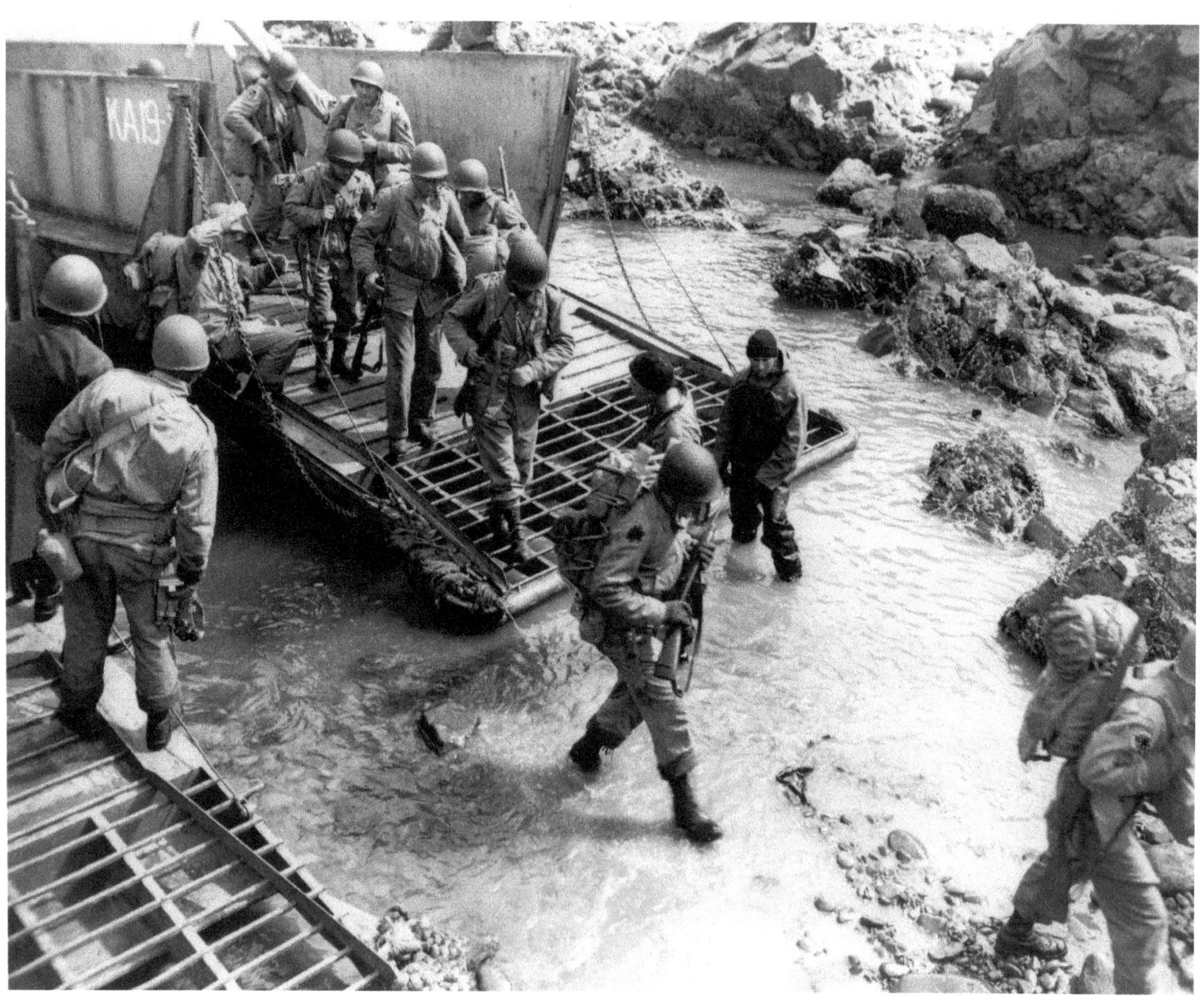

Imperial Japanese troops captured Kiska Island in the Aleutians on June 6, 1942, and seized the island of Attu the next day. American troops recaptured Attu in May 1943 after heavy fighting. On August 15, an American and Canadian force invaded Kiska, but unbeknownst to them, the Japanese had already evacuated the island. Small groups of Japanese troops remained in the Aleutians to war's end. This photo shows American soldiers disembarking during the Kiska invasion.

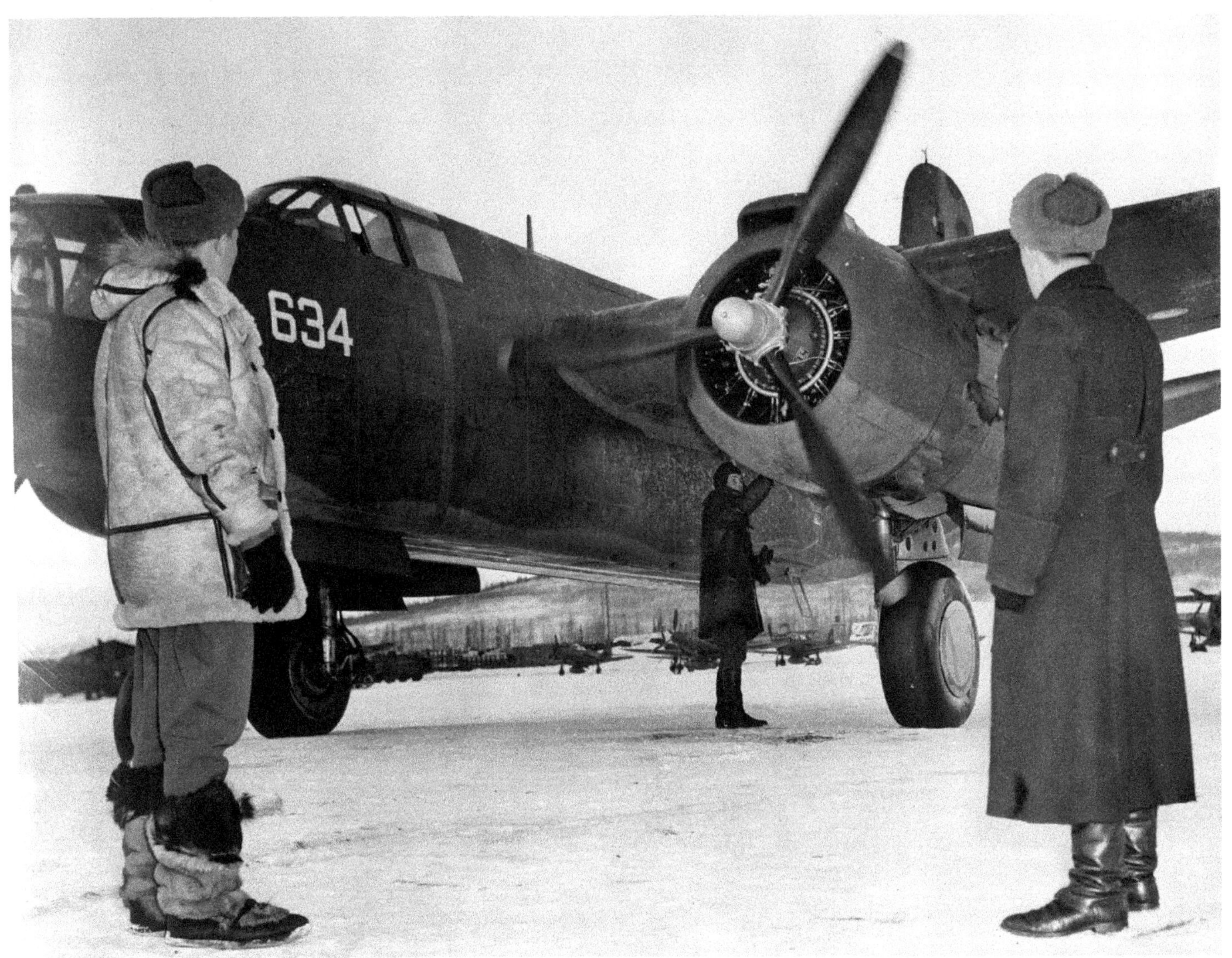

An A-20 aircraft is checked out before being turned over to the Soviets at Ladd Air Field in Fairbanks as part of the Lend-Lease aid program during World War II.

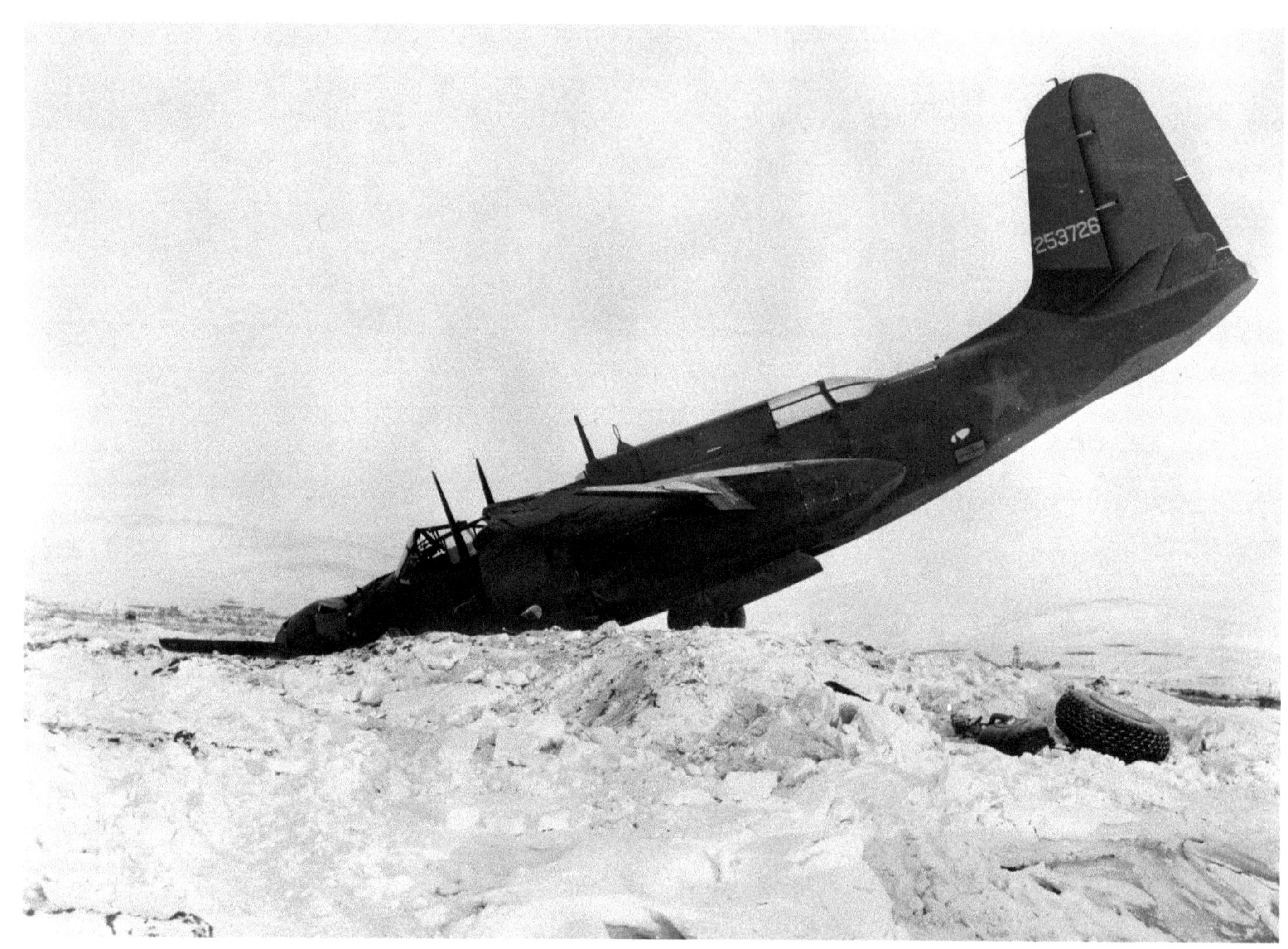

A plane delivered to the Russians crash-landed in Nome, but was repaired and sent on its way to the German Front during the war.

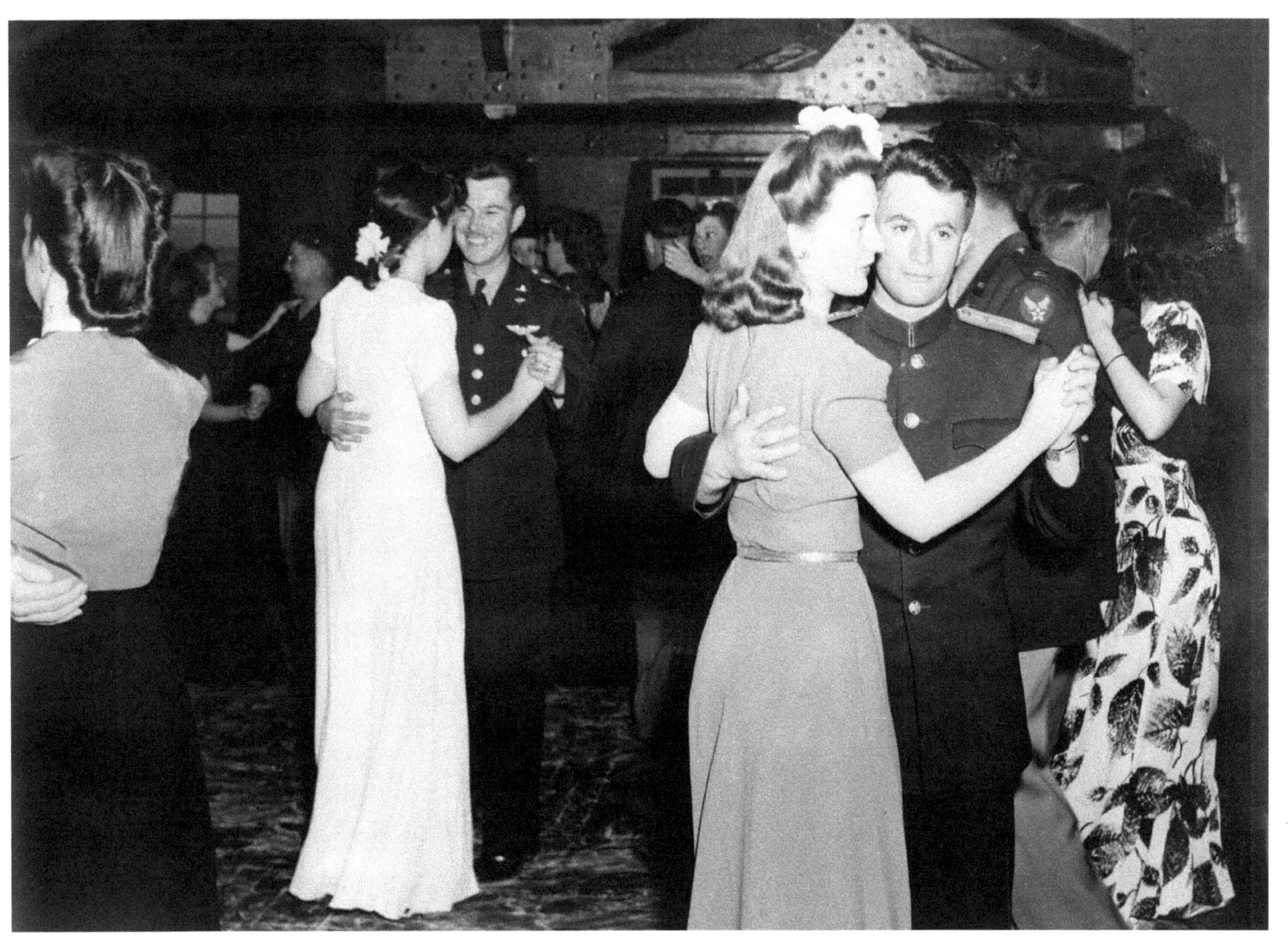

American and Soviet officers enjoy a dance at the officers' club in Nome. The Russian presence in Alaska was an official secret early in the war but was heavily publicized later.

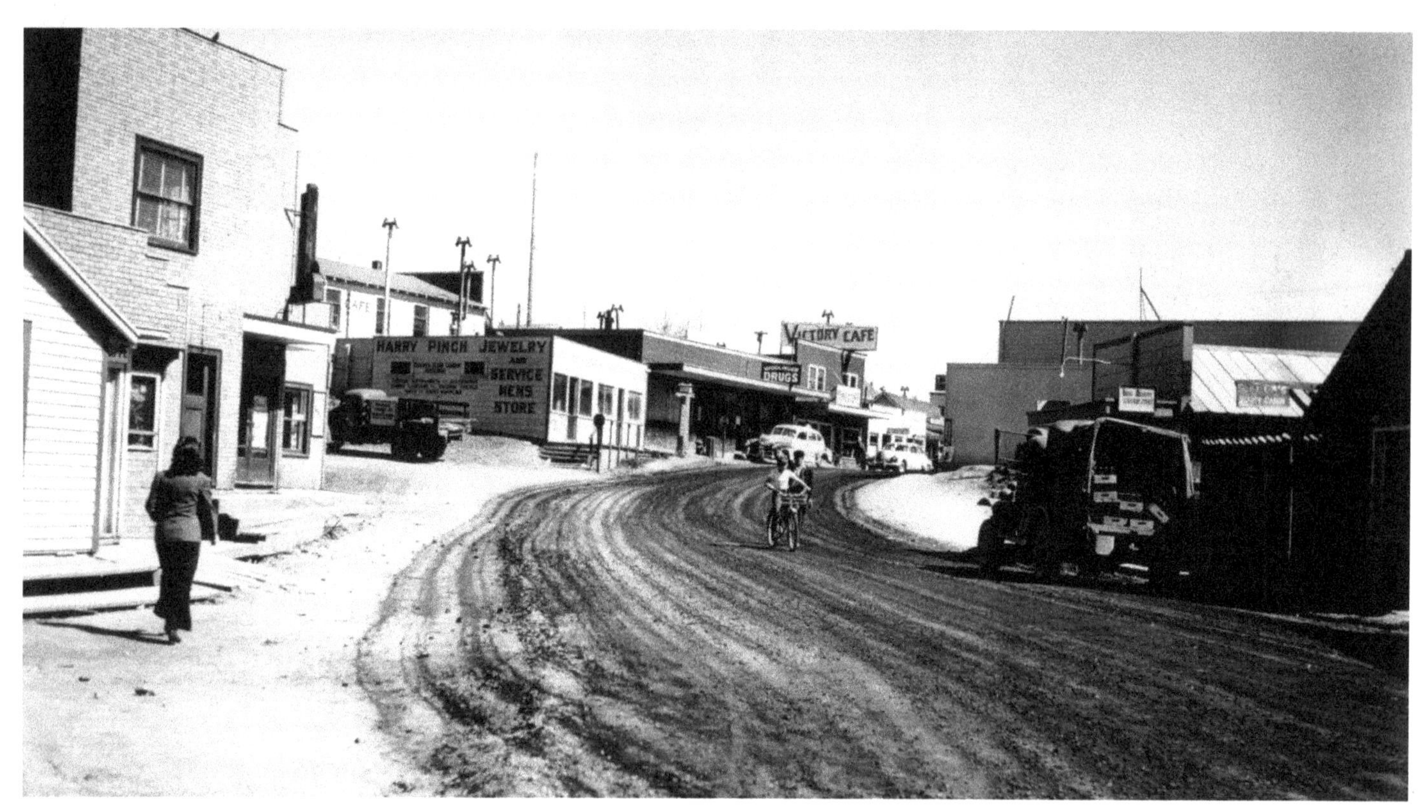

A female pedestrian makes her way along a main street in Kodiak about 1945.

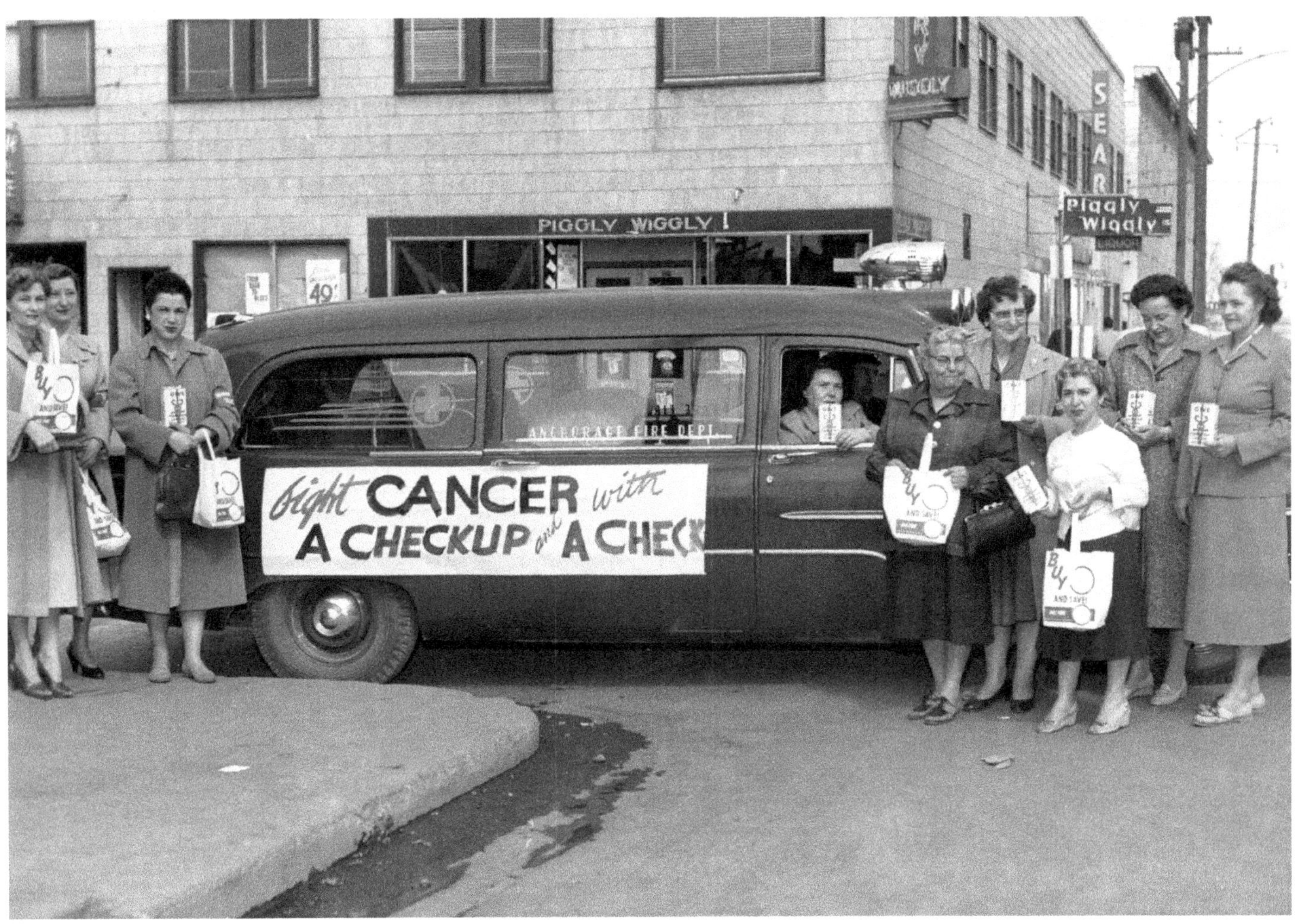

A postwar American Cancer Society campaign to "Fight Cancer with a Checkup and a Check" prompts volunteers to take to the streets of Anchorage across from the Piggly Wiggly store to gather donations.

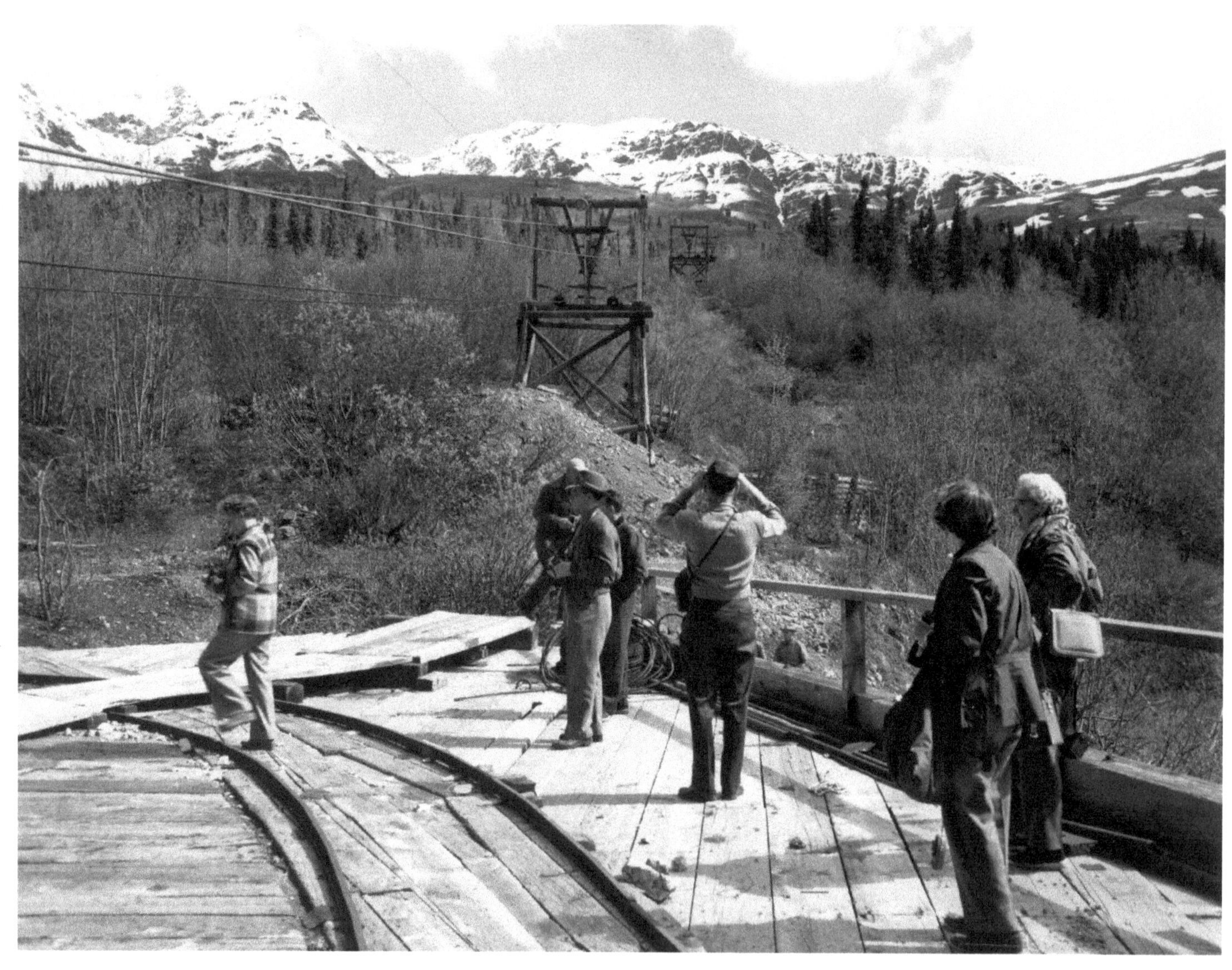

Tourists to the abandoned Kennecott Copper Mine in 1953 inspect a tram that once conveyed ore to the Copper River & Northwestern Railway that closed in 1938.

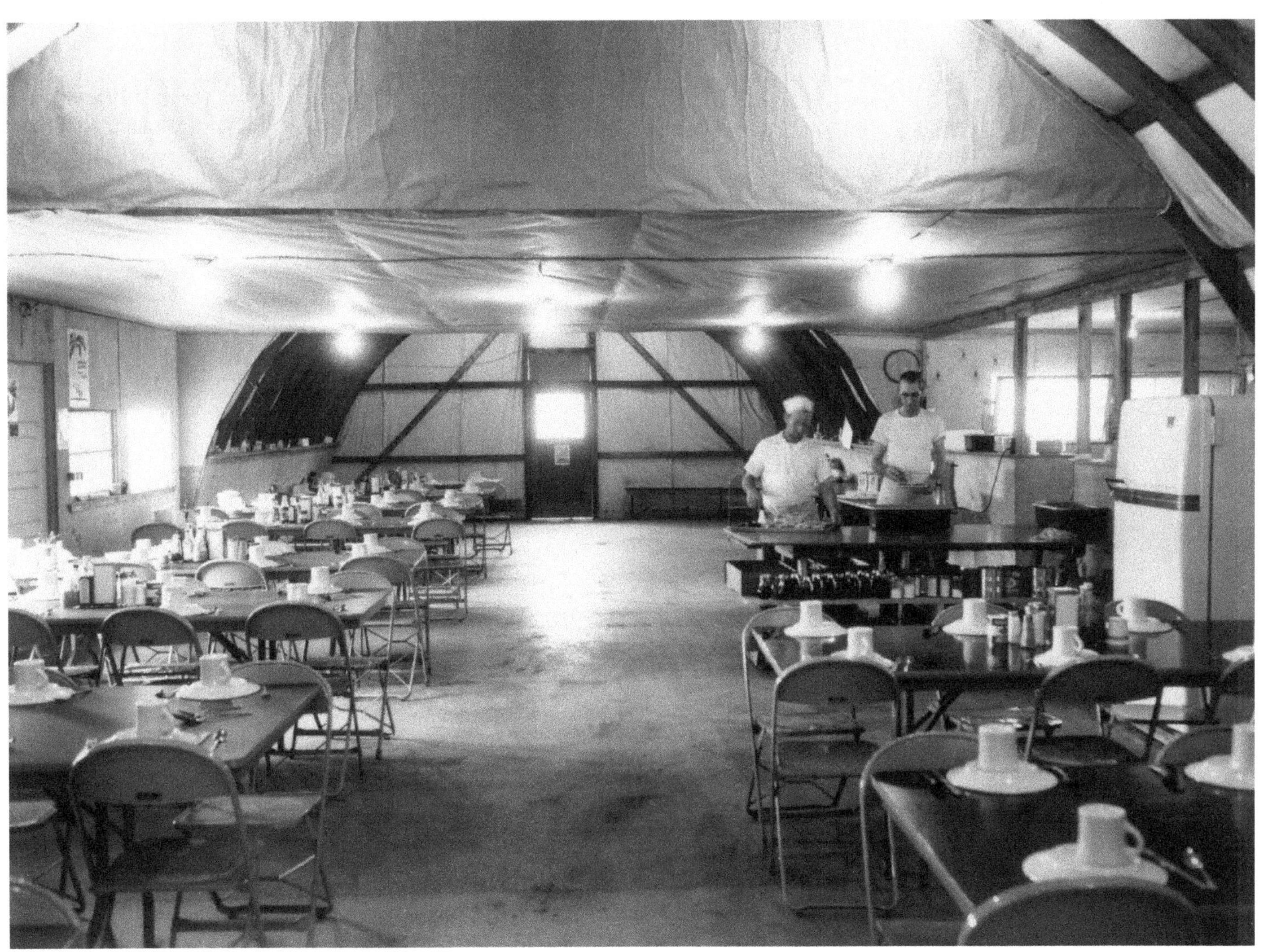

Driftwood Bay in the Aleutian Islands was home to one of the Distant Early Warning or DEW Line sites constructed in the 1950s to give warning of a Soviet air attack. This is the construction camp dining hall on Unalaska.

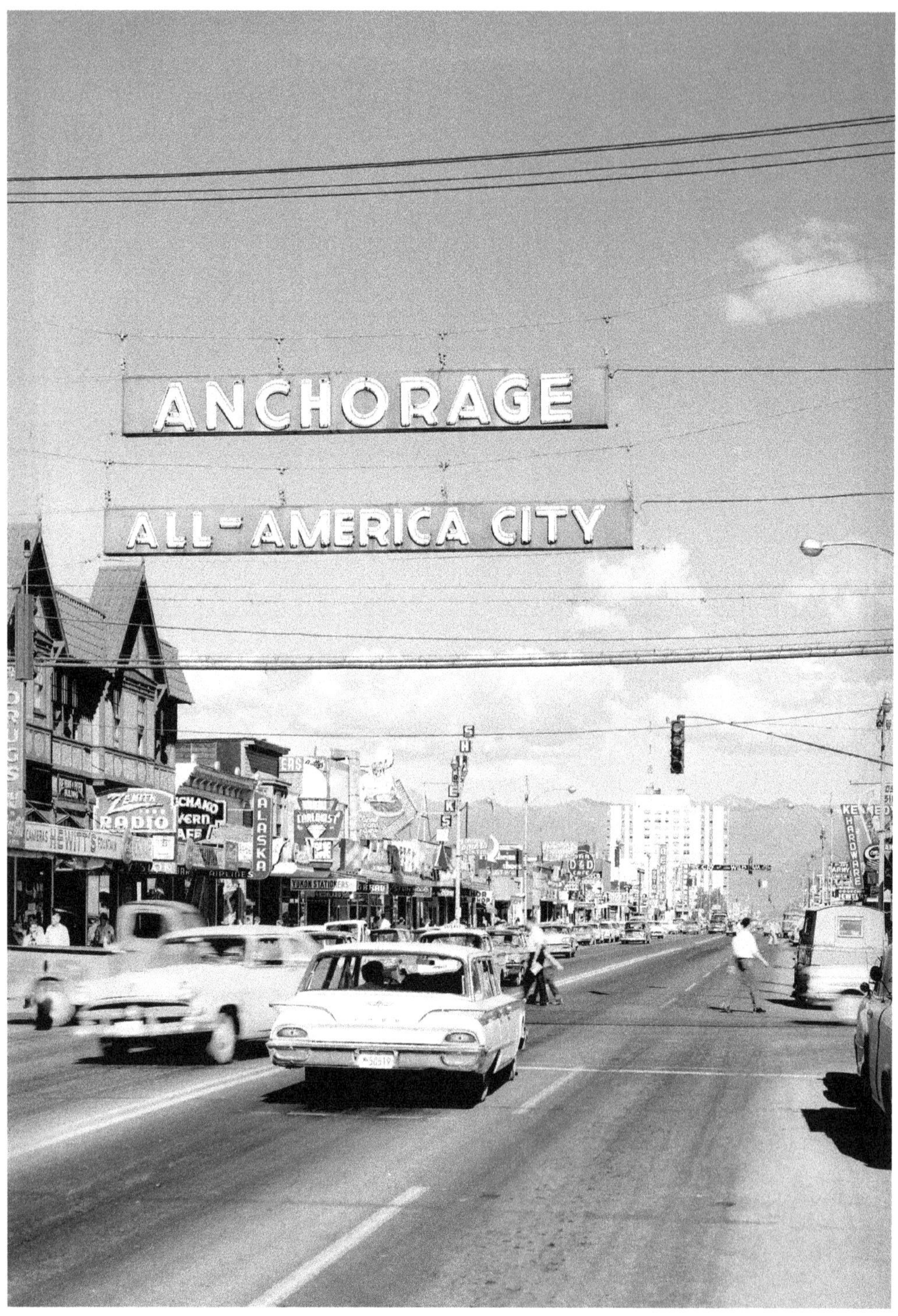

First named an "All-America City" in 1956, Anchorage emerged as the state's chief business and population center, thanks largely to its position as an important center for air travel, communications, rail traffic, and the military.

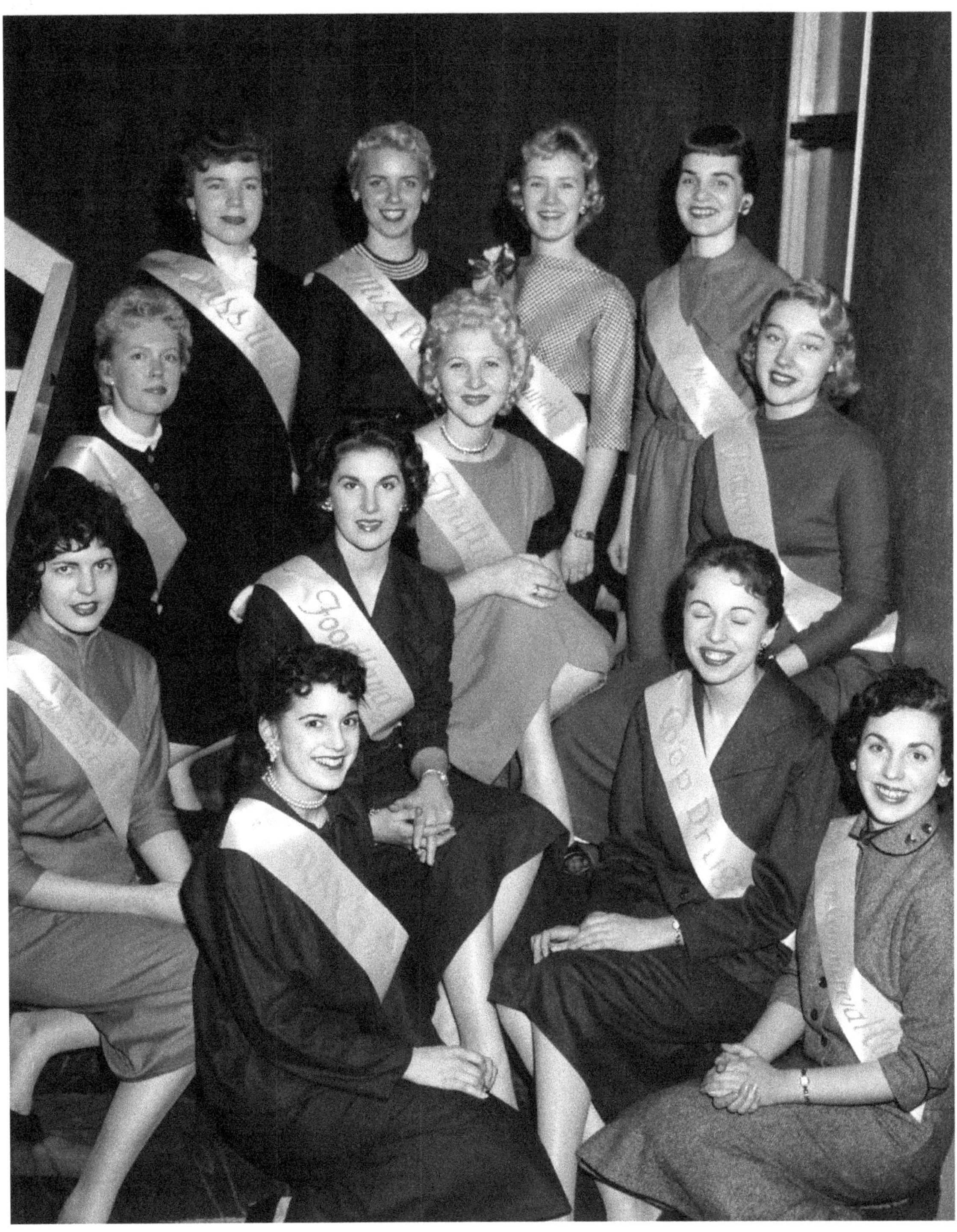

A dozen of the fifteen candidates for the title of Fairbanks Winter Carnival Queen of 1958 enjoy a moment together at the Travelers Inn.

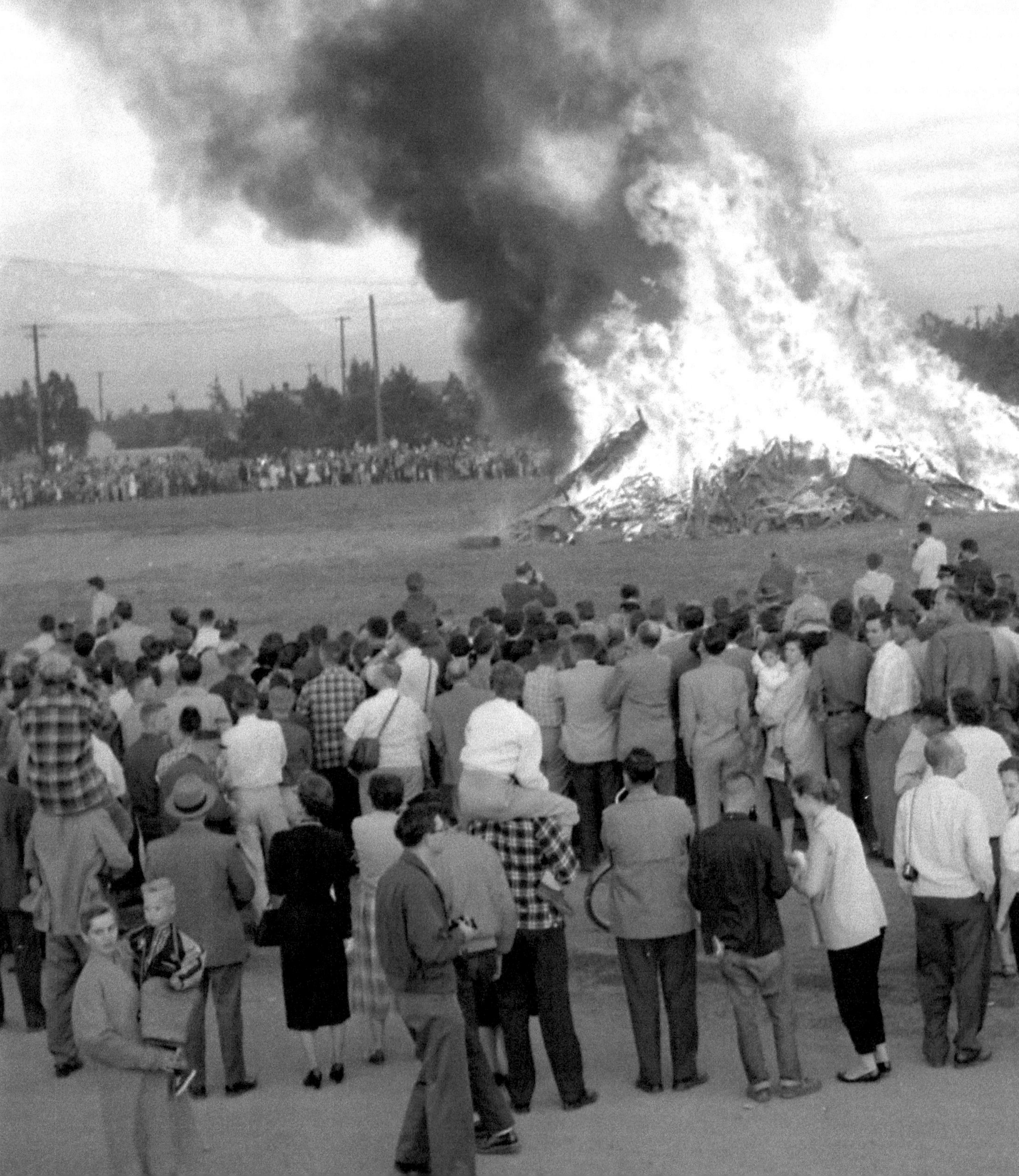

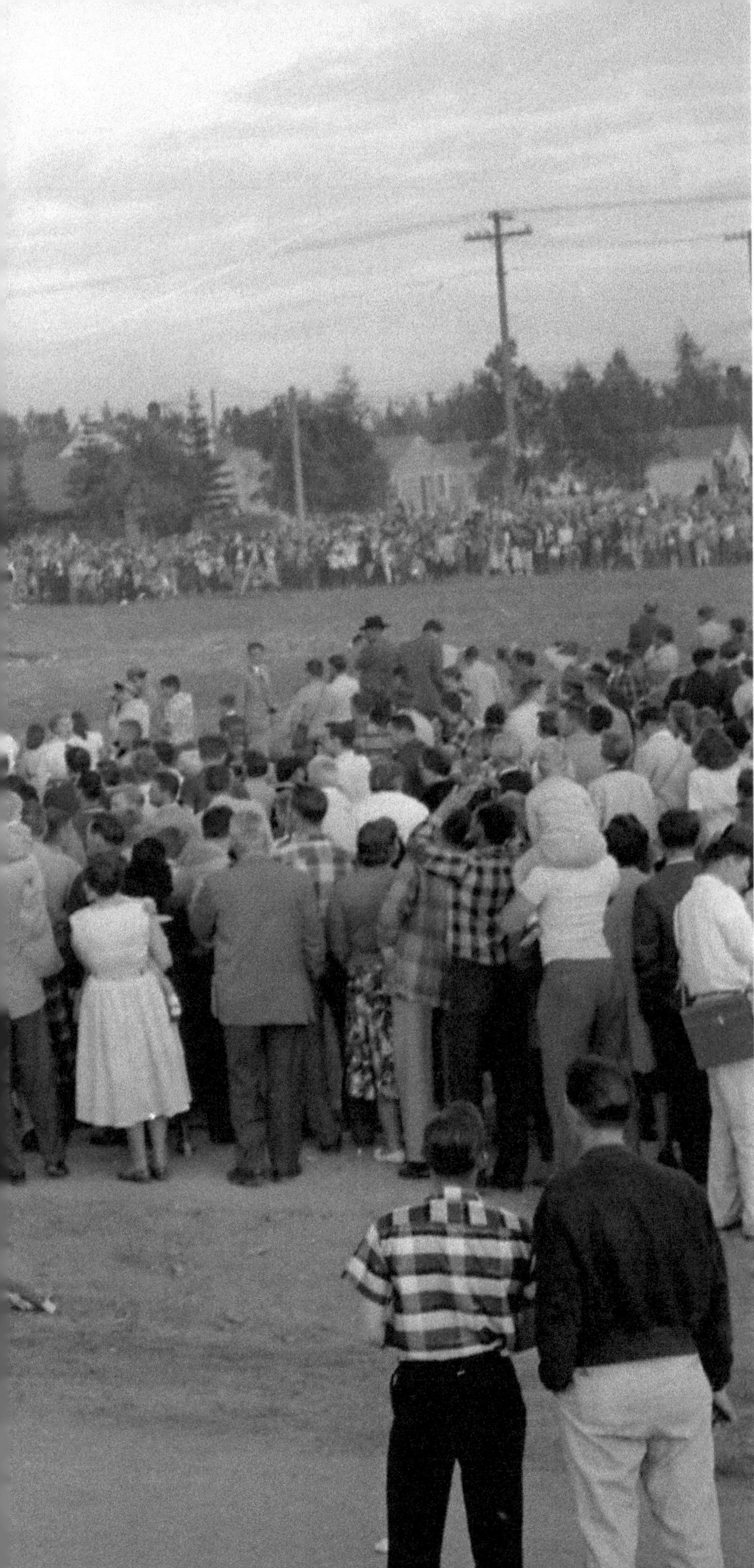

Anchorage residents mark the U.S. Congress' approval of statehood for Alaska with a giant bonfire on the park strip on June 30, 1958.

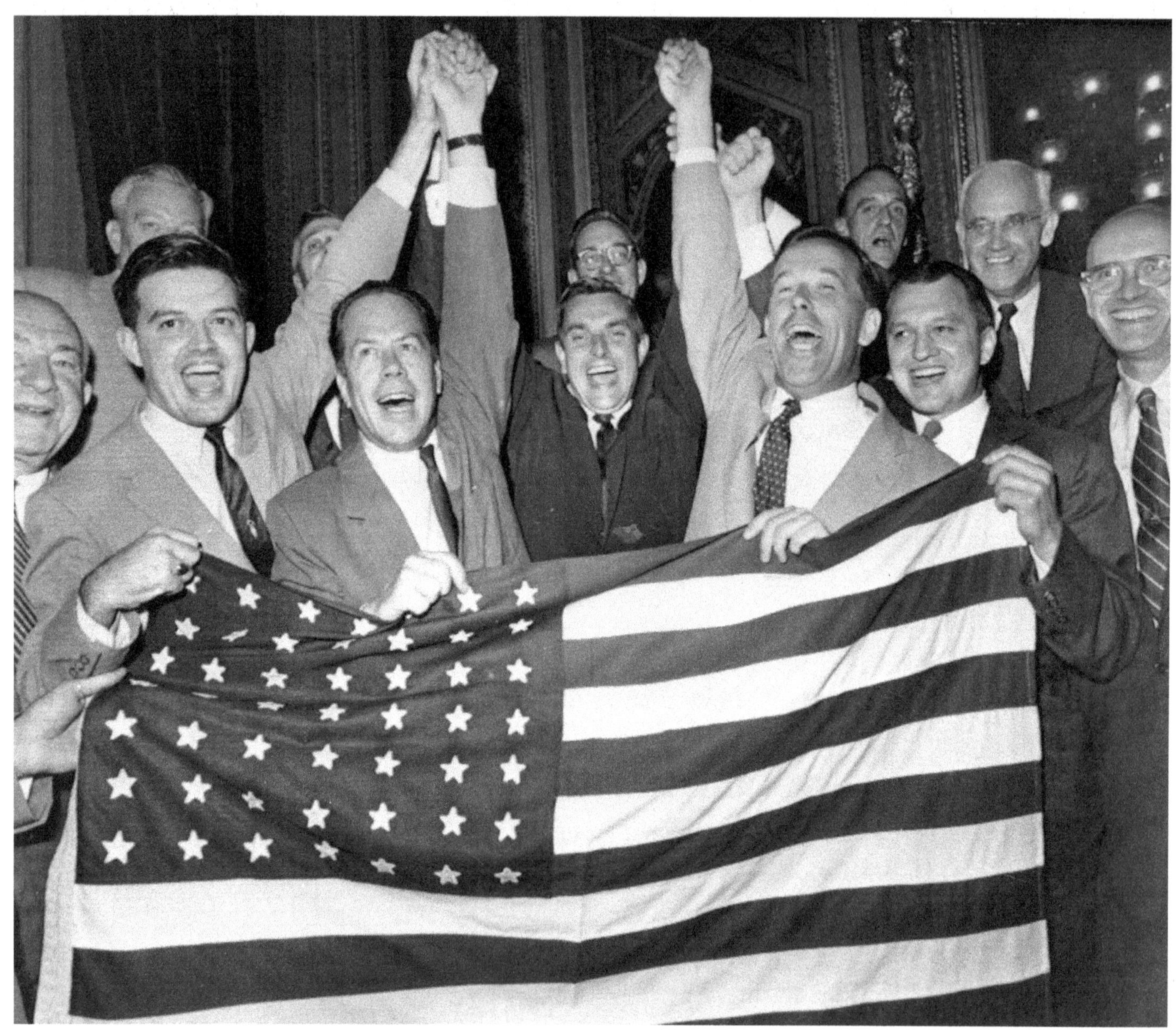

Alaska statehood advocates celebrate the passage of the bill to create the forty-ninth state by displaying an unofficial forty-nine-star flag on June 30, 1958. From left to right: Ernest Gruening, former Alaska governor; Senator Frank Church, D-Idaho; Senator Thomas Kuchel, R-California; Alaska Governor Mike Stepovich; Senator Henry Jackson, D-Washington; Wally Hickel, GOP chairman for Alaska; Senator Arthur Watkins, R-Utah; and Senator Richard Neuberger, D-Oregon.

Alaska Governor Bill Egan, left, inspects damage in the Turnagain Heights neighborhood caused by the devastating earthquake on March 27, 1964. Turnagain Heights, which had been home to some of the finest homes in Anchorage, was the site of a major landslide along 4,300 feet of the subdivision. The bluff collapsed, destroying seventy-five homes as the ground slid down toward Knik Arm.

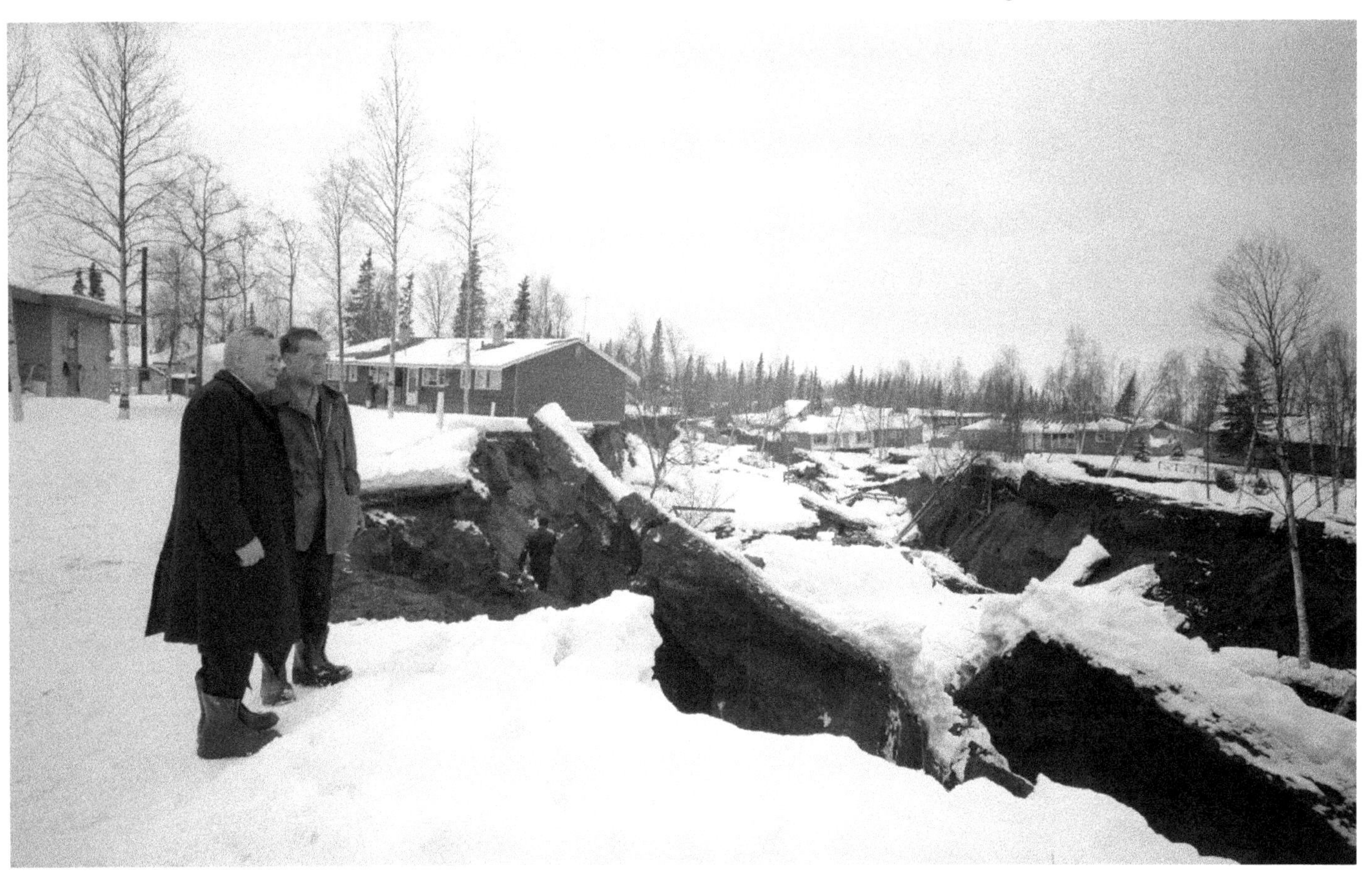

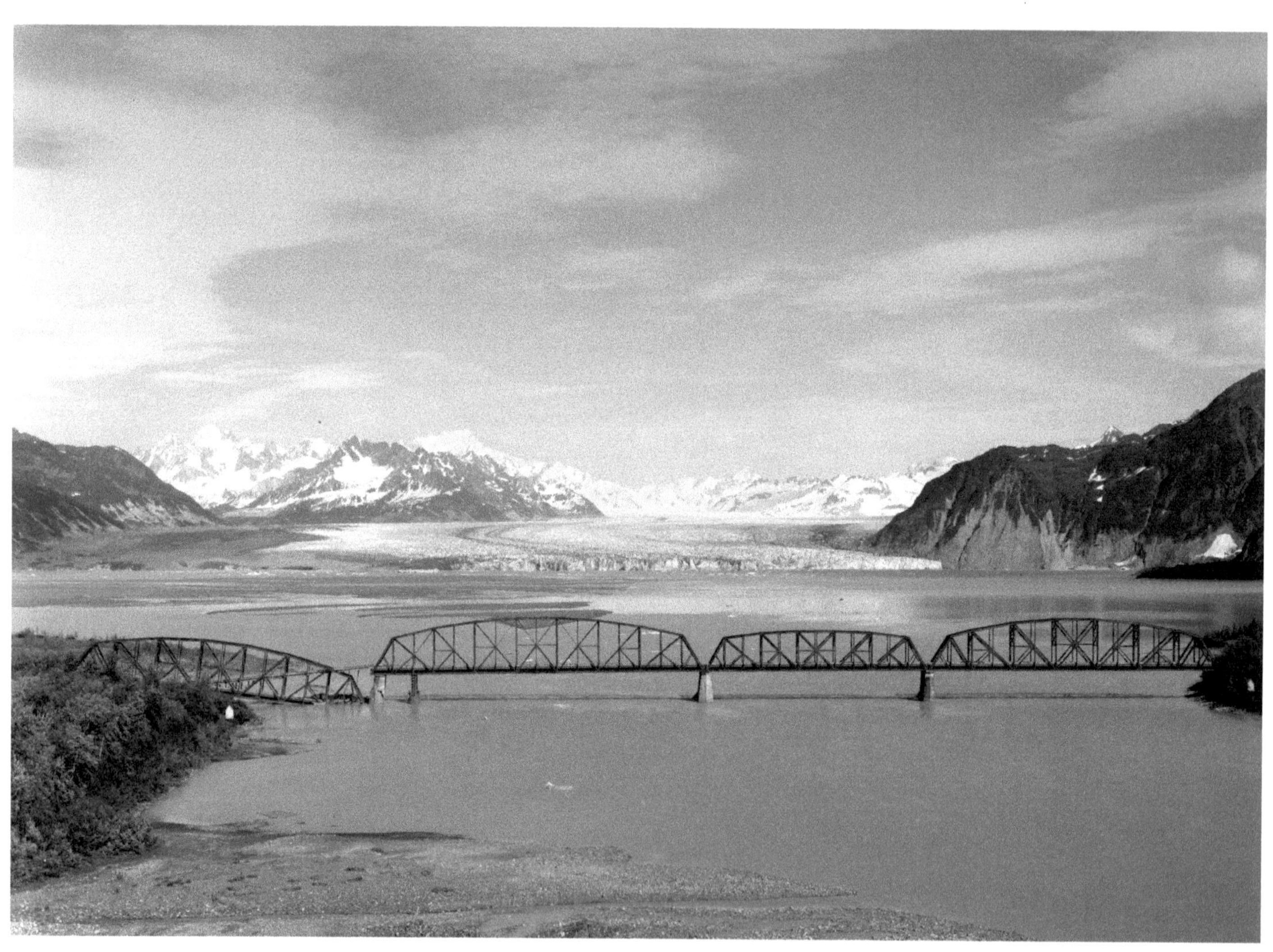

The "Million Dollar Bridge" over the Copper River, an engineering marvel when it was completed in 1908 at a cost of more than $1.4 million, collapsed during the 1964 earthquake. It was built by the Copper River & Northwestern Railway but was converted to a highway bridge in the 1950s. The bridge was repaired in 2004–05 because state engineers figured it would be cheaper to fix it than to remove it.

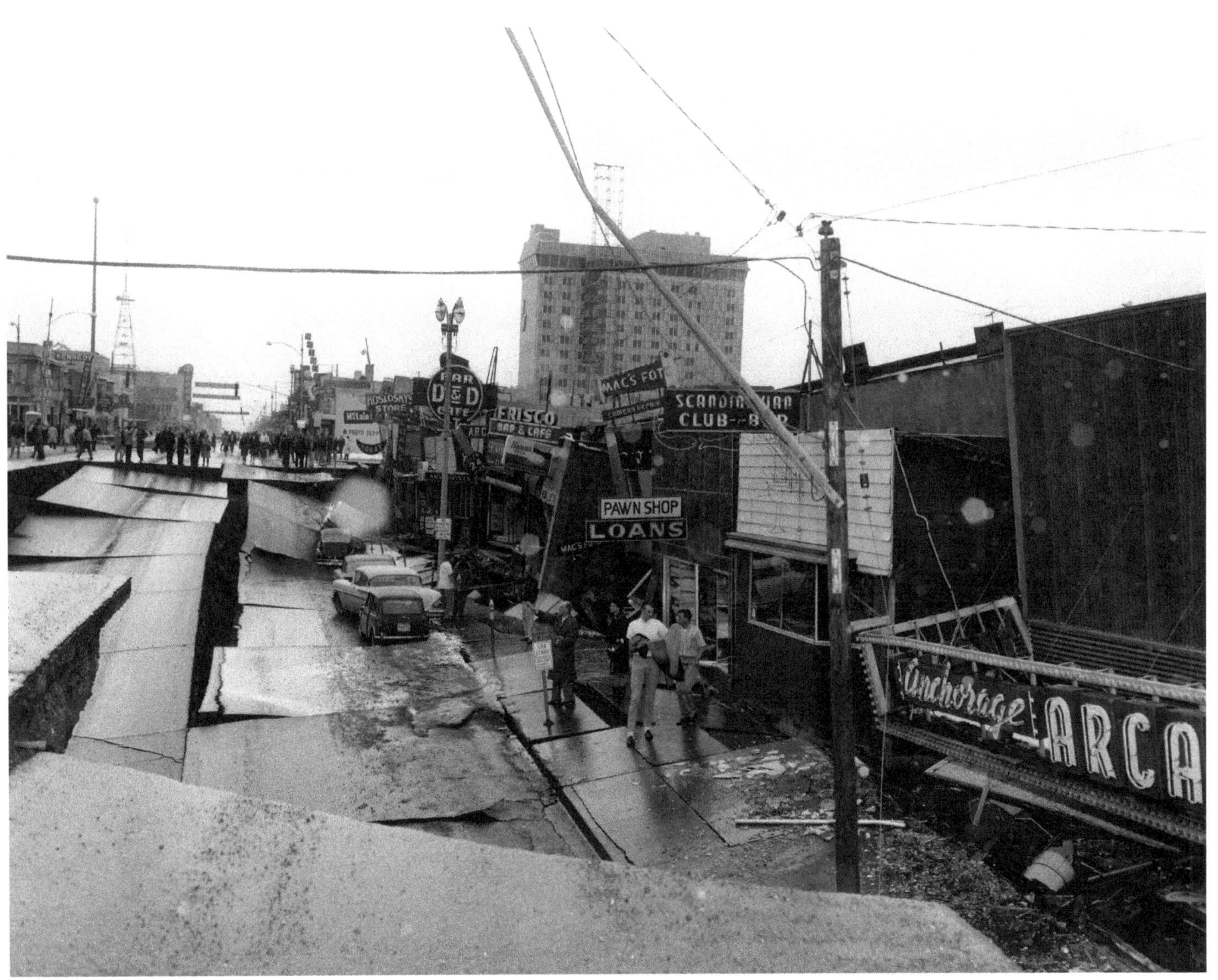

Fourth Avenue in downtown Anchorage collapsed during the quake. In this area the buildings sank straight down until their entrances were below street level.

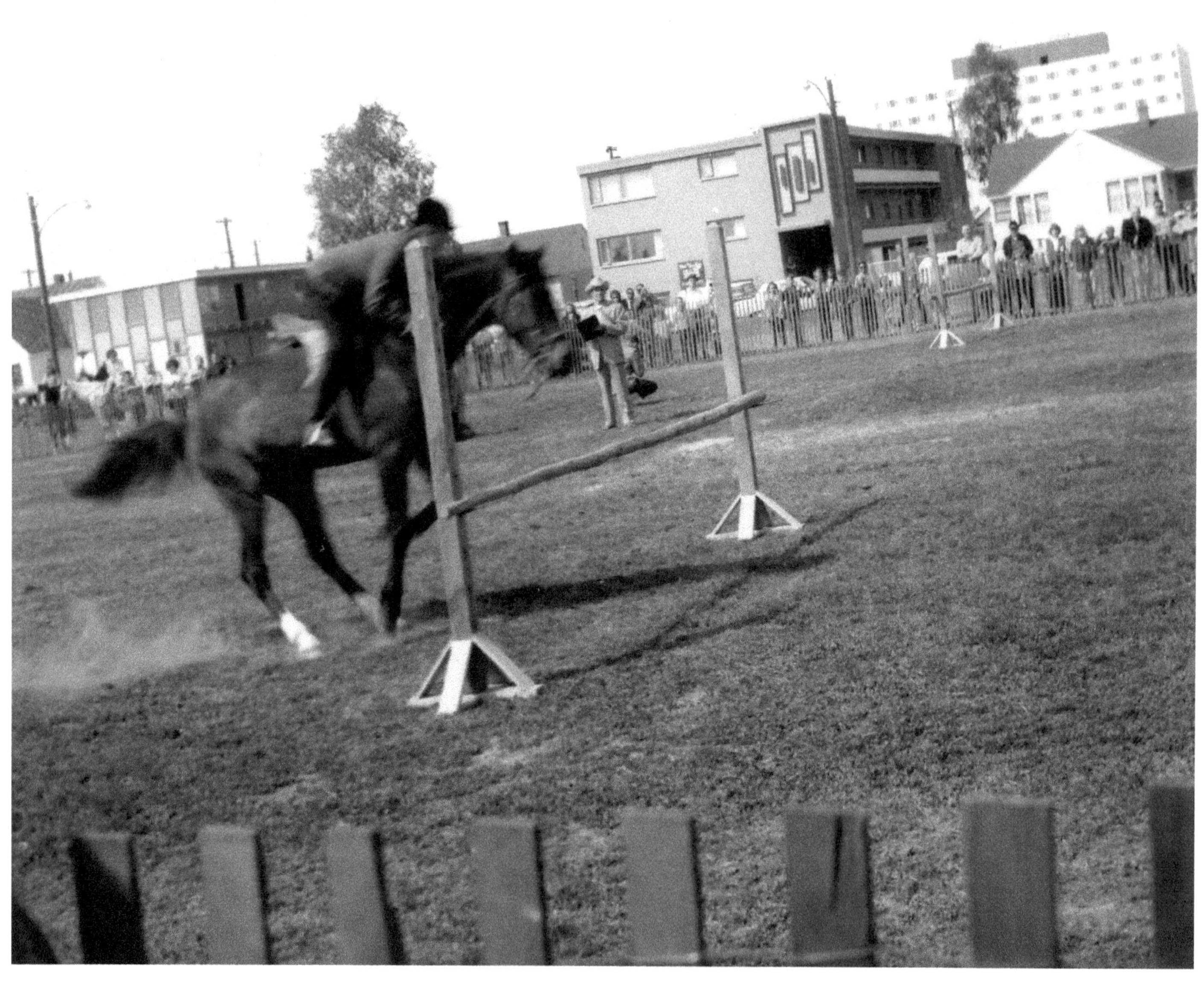

A horse-jumping demonstration on the Anchorage Park Strip in the early 1960s.

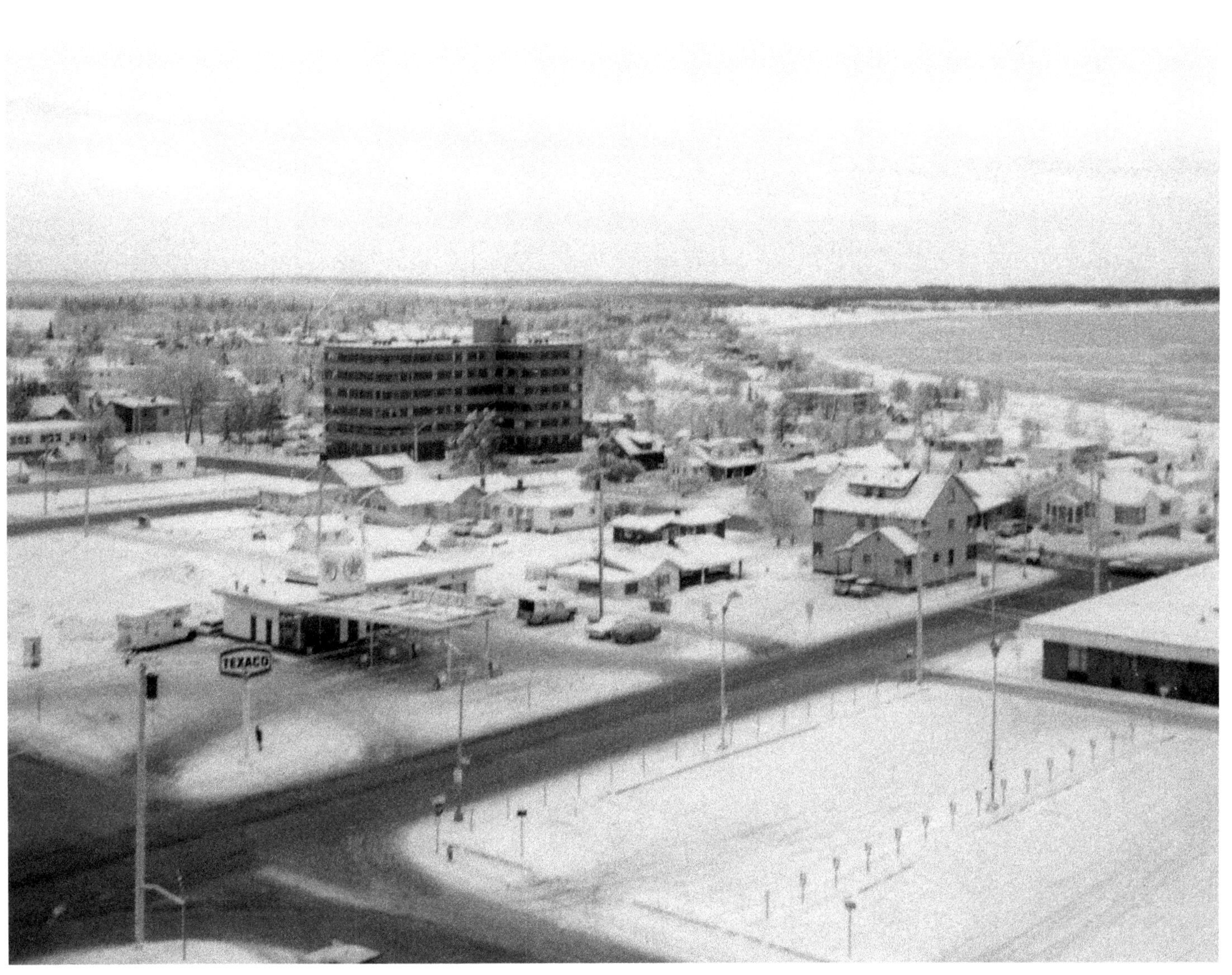

Anchorage, with Cook Inlet in the distance on a cold December day in 1968, the year that the Prudhoe Bay oil discovery set in motion a chain of events that would bring monumental changes to Alaska.

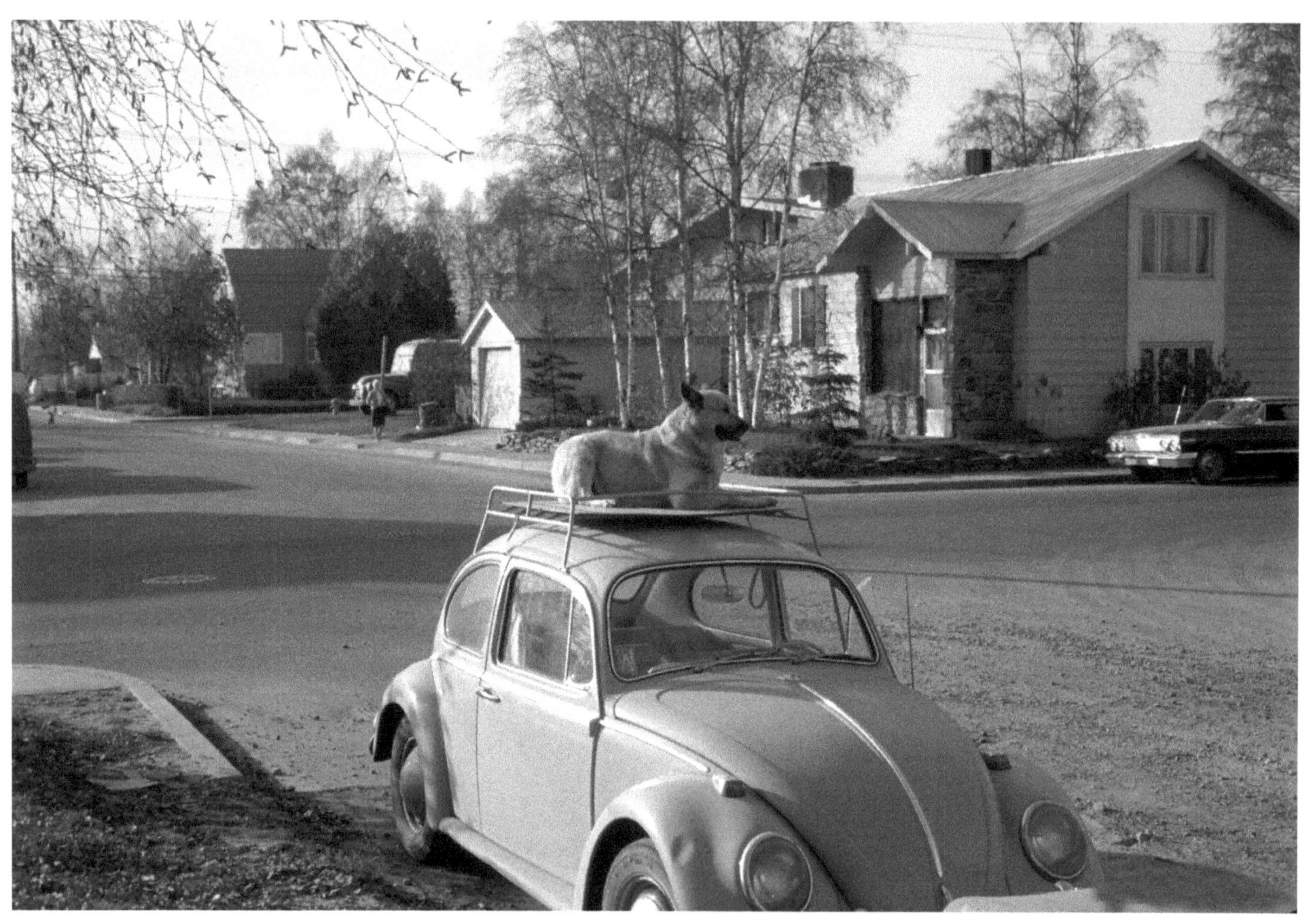

A Fairbanks dog rides in style on a car-top carrier. He regularly traveled around town this way in 1967. The photograph was taken by Mark C. Glunz, who was serving in the 171st Infantry at Fort Wainwright, which was formerly named Ladd Field.

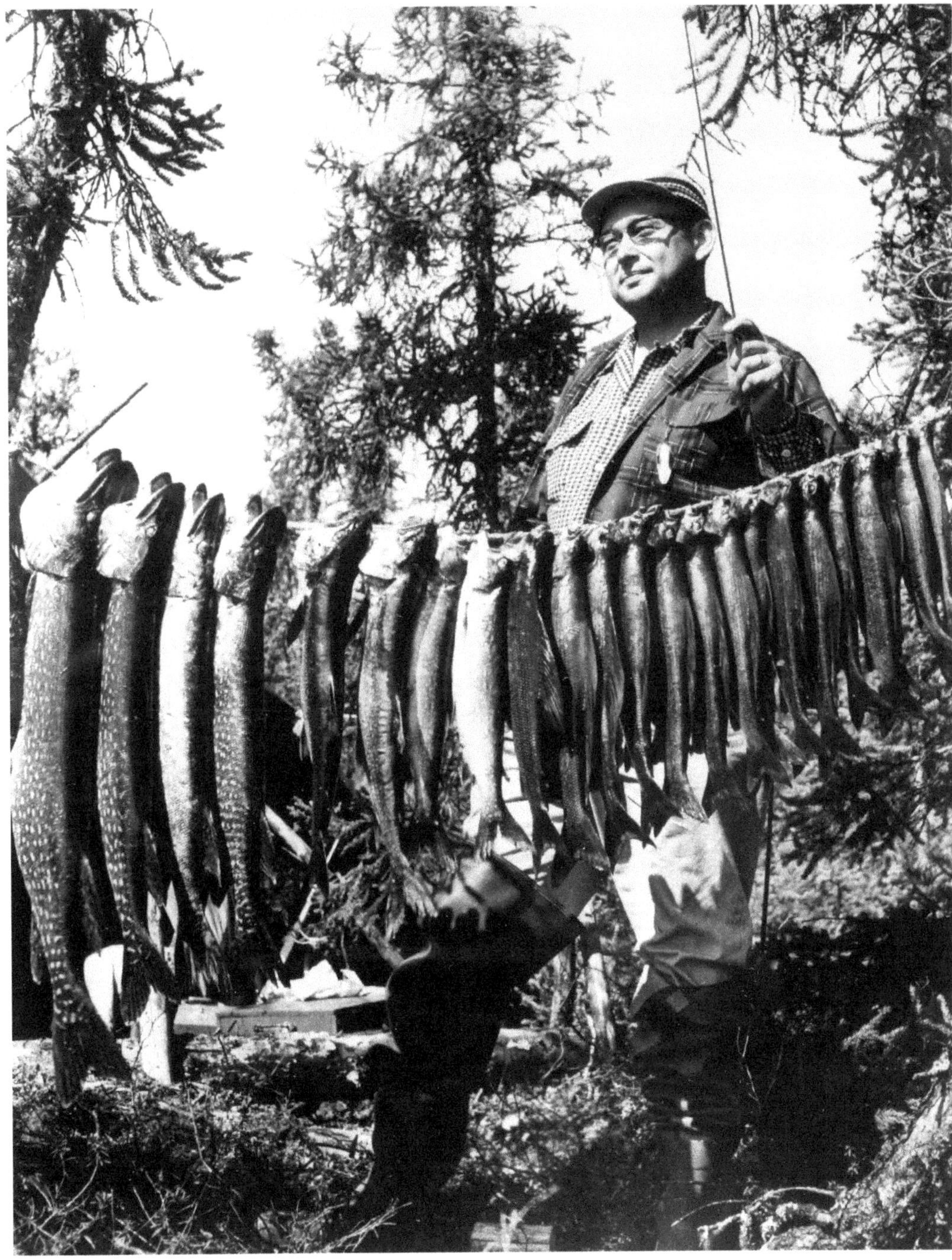

Bud Hagberg of Wien Air Alaska displays the catch of the day on Selby Lake in the 1960s.

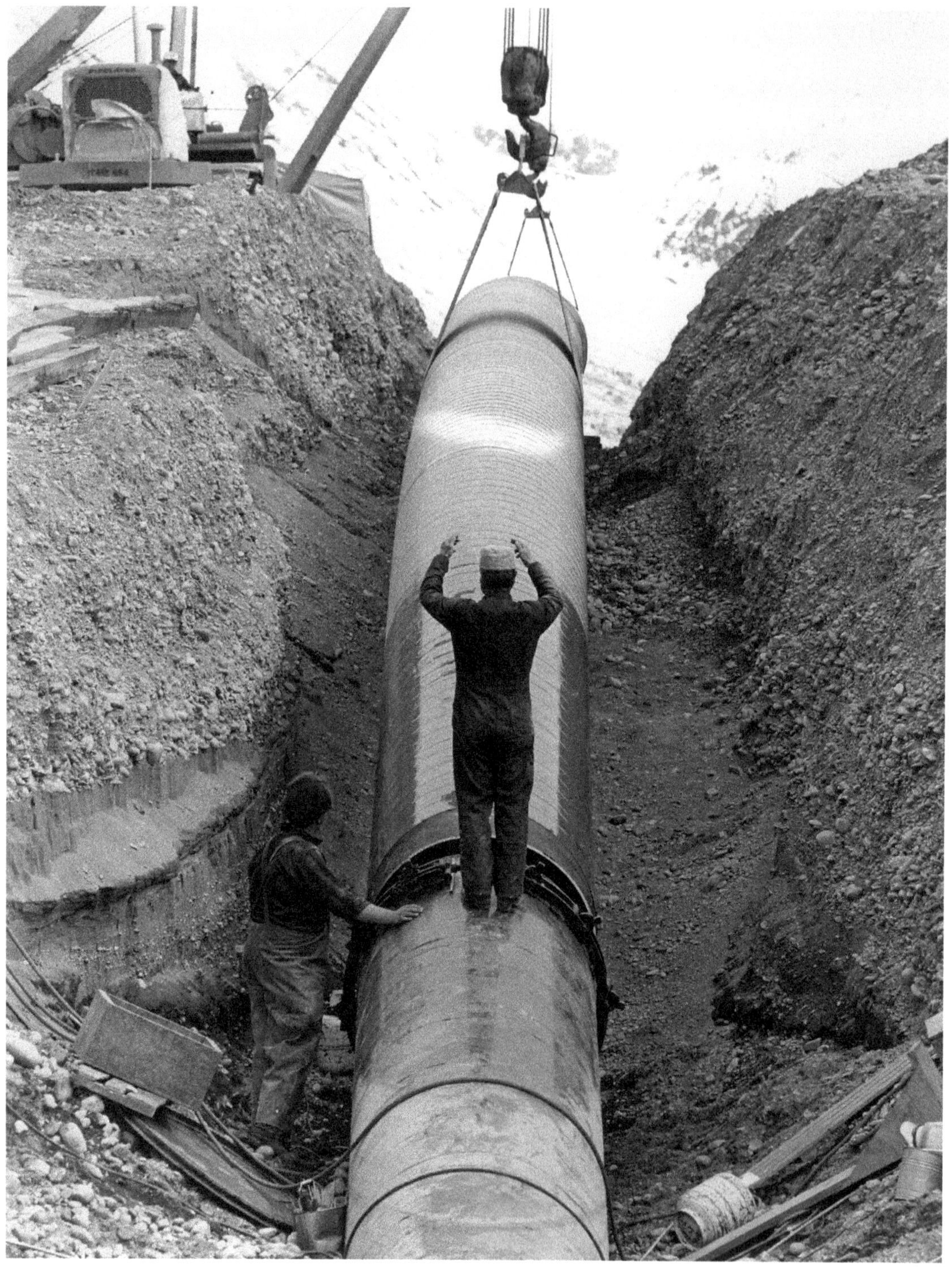

Construction workers lay pipe near the Little Tonsina River in 1975 on the project that redefined Alaska in the latter stages of the twentieth century.

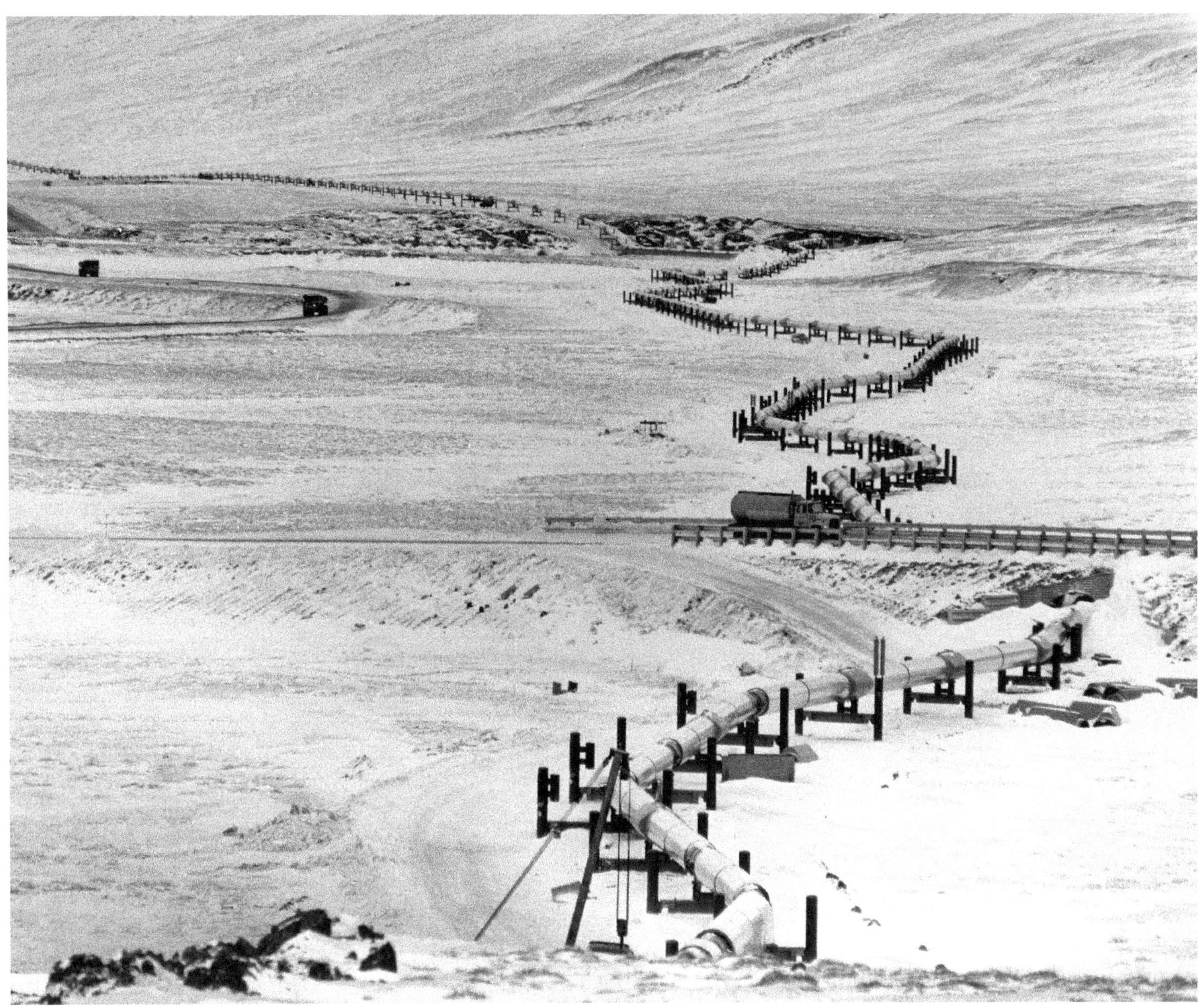

The trans-Alaska oil pipeline, built in a zigzag manner so that the metal could withstand contraction and expansion from extreme swings in temperature, passes near Galbraith Lake on the north side of the Brooks Range.

The eight-hundred-mile trans-Alaska oil pipeline crosses three mountain ranges, thirty-four rivers, and hundreds of streams between Prudhoe Bay and Valdez. The pipe is elevated wherever the soil is unstable. The fins on the steel posts release heat into the air, which helps keeps the soil frozen.

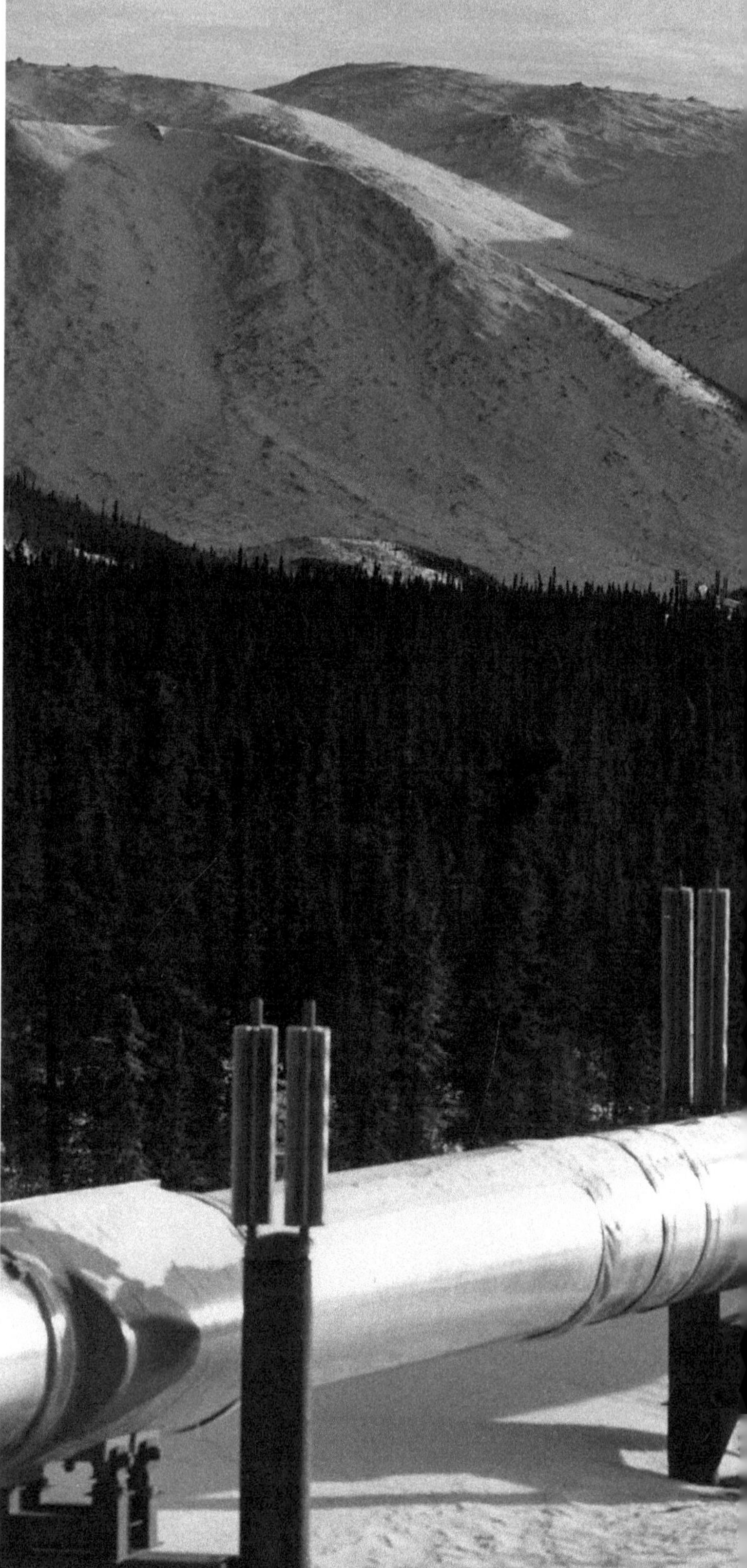

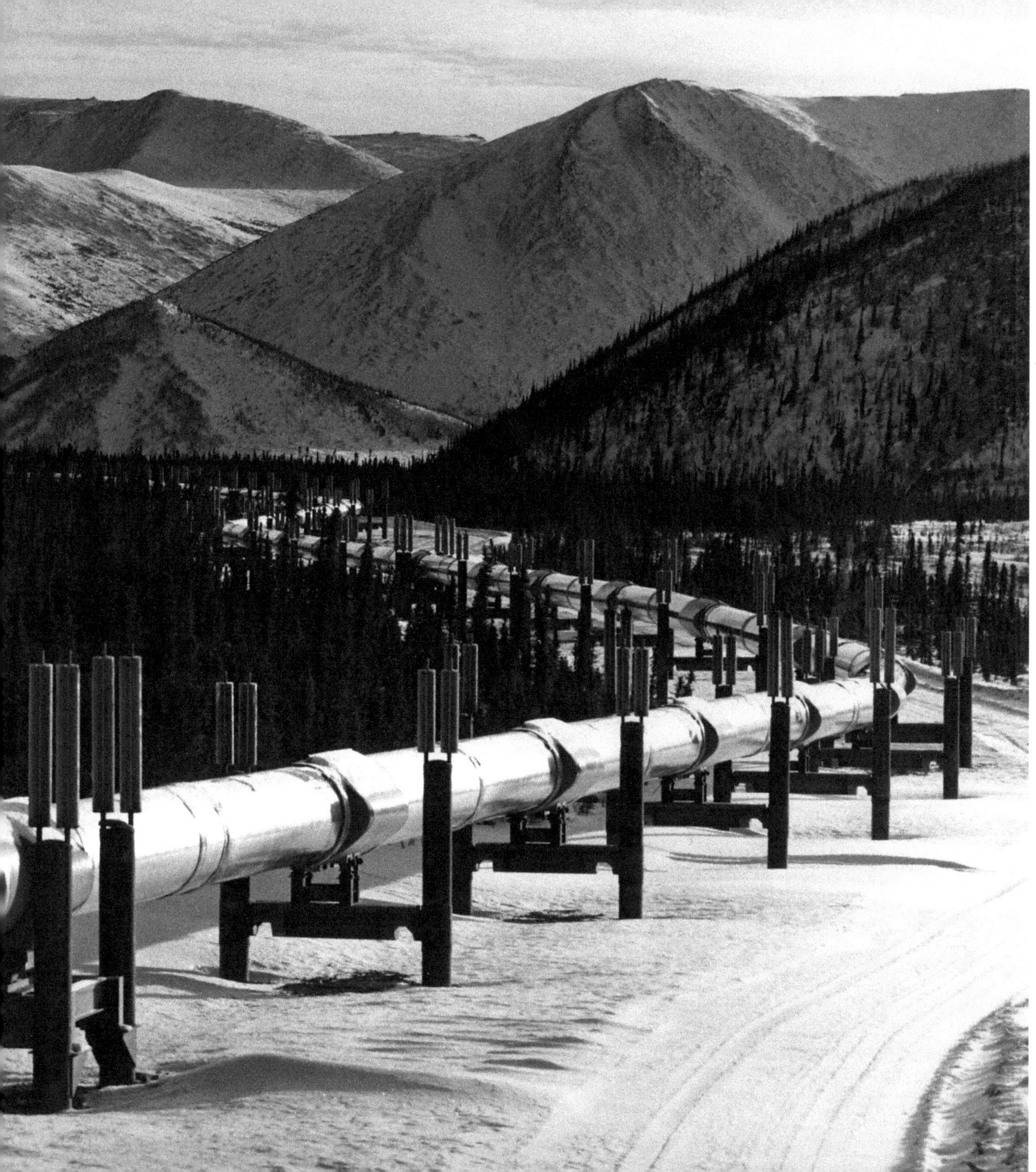

Notes on the Photographs

These notes, listed by page number, attempt to include all aspects known of the photographs. Each of the photographs is identified by the page number, photograph's title or description, photographer and collection, archive, and call or box number when applicable. Although every attempt was made to collect all available data, in some cases complete data was unavailable due to the age and condition of some of the photographs and records.

II **Taku Glacier**
Library of Congress
ppmsc 02046

VI **Dogs Pulling Cart**
Library of Congress
LC-DIG-ppmsc-01575

X **Map**
Alaska and Polar Regions Collections, Rasmuson Library, University of Alaska Fairbanks
G3351/H2/1897/L361

2 **Castle and Barracks**
Fred Wildon Fickett Collection
University of Alaska Anchorage Consortium Library, Archives & Special Collections Department
UAA-HMC-0108-series8d-1

3 **Totem Poles**
Library of Congress
cph 3c02219

4 **Ketchikan**
Julia Willma Weber Collections
University of Alaska Anchorage Consortium Library, Archives & Special Collections Department
UAA-hmc-0344-13-a

5 **Shaman's Grave**
Library of Congress
cph 3c36004

6 **Steamer Topeka**
Library of Congress
cph 3b01942

7 **Hose Co. 1**
Library of Congress
cph 3a48630

8 **After Snowslide**
Library of Congress
cph 3c17014

9 **July Fourth, 1898**
Julia Willma Weber Collections
University of Alaska Anchorage Consortium Library, Archives & Special Collections Department
UAA-hmc-0344-29-c

10 **Schooner Olga**
Edwin Forbes Glenn Collections
University of Alaska Anchorage Consortium Library, Archives & Special Collections Department
UAA-HMC-0116-series3a-47-3

11 **Circle City**
Library of Congress
pan 6a00375

12 **Harriman Alaska Expedition**
Library of Congress
cph 3g08288

13 **Surveyor**
Library of Congress
cph 3c30715

14 **Camping**
Library of Congress
cph 3c30717

15 **Expedition Vessel**
Library of Congress
cph 3c30719

16 **Forest**
Library of Congress
cph 3c30726

17 **Unalaska**
Library of Congress
cph 3c24568

18 **Driftwood Shelter**
Library of Congress
cph 3c30716

19 **Ketchikan**
Library of Congress
ppmsc 01886

20 **Resurrection Bay**
Library of Congress
ppmsc 01958

21 **Scenery at Resurrection Bay**
Library of Congress
ppmsc 01778

22 **Aerial Tramway**
Library of Congress
ppmsc 02232

23 **Log Cabin Club**
Library of Congress
ppmsc 01955

24 **Anvil Rock**
Library of Congress
ppmsc 02227

25 **St. Michael Army Post**
Library of Congress
ppmsc 02002

26 **Steamer U.S.R.C. McCulloch**
Library of Congress
ppmsc 01905

27 **Valdez Trail**
Library of Congress
ppmsc 02490

28 **Yukon Boundary**
Library of Congress
ppmsc 01615

29 **Holy Cross Mission**
Library of Congress
ppmsc 01871

30 **Nome, Alaska**
Library of Congress
fsa 8e03688

31 **Clouds on Main Street**
Library of Congress
ppmsc 02239

32 **Camp**
Library of Congress
ppmsc 01733

33 **Eskimos Hunting**
Library of Congress
ppmsc 02408

34 **Hauling Logs**
Library of Congress
ppmsc 01617

35 **Miners and Merchants**
Library of Congress
ppmsc 01669

36 **Waterfront, Valdez, and Mountains**
Library of Congress
ppmsc 01970

38 **Valdez Business District**
Frederick John Date Collections
University of Alaska Anchorage Consortium Library, Archives & Special Collections Department
UAA-hmc-0379-series2-v1-13b

39 **Public School**
Library of Congress
ppmsc 01580

40 **Unexpected Shore Ice**
Library of Congress
cph 3b3350

41 **Eskimo and Captured Reindeer**
Library of Congress
ppmsc 02391

42 **Reindeer Herd**
Library of Congress
ppmsc 01749

43 **Chariot Race**
Library of Congress
ppmsc 01892

44 **Trapper**
Library of Congress
ppmsc 01998

46 **Eskimo Dance**
Library of Congress
ppmsc 02390

47 **View of Sitka**
Library of Congress
ppmsc 02106

48 **U.S. Public School for Eskimos**
Library of Congress
ppmsc 02459

49 **Carpenter Work**
Library of Congress
ppmsc 02463

50 **Northern Commercial Co.**
Library of Congress
ppmsc 02072

51 **Skagway**
Library of Congress
ppmsc 02004

52 **McCabe Building**
Library of Congress
ppmsc 02003

53 **Public School**
Library of Congress
ppmsc 01581

54 **Snow River**
Library of Congress
ppmsc 01868

55 **Drying Salmon**
Library of Congress
ppmsc 01750

56 **Aerial of Kodiak**
Library of Congress
ppmsc 01747

57 **Alaska Commerical Co.**
Library of Congress
ppmsc 01883

58 **Nome to Seward**
Library of Congress
ppmsc 01575

60 **Schoolhouse**
Library of Congress
ppmsc 01924

61 **Sewing Class**
Library of Congress
ppmsc 02457

62 **Miocene Ditch Company "Giants"**
Library of Congress
ppmsc 01701

63 **Tunnel at Juneau Mine**
Library of Congress
ppmsc 01645

64 **Loading Copper**
Library of Congress
ppmsc 01756

65 **View of Wrangell**
Library of Congress
ppmsc 0228

66 **SS Princess May**
Library of Congress
ppmsc 01752

67 **Dog-Sled Team**
Library of Congress
ppmsc 01601

68 **Transportation**
Library of Congress
ppmsc 01569

69 **U.S. Mail Sled**
Library of Congress
ppmsc 01563

70 **Child's Glacier**
Library of Congress
ppmsc 01732

71 **U.S. Marshal's Office**
Library of Congress
ppmsc 01912

72 **Freighting with Dog Teams**
Library of Congress
cph 3c23941

73 **Fourth of July, Skagway**
Library of Congress
cph 3b1672

74 **Tug-of-War**
Library of Congress
cph 3b16873

76 **Mount McKinley**
Library of Congress
ppmsc 01972

77 Three Sisters Mountains
Library of Congress
ppmsc 02056

78 Russian Orthodox Church
Library of Congress
ppmsc 01947

79 W. A. Hesse at Katmai Volcano
Library of Congress
ppmsc 01940

80 Sixth All-Alaska Sweepstakes
Library of Congress
ppmsc 02233

82 SS Corwin
Library of Congress
ppmsc 01611

83 Taku Glacier
Library of Congress
ppmsc 02199

84 Street Scene
Library of Congress
ppmsc 02220

85 SS Alameda
Library of Congress
ppmsc 02042

86 Anchorage
Library of Congress
ppmsc01941

87 Street Scene
Library of Congress
ppmsc 01772

88 Alaska Clothing Co.
Library of Congress
ppmsc 01616

89 Hospital
Library of Congress
ppmsc 02110

90 Mattress Factory
Library of Congress
ppmsc 02225

91 Two Girls Waffle House
Library of Congress
ppmsc 02057

92 Haly's Road House
Library of Congress
ppmsc 02147

93 Street Scene
Library of Congress
ppmsc 01620

94 Children on Sleigh
Library of Congress
ppmsc 02481

95 ANB's First Basketball Team
Alaska State Library
Alaska Native Organizations,
Photographs ASL-PCA33
ASL-P33-02

96 Firebox
Library of Congress
ppmsc 01741

97 Horses Pulling Tent
Library of Congress
02085

98 Tower House, Tanana
Library of Congress
ppmsc 02234

99 Fire Drill
Library of Congress
ppmsc 01738

100 Auto Wood Saw Machine
Buzby and Metcalf
Photograph Album
Alaska and Polar Regions
Collections, Rasmuson
Library, University of
Alaska Fairbanks
UAF-1963-0071-35

101 Fourth of July Footrace
National Geographic
Society, Katmai
Expeditions Collections
University of Alaska
Anchorage Consortium
Library, Archives & Special
Collections Department
UAA-hmc-0186-
volume1-3554

102 July Fourth Parade
Library of Congress
ppmsc 02486

103 Umaik Racers
Library of Congress
ppmsc 02397

104 Fourth Street
Library of Congress
ppmsc 02224

105 Eskimo Women
Library of Congress
ppmsc 02423

106 Miner Panning Gold
Library of Congress
ppmsc 01635

108 Government Railway Office Building
Library of Congress
ppmsc 02092

109 July Fourth Celebration
Library of Congress
ppmsc 01867

110 Nome
Library of Congress
ppmsc 01899

111 Front Street
Library of Congress
ppmsc 01677

112 "110-Pound Auto"
Buzby and Metcalf
Photograph Album
Alaska and Polar Regions
Collections, Rasmuson
Library, University of
Alaska Fairbanks
UAF-1963-0071-42

113 Height of Grain
Library of Congress
ppmsc 01966

114 Snow-Covered Trail
Library of Congress
ppmsc 01960

115 July Fourth on Front Street
Library of Congress
ppmsc 01647

116 Ball Game with Prince Rupert
Library of Congress
ppmsc 02047

117 High Tide
Library of Congress
ppmsc 01794

118 Chitina and Mountains
Library of Congress
ppmsc 02222

119 Tanana Club House
Library of Congress
ppmsc 01915

120 Cordova Night
Library of Congress
cph 3b43828

121 MOUNT MCKINLEY
Library of Congress
ppmsc 01734

122 THE BONES OF MASTODONS
Library of Congress
ppmsc 01751

123 CARLSON'S MAIL TRUCK
George B. Nelson Collection
University of Alaska Anchorage Consortium Library, Archives & Special Collections Department
UAA-hmc-0187-series4-9-I35

124 MARSHALL ERWIN
Library of Congress
ppmsc 02190

125 REVILLA HOTEL
Library of Congress
ppmsc 02109

126 CITY HALL AND COURTHOUSE
Library of Congress
ppmsc 01671

128 DOG-SLED TEAM BARKING
Library of Congress
ppmsc 01576

129 SOURDOUGH OUTFIT
George A. Parks Collection
Alaska State Library
ASL-P240-239

130 EDDYSTONE ROCK
Library of Congress
ppmsc 01959

131 FISHING BOAT
Library of Congress
ppmsc 01626

132 COMMERCIAL AIRPLANES, FAIRBANKS
Edward Lewis Bartlett Papers Collection
Alaska and Polar Regions Collections, Rasmuson Library, University of Alaska Fairbanks
UAF-1969-95-534

133 PULLEN HOUSE
Library of Congress
cph 3c20296

134 TOONERVILLE TROLLEY
Wilson W. Brine Collection
University of Alaska Anchorage Consortium Library, Archives & Special Collections Department
UAA-hmc-0074-72-1

135 VIEW OF CITY
Library of Congress
ppmsc 02100

136 REINDEER TEAM
Library of Congress
ppmsc 02393

137 FARM
Library of Congress
ppmsc 02049

138 WARREN G. HARDING
Library of Congress
cph 3b36748

139 CORNERSTONE OF ODD FELLOWS' TEMPLE
Alaska Pacific University Collection, University of Alaska Anchorage Consortium Library, Archives & Special Collections Department
APU-AHP-f10-26

140 CUTTING ICE
Buzby and Metcalf Photograph Album
Alaska and Polar Regions Collections, Rasmuson Library, University of Alaska Fairbanks
UAF-1963-0071-34

141 RICHARDSON HIGHWAY
Library of Congress
ppmsc 108346

142 MAIN STREET, JUNEAU
Library of Congress
cph 3b36748

143 YUKON RIVER BOAT
Estelle and Philip Garges Collection
University of Alaska Anchorage Consortium Library, Archives & Special Collections Department
UAA-hmc-0381-series2 58-1

144 OPERATION OF BUCKETS
Walter W. Hodge Collection
Alaska and Polar Regions Collections, Rasmuson Library, University of Alaska Fairbanks
UAF-2003-63-40

145 BALD EAGLE
Library of Congress
ppmsc 02059

146 WALRUS TUSKS
Library of Congress
ppmsc 01837

147 FILM CREW
Michael Philip Collection
University of Alaska Anchorage Consortium Library, Archives & Special Collections Department
UAA-hmc-0430-3a-149

148 FRANK YASUDA
Alaska's Japanese Pioneers Research Project Collection
Alaska and Polar Regions Collections, Rasmuson Library, University of Alaska Fairbanks
UAF-1991-0045-6

150 KETCHIKAN
Library of Congress
LC-USZ62-97175

151 PARADE AT FAIRBANKS ICE CARNIVAL
Thomas Culhane Collection
University of Alaska Anchorage Consortium Library, Archives & Special Collections Department
UAA-hmc-0096-series2-1-37-2

152 FAIRBANKS DOG DERBY
Thomas Culhane Collection
University of Alaska Anchorage Consortium Library, Archives & Special Collections Department
UAA-hmc-0096-series2-1-37-1

153 GRANGE FLOAT
Almer J. Peterson Collection
University of Alaska Anchorage Consortium Library, Archives & Special Collections Department
UAA-hmc-0413-series2-2-26c

154 JULY FOURTH GAMES
Thomas Culhane Collection
University of Alaska Anchorage Consortium Library, Archives & Special Collections Department
UAA-hmc-0096-series2-1-16-2

155 **Walt's Transfer Company**
Thomas Culhane Collection
University of Alaska Anchorage Consortium Library, Archives & Special Collections Department
UAA-hmc-0096-series2-2-3-4

156 **4-H Club**
Almer J. Peterson Collection
University of Alaska Anchorage Consortium Library, Archives & Special Collections Department
UAA-hmc-0413-series2-2-26a

157 **Anchorage/Fairbanks Hockey Game**
Thomas Culhane Collection
University of Alaska Anchorage Consortium Library, Archives & Special Collections Department
UAA-hmc-0096-series2-2-1-2

158 **View of Campus**
General Collections
Alaska and Polar Regions Collections, Rasmuson Library, University of Alaska Fairbanks
UAF-1958-1026-1008

159 **Fur Rendezvous**
Thomas Culhane Collection
University of Alaska Anchorage Consortium Library, Archives & Special Collections Department
UAA-hmc-0096-series2-2-2-4

160 **Main Street Valdez**
Russell W. Dow Collection
University of Alaska Anchorage Consortium Library, Archives & Special Collections Department
UAA-hmc-0396-14f-193

161 **Nome, After Fire**
Glenn H. Bowersox Collection
University of Alaska Anchorage Consortium Library, Archives & Special Collections Department
UAA-hmc-0731-154

162 **Mentasta Reflections**
National Park Service Collections
University of Alaska Anchorage Consortium Library, Archives & Special Collections Department
UAA-hmc-0285-23

163 **Anchorage Street Scene**
Russell W. Dow Collection
University of Alaska Anchorage Consortium Library, Archives & Special Collections Department
UAA-hmc-0396-14o-f3-2

164 **Aleut Boy**
Library of Congress
fsa 8e09144

165 **Somersaulting**
Russell W. Dow Collection
University of Alaska Anchorage Consortium Library, Archives & Special Collections Department
UAA-hmc-0396-14f-618

166 **Army Band**
Russell W. Dow Collection
University of Alaska Anchorage Consortium Library, Archives & Special Collections Department
UAA-hmc-0396-14f-867

168 **Soldiers Doing Ski Calisthenics**
Russell W. Dow Collection
University of Alaska Anchorage Consortium Library, Archives & Special Collections Department
UAA-hmc-0396-14f-777

169 **Anchorage Ski Club**
Anchorage Ski Club Collections
University of Alaska Anchorage Consortium Library, Archives & Special Collections Department
UAA-hmc-0055-series6-3

170 **U.S. Planes**
Library of Congress
fsa 8e09144

171 **Operations During Snowstorm**
Library of Congress
LOT 8754

172 **Tanks on Mountain Pass**
Library of Congress
fsa-8e09169

173 **Russian Military Mission, Nome**
Library of Congress
LC-USW33-053763-ZC

174 **Alaska Highway**
Library of Congress
fsa 8e00445

175 **Alaska Highway Camp**
Library of Congress
fsa 8e00463

176 **Kiska Landing**
Library of Congress
LOT 803

177 **Checking A-20**
Library of Congress
fsa 8e02415

178 **Crash**
Library of Congress
fsa 8e02404

179 **American and Soviet Officers**
Library of Congress
fsa 8e02394

180 **Kodiak**
Hans and Margaret Hafemeister Collections
University of Alaska Anchorage Consortium Library, Archives & Special Collections Department
UAA-hmc-0126-m1-2-39

181 **Fund Raiser**
Christine M. McClain Collection
University of Alaska Anchorage Consortium Library, Archives & Special Collections Department
UAA-hmc-0370-series15a-2-1

182 **Aerial Tramway**
Robert and Wilma Knox Collections
University of Alaska Anchorage Consortium Library, Archives & Special Collections Department
UAA-hmc-0461-series15-1-9

183 Construction Camp Dining Hall
Howard and Mabel Jonish Collections
University of Alaska Anchorage Consortium Library, Archives & Special Collections Department
UAA-hmc-0428-series5-f12-26

184 Fourth Avenue
Ward W. Wells Collection
Anchorage Museum at Rasmuson Center
AMRC-wws-3145

185 A Dozen Alaskan Beauties
Earnest H. Gruening Collection
Alaska and Polar Regions Collections, Rasmuson Library, University of Alaska Fairbanks
UAF-1976-21-1013

186 Bonfire Celebration
Ward W. Wells Collection
Anchorage Museum at Rasmuson Center
AMRC-wws-2023-41

188 Statehood
Alaska State Library General Collections
ASL P01 3918

189 Earthquake Damage
Ward W. Wells Collection
Anchorage Museum at Rasmuson Center
AMRC-wws-4176-84

190 "Million Dollar Bridge"
Library of Congress
HAER AK,20-CORD.V,1-1

191 1964 Earthquake
Ward W. Wells Collection
Anchorage Museum at Rasmuson Center
AMRC-wws-4176-19

192 Horse Jumping
Christine M. McClain Collections
University of Alaska Anchorage Consortium Library, Archives & Special Collections Department
UAA-hmc-0370-series15a-4-96

193 Anchorage
Christine M. McClain Collections
University of Alaska Anchorage Consortium Library, Archives & Special Collections Department
UAA-hmc-0370-series15a-4-182

194 Dog Rides VW
Mark C. Glunz Slide Collection
Alaska and Polar Regions Collections, Rasmuson Library, University of Alaska Fairbanks
UAF-1996-167-29

195 Bud Hagberg
Kay J. Kennedy Collections
Alaska and Polar Regions Collections, Rasmuson Library, University of Alaska Fairbanks
UAF-1991-98-1129

196 South of Little Tonsina River Crossing
Steve McCutcheon Trans Alaska Pipeline System Construction Collections
Anchorage Museum at Rasmuson Center
AMRC-b90-14-3-1305

197 North of Pump 4
Steve McCutcheon Trans Alaska Pipeline System Construction Collections
Anchorage Museum at Rasmuson Center
AMRC-b90-14-3-345

198 Approach to South Fork of Koyukuk River
Steve McCutcheon Trans Alaska Pipeline System Construction Collections
Anchorage Museum at Rasmuson Center
AMRC-b90-14-3-599

HISTORIC PHOTOS OF ALASKA

Just over 140 years ago, the United States made one of the greatest land deals of all time, purchasing from Russia a massive piece of property near the Arctic Circle. Since then, the land known as Alaska has been the site of a gold rush and an oil boom, but even those great events comprise only a small portion of what makes America's largest and most northern state a place that continues to capture the imagination and the hearts of residents and visitors alike.

Historic Photos of Alaska portrays the majesty, the history, and the awe-inspiring beauty of this unique section of America through rarely seen, stunning, black-and-white photographs selected from local, state, and national collections.

Climb the snow-filled Chilkoot Pass with gold-seekers. Hunt with Native tribesmen. See cities like Anchorage and Fairbanks grow from a cluster of tents and wooden shacks. Stand with American soldiers as they repel the only invasion of North America during World War II. Observe the engineering feat of constructing the trans-Alaska oil pipeline through frozen wilderness. Marvel at pristine natural beauty, celebrate the long-awaited statehood, and witness the incredible destruction wrought by the 1964 earthquake, in this unique collection of historic photographs.

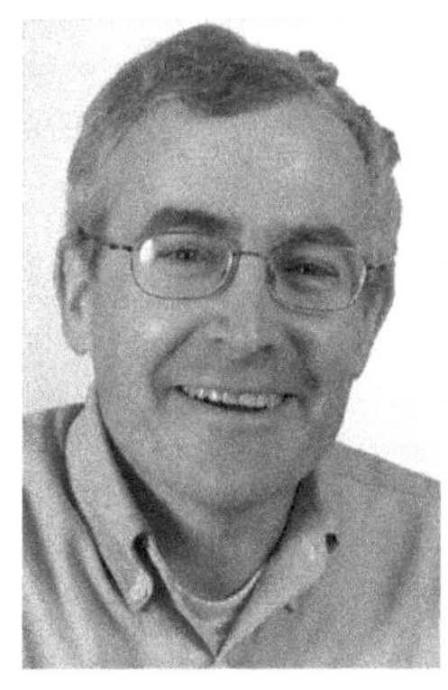

Dermot Cole has been researching and writing about Alaska's history and its people for more than 30 years and has written a daily newspaper column about life in Alaska for 15 of those years. Originally from Pennsylvania, he traveled to Fairbanks in 1974 at age 21 to visit his identical twin brother Terrence, his older brother Patrick, and his sister Maureen, who had converged in Fairbanks to study at the University of Alaska. Deciding to stay, he enrolled at the university, earned a degree in journalism, and developed a fascination for Alaska politics, history, and journalism. He began work at the *Fairbanks Daily News-Miner* in 1976 as a sports writer and has held almost every editing and reporting position at the newspaper. A Michigan Journalism Fellow, he worked for the Associated Press in Seattle for a year, but he and his wife Debbie, also a writer, decided to move back to Fairbanks to raise their family, Connor, Aileen and Anne. Cole wrote his first book, a biography of Alaska bush pilot Frank Barr, more than 25 years ago. He has also written two histories of Fairbanks, a social history of the trans-Alaska oil pipeline and a book about the great 1908 auto race from New York to Paris. Other favorite projects included writing a portion of an Alaska history course for high school students.

WWW.TURNERPUBLISHING.COM

www.ingramcontent.com/pod-product-compliance
Lightning Source LLC
LaVergne TN
LVHW070459120826
845154LV00019BA/30

* 9 7 8 1 6 8 4 4 2 0 0 0 1 *